THE DEVOTED LIFE

An Invitation to the Puritan Classics

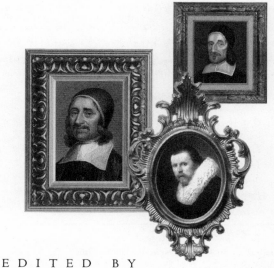

EDITED BY

Kelly M. Kapic and Randall C. Gleason

InterVarsity Press
Downers Grove, Illinois

InterVarsity Press
P.O. Box 1400, Downers Grove, IL 60515-1426
World Wide Web: www.ivpress.com
E-mail: mail@ivpress.com

InterVarsity Press® *is the book-publishing division of InterVarsity Christian Fellowship/USA*®*, a student movement active on campus at hundreds of universities, colleges and schools of nursing in the United States of America, and a member movement of the International Fellowship of Evangelical Students. For information about local and regional activities, write Public Relations Dept., InterVarsity Christian Fellowship/USA, 6400 Schroeder Rd., P.O. Box 7895, Madison, WI 53707-7895, or visit the IVCF website at* <www.intervarsity.org>.

Scripture quotations, unless otherwise noted, are from the New Revised Standard Version of the Bible, *copyright 1989 by the Division of Christian Education of the National Council of the Churches of Christ in the USA. Used by permission. All rights reserved.*

We gratefully acknowledge the permission granted by Peter Lang Publishing for using material from Randall C. Gleason's work John Calvin and John Owen on Mortification: A Comparative Study in Reformed Spirituality *(1995).*

Design: Cindy Kiple
Images: Man at desk: Alexander Burkatovski/CORBIS
   Oval frame: Photodisc/Getty Images
   John Milton: Hulton Archive/Getty Images
   Various frames: Rick Franklin/InterVarsity Press
   John Bunyan: Thomas Adler/National Portrait Gallery
   Richard Baxter: National Portrait Gallery
   Jonathan Edwards: Roberta Polfus

ISBN 0-8308-2794-3

Printed in the United States of America ∞

Library of Congress Cataloging-in-Publication Data

The devoted life : an invitation to the Puritan classics / edited by Kelly
M. Kapic and Randall Gleason.
 p. cm.
Includes bibliographical references and index.
ISBN 0-8308-2794-3 (pbk. : alk. paper)
1. Puritans. I. Kapic, Kelly M., 1972- II. Gleason, Randall C., 1958-
BX9323.D48 2004
285'.9--dc22

                  2004011516

P	18	17	16	15	14	13	12	11	10	9	8	7	6	5	4	3	2	1
Y	19	18	17	16	15	14	13	12	11	10	09	08	07	06	05	04		

To our wives,
Cathy Gleason and Tabitha Kapic

CONTENTS

Acknowledgments

We the editors have each experienced occasions while reading a Puritan when a passage caused us to stop, put down the book, and contemplate an unexpected theological, pastoral or psychological insight that had leaped off the page and through the centuries into our lives. Although the Puritans have their share of weaknesses and shortcomings, it is a thrilling possibility that this book may help introduce many of these theologians and pastors to contemporary evangelicals. Although our goal is certainly not to convince our readers to return to the seventeenth century, it is our hope that some of the richness of this heritage will be freshly remembered or perhaps experienced for the first time. We are profoundly grateful to the Puritans, many of whom are represented in this volume, for stirring our souls, challenging our minds, moving our wills and informing our worship.

This volume was designed to be enjoyed by scholars and educated lay people alike. To help us achieve this, we enlisted the help of a small army of undergraduate and graduate students. The following group from Covenant College spent considerable time reading through and giving invaluable feedback on each of the chapters: Ellis Chaplin, Justin Johnson, Cameron Moran, Dave Rooy, Rebekah Tuggy, Wesley Vander Lugt and Paul Weinhold, with special mention given to Wilhelmus Codington, who took the title "work-study student" to a whole new level. The time and effort volunteered by these students not only strengthened the finished volume but made the work a joy.

We also appreciate the inspiration and helpful feedback on several chapters from David Darwin, who has for several years taught with Randall an elective class on Reformed spirituality to an enthusiastic group of Asian students at the International School of Theology in Manila, Philippines. Their passionate interest in Puritan authors suggests the potential impact of Puritan spirituality throughout the global Christian community.

One of the great pleasures of editing this book has been the opportunity to work with a group of fantastic and diverse scholars who have inspired us with their previous work, and their contributions here are no exception. We wish to express our deepest thanks to our contributors for their kindness and patience throughout the process of completing this book—their grace and friendship is much appreciated.

Beyond the scholars contributing to this particular volume, there are others who have influenced and encouraged us along the way, a few of whom we particularly wish to name: William (Bill) Black, John Brouwer, Lunette Fleming, John Hannah, Frank James III, Susan Hardman Moore and Roger Nicole. Furthermore, Gary Deddo and IVP have been an exceptional team to work with on this project. Kelly would like to acknowledge the generous support he received from the Kaleo Center at Covenant College which is funded through Lilly Endowment Inc. Randall would like to express his gratitude for the encouragement of his parents, Gerald and Shirley Gleason, who enthusiastically listened to the chapters read aloud and especially to his ailing father who now awaits Bunyan's "Celestial City" with such confidence.

Finally, we wish to express our unending gratitude to our wives, Cathy Gleason and Tabitha Kapic. The tremendous compassion and strength of these two remarkable women leaves us humbled and thankful beyond measure. We believe that they, more than anyone else, have pointed us to the loveliness of Christ and the hope of the gospel.

KEY EVENTS IN PURITAN HISTORY

1509	Henry VIII becomes king of England
1521	Lutheran books start appearing in England
	Students begin studying Reformers
1526	Cardinal Wolsey burns Lutheran books
1532	Thomas Cranmer becomes archbishop of Canterbury
1534	*Act of Supremacy* declaring the king supreme head of the Church of England
1538	Edward VI, Henry VIII's only legitimate son, is born
1547	Henry VIII dies and is succeeded by Edward VI
1549	Cranmer publishes *First Book of Common Prayer*
1552	*Book of Common Prayer* revised
1553	*Forty-Two Articles of Religion* adopted
	Edward VI dies and is succeeded by Mary Tudor
1555	Mary Tudor begins to burn Protestants as heretics
	Many Protestants flee England to Europe
1558	Mary Tudor dies and is succeeded by Elizabeth I
	Marian exiles return to England
1559	*Book of Common Prayer* revised
	Act of Supremacy and Uniformity instituted by Elizabeth
1563	*Thirty-Nine Articles of Religion* adopted
1570	Thomas Cartwright lectures on Presbyterian reforms in Cambridge
1593	*Act Against Puritans* accuses them of sedition and disloyalty
1603	Elizabeth dies and is succeeded by James I (James VI of Scotland)
	The Millenary Petition submitted to James I
1604	*Hampton Court Conference* held by James I
1605	"Gunpowder plot" to blow up the king and Parliament exposed
1611	*King James Version of the Bible* published
1618-1619	Synod of Dort held in the Netherlands

1625   James I succeeded by Charles I
1628   William Laud appointed Bishop of London
1629   Charles I dissolves Parliament
1630   John Winthrop leads Puritan exodus to New England
1633   William Laud appointed Archbishop of Canterbury
1638   *National Covenant* adopted by Scottish Presbyterians
1640   Long Parliament convenes
1641   *Grand Remonstrance* is passed in response to the Irish Rebellion
1642   Civil War begins and Charles I flees from London
1643   Westminster Assembly convenes
            Scots adopt the *Solemn League and Covenant*
1645   William Laud executed
            Formation of New Model Army
1647   *Westminster Confession* completed
1648   Civil War ends
1649   Charles I beheaded
            Oliver Cromwell assumes leadership
1653   Cromwell dissolves Parliament and establishes himself as Lord Protector
1658   Cromwell dies
1660   Monarchy restored under Charles II
1662   *Act of Uniformity* enforces Anglican ordination
            2000 ministers ejected on St. Bartholomew's Day (August 24)
1664   *Conventicle Act* bans preaching by nonconformists
1665   *Five Mile Act* prohibits nonconformists from parishes and towns
1685   Charles II succeeded by James II
1688   Bloodless (Glorious) Revolution
            William III (of Orange) called by Parliament to succeed James II
1689   *Act of Toleration* ends religious persecution

PURITAN PUBLICATIONS
DISCUSSED IN THIS VOLUME

❧ I ❧

WHO WERE THE PURITANS?

Randall C. Gleason and Kelly M. Kapic

APART FROM NOSTALGIC PORTRAITS OF NEW ENGLAND PILGRIMS feasting with American Indians, the word *Puritan* typically conjures up images representing the worst sort of religious hypocrite. C. S. Lewis's demon Screwtape claims credit for this modern caricature in his correspondence to Wormwood, "The value we have given to that word [*Puritanism*] is one of the really solid triumphs of the last hundred years."[1] Yet history indicates that since the time of Shakespeare, Puritans were viewed as sexually repressed killjoys. In his comedy *Twelfth Night*, which first played in 1602, the playwright used the term to poke fun at Malvolio who squelched the mirth and merriment of others:

Maria:	Sir, sometimes his is a kind of Puritan.
Sir Andrew:	Oh! If I thought that, I'd beat him like a dog.
Maria:	The devil a Puritan that he is, . . . so crammed, as he thinks, with excellencies, that it is his grounds of faith that all that look on him love him.[2]

Two decades later the public image of Puritans had changed little when James I warned his son Charles:

Take heed of these Puritans, the very pests (or plagues) of the Church and Commonwealth, whom no deserts can oblige, nor oaths, or promises bind; one that breathes nothing but sedition and calumnies. . . . He is a fanatic spirit; with whom you may find greater ingratitude, more lies, and viler perjuries, than amongst the most infamous thieves.[3]

---

[1] C. S. Lewis, *The Screwtape Letters* (London: Mentor, 1988), pp. 38-39.
[2] William Shakespeare, *Twelfth Night* (New York: Bantam, 1988), 2.3.139-52.
[3] Anonymous, *A Puritane Set Forth in His Lively Colours* (London: n.p., 1642), pp. 2-3.

Many readers in the twenty-first century will fairly wonder why they should care about the Puritans. Were not the Puritans just some fanatical group that forced public religiosity without concern for authentic spirituality? Although an inaccurate stereotype, this misconception has had enduring power that is not easily set aside. In this book we hope to introduce readers to *real* Puritans, a wide variety of them, and to present them by looking at what they *really* said. This means becoming acquainted with some of their key writings. Our belief is that if readers develop a familiarity with a sampling of significant Puritan literature they will begin to have a much healthier and more accurate view of the Puritans, and this discovery could positively influence and challenge contemporary understandings of the Christian life. That does not mean we are arguing for an uncritical view of the Puritans; rather, we are hoping to cultivate an informed appreciation for this important, although often neglected, movement in the history of Christianity.

Before moving to the later chapters on particular Puritan classics some background is necessary. In this chapter we will begin by exploring the history of the name *Puritan*, since this title can mean so many different things to different people. From there we will give a brief history of Puritanism, covering roughly the period from the 1550s to 1700. This overview aims to help readers appreciate the historical and political soil from which Puritanism grew. We will next turn our attention to the idea of Puritan spirituality, arguing that amid the countless differences between the various Puritans there are some unifying features: we shall argue for a cluster of characteristics to fairly describe the Puritans in general. Once readers are familiar with this basic material, we believe they will be equipped to interact thoughtfully with some Puritan classics.

THE NAME *PURITAN*

Taking into consideration the comments noted above of Lewis, Shakespeare, and Charles I, we now turn to a fuller consideration of the word *Puritan*. Since some applied this term to those considered notorious separatists like the Anabaptists and Brownists,[4] Henry Parker in 1641 warned that "if the confused misapplication of this foul word Puritan be not reformed in England, . . . we can expect nothing but a sudden universal downfall of all goodness."[5] Historian Patrick Collinson clarifies that the "hotter sort of Protestants" who were called Puritans in the Elizabe-

---

[4]Giles Widdowes listed ten kinds of Puritans, including "the Perfectist, the factious Sermonist, the Separatist, the Anabaptist, the Brownist, Loves-familist, the Precisian, the Sabbatarian, the Ante-disciplinarian, [and] the Presuming Predestinatist" in his tract *The Schysmatical Puritan* (Oxford: n.p., 1630), p. B2.

[5]Henry Parker, *A Discourse Concerning Puritans* (n.p., 1641), p. 57.

than tabloids preferred to call themselves "the godly," "the faithful" or "God's elect."[6] Some wished to abolish the term *Puritan* altogether because of its pejorative connotations. Once the English revolution was underway others attempted to redefine the term as a worthy title for those patriotic nonconformists seeking to reform the church.[7]

In spite of the fact that few individuals ever boasted of being a Puritan, modern historians agree that Puritanism was a genuine movement that wielded considerable force within seventeenth-century England and New England. However, because the name *Puritan* had a variety of historical meanings, agreement on a definition of Puritanism has continued to be elusive.[8] As Basil Hall demonstrates with examples from Thomas Fuller (1508-1561) and Richard Baxter (1615-1691), prior to the English Civil War (1642-1648) the term *Puritan* applied to "restlessly critical and occasionally rebellious members of the Church of England who desired some modifications in church government and worship, but not . . . those who deliberately removed themselves from that Church."[9] However, this narrow definition technically excludes the New England-bound *Separatists* who settled Plymouth colony, along with other early Puritan sympathizers who chose exile in the Netherlands rather than compromise their religious convictions.[10]

Here we offer a more inclusive definition that fits a growing scholarly consensus. Puritans should not be limited strictly to radical Protestant nonconformists, but rather to a much broader movement of individuals distinguished by a cluster of characteristics that transcends their political, ecclesiastical, and religious differences.[11] Some who we include as Puritans in this collection of essays (e.g., Thomas

---

[6]Patrick Collinson, *The Elizabethan Puritan Movement* (Oxford: Clarendon, 1967), pp. 22-28.

[7]For example see the anonymous *The Old Puritan, Godly, Honest, and Loyal* (London: n.p., 1642), and John Geree, *The Character of an Old English Puritan or Non-Conformist* (London: n.p., 1646).

[8]On the problems defining Puritanism see Basil Hall, "Puritanism: the Problem of Definition," in *Studies in Church History*, ed. G. J. Cuming (Edinburgh: Thomas Nelson, 1965), 2:283-96; Lawrence A. Sasek, *Images of English Puritanism: A Collection of Contemporary Sources 1589-1646* (Baton Rouge: Louisiana State University Press, 1989), pp. 1-27; Peter Lake, "Defining Puritanism: Again?" in *Puritanism: Trans-Atlantic Perspectives on a Seventeenth-Century Anglo-American Faith* (Boston: Massachusetts Historical Society, 1993), pp. 3-29; and John Spurr, *English Puritanism 1603-1689* (London: Macmillan, 1998), pp. 1-27.

[9]Hall, "Puritanism: the Problem of Definition," p. 290.

[10]William Bradford clearly includes the Plymouth colonialists among those (e.g., William Perkins) who were called Puritans in his *History of Plymouth Plantation 1606-1647*, ed. Samuel Eliot Morrision (New York: Random House, 1952), p. 7. For information on the Dutch Second Reformation (*De Nadere Reformatie*) and how it fits into a discussion of Puritanism, see Joel R. Beeke, *The Quest for Full Assurance: The Legacy of Calvin and His Successors* (Edinburgh: Banner of Truth Trust, 1999), pp. 286-309.

[11]See for example Christopher Durston and Jacqueline Eales, "Introduction: The Puritan Ethos, 1560-1700," in *The Culture of English Puritanism 1560-1700*, ed. C. Durston and J. Eales (London: Macmillan, 1996), pp. 1-31 and Spurr, *English Puritanism 1603-1689*, pp. 28-45.

Boston and Jonathan Edwards) lived long after the age of Puritan dissent had ended with the *Act of Toleration* in 1689. Yet they exhibited in their lives and ministries the same distinctive mindset, vibrant spirituality, and dynamic religious culture of their Puritan forebears. Similarly, although Richard Baxter and John Owen could have significant theological differences on how best to understand the atonement and justification, there is no debate that both men are rightly considered leading Puritans. Any proposed definition must also be flexible enough to affirm real differences that existed among those who are in some way represented by this name. For our purposes John Spurr comes closest to defining the "essence of Puritanism."

> It grows out of the individual's conviction that they have been personally saved by God, elected to salvation by a merciful God for no merit of their own; and that, as a consequence of this election, they must lead a life of visible piety, must be a member of a church modeled on the pattern of the New Testament, and must work to make their community and nation a model Christian society.[12]

Though these marks are primarily theological, and we will return to such common characteristics later, we cannot neglect the historical narrative from which they arose. Although Puritanism sprung from a matrix of religious, social and political events in sixteenth-century Europe, we will begin with the arrival of the Protestant Reformation in England.

A BRIEF HISTORY OF PURITANISM (1558-1700)

Protestant ideas from Wittenberg spread rapidly throughout Europe, reaching England during the reign of Henry VIII (1509-1547).[13] The English monarch used the pretense of religious reform as an opportunity to break with the Catholic Church so he could legally divorce, remarry and hopefully produce a male heir. During the short reign of his sickly son Edward VI (1547-1553), the theology of Luther and Calvin was introduced into the English Church by Archbishop Thomas Cranmer (1489-1556) through his book of *Homilies* (1547), his *Book of Common Prayer* (1552), and his *Forty-Two Articles of Religion* (1553). However, these reforms were quickly reversed during the "bloody" reign of Mary Tudor (1553-1558). She reinstated the Latin mass and enforced English allegiance to the Roman pope at the cost of 270 Protestant martyrs, including Thomas Cranmer.

When Queen Elizabeth (1533-1603) came to the throne in 1558, many who had fled to Europe in order to escape persecution under Mary returned to England

---

[12]Spurr, *English Puritanism 1603-1689*, p. 5.
[13]See Carl R. Trueman, *Luther's Legacy: Salvation and the English Reformers 1525-1556* (Oxford: Clarendon, 1994).

with hopes of continuing the reforms begun under Edward VI. Though the Queen appointed some of the "Marian exiles" to positions of influence (including six bishops), many felt that her *Acts of Uniformity* (1659-1662) left the Church only "half reformed," since she failed to rid England of the clerical vestments and ceremonies remaining from Catholicism. Her demand for strict observance of Cranmer's *Book of Common Prayer* and *Articles of Religion* did little to satisfy their longing for the sort of biblical preaching they had experienced in the great Reformed churches on the continent. Horrified by the immoral and incompetent clergy tolerated by the English episcopacy, Thomas Cartwright (1535-1603) convinced many through his Cambridge lectures in 1570 that the road to reform required the more disciplined Presbyterian model practiced in Geneva. By 1586 a *Book of Discipline* began to circulate quietly among concerned ministers; it outlined new patterns for public worship that insured the preaching of the Word and proper administration of the sacraments.

Once the Queen overcame the international threat of Catholicism by defeating the Spanish Armada in 1588, she turned her attention again to reinforce conformity within the English Church. Her new Court of High Commission under Archbishop John Whitgift (1530-1604) suspended hundreds of clergy, accusing them of sedition and disloyalty in her *Act Against Puritans* issued in 1593.[14] Some of the ejected ministers continued preaching in lectureships sponsored by sympathetic Puritan gentry while a few began to gather congregations in private homes. Although Elizabeth successfully ended any organized efforts to reform the Church, a "spiritual brotherhood" of reform-minded moderates continued to flourish. Collinson explains that this was especially true in Cambridge where students flocked to hear the sermons of William Perkins (1558-1602), the "prince of Puritan theologians." During his ministry at Great St. Andrews Church, Perkins kept the university press busy printing his books on Reformed theology and practical divinity that were eagerly read throughout England. Equally influential was Laurence Chaderton (1538-1640), the "pope of Cambridge Puritanism," who for nearly forty years as master of Emmanuel College trained many of the most talented Puritan preachers of the next generation.[15]

Since James I (1566-1625) was a Calvinist, his accession to the throne in 1603 revived Puritan hopes for further reforms. Denying accusations that they were

---

[14]See *Documents of the Christian Church*, ed. Henry Bettenson, 2nd ed. (London: Oxford University Press, 1963), pp. 242-43.

[15]On the importance of Cambridge to the growth of Puritanism, see Patrick Collinson, *The Elizabethan Puritan Movement* (Oxford: Clarendon, 1967), pp. 122-30.

"schismatics aiming at the dissolution" of the English Church, the Puritan brotherhood presented their requests to the new king in *The Millenary Petition* (1603),
which was signed by a thousand ministers. They appealed for changes in the administration of baptism and use of vestments, the need for self-examination before
Communion, the replacement of absent bishops with clergy able to preach and
greater restraint by the ecclesiastical courts in excommunicating laypersons and
suspending ministers.[16]

In 1604 James I held a conference at Hampton Court to consider their requests.
However, recognizing that his royal supremacy was tied to the English episcopacy,
James openly declared his fears: "No bishop, no king." Although he agreed to produce a fresh translation of the Bible to assist English preachers (the King James
Version), he demanded that all clergy conform to the liturgy and government of
the Church of England. To insure this, the king began a new campaign to impose
ceremonial conformity through his bishops. From 1604 to 1609 nearly ninety
ministers were suspended from office, including John Robinson (1575-1625),
who migrated to the Netherlands with fellow separatist William Bradford (1589-
1657), the future governor of Plymouth colony. In 1609 William Ames (1576-
1633) was also ejected from Cambridge University and fled to the Netherlands
where he became one of the greatest Puritan theologians.

After these initial suspensions, James I grew more tolerant toward Puritan pastors due to pressure from sympathetic members of Parliament.[17] Tensions were further eased by the king's support of Calvinism at the Synod of Dort (1618-1619)
and by a growing number of moderate Puritans who found ways to compromise in
order to continue their service within the English Church. They were led by Laurence Chaderton, who continued as master of Emmanuel College until 1622, and
Richard Sibbes (1577-1635), who served as preacher at Holy Trinity Church in
Cambridge and later at Gray's Inn in London. Sibbes's moderate stance on ecclesiastical matters allowed his popularity as a preacher to grow even during the con-
tentious reign of King Charles I (1625-1640).[18]

Charles's marriage in 1625 to Henrietta Maria, a devout Catholic, sparked immediate fears among Puritan ministers and Parliament that the new king intended
to lead England back to Rome. Suspicions grew when Charles appointed his

---

[16]"The Millenary Petition (1603)" in *Documents of the Christian Church*, ed. Henry Bettenson, 2nd ed. (London: Oxford University Press, 1963), pp. 282-84.

[17]Spurr, *English Puritanism 1603-1689*, p. 61.

[18]Mark E. Dever, *Richard Sibbes: Puritanism and Calvinism in Late Elizabethan and Early Stuart England* (Macon, Ga.: Mercer
University Press, 2000), pp. 27-85.

trusted adviser, William Laud (1573-1645), as the bishop of London in 1628. Although Laud opposed the authority of the pope, his reintroduction of many Catholic forms of worship and support of Arminian theology distressed the Puritan clergy. After Charles dissolved Parliament and assumed personal rule in 1629, Bishop Laud unleashed a bitter persecution of Puritans. He prohibited the preaching of predestination, required all clergy to use the prayer book and clerical dress, and made the laity kneel while receiving Communion. After his appointment as archbishop of Canterbury in 1633, Laud opposed the Puritan observance of the sabbath by demanding that the *Book of Sports* be read from every pulpit upon threat of suspension.[19]

Hounded by Laud's agents, many Puritans chose to emigrate either to the Netherlands or to New England. In 1630, John Winthrop (1588-1649) led the first great Puritan exodus to Massachusetts aboard the *Arbella* (with Simon and Anne Bradstreet) as part of a seven-ship flotilla. During the next decade, some of the most esteemed preachers in England, including John Cotton, Thomas Hooker and Thomas Shepard joined more than thirteen thousand emigrants who sailed to New England.[20]

The escalation of Laud's repressive tactics in 1637 proved disastrous for King Charles. His barbaric treatment of Puritan nonconformists like William Prynne (1600-1669), whose ears were cut off and face branded with hot irons, brought back memories of the brutal persecutions against Protestants under Queen Mary.[21] Laud's attempt to enforce Anglican liturgy on the Scottish Presbyterians galvanized their national resistance leading to their adoption in 1638 of the *National Covenant* that affirmed the Reformed faith and freedom of the Church in Scotland. The king's failed war against the Scottish "Covenanters" and his refusal to work with Parliament incited more opposition, ultimately forcing Charles to flee London in May 1642. In league with the Scottish Presbyterians and with the support of the Puritan clergy, the Long Parliament rejected Charles's claim of the divine right of kings, plunging the country into civil war. Charles and his cavalier army proved no match for the brilliant leadership of Oliver Cromwell (1599-1658) and his New Model Army of Puritan soldiers. Parliament arrested Archbishop Laud and executed him for treason in 1645. After the defeat of the Roy-

---

[19] *The Book of Sports,* first issued by James I in 1618, encouraged dancing and recreation on Sundays. See *Documents of the Christian Church,* pp. 284-86.

[20] See John Coffey, *Persecution and Toleration in Protestant England 1558-1689* (Harlow, England: Longman, 2000), pp. 125-30 and Spurr, *English Puritanism 1603-1689,* pp. 86-93.

[21] On Prynne's persecution and public sentiment leading to the Civil War, see William Lamont, *Puritanism and Historical Controversy* (Los Angeles: UCLA Press, 1996), pp. 16-25.

alists, Charles negotiated from prison a secret treaty with the Scots that led to further hostilities. For his role in prolonging the civil war, the king was tried and executed on January 30, 1649.

Throughout the English Civil War (1642-1648), under the direction of Parliament, over one hundred Puritan leaders assembled at Westminster Abbey to draft a new confession of faith for the national Church. Although they generally agreed on Calvinistic theology, differences arose between the majority who advocated a national Presbyterian Church, and a small but vocal minority of Independents, led by Thomas Goodwin, who argued for the right of congregations to govern themselves. They finally reached a compromise that advocated the voluntary formation of congregational presbyteries throughout the country. The Church of Scotland immediately approved the *Westminster Confession* upon its completion in 1647, followed by Congregationalists in New England in 1648. A decade later, English Congregationalists meeting in London adopted the Westminster Confession in their *Savoy Declaration* (1658) with only minor modifications on church government.[22] Thus, the Westminster Confession became the doctrinal standard for Puritan theology.

In spite of the great achievement at Westminster, any semblance of solidarity among nonconformists quickly disappeared with the end of the monarchy. After the creation of a new Commonwealth, the political tensions between Presbyterians and Independents in Parliament continued to escalate. To avoid political gridlock Cromwell dissolved Parliament in 1653 and ruled the country as Lord Protector until his death in 1658. Cromwell's guarantee of religious freedoms allowed unprecedented growth among nearly all religious sects. Independents were promoted to positions of great power within the Puritan Commonwealth. John Owen, for example, was appointed vice chancellor of Oxford, a former royalist stronghold. Unfortunately the new religious freedoms were short lived. Richard Cromwell's failed attempt to succeed his father created a complex political crisis that precipitously led to the restoration of the monarchy in 1660. In spite of promises by Charles II to preserve liberty of conscience, Anglican loyalists driven by revenge pressured the king to restore religious conformity through a series of acts known as the Clarendon Code (named after Lord Chancellor Edward Hyde, earl of Clarendon).

Thus began the period of dissent that resulted in the persecution and imprisonment of many famous Puritan pastors, including John Bunyan and Richard Bax-

---

[22]See *Documents of the English Reformation*, ed. Gerald Bray (Minneapolis: Fortress, 1994), pp. 521-42.

ter. In 1662 the *Act of Uniformity* required Puritan ministers to repudiate their denominational ordinations, renounce their oath to the *Solemn League and Covenant*, and be reordained under the bishops.[23] Nearly two thousand ministers (a fifth of all the clergy) refused to conform and were ejected from their parishes on St. Bartholomew's day, August 24, 1662. The *Conventicle Act* in 1664 banning nonconformists from preaching in the fields or conducting services in homes was followed in 1665 by the *Five Mile Act*, which prohibited ejected ministers from coming within five miles of their former parishes or any city or town.

Although Puritans were barred from the pulpits and universities, the repressive measures could not silence their pens. After 1662, under the shadow of persecution, they produced some of their most cherished devotional and theological works (e.g., *Pilgrim's Progress*). Although the hopes of a Puritan commonwealth continued to flicker in New England, the strength of Puritanism was quickly fading in old England. Sadly, most of the leading Puritans died before the lifting of persecution in 1689 by the *Toleration Act* under William and Mary. Banned from English churchyards even after their death, many Puritans, including John Bunyan, Thomas Goodwin and John Owen, were buried in a special nonconformist cemetery in Bunhill Fields, London. By the end of the century, much of the Puritan passion to reform the Church of England was redirected into the forming of various dissenting denominations then lawfully permitted by the English government.

PURITAN SPIRITUALITY

The history of Puritanism illustrates the fact that Puritans were not of one mind on ecclesiastical issues, for they included Anglicans (e.g., William Perkins, Richard Sibbes), Separatists (e.g., William Bradford), Independents (e.g., Thomas Goodwin, John Cotton and John Owen), Presbyterians (e.g., John Howe and Thomas Watson) and Baptists (e.g., John Bunyan). Neither could Puritans agree on such doctrines as the eternal decrees of predestination, for they included Dortian Calvinists (e.g., John Owen and Thomas Goodwin),[24] moderate Calvinists (e.g., Richard Baxter),[25] and even a few Arminians (e.g., John Goodwin).[26] Furthermore the Puritans did not share a common sociopolitical

---

[23]See *Documents of the English Reformation*, pp. 546-59.

[24]These included Puritans who affirmed particular redemption along with total depravity, unconditional election, irresistible grace and perseverance of the saints as expressed in the canons adopted at the Synod of Dort (1618-1619).

[25]On Baxter's "moderate Calvinism" see Dewey D. Wallace, *Puritans and Predestination: Grace in English Protestant Theology 1525-1695* (Chapel Hill: University of North Carolina Press, 1982), pp. 132-40.

[26]Foremost among those sectarians sympathetic toward the views of Jacob Arminius was John Goodwin (1594-

agenda, for loyalists as well as revolutionaries were numbered among their ranks. Consequently historians have often focused on the varieties within Puritanism.[27] However, here we offer a cluster of characteristics that describe the overall ethos that united the various theological, political and ecclesiastical streams of Puritanism. Each characteristic builds on another and should be seen as necessarily interrelated with the others, since all in some way represent core Puritan values and beliefs.

First, *many understand Puritanism as a movement of spirituality.* William Haller stressed that Puritans were foremost a "brotherhood" of preachers detailing the spiritual life for their listeners.[28] Charles E. Hambrick-Stowe affirms, "The rise of Puritanism [in] New England ought to be understood as a significant episode in the ongoing history of Christian spirituality."[29] E. Glenn Hinson simply declares "Puritanism was spirituality."[30] The variety of "spiritualities" in postmodern society requires we clarify that we refer here to a *Christian* spirituality that seeks a deeper awareness of God's presence as defined by the Christian faith according to the Bible.[31] Although the term *spirituality* was not in vogue among the Puritans, their emphasis upon daily communion with Christ, energized by the Spirit and guided by a biblically ordered set of beliefs and values, includes all the essential elements of a truly Christian spirituality.[32] This is particularly true of Puritanism during the period following the bitter civil war and in light of the theological debates of the Puritan revolution. Dewey Wallace explains that following 1660, "The piety and spirituality that had always been at the core of Puritanism . . . now [became] the point of concentration for the still-considerable Puritan energies."[33] The funda-

---

1665), who denied predestination, particular redemption and irresistible grace, though he practiced the same piety and commitment to reform the English Church as other Puritans. Wallace also includes John Milton among the "sectarian Arminians" because of his statements in his *De Doctrina Christiana.* See Wallace, *Puritans and Predestination,* pp. 130-32.

[27]See Leonard J. Trinterud, ed., *Elizabethan Puritanism* (New York: Oxford University Press, 1971), p. 9; H. C. Porter, ed. *Puritanism in Tudor England* (Columbia: University of South Carolina Press, 1971), p. 10; and Jerald C. Brauer, "Types of Puritan Piety," *Church History* 56:1 (1987): 39-58.

[28]William Haller, *The Rise of Puritanism* (New York: Columbia University Press, 1938), pp. 49-82.

[29]Charles E. Hambrick-Stowe, *The Practice of Piety: Puritan Devotional Disciplines in Seventeenth-Century New England* (Chapel Hill: University of North Carolina Press, 1982), p. 25.

[30]E. Glenn Hinson, "Puritan Spirituality," in *Protestant Spiritual Traditions,* ed. Frank C. Senn (New York: Paulist, 1986), p. 165.

[31]On defining *spirituality* in light of its postmodern usage see D. A. Carson, *The Gagging of God: Christianity Confronts Pluralism* (Grand Rapids: Zondervan, 1996), pp. 555-69.

[32]On defining "Christian spirituality" according to "a set of beliefs and values" expressed as "a way of life," see Alister McGrath, *Christian Spirituality: An Introduction* (Oxford: Blackwell, 1999), pp. 1-5.

[33]Dewey D. Wallace Jr., *The Spirituality of the Later English Puritans: An Anthology* (Macon, Ga.: Mercer University Press, 1987), p. xiii.

mental nature of spirituality within Puritanism is found in its insistence that the converted soul must go beyond conversion to actual holiness of life. This preoccupation with growth and progressive sanctification is often described in terms of a pilgrimage, as illustrated by John Bunyan's *Pilgrim's Progress* (1678), a work that J. I. Packer ably discusses later in this book.[34] The Puritan concern with a growing spirituality toward personal holiness cannot be overstated, and this naturally takes us to the next characteristic.

Second, *Puritanism, at its heart, lays stress on experiencing communion with God.* Richard F. Lovelace states, "Recent scholarship has increasingly concluded that throughout most of its history English Puritanism can best be understood by examining its predominating stress on Christian experience."[35] Geoffrey Nuttall defines Puritanism as "a movement towards immediacy in relation to God,"[36] and Charles Hambrick-Stowe describes it as "a devotional movement, rooted in religious experience."[37] "The practical bent of the Puritans," says Leland Ryken, "led them to emphasize the experiential nature of the Christian faith."[38] For the Puritan, intellectual assent to Christian doctrine had to be balanced with the practical outworking of God's grace in life experiences.

This was commonly expressed by the Puritan term *experimental*, which meant "experiential." Thomas Shepard (1605-1649) wrote, "Saints have an experimental knowledge of the work of grace, by virtue of which they come to know it as certainly . . . as by feeling heat, we know that fire is hot; by tasting honey, we know it is sweet."[39] "Experience is the life of a Christian," declared Richard Sibbes (1577-1635).[40] John Bunyan (1628-1688) explained that he preached "what I felt, what I smartingly did feel."[41] James Maclear notes that this stress upon experience which "sounded again and again in Puritan sermons, diaries, biographies, and guides to

---

[34]Hambrick-Stowe regards the pilgrimage theme as "the principle metaphor running through Puritan spirituality" (*The Practice of Piety*, p. 54).

[35]Richard C. Lovelace, *The American Pietism of Cotton Mather: Origins of American Evangelicalism* (Grand Rapids: Christian University Press, 1979), p. 36.

[36]Geoffrey Nuttall, *The Holy Spirit in Puritan Faith and Experience*, 2nd ed. (London: University of Chicago Press, 1992), p. 134.

[37]Hambrick-Stowe, *The Practice of Piety*, p. vii.

[38]Leland Ryken, *Worldly Saints: The Puritans as They Really Were* (Grand Rapids: Zondervan, 1986), p. 214. See also Gordon Rupp, "A Devotion of Rapture in English Puritanism," in *Reformation, Conformity, and Dissent: Essays in Honour of Geoffrey Nuttall*, ed. R. Buick Knox (London: Epworth, 1977), p. 120.

[39]Thomas Shepard, *The Parable of the Ten Virgins Opened and Applied* (1659; reprint, Morgan, Penn.: Soli Deo Gloria, 1990), p. 222.

[40]Richard Sibbes, *The Complete Works of Richard Sibbes*, ed. Alexander B. Grosart (1862-1864; reprint, Edinburgh: Banner of Truth Trust, 1983), 4:412.

[41]John Bunyan, *Grace Abounding to the Chief of Sinners* (1666; reprint, London: SCM Press, 1955), p. 124.

the spiritual life, attained its climax in the conversion experience, which was not an ornament but a norm of the religious life."[42] Hence, rather than being merely interested in an intellectual knowledge of theology or the outward observance of a moral code, the Puritans were united in their commitment to integrate their personal experience of God into their daily living.

Third, *Puritans were united in their dependence upon the Bible as their supreme source of spiritual sustenance and guide for the reformation of life.*[43] They based this commitment on their belief that the Bible was the inspired Word of God. "Think in every line you read that God is speaking to you," said Thomas Watson.[44] For John Owen, "The whole authority of the Scriptures . . . depends solely on its divine original [*sic*]. . . . The Scripture hath all its authority from its Author."[45] Puritans further reasoned that biblical authority was absolute because of the infallibility of Scripture. Concerning the human authors of Scripture, William Ames stated, "Only those could set down the rule of faith and conduct, who . . . were free from all error because of the direct and infallible direction they had from God."[46] According to Richard Baxter, the apostles wrote "without errors,"[47] and for John Owen the Bible was "a stable, infallible revelation of [God's] mind and will."[48] However, the Puritans were concerned with far more than the infallibility of the Bible.

Puritan preachers stressed the need for their listeners to cultivate an intense appetite for the Scriptures. "Feed upon the Word," John Cotton told his congregation.[49] Richard Baxter implored his readers to "love, reverence, read, study, obey and stick close to the Scriptures."[50] The Puritan conviction that the Bible was the source of spirituality is evidenced in their commitment to a vernacular Bible available to all literate Christians. This was initially expressed by their use of the *Geneva Bible* produced by Protestant exiles during the reign of Queen Mary in 1560, but ultimately realized in the production of the Authorized Version under King James

---

[42] James Maclear, "The Birth of the Free Church Tradition," *Church History* 26 (1957): 101.

[43] For a helpful overview of the Puritan view of the Bible, see Allen Carden, "The Word of God in Puritan New England: Seventeenth-Century Perspectives on the Nature and Authority of the Bible," *Andrews University Seminary Studies* 18 (1980):1-16; and Brian G. Armstrong, "Puritan Spirituality: The Tension of Bible and Experience," in *The Spirituality of Western Christendom*, vol. 2, ed. E. Rozanne Elder (Kalamazoo, Mich.: Cistercian Publications, 1984), pp. 243-48.

[44] Thomas Waston, *A Body of Divinity* (1692; reprint, London: Banner of Truth Trust, 1958), p. 25.

[45] John Owen, *The Works of John Owen*, ed. William H. Goold, 24 vols. (1850-1855; republished, Edinburgh: Banner of Truth, 1965, 1991), 16:297, 309.

[46] William Ames, *The Marrow of Theology* (1629; reprint, Boston: Pilgrim, 1968), pp. 185-86.

[47] Richard Baxter, *The Practical Works of Richard Baxter*, ed. William Orme (London: J. Duncan, 1830), 20:115.

[48] Owen, *Works*, 14:273.

[49] John Cotton, *Christ the Fountaine of Life* (London: n.p., 1651), p. 134.

[50] Baxter, *Practical Works*, 22:239.

I in 1611. The Puritans not only originated the idea of a new translation, but they also played a prominent role in its actual publication, for half of the committee of fifty-four translators were Puritan scholars.[51]

Their commitment to a biblically based spirituality can further be seen in their emphasis upon the spoken and written sermon as a means to communicate and meditate upon the Scriptures.[52] Chaderton called their style "a plain but effectual way of preaching."[53] Ideally the Puritan preacher's aim was not to impress listeners by their wit and learning, but rather to relate biblical truth to everyday life. This required not only the careful study of Scripture but also a perceptive understanding of human nature. They spoke of themselves as "physicians of the soul" who sought to apply the medicine of the Bible to the wounded consciences and broken hearts among their congregations. Puritan spirituality was supremely rooted in the Bible.

Fourth, *the Puritans were predominantly Augustinian in their emphasis upon human sinfulness and divine grace.*[54] Few have challenged Perry Miller's claim that Puritanism was primarily a manifestation of "the Augustinian strain of piety."[55] Augustine's restless path toward conversion and meditative purging of heart and soul eloquently recounted in his *Confessions* is echoed throughout numerous Puritan autobiographies and personal journals. But more importantly, Puritans followed Luther and Calvin's emphasis on an Augustinian view of human depravity that requires God's gracious initiative to work out salvation in the human heart. In his discussion of original sin in *The Golden Chaine* (1591), William Perkins (1558-1602) declared:

> The will received an impotence whereby it cannot will, or so much as lust after that which is indeed good, that which may please and be acceptable to God; . . . an inward rebellion whereby it utterly abhorreth that which is good, desiring and willing that alone which is evil. By this appeareth that the will is no agent, but a mere patient in the first act of conversion to God and that by itself it can neither begin that conversion, or any other inward and sound obedience due to God's law.[56]

---

[51]Ralph Barton Perry, *Puritanism and Democracy* (New York: Vanguard, 1944), p. 238.

[52]On the importance of preaching to Puritan spirituality see J. I. Packer, *A Quest for Godliness* (Wheaton, Ill.: Crossway, 1994), pp. 277-89, and Harry S. Stout, *The New England Soul: Preaching and Religious Culture in Colonial New England* (New York: Oxford University Press, 1988), pp. 3-64.

[53]Cited by John Adair, *Puritans: Religion and Politics in Seventeenth-Century England and America* (Gloucestershire, England: Sutton, 1998), p. 92.

[54]Against Pelagius, Augustine (354-430) declared that, with the Fall, man lost the ability to do good apart from God's grace (see Augustine *The Spirit and the Letter* 4-11). Hence, Augustine affirmed man's need of divine grace both to believe and obey God's commands (see Augustine *Enchiridion* 30-32, 106-7; *Confessions* 10:29-30, 37).

[55]Perry Miller, *The New England Mind: The Seventeenth Century* (1939; reprint, Boston: Beacon, 1961), pp. 4-5.

[56]William Perkins, *A Golden Chaine* (Cambridge: John Legate, 1591), p. 29.

The human inability that requires God's grace is stressed in the Westminster Confession (1647):

> Man, by his fall into a state of sin, hath wholly lost all ability of will to any spiritual good accompanying salvation; so as a natural man, being altogether averse from that good; and dead in sin, is not able, by his own strength, to convert himself, or to prepare himself thereunto. When God converts a sinner, and translates him into the state of grace, he freeth him from his natural bondage under sin, and by his grace alone enables him freely to will and to do that which is spiritually good.[57]

The Puritan stress on human inability led to their emphasis upon the necessity of God's gracious renovation of human nature. By his Spirit, God equips the redeemed person with the power to live righteously. Thus John Cotton concluded, "That there be in all such as are effectually called and united unto Christ, in-dwelling spiritual gifts of grace, wrought and created in us by the Holy Spirit, that is, by the begetting whereof, we are begotten and renewed to a spiritual life unto God, and so become fit members of his Church."[58] This need for regeneration became a dominant theme within Puritan spirituality. For example, Thomas Goodwin wrote, "There are inwrought and infused in the soul at regeneration, inherent and abiding principles of spiritual life, by which the soul is inwardly fitted, capacitated, inclined, and quickened unto the operations of a spiritual life."[59] Similarly, John Owen described regeneration as

> the infusion of a new, real, spiritual principle into the soul and its faculties, of spiritual life, light, holiness, and righteousness, disposed unto and suited for the destruction or expulsion of a contrary, inbred, habitual principle of sin and enmity against God, enabling unto all acts of holy obedience.[60]

Therefore, Puritan spirituality was rooted in an inner renewal that empowers the soul with spiritual life, but this could only be understood in light of the Spirit's activity.

Fifth, *the Puritans placed great emphasis upon the work of the Holy Spirit in the believer's life.* Richard Baxter declared that since the Holy Spirit is "our Guide, and Sanctifier, and Comforter," the doctrine of the Holy Spirit "is a most practical article of our belief."[61] There can be no doubt that for the Puritans reflection on the Holy Spirit was essential—not accidental—to understanding the Christian life.

---

[57]See *Documents of the English Reformation*, p. 595.

[58]John Cotton, *The Covenant of God's Free Grace* (London: n.p., 1645), p. 27.

[59]Thomas Goodwin, *The Works of Thomas Goodwin*, ed. Thomas Smith (1863; reprint, Edinburgh: Banner of Truth Trust, 1979), 6:187. See also Stephen Charnock, *The Doctrine of Regeneration* (1840; reprint, Grand Rapids: Baker, 1980).

[60]Owen, *Works*, 3:218-19.

[61]Baxter, *Practical Works*, 1:69.

B. B. Warfield, the brilliant Princeton theologian writing in 1900, made the startling comment that "the developed doctrine of the work of the Holy Spirit is an exclusively Reformation doctrine, and more particularly a Reformed doctrine, and more particularly still a Puritan doctrine."[62] Although one can argue that Warfield's case is overstated, he nevertheless does rightly acknowledge just how clearly Puritans focused on the Spirit's activity. Although this may surprise many who assume the Puritans were rationalists with no concern for the Spirit, nothing could be further from the historical truth. Geoffrey F. Nuttall, one of the most respected scholars of Puritanism in the twentieth century, made the point without hesitation: "the doctrine [of the Holy Spirit], with its manifold implications, received a more thorough and detailed consideration from the Puritans of seventeenth-century England than it has received at any other time in Christian history."[63]

Consistently Puritan pastors and theologians found themselves diving afresh into explorations of the person and work of the Spirit, for here they found insight into how faithfully to shepherd the people of God. The Holy Spirit's critical role in sanctification was rooted in the Puritan belief that all spirituality resulted from the work of the Holy Spirit. Thus, for the Puritans, the Spirit's work became the manner through which spirituality was initiated by God as an act of divine grace. Through the chapters of this book the reader will encounter creative ways in which the Puritans sought to have their thinking informed by a high view of the Spirit. Their interest in the work of the Holy Spirit is evidenced by a number of lengthy treatises written on the subject, the greatest of which were Thomas Goodwin's *The Work of the Holy Spirit in Our Salvation* (1663)[64] and John Owen's *Pneumatologia: A Discourse on the Holy Spirit* (1674).[65]

Sixth, *the Puritans were deeply troubled with sacramental forms of Catholic spirituality fostered within the Anglican Church.* They vigorously spoke out against what they labeled as "popish" forms of piety, regarding them, according to Richard Lovelace, "as a kind of rust to be scrubbed off the church rather than as furniture for its devotional life."[66] For example, speaking against the influx of Roman Catholic devotional practices into England, Henry Burton (1578-1648) wrote:

---

[62]B. B. Warfield, introduction to Abraham Kuyper, *The Work of the Holy Spirit*, trans. Henri De Vries (London: Funk & Wagnalls, 1900), p. xxxviii.

[63]Geoffrey F. Nuttall, *The Holy Spirit*, p. xxviii.

[64]Goodwin, *Works*, 6:1-522.

[65]Owen, *Works*, 3:1-651.

[66]Richard C. Lovelace, "Puritan Spirituality: The Search for a Rightly Reformed Church," in *Christian Spirituality: Post-Reformation and Modern*, ed. Louis Dupré and Don E. Saliers (New York: Crossroad, 1989), p. 296.

There is as well a Devotion blind and superstitious, breathed from the Bottomlesse-pit by him, who can transforme himself into an Angel of Light: as a Devotion illu-minate, and truly religious, like Elias his Sacrifice, inspired and inflamed by Fire from Heaven. Nor doth the Old Serpent either so usually or effectually infuse his poyson-ous enchantments into men's minds, as when he propineth them in the Golden Cup of demure Devotion. . . . What rabbles and swarmes of vowed disciples did these two, St Francis, and St Dominicke draw after them, and all by the strong incantations of their deepe Devotion.[67]

This critique of Anglo-Catholic piety is also evident in John Owen's rejection of the vows, orders, fastings and penances of "popish religion" as the "mistaken ways and means of mortification."[68] For it was "such outside endeavours, such bodily exercises, such self-performances, such merely legal duties, without the least mention of Christ or his Spirit" that inspired Owen to publish his treatise *On the Mortification of Sin in Believers.*[69] Thus the Puritan enthusiasm to promote a spirituality that was biblical must be seen in part as an attempt to counteract the various ele-ments of Catholic piety found within the Church of England.

Seventh, *Puritanism can also be understood as a revival movement.* J. I. Packer strongly em-phasizes this by asserting, "spiritual revival was central to what the Puritans pro-fessed to be seeking." Packer defines revival "as a work of God by his Spirit through his word bringing the spiritually dead to living faith in Christ and renewing the in-ner life of Christians who have grown slack and sleepy."[70] He bases his definition of Puritanism as "a movement of Revival" on three evidences. The first is that, al-though "revival" is not commonly found in their writings, Puritans repeatedly used the terms *reform, reformation* and *reformed,* to express the inward renewal of the heart and life that they sought to promote. The Puritans urged rulers "to reform their countries,"[71] citizens to promote "the reformation of religion,"[72] and fathers "to reform families."[73] When Richard Baxter published his classic work on the minis-try, *The Reformed Pastor* (1656), his purpose was not to encourage pastors to be

---

[67] Henry Burton, *A Tryall of Private Devotions* (1628; reprint, Norwood, N.J.: Walter J. Johnson, 1977), p. C-1, quoted in Lovelace, "Puritan Spirituality," p. 297.

[68] Owen, *Works,* 6:16.

[69] Ibid., 6:17.

[70] Packer, *Quest for Godliness,* pp. 36-37.

[71] See the preface of the *Geneva Bible* addressed "To the Most Virtuous and Noble Queen Elizabeth" (1560) in *Documents of the English Reformation,* ed. Gerald Bray (Minneapolis: Fortress, 1994), p. 358.

[72] "The Solemn League and Covenant, 1643," in *Documents of the English Reformation,* ed. Gerald Bray (Minneapolis: Fortress, 1994), pp. 483-84.

[73] The promise made by the church of Dorchester in 1677 according to the records of the First Church in Dorches-ter (Boston, 1891), p. 19, quoted in Packer, *Quest for Godliness,* p. 36.

Calvinistic in doctrine, but rather to be "renewed in vigour, zeal and purpose, in other words [be] *revived*."

The second evidence is that "personal revival was the central theme of Puritan devotional literature."[74] The vast number of printed sermons, manuals for godliness, treatises on conversion, and autobiographies written by the "affectionate practical English writers" substantiates this claim.[75]

Packer's third evidence that Puritanism must be considered a revival movement is that "the ministry of Puritan pastors under God brought revival."[76] He illustrates this by contrasting the faithful ministry of Richard Greenham from 1570 to 1590, which "was virtually fruitless," with the revivalistic nature of Richard Baxter's ministry in Kidderminster from 1641 to 1660 (during the Puritan revolution), where most of the two thousand adults in town "were converted under his ministry."[77] This reveals that sometimes revival did come as a result of Puritanism in England. Hence, as Wallace suggests, the "evangelical revivals of the eighteenth century" should not be regarded "as a new departure after generations of religious deadness," but rather as "continuations of [the] seventeenth-century . . . revival of spirituality" among the Puritans.[78] This is an argument Richard Lovelace will build upon in the final chapter of this book, which focuses on the Puritans and spiritual renewal.

Let us review the cluster of characteristics we have highlighted above:

- Many understand Puritanism as a movement of spirituality.

- Puritanism, at its heart, lays stress on experiencing communion with God.

- Puritans were united in their dependence upon the Bible as their supreme source of spiritual sustenance and guide for the reformation of life.

- The Puritans were predominantly Augustinian in their emphasis upon human sinfulness and divine grace.

- The Puritans placed great emphasis upon the work of the Holy Spirit in the believer's life.

---

[74]Packer, *Quest for Godliness*, pp. 38-39.

[75]Richard Baxter, *Baxter's Practical Works* (1673; reprint, Ligonier, Penn.: Soli Deo Gloria, 1990), 1:732. After stating that the "poorest library" must include a Bible, concordance, a "sound commentary" and "some English catechisms," Baxter concluded with the names of some sixty works, all but three of them written by Puritans.

[76]Packer, *Quest for Godliness*, p. 42.

[77]Ibid., p. 43-44.

[78]Wallace, *Spirituality of the Later English Puritans*, p. xii.

- The Puritans were deeply troubled with sacramental forms of Catholic spirituality fostered within the Anglican Church.

- Puritanism can also be understood as a revival movement.

These seven characteristics avoid blurring the theological, political and ecclesiastical differences that existed among Puritans while capturing their ethos of renewal and personal piety. The works introduced in this collection of essays are *Puritan* because each one reflects threads of a common spirituality that emphasized Christian experience and promoted corporate revival based upon the preaching of the Bible and wrought by the Holy Spirit.

A PURITAN CLASSIC

We have sought to define the meaning of *Puritan* both historically and theologically. However, we feel that the best way to experience the essence of Puritanism is through reading its classic texts. If a *classic* is a work of enduring popularity to all generations, few of the works we have selected in this book would qualify. With the exceptions of Bunyan's *Pilgrim's Progress* and Milton's *Paradise Lost*, most of the classics introduced here were selected more because of their neglect than their familiarity, although almost all of the volumes included have been reprinted numerous times since their original publication. Each classic included in this book has served and nourished previous generations in ways that offer great promise for generations to come. Contemporary neglect of these volumes should not disqualify them from requiring the attention they deserve.

Contemporary debates rage regarding the questionability of there being such a thing as a canon of Western literature, that is, an agreed upon set of texts every educated reader should be familiar with. Educators have become keenly aware of the difficulty of selectivity and bias.[79] Nevertheless it seems fair to suggest that one of the tasks of a scholar is to read widely, find some of the very best literature and then suggest a distilled list of texts worthy of the layperson's time. With this in mind, in this book we invite you to discover the Puritans and some of what we consider to be their most significant literary contributions. Ultimately it is you the reader who will determine which of these texts are truly classics when you read them for your own enrichment. This is certainly true of the contributors to this book, for in each case the work they introduce is, in some sense, a personal classic in their own lives.

---

[79]See, for example, the differing views represented by Harold Bloom, *The Western Canon: The Books and School of the Ages* (New York: Harcourt Brace, 1994), esp. pp. 15-39, and Lillian S. Robinson, "Treason Our Text: Feminist Challenges to the Literary Canon," in *The New Feminist Criticism: Essays on Women, Literature, and Theory*, ed. Elaine Showalter (New York: Pantheon, 1985), pp. 105-21.

Our primary intention here is to encourage you to read the original works for yourself. However, we also realize that Mark Twain's quip that a classic is what "everyone wishes they have read but never takes the time to read" will remain true for many. It is for this reason that many of the chapters, especially those dealing with the more difficult to read volumes, spend so much time surveying the actual work. Although a person may not have the time to read the thousands of pages represented in these classics, simply reading *The Devoted Life* may lead in the right direction. For those unable to read the original texts, this collection of essays offers access to a vast treasure of Puritan wisdom and theology that would remain otherwise out of reach.

The process of selecting texts proved difficult because of the numerous works that could have been included. Many other Puritan works qualify as classics, including William Gurnell's *Christian in Complete Armour*, Stephen Charnock's *Existence and Attributes of God* and John Preston's *The Saints' Daily Exercise*, just to name a few. Our selection was an attempt to provide examples of works on various themes throughout the history of Puritanism.

There are certain difficulties encountered when reading classic texts from centuries past. The following essays attempt to neutralize some of these difficulties by introducing the authors within their historical contexts in ways that illumine their goals. Often an understanding of the original circumstances will help guide modern readers in not only understanding the author's meaning, but also determining how to apply it to modern life. Because of the change of times and circumstances, we should not presume that we must agree with every point of Puritan authors in order to benefit from their message. Yet we believe that none of these Puritan classics should be preserved only for the academic elite. We have selected these classics because they have proven to be helpful, stimulating, encouraging or challenging to many who have taken the time to read them. After you read through this volume, you might choose to read a few of the original Puritan works that captured your imagination. We suspect that the more you read of the original texts, the more you will find the Puritans as healthy dialogue partners for understanding the Christian faith and life in our own day.

C. S. Lewis memorably noted the "mistaken preference for the modern books and this shyness of the old ones is nowhere more rampant than in theology."[80] This was the opposite of how it should be, argued Lewis, since "old books" not specifically addressed to us may speak more powerfully to our own day because they are

---

[80]C. S. Lewis, "On the Reading of Old Books," in *God in the Dock: Essays on Theology and Ethics* (Grand Rapids: Eerdmans, 1970), p. 201.

not bound by the same cultural blinders. We can do no better than to listen to Lewis powerfully make his case.

> None of us can fully escape this blindness [of our age], but we shall certainly increase it, and weaken our guard against it, if we read only modern books. Where they are true they will give us truths which we half knew already. Where they are false they will aggravate the error with which we are already dangerously ill. The only palliative is to keep the clean sea breeze of the centuries blowing through our minds, and this can be done only by reading old books. Not, of course, that there is any magic about the past. People were no cleverer then than they are now; they made as many mistakes as we. But not the *same* mistakes. They will not flatter us in the errors we are already committing; and their own errors, being now open and palpable, will not endanger us. . . . To be sure, the books of the future would be just as good a corrective as the books of the past, but unfortunately we cannot get at them.[81]

We must avoid being engaged in what has been called "chronological snobbery," in which we assume our age has the correct perspective. Reading from different generations allows us to see what was previously hidden, and the best way to avoid darkness is to turn on the lights. May this volume be the switch that illumines the world of the Puritans for you.

A GENERAL BIBLIOGRAPHY ON PURITANISM

Adair, John. *Puritans: Religion and Politics in Seventeenth-Century England and America.* Gloucestershire, England: Sutton, 1998.

Barker, William S. *Puritan Profiles: 54 Influential Puritans at the Time When the Westminster Confession of Faith Was Written.* Fearn, Ross-shire, Scotland: Christian Focus, 1996.

Beeke, Joel R. *The Quest for Full Assurance: The Legacy of Calvin and His Successor.* Edinburgh: Banner of Truth Trust, 1999.

Brachlow, Stephen. *The Communion of Saints: Radical Puritan and Separatist Ecclesiology, 1570-1625.* Oxford: Oxford University Press, 1988.

Caldwell, Patricia. *The Puritan Conversion Narrative: The Beginnings of American Expression.* New York: Cambridge University Press, 1983.

Carden, Allen. *Puritan Christianity in America: Religion and Life in Seventeenth Century Massachusetts.* Grand Rapids: Baker, 1990.

Coffey, John. *Persecution and Toleration in Protestant England 1558-1689.* Harlow, England: Longman, 2000.

Cohen, Charles. *God's Caress: The Psychology of Puritan Religious Experience.* New York: Ox-

---

[81]Ibid., p. 202.

ford University Press, 1986.

Chan, Simon R. H. "The Puritan Meditative Tradition, 1599-1691: A Study of Ascetical Piety." Ph.D. Dissertation, University of Cambridge, 1986.

Collinson, Patrick. *The Elizabethan Puritan Movement.* Oxford: Clarendon, 1967.

————. *Godly People: Essays on English Protestantism and Puritanism.* London: Hambledon, 1983.

————. *The Religion of Protestants: The Church in English Society 1559-1625.* Oxford: Clarendon, 1982.

Durston, Christopher, and Jacqueline Eales, eds. *The Culture of English Puritanism 1560-1700.* London: Macmillan, 1996.

Haller, William. *Liberty and Reformation in the Puritan Revolution.* New York: Columbia University Press, 1955.

————. *The Rise of Puritanism.* New York: Columbia University Press, 1938.

Hambrick-Stowe, Charles. *The Practice of Piety: Puritan Devotional Disciplines in Seventeenth-Century New England.* Chapel Hill: University of North Carolina Press, 1982.

————. "Puritan Spirituality in America." In *Christian Spirituality: Post-Reformation and Modern,* edited by Louis Depré and Don Saliers, pp. 338-53. London: SCM Press, 1990.

Helm, Paul. *Calvin and the Calvinists.* Edinburgh: Banner of Truth Trust, 1982.

Hill, Christopher. *Society and Puritanism in Pre-Revolutionary England.* New York: St. Martins, 1997.

————. *Puritanism and Revolution.* London: Secker and Warburg, 1965.

Hindson, Edward, ed. *Introduction to Puritan Theology.* Grand Rapids: Baker, 1976.

Hinson, E. Glenn. "Puritan Spirituality." In *Protestant Spiritual Traditions,* edited by Frank C. Senn, pp. 165-82. New York: Paulist, 1986.

Holifield, E. Brooks. *The Covenant Sealed: The Development of Puritan Sacramental Theology in Old and New England, 1570-1720.* New Haven, Conn.: Yale University Press, 1974.

Hulse, Errol. *Who Are the Puritans? And What Do They Teach?* Darlington, England: Evangelical Press, 2000.

Kendall, Robert T. *Calvin and English Calvinism to 1649.* Oxford: Oxford University Press, 1979.

Lake, Peter. *Anglicans and Puritans? Presbyterianism and English Conformist Thought from Whitgift to Hooker.* London: Unwin Hyman, 1988.

————. *Moderate Puritans and the Elizabethan Church.* Cambridge: University of Cambridge Press, 1982.

Lamont, William. *Puritanism and Historical Controversy.* McGill-Queen's Studies in the History of Religion 26. Los Angeles: UCLA Press, 1996.

Lloyd-Jones, D. Martyn. *The Puritans: Addresses Delivered at the Puritan and Westminster Conferences 1959-1978*. Edinburgh: Banner of Truth Trust, 1987.

Lovelace, Richard F. *The American Pietism of Cotton Mather: Origins of American Evangelicalism*. Grand Rapids: Christian University Press, 1979.

————. "The Anatomy of Puritan Piety: English Puritan Devotional Literature." In *Christian Spirituality: Post-Reformation and Modern*, edited by Louis Dupré and Don E. Saliers, pp. 294-323. New York: Crossroad, 1989.

Martin, Robert P. *A Guide to the Puritans*. Edinburgh: Banner of Truth Trust, 1997.

Miller, Perry. *Errand into the Wilderness*. Cambridge, Mass.: Harvard University Press, 1950.

————. *The New England Mind: The Seventeenth Century*. 1939. Reprint. Boston: Beacon Press, 1961.

Morgan, Edmund S. *The Puritan Family: Religion and Domestic Relations in Seventeenth-Century New England*. New York: Harper & Row, 1966.

————. *Visible Saints: The History of a Puritan Idea*. Ithaca, N.Y.: Cornell University Press, 1963.

Morgan, Irvonwy. *Puritan Spirituality: Illustrated from the Life and Times of the Rev. Dr. John Preston*. London: Epworth, 1973.

Morgan, John. *Godly Learning: Puritan Attitudes towards Reason, Learning, and Education, 1560-1640*. Cambridge: Cambridge University Press, 1986.

Muller, Richard A. *After Calvin: Studies in the Development of a Theological Tradition*. New York: Oxford University Press, 2003.

————. *Christ and the Decree: Christology and Predestination in Reformed Theology from Calvin to Perkins*. Grand Rapids: Baker, 1986.

————. *Post-Reformation Reformed Dogmatics: Volumes 1-4*. Grand Rapids: Baker, 1987-2003.

Murray, Iain H. D. *The Puritan Hope*. London: Banner of Truth Trust, 1971.

New, John F. H. *Anglican and Puritan: The Basis of Their Opposition, 1558-1640*. Stanford, Calif.: Stanford University Press, 1964.

Nuttall, Geoffrey F. *The Holy Spirit in Puritan Faith and Experience*. 2nd ed. London: University of Chicago Press. Reprint, 1992.

————. *Visible Saints: The Congregational Way, 1640-1660*. Oxford: Basil Blackwell, 1957.

Packer, J. I. *A Quest for Godliness: The Puritan Vision of the Christian Life*. Wheaton, Ill.: Crossway, 1994.

Pettit, Norman. *The Heart Prepared: Grace and Conversion in Puritan Spiritual Life*. New Haven, Conn.: Yale University Press, 1966.

Porterfield, Amanda. *Female Piety in Puritan New England: The Emergence of Religious Humanism*.

New York: Oxford University Press, 1992.

Puritan Bookshelf: Volumes 1-32. Still Waters Revival Books, 2001. CD-ROM.

Reformation Bookshelf: Volumes 1-30. Still Waters Revival Books, 2002. CD-ROM.

Rupp, Gordon. "A Devotion of Rapture in English Puritanism." In *Reformation, Conformity, and Dissent: Essays in Honour of Geoffrey Nuttall,* edited by R. Buick Knox, pp. 115-31. London: Epworth, 1977.

Ryken, Leland. *Worldly Saints: The Puritans as They Really Were.* Grand Rapids: Zondervan, 1986.

Sasek, Lawrence. ed. *Images of English Puritanism: A Collection of Contemporary Sources 1589-1646.* Baton Rogue: Louisiana State University Press, 1989.

Spurr, John. *English Puritanism 1603-1689: Social History in Perspective.* London: Macmillan, 1998.

Stout, Harry S. *The New England Soul: Preaching and Religious Culture in Colonial New England.* New York: Oxford University Press, 1988.

Toon, Peter. *The Emergence of Hyper-Calvinism in English Nonconformity, 1689-1765.* London: Olive Tree, 1967.

————. *Puritans and Calvinism.* Swengel, Penn.: Reiner, 1973.

Trinterud, Leonard J., ed. *Elizabethan Puritanism.* New York: Oxford University Press, 1971.

Trueman, Carl R. "Puritan Theology as Historical Event: A Linguistic Approach to the Ecumenical Context." In *Reformation and Scholasticism: An Ecumenical Enterprise,* edited by Willem J. van Asselt and Eef Dekker, pp. 253-75. Grand Rapids: Baker, 2001.

Tyacke, Nicholas. *The Fortunes of English Puritanism, 1603-1640.* London: Dr. Williams's Library Lecture, 1990.

Van Til, John L. *Liberty of Conscience: The History of a Puritan Idea.* Philadelphia: Presbyterian & Reformed, 1992.

Von Rohr, John. *The Covenant of Grace in Puritan Thought.* Atlanta: Scholars Press, 1986.

Wakefield, Gordon F. *Puritan Devotion: Its Place in the Development of Christian Piety.* London: Epworth, 1957.

Wallace, Dewey D., Jr. *Puritans and Predestination: Grace in English Protestant Theology 1525-1695.* Chapel Hill: University of North Carolina Press, 1982.

————. *The Spirituality of the Later English Puritans.* Macon, Ga.: Mercer, 1987.

Watts, Michael. *The Dissenters: From the Reformation to the French Revolution.* Oxford: Oxford University Press, 1978.

Webster, Tom. *Godly Clergy in Early Stuart England: The Caroline Puritan Movement c. 1620-1643.* Cambridge: Cambridge University Press, 1997.

❧ 2 ❧

THE ARTE OF PROPHESYING

BY WILLIAM PERKINS

(1558-1602)

Paul R. Schaefer

ALTHOUGH WILLIAM PERKINS WAS ONE OF THE MOST WIDELY READ preachers of his own age, and one of the most outstanding theological thinkers of the Elizabethan era, many, even among those who regularly buy and read Puritan reprints, scarcely know of him. Part of the reason for this might be that unlike the writings of notables such as Owen, Baxter and Sibbes, few of Perkins's works actually have been reprinted in either of the Puritan reprint revivals of the nineteenth or twentieth centuries.[1] Another reason for this might be the quandary of exactly how to understand Perkins, a man whose scant forty-four years (1558-1602) nevertheless spanned almost the entirety of the religiously tumultuous reign of Elizabeth I (reigned 1558-1603). While he was a Cambridge man who came to faith under the great Puritan leader Laurence Chaderton at Christ's College, he matured after the Cambridge and southeastern England controversies over vestments and church government and he died before the rise of more vocal Puritan protest during the Stuart years of James I and especially Charles I. Perkins always viewed himself as a loyal son of the established Church and although it is true that he never directly praised the Elizabethan settlement, episcopal government or the *Book of Common Prayer*, he poured scorn on any who separated from the established Church of Eng-

---

[1] There are a few exceptions to this. See, for example, William Perkins, *A Commentary on Galatians*, ed. Gerald Sheppard (New York: Pilgrim, 1989); William Perkins, *A Commentary on Hebrews 11*, ed. John Augustine (New York: Pilgrim, 1991); William Perkins, *The Work of William Perkins* (edited selections from some notable texts), ed. Ian Breward (Appleford, England: Sutton Courtenay, 1970).

land, which he considered to be "God's cornfield."[2]

Nevertheless one can see something of the Puritan in him simply by noting the title of the particular Puritan classic under review here, namely *The Arte of Prophesying* (1592).[3] *Prophesying* was the Elizabethan term for penetrating preaching, preaching that expressed correct doctrine but also convicted of sin and gloried in God's sovereign grace. "Prophesying movements" formed part of the way that those uncomfortable with Elizabeth's "settlement of religion" in the early 1560s expressed their concern for reformational preaching of the Word. These movements were concerned that the reading of the *Homilies* (fine in and of themselves to these people) produced during the reign of Elizabeth's half-brother Edward VI could not fully replace vibrant preaching. (These homilies, many of them written by Archbishop Thomas Cranmer, primary author of the original *Book of Common Prayer*, were full-length sermons drafted because early English Reformers such as Cranmer as well as Hugh Latimer, Nicholas Ridley and John Hooper found the overall state of preaching in the mid-sixteenth century so abominable. The authors of the homilies themselves would have believed that this was merely a temporary measure.) Elizabeth herself basically censured her archbishop of Canterbury, Edmund Grindal, in 1575 for failure to root out "prophesiers" and other disturbers of the peace of the church.[4] Yet Grindal knew that such gatherings to hear known clergy preach and allow novices to gain experience would prove necessary to make England a truly Reformed land as they had helped many in the Swiss and German Reformed movements.[5] Grindal even willingly admonished Elizabeth:

> Where it is thought that the reading of godly homilies, set forth by public authority, may suffice, I continue of the same mind as I was when I attended last upon your

---

[2]See, for example, William Perkins, "The Symbol: An Exposition of the Creed," *The Workes of the Famous and Worthie Divine William Perkins* (Cambridge: Legate, 1616-1618), 1:310-12. Hereafter references to the original three-volume Legate edition will simply give Perkins's name, the title of the treatise, and the volume and page number.

[3]Perkins, "The Arte of Prophesying," 2:644-73. Reprint: William Perkins, *The Art of Prophesying* (Edinburgh: Banner of Truth Trust, 1996), pp. 3-79. The reprint also contains Perkins's "The Calling of the Ministry." The reprint version will be used throughout this chapter since that is the one accessible to the reading audience today. The reprint generally follows the original text, usually only updating grammar. There are some places where the phraseology has been slightly altered to accommodate modern readers. One excision that this author believes should have been left in is a concluding remark in the original on page 673 where Perkins lists those who helped him organize his thoughts. The list is remarkable in its depth and breath: "Augustine, Hemingus, Hyperius, Erasmus, Illyricus, Wigandus, Jacobus Mathias, Theodore Beza, Franciscus Junius."

[4]See Patrick Collinson, *Archbishop Grindal: 1519-1583* (London: Jonathan Cape, 1979), pp. 219-52.

[5]For a fascinating study of preaching during the Reformation era that contains an account of the Reformed "prophesyings" as well as a separate chapter on Perkins's *The Arte of Prophesying*, see Hughes Oliphant Old, *The Reading and Preaching of Scriptures in the Worship of the Christian Church Volume 4: The Age of Reformation* (Grand Rapids: Eerdmans, 2002), esp. pp. 50-52, 251-69.

Majesty. The reading of homilies hath its commodity, but is nothing comparable to the office of preaching. The godly preacher . . . can apply his speech according to the diversity of times, places and hearers, which cannot be done in homilies: exhortations, reprehensions, and persuasions are uttered with more affection, to the moving of the hearers. . . . Besides, homilies were devised by the godly bishops in your brother's time only to supply necessity, for want of preachers, and are by statute not to be preferred but to give place to sermons . . . and were never thought in themselves alone to contain sufficient instruction for the Church of England.[6]

Perkins obviously shared this concern. He even once lamented that some of his students neglected the "famous and clear lights whom the Lord raised up for the reforming of religion, such as Luther, Calvin, Bucer, Martyr, &c."[7] Thus Perkins's addressing a subject like reformational preaching and calling it "prophesying" entailed a risk of governmental displeasure. In fact, when the work first appeared (in Latin) in the 1590s, Grindal was dead and John Whitgift was archbishop of Canterbury. Although a Calvinist in doctrine, Whitgift followed Elizabeth's lead and sought to bring full conformity to the settlement of religion.[8]

As noted above, Perkins's life spanned almost the entire reign of Elizabeth I.[9] For such a short life, he produced a large quantity of work. The Legate editions (first edition 1608-1609, second edition 1616-1617), the standard editions used in scholarly research, comprised three lengthy folio volumes. Originally delivered as sermons and lectures at Great St. Andrews Church, Cambridge, to an audience both town and gown, these treatises contained materials coming directly from his pen as well as some taken from notes and published posthumously. These published treatises, which covered a ministry of eighteen years, 1584-1602, exhibited a remarkable breadth of interest, dealing with topics ranging from predestination to the right ordering of the family.

Perkins's fame spread well beyond the borders of his beloved England. Churchmen from other lands quickly translated his treatises into a number of languages including Dutch, German and Polish. In the land of his birth, sales of his works soon eclipsed even those of Calvin's and lined the bookshelves of "the godly." Somewhat remarkably, given the wide variety of topics discussed, his own theolog-

---

[6]Edmund Grindal, *Remains* (Cambridge: Parker Society, 1843), p. 382.

[7]Perkins, "An Exposition of the Whole Epistle of Jude," *Works,* 3:2:552.

[8]See Patrick Collinson, *The Elizabethan Puritan Movement* (Oxford: Oxford University Press, 1967), pp. 432-67, and H. C. Porter, *Reformation and Reaction in Tudor Cambridge* (Cambridge: Cambridge University Press, 1958), pp. 277-343.

[9]For modern biographical sketches of Perkins, see Porter, *Reformation and Reaction,* pp. 288-313 and Ian Breward, "General Introduction," *The Work of William Perkins,* pp. 1-129.

ical understanding generally remained constant.

Anyone familiar with Perkins has probably heard of the following notation by his seventeenth-century biographer Thomas Fuller: "[Perkins] would pronounce the word *damn* with such emphasis, as left a doleful echo in his auditors' ears a good while after; and when a catechist of Christ's College, in expounding the Commandments, applied them so home . . . almost to make his hearers' hearts fall down, and bring to stand upright." One should be cautious in evaluating Perkins as preacher or pastoral counsellor from this remark because Fuller immediately adds that when the fiery young Cambridge don became a more seasoned preacher and pastor at Great St. Andrews, "in older age he altered his voice, and remitted much of his former rigidness, often professing that to preach mercy was [the] proper office of ministers of the Gospel."[10]

An entire generation of preachers was indeed shaped by Perkins, not only through this small tract on hermeneutics and homiletics, but also through his own deep piety mixed with his exacting and penetrating preaching. William Haller, who, along with Perry Miller and M. M. Knappen, helped bring Puritan studies out of scholarly obsolescence, coined the phrase "the spiritual brotherhood" for this younger generation of preachers who absorbed the instruction of those like Chaderton and his pupil Perkins.[11] In fact a succession of "Puritan worthies" arose directly from Perkins's ministry. Perkins himself contributed to the spiritual awakening of his successor at Great St. Andrews, Paul Baynes, and Baynes in turn witnessed the awakening of Richard Sibbes who in turn witnessed to John Cotton who in turn witnessed to John Preston who in turn saw the conversions of both Thomas Shepard and Thomas Goodwin.

God uses preaching, Perkins claimed in his preface to *The Art of Prophesying*, as the means "instrumental in gathering the church" and "driv[ing] away the wolves from the folds of the Lord." It allures the soul by subduing "our self-willed minds" and changing people from "an ungodly and pagan lifestyle to a life of Christian faith and repentance." He therefore believed that of all the gifts given to the church by the Spirit, "prophesying" stood as "the most excellent." One should, moreover, never despise this great gift but should reflect on the "tremendous responsibility" and the difficulty of the task of those who would shepherd souls through the Word of God. Not only so, but "prophesying . . . a solemn public utterance" relates "to the worship of God and the salvation of our neighbors." Those who scorn discus-

---

[10]Thomas Fuller, *The Holy State and the Profane State*, ed. J. Nichols (1648; reprint, London: William Pickering, 1840), 2:81.

[11]William Haller, *The Rise of Puritanism* (New York: Harper, 1938), pp. 49-82.

sion of such a vital means of grace prove that they do "not like godly and moderate-minded men." Such prophesying for Perkins was not receiving a new word from the Lord but rather correctly handling what God has given in the Scriptures. It is to this reflection on preaching that we now turn.[12]

CANON AS CONTENT

The Reformation watchwords *sola Christi* and *sola Scriptura*—Christ alone, Scripture alone—serve as the twin foundation stones for what Perkins conceived as biblical preaching: "Preaching the Word is prophesying in the name and on behalf of Christ. Through preaching those who hear are called into a state of grace, and preserved in it."[13] Citing a number of passages, Perkins closed his exhortation by arguing that the recognition of Christ in the Word forms the all-important basis of preaching. Thus he quoted Romans 10:14: "How are they to call on one in whom they have not believed? And how are they to believe in one of whom they have never heard? And how are they to hear without someone to proclaim him?"

At this juncture, however, a stylistic point should be noted. Readers of this piece will consistently note that Perkins constantly divided everything into twos and makes regular definitional distinctives. Given the times in which he lived (namely the heart of the English Renaissance), Perkins's training at Tudor Cambridge included a wide variety of methods and styles fitted together, albeit sometimes uncomfortably, namely, the older scholasticism, the Christian humanism of the northern Renaissance[14] and the philosophical work of the French Calvinist logician Peter Ramus. Perkins's works actually show elements of all of these styles although he never allowed style to shape substance but rather desired style to rivet the listener's attention to substance.[15] Thus while it is very apparent that Perkins made substantial use of certain Ramist techniques in *The Art of Prophesying* such as divisions, definitions and dialectics, his theological awareness followed that of Calvin. Donald McKim, an expert on Perkins's relationship to the Ramist system, openly acknowledges this: "Ramism as adapted by the Puritans did not give specific content to theology as such. The sources of theology for the English Puritans

---

[12]Perkins, *Art of Prophesying*, pp. 3-5.

[13]Ibid., p. 7.

[14]For a fascinating study on the Puritans and Renaissance humanism, see Margo Todd, *Christian Humanism and the Puritan Social Order* (Cambridge: Cambridge University Press, 1987).

[15]For a general introduction to Perkins in the context of Cambridge University see my "Protestant Scholasticism at Elizabethan Cambridge: William Perkins and a Reformed Theology of the Heart," in *Protestant Scholasticism: Essays in Reassessment*, ed. Scott Clark and Carl Trueman (Carlisle, U.K.: Paternoster, 1999), pp. 148-64.

were more from Calvin's Geneva [than] from Ramus's Paris."[16] What Ramism did for Perkins—in this handbook at least—was allow a greater clarity and potency to come through the substance of the argument.

Moving past the question of the use of Ramist techniques, Perkins clearly demanded that the Scriptures alone form "the exclusive subject of preaching" because Scripture displays "God's Wisdom revealing from heaven the truth which is in accord with godliness." Such wisdom from God has "power to penetrate the spirit of man" and "bind the conscience" because Scripture in itself has "purity" and "clarity" and because the Holy Spirit uses Scripture to move people to see the "sum and substance of the Bible." At the heart of this wisdom stands Christ, a wisdom that Perkins laid out in syllogistic form:

> Major Premise: The true Messiah shall be both God and man, from the seed of David. He shall be born of his heavenly Father's bosom. He shall satisfy the law. He shall offer himself as a sacrifice for the sins of the faithful. He shall conquer death by dying and rising again. He shall ascend into heaven. In due time he shall return for judgment.
>
> Minor Premise: Jesus of Nazareth, the son of Mary, meets all these requirements.
> Conclusion: Therefore Jesus is the true Messiah.[17]

Perkins contended that the major premise derives from the Old Testament while the minor derives from the New.[18] Perkins insisted, moreover, that this unity of Old and New formed the vital center for the apostolic writers as they themselves looked back on the Old Testament. For example, one passage Perkins noted in passing is Luke 24:44-47:

> Then [Jesus] said to them, "These are my words that I spoke to you while I was still with you—that everything written about me in the law of Moses, the prophets, and the psalms must be fulfilled." Then he opened their minds to understand the scriptures, and he said to them, "Thus it is written, that the Messiah is to suffer and to rise from the dead on the third day, and that repentance and forgiveness of sins is to be proclaimed in his name to all nations, beginning from Jerusalem."

Thus the Bible contains one message, one covenant of grace, seen in ways of promise and deliverance, now and not yet to be sure, but one message nonetheless.[19]

---

[16]Donald K. McKim, *Ramism in William Perkins' Theology* (New York: Harper, 1987), p. 132.

[17]Perkins, *Art of Prophesying*, pp. 9-11.

[18]Ibid., p. 11.

[19]A modern writer who has done much in this area of having a Christocentric reading of the Old Testament is Sidney Greidanus. See his *Preaching Christ from the Old Testament* (Grand Rapids: Eerdmans, 1999).

Perkins also took his readers through a brief tour of the canonical Scriptures and later, after discussing the issue of canon, explained why the Apocrypha is not canonical.[20] One must remember that preaching had not been a priority in many English parishes and thus Perkins took nothing for granted. After doing his canonical overview, Perkins reminded his readers that defense of the canon begins with the "inward testimony of the Holy Spirit" because in these books the Spirit seals to our hearts the "voice of Christ." Secondary testimonies such as the "voice of the church" or Scripture's "antiquity," "harmony of parts" or enunciation of "fulfilled prophecy" all help buttress the claim of the supreme authority of Scripture, but none of these can have first place. Rather, the "sovereign and supreme judgment" must rest with the Scripture's testimony "to itself" and the "prerogative of the Holy Spirit speaking in the Scriptures." Such teaching, Perkins believed, safeguards the final authority of Scripture in matters of faith and practice yet allows for the church to grapple with said Scripture through the give and take of interpretation. Perkins even admitted a "ministerial judgment" given to the church for order and discipline but demanded that such judgment must never go out on its own but always "judge according to the Scriptures."[21] Although shorter in length than Calvin's exposition in the 1559 *Institutes*, Perkins's teaching on scriptural authority clearly parallels that of Calvin.[22]

CONSIDERATION OF CONTEXT

Perkins moved from his undergirding doctrinal concerns, found in the first three chapters, to three chapters (four to six) concerning methodological issues facing the exegete of Scripture. In chapter four, titled "The Interpretation of Scripture," one detects the fine nuances in Perkins's advocacy of *sola Scriptura*. Perkins, like the Protestant Reformers before him, rejected the medieval fourfold approach to biblical study. The "fourfold approach" was a method of biblical interpretation that started with the "literal" or "plainest" sense as a foundation but then allowed the exegete to move into "allegorical," "tropological" (moralistic maxims), and "anagogical" (stylized apocalyptic speculations) interpretations. While the Reformers and their heirs certainly believed that one could find Old Testament "types" or "shadows" (like the Passover lamb) that pointed to Christ, they found the fourfold approach dangerous because it was too speculative.

---

[20]Perkins follows the lead of his own Church of England Articles of Religion, *The Thirty-Nine Articles*, Article VI.

[21]All references from Perkins in this paragraph are from *The Art of Prophesying*, pp. 18-22.

[22]See John Calvin, *Institutes of the Christian Religion*, ed. John McNeill, trans. Ford Lewis Battles (Philadelphia: Westminster Press, 1960), 1:69-92.

Perkins clearly recognized that Scripture as writing, even if inspired writing, needs interpretation that calls for care. Part of this included a liberal arts education, since correct interpretation of Scripture demands "grammatical, rhetorical and logical analysis, and the relevant ancillary studies" and keeping a "commonplace" book on one's findings. Furthermore, Perkins highlighted the importance of Paul's letter to the Romans and the Gospel of John as key to understanding the New Testament, and thus they deserve special attention. Not only so, but Perkins argued "we ought to get help from orthodox Christian writers, not only from modern times but also from the ancient church. For Satan raises old heresies from the dead in order to retard the restoration of the church which has begun in our own time." One interesting feature of this short book is its liberal use of quotations from the church fathers, especially Augustine, Gregory of Nazianzus and John Chrysostom.[23]

Since the church councils and early Christian writers "reliably" refuted the heresies that Perkins believed in his day were the same as the old, only "painted with a new coat of varnish," Perkins even incorporated the Apostles' Creed as part of his understanding of the "analogy of faith"; in other words, where the exegete should turn when encountering a difficult passage.[24] While such a use of tradition within a *sola Scriptura* framework might seem odd at first to a modern evangelical, it actually fits the standard sixteenth-century way of explaining the final normativeness of Scripture. To the sixteenth-century Reformed mind, the interpreter never stands alone but rather embraces a trinitarian and redemptive reading as the matrix in which sound understanding arises.[25]

Such reflection in no way denudes the final authority of Scripture in matters of faith and practice, they claimed, because all such creedal expressions and teachings of humans finally must come under the searchlight of Scripture as final and only infallible authority. Human teaching derives authority only secondarily as both the individual exegete and the church catholic hold to the sure testimony of Scripture with humble and prayerful commitment. Perkins's own confessional standard, *The Thirty-Nine Articles*, clearly expressed this for him.[26] Moreover, while approving the creeds and fathers as helps, Perkins also admonished his hearers (even quoting Augustine as a support) that "[we] should not rest our faith on human testimonies,

---

[23]Perkins, *Art of Prophesying*, pp. 23-25.

[24]Ibid., p. 27.

[25]For a fine modern study in this regard, see Keith Mathison, *The Shape of Sola Scriptura* (Moscow, Idaho: Canon, 2001).

[26]*The Thirty-Nine Articles*, Articles VI, VIII.

either from the philosophers or the fathers."[27]

Essentially interpretation meant for Perkins an "opening up of the words and statements of Scripture in order to bring out its single, full and natural sense." Given this, Perkins contended that not only should the rule of faith give boundaries for clear interpretation, but also those seeking to bring forth true meaning need to view the passage within its own literary and historical circumstances, within the Christian ethic of love and with an eye toward other passages of comparison that might elucidate the meaning. He also declared, "The principal interpreter of Scripture is the Holy Spirit." Thus even with the other tools, the biblical interpreter's work would be severely diminished if not depleted altogether without prayerful seeking of illumination from the One who inspired the biblical books in the first place.[28]

Perkins further supplied his readers with an astonishing number of contextual, linguistic and comparative helps to aid in the task of exegesis. Space does not permit a thorough examination of all these helps but some reflection surely is in order. One notices that Perkins had indeed made great use of many of the advances of the Renaissance in terms of textual studies. Not only so, but he freely admitted that while many passages are plain and can be seen to have clear analogies to other parts of the Bible, some parts are more "cryptic and dark." For the Reformers, perspicuity never meant that all places plainly expressed their meaning but rather that the basic teachings on God and redemption could be grasped clearly. Although he never mentioned in chapters four through six that the exegete should be knowledgeable in the original languages, he did show how such knowledge can often be beneficial, especially in noting certain linguistic and cultural nuances in the text.[29] Ultimately the concern for "right 'cutting'" of the Bible should be "to edify the people of God: 'Study to show thyself approved unto God, a workman that needeth not to be ashamed, rightly dividing [or cutting (the note is Perkins's)] the word of truth' (2 Tim 2:15 KJV)."[30]

COMMITMENT TO CONFRONT AND TO COMFORT

Perkins closed his short treatise with five chapters (seven through eleven) on the movement from the study to the pulpit. He began by arguing that the doctrines

---

[27]Perkins, Art of Prophesying, p. 53.

[28]Ibid., pp. 26-27.

[29]Ibid., pp. 30-50. The reader may also wish to consult chapter one of the Westminster Confession of Faith. Although written over a generation after Perkins's death, it reflects many of his thoughts on the nature and interpretation of Holy Scripture.

[30]Perkins, Art of Prophesying, p. 48.

drawn from one's study should be applied "appropriately to the circumstances of the place and time and to the people in the congregation." He further contended that passages when applied fit either the category of law or gospel and should be brought forth in a manner to instruct and upbuild the congregation: "The basic principle in application is to know whether the passage is a statement of the law or of the gospel."[31] From this perspective, Perkins masterfully wove together the concerns of the earlier Reformers Luther and Calvin and also their heirs.

In much the same way as Luther in the treatise *On Christian Liberty*,[32] Perkins contended that the law "exposes the disease of sin . . . [but] provides no remedy for it." On the other hand, he admonished:

> The gospel not only teaches us what is to be done; it also has the power of the Holy Spirit joined to it. When we are regenerated by him we receive the strength we need both to believe the gospel and do what it commands. The law is, therefore, first in the order of teaching; then comes the Gospel.

Thus, since the law demands the "need for perfect inherent righteousness," the preacher should use it to show that all are under a curse from which they cannot escape through their own efforts. Then once the futility of merit and the curse arising from sin is clearly known, then the gospel can shine forth as the "contrast" that proclaims "Christ and his benefits, and of faith being fruitful in good works."[33]

Perkins then continued this discussion about the place of good works in the life of the Christian by stating that the law has application for the justified believer not in terms of a "legal" character but in terms of "evangelical" character "in light of Christ."[34] This evangelical character contains no merit of its own and thus cannot be the way of salvation, but rather uses the law now to show a true believer a guide to godly walking. Such an emphasis fits well with Calvin's discussion of the "third use of the law" in the *Institutes*. And by way of an intriguing parallel—intriguing because Perkins did not mention it as a source—his discussion of law and gospel as a whole appears to follow the basic outline of the *Heidelberg Catechism* (1563) with its three-part structure of guilt-grace-gratitude.[35]

In this same chapter (chapter seven) on use and application, Perkins then supplied potential preachers with a detailed list of "categories of hearers." Of the seven

---

[31] Ibid., p. 54.

[32] Martin Luther, *On Christian Liberty* (Minneapolis: Augsburg/Fortress, 2003).

[33] Perkins, *Art of Prophesying*, pp. 54-55.

[34] Ibid., p. 55.

[35] See Calvin *Institutes* 2.7.12 (1:360-61 in the Battles edition) and *The Heidelberg Catechism* (Grand Rapids: CRC Publications, 1975).

categories, six apply to individual hearers thus providing instruction for sensitive listening as a pastoral counselor to the individual as well as a call to know the makeup of one's whole congregation. The seventh gives a summation of the basic congregational setting within an Augustinian framework of a "mixed church" of believers and unbelievers:[36] "Churches with both believers and unbelievers . . . is the typical situation in our congregations. Any doctrine may be expounded to them, either from the law or the gospel, so long as its biblical limitations and circumspections are observed."[37]

And just what are these biblical limitations and circumspections? Perkins answered this in a variety of ways throughout this section. The preacher of the Word as prophet, as one who brings forth God's Word to bear on the present life situations of a multivariate congregation, must be thunderer and therapist, confronter and comforter, exhorter and encourager. People have different needs and so different ways of bringing home law and gospel must be applied. The hardhearted must be threatened with the law. The humbled unbeliever must hear the tenderness of the gospel. The believer living in assurance of faith must be reminded of the gospel that saved and be exhorted to continual fruitfulness. Those professors of the gospel who have no peace because they have "fallen back" must have their temptation or struggle diagnosed and be called to repent, but also given the assurance that "sin does not abolish grace" and that in this "fallen and sinful world all of God's works are done by means which are contrary to him" (i.e., "all things work together for good for those who love God, who are called according to his purpose" [Rom 8:28]).[38]

Finally, Perkins addressed the preacher in the pulpit. He remarked that "two things are essential: (i) the hiding of human wisdom and (ii) demonstration or manifestation of the Spirit." From what has been noted previously, such "hiding of human wisdom" in no way prohibits study; in fact, Perkins again admonished the preacher to study in the strongest terms: "The minister . . . must privately make free use of the general arts and of philosophy as well as employ a wide variety of reading while he is preparing his sermon." Nevertheless since the minister presents Christ, his own skills and knowledge must recede to the background. Perkins even quoted an old Latin proverb: "[It] is also a point of art to conceal art."[39]

---

[36]For Augustine on the idea of a "mixed church," see Peter Brown, *Augustine of Hippo* (Berkeley: University of California Press, 1967), especially chapter 19.

[37]Perkins, *Art of Prophesying*, p. 62.

[38]Ibid., pp. 56-62.

[39]Ibid., pp. 70-71.

"Demonstrating the Spirit" means that the preacher will speak graciously, simply, and clearly, with the message tailored "to the understanding of the hearers and appropriate for expressing the majesty of the Spirit." Perkins criticized those who focus attention on "Greek and Latin phrases" or who try to impress with "odd turns of phrase." He contended that such speaking only serves to "distract the minds of those listeners who cannot see the connection between what has been said and what follows." Not only should the minister delete these ways from the sermon, but the minister should also avoid "mere story telling as well as vulgar [*vulgar* in the sixteenth century meant something more akin to "common"] or foolish statements."[40]

Perkins assumed that his readers preparing for the ministry would be serious about their calling. Nevertheless, he warned those who have no sense of grace to abandon such a calling because "God abhors godly speech which is not joined with a godly life." Such does not mean "perfection" because Perkins limited perfection to the saints in glory. Still the preacher should grow in "good conscience," in "an inward sense of the doctrine" being preached, in "the fear of God" and a "love for the people." Speaking to those younger in his audience, who were just beginning to sense a call to the ministry, Perkins paraphrased I Timothy 4:7: "Those who are younger must devote themselves to godliness, and reject the lusts of youth." The preacher must be a person of thoughtful and ardent prayer as well.[41]

Perkins concluded his book with a short overview of his main points in the treatise. He then turned again to the dynamic center of the whole: "The heart of the matter is this: Preach one Christ, by Christ, to the praise of Christ." He then added a simple but powerful reminder: "*Soli Deo Gloria*—To God alone be the glory!"[42]

CONCLUSION: CALLING THE CHURCH BACK TO CHRIST-CENTEREDNESS

The Arte of Prophesying surely is a Puritan classic. In short compass, it explains many of the concerns that the variegated movement we call Puritanism shared and ideas that we, too, need to hear again and again: deep commitment to the word of God in Scripture as supreme authority; a commitment to both ardor and order in life; a passion for godliness placed within a Christ-centered theology that constantly reminds the believer that salvation is all of grace from beginning to end; and that fine

---

[40]Ibid.
[41]Ibid., pp. 72-78.
[42]Ibid., p. 79.

balance between justification and sanctification that refuses to separate the two when speaking of the Christian life, but that also always distinguishes between them so that a true believer will not wallow in despair.

Perkins's ability to merge the hermeneutical process with teachings on homiletics also has much to commend it to our age. We live in a day of specialists and indeed have reaped many rewards because of that. Nevertheless, Perkins draws us back to the biblical model of the preacher as one "apt to teach," which means that such a person must be knowledgeable of the tools to "cut rightly" the Word as well as prepared to grow in learning how "to admonish" in all earnestness and sincerity. The balance that Perkins provides proves an admonishment to those in the education and training of future clergy to help give both emphases their due concern.

Also Perkins's emphasis on law and gospel provides the modern church with a much needed reminder on what is really of importance in this end of modernity/ beginning of postmodernity age. The one triune God who created and sustains the heavens and the earth still lives and reigns and in him is found the wealth of wisdom and truth. His Word provides a way into relationship with him because it tells us of Christ the Son who gave his life that we might stand forgiven through faith and who rose again in power and from that power gives his people the Spirit to empower them to grow in the fruit of the Spirit (Gal 5:22). Perkins's work also sensitizes us to the need to provide thoughtful rather than superficial answers in the variety of situations we face in relationships each day with fellow believers and unbelievers alike. Since we do not live in sixteenth-century Elizabethan society, some of our applications might differ from those advocated by Perkins, but the truth of the gospel message he brings will last.

SELECT BIBLIOGRAPHY

Primary Sources

Perkins, William. *The Art of Prophesying.* Edinburgh: Banner of Truth Trust, 1996.

————. *A Commentary on Galatians.* Edited by Gerald Sheppard. New York: Pilgrim, 1989.

————. *The Work of William Perkins.* Selections with biographical introduction edited by Ian Breward. Appleford, England: Sutton Courtenay, 1970.

Secondary Sources

Collinson, Patrick. *The Elizabethan Puritan Movement.* Oxford: Oxford University Press, 1967.

Muller, Richard. *Christ and the Decree: Christology and Predestination in Reformed Theology from Calvin to Perkins.* Grand Rapids: Baker, 1986.

Old, Hughes Oliphant. *The Reading and Preaching of the Scriptures in the Worship of the Christian Church, Volume IV: The Age of the Reformation.* Grand Rapids: Eerdmans, 2002.

Schaefer, Paul. "Protestant Scholasticism at Elizabethan Cambridge: William Perkins and a Reformed Theology of the Heart." In *Protestant Scholasticism: Essays in Reassessment,* edited by Carl R. Trueman and R. S. Clark, pp. 148-64. Carlisle, U.K.: Paternoster, 1999.

❧ 3 ❧

THE MARROW OF THEOLOGY

BY WILLIAM AMES
(1576-1633)

Joel R. Beeke and Jan van Vliet

WHEN ABRAHAM KUYPER JR. EXAMINED THE ANTAGONISTIC RELA-
tionship between William Ames (1576-1633) and Johannes Maccovius (1588-
1644), two theological teachers at Franeker, the Netherlands, he concluded that
Ames had deviated from the Reformed position that Maccovius defended.[1] Robert T.
Kendall goes so far as to say that through Ames's influence, "Calvin's doctrine of
faith, for all practical purposes, was now dead and buried. Ames espoused a voluntaristic doctrine of faith [i.e., emphasized the role of the will or volition more than
the intellect in the doctrine of saving faith] within a tradition that had already been
shaking off Calvin's influence anyway." Kendall goes on to conclude, "Ames's voluntarism appears to be the key to all he believes."[2]

Though Ames did make occasional statements that sounded as though he were
a voluntarist who had strayed from the path of Reformed orthodoxy that usually
put more focus on the intellect, scholars who charge Ames with voluntarism (i.e.,
teaching that one is saved by an act of the will) betray a lamentable lack of understanding of his entire work. Within the parameters of orthodox Reformed theology, Ames stressed that Christianity is a Spirit-worked, vital, heartfelt faith that
produces a genuine Christian walk.

---

[1] Abraham Kuyper Jr., *Johannes Maccovius* (Leiden: D. Donner, 1899), pp. 315-96. Abraham Kuyper Jr. was the son
of the famous Abraham Kuyper Sr. (1837-1920), Dutch Reformed theologian and political leader who served
as prime minister in the Netherlands from 1901 to 1905.
[2] Robert T. Kendall, *Calvin and English Calvinism to 1649* (Oxford: Oxford University Press, 1979), pp. 151, 154.

After we sketch Ames's life and teaching career, we will show that an examination of the system and content of Ames's classic work *The Marrow of Theology* reveals that Ames was one of the first to build an entire system of Reformed covenant theology. Although a theology of covenant is discernible in Calvin and other Reformers, Ames went beyond them, turning a covenantal theology (i.e., covenant treated as an important aspect of theology) into a theology of the covenant (i.e., covenant as the overarching principle and framework of theology). Within the framework of covenant theology, Ames wedded doctrine and life to promote practical Puritan piety.

Biographical Sketch

William Ames (Latinized as "Amesius") was born in 1576 at Ipswich, chief city of England's Suffolk County, then a center of the robust Puritanism introduced by William Perkins (1558-1602).[3] Ames's father, also named William, was a well-to-do merchant with Puritan sympathies; his mother, Joan Snelling, was related to families that helped to found Plymouth Plantation in the New World. Since both parents died when he was young, he was reared by his maternal uncle, Robert Snelling, a Puritan from nearby Boxford. From childhood Ames was steeped in the vigorous Puritanism of his age and place.

Ames's uncle sent him in 1593/94 to Christ's College at Cambridge University, known for its undiluted Puritanism and Ramist philosophy. Ames rapidly displayed his proclivity to learn. He graduated with a Bachelor of Arts degree in 1598. In 1601, he received a Master of Arts degree, was elected fellow at Christ's

---

[3]The definitive biographical account of Ames is Keith L. Sprunger, *The Learned Doctor William Ames: Dutch Backgrounds of English and American Puritanism* (Chicago: University of Illinois Press, 1972), a revision of his "The Learned Doctor Ames" (Ph.D. dissertation, University of Illinois, 1963). Also helpful is Benjamin J. Boerkoel Sr., "William Ames (1576-1633): Primogenitor of the *Theologia-Pietatis* in English-Dutch Puritanism" (Th.M. thesis, Calvin Theological Seminary, 1990). For briefer accounts of Ames's life and work, see Eusden's introduction in William Ames, *The Marrow of Theology*, trans. and ed. John H. Eusden (1968; reprint, Grand Rapids: Baker, 1997), pp. 1-66; introduction by Lee W. Gibbs in William Ames, *Technometry* (Philadelphia: University of Pennsylvania Press, 1979), pp. 3-17; Jan van Vliet, "William Ames: Marrow of the Theology and Piety of the Reformed Tradition" (Ph.D. dissertation, Westminster Theological Seminary, 2002), pp. 15-40. The best Dutch sources are Hugo Visscher, *Guilielmus Amesius, Zijn Leven en Werken* (Haarlem: J. M. Stap, 1894); Willem van't Spijker, "Guilielmus Amesius," in *De Nadere Reformatie en het Gereformeerd Piëtisme* ('s-Gravenhage: Boekencentrum, 1989), pp. 53-86.

Three biographical works on Ames were translated and edited by Douglas Horton, and published in one volume as *William Ames by Matthew Nethenus, Hugo Visscher, and Karl Reuter* (Cambridge: Harvard Divinity School Library, 1965). These include Matthias Nethenus, *Introductory Preface in Which the Story of Master Ames Is Briefly Narrated and the Excellence and Usefulness of His Writings Shown* (Amsterdam: John Jansson, 1668), Hugo Visscher, *William Ames: His Life and Works* (Haarlem: J. M. Stap, 1894), and Karl Reuter, *William Ames: The Leading Theologian in the Awakening of Reformed Pietism* (Neukirchen: Neukirchener Verlag des Erziehungsvereins, 1940). Notes from these biographies reference Horton's volume. See also Horton, "Let Us Not Forget the Mighty William Ames," *Religion in Life* 29 (1960): 434-42, and John Quick's (1636-1706) unpublished manuscript, "Icones Sacrae Anglicapae" at Dr. Williams's Library in London, which includes a chapter, "The Life of William Ames, Dr. of Divinity."

College and ordained to the ministry, and underwent a dramatic conversion experience under the "rousing preaching" of Master William Perkins, father of experimental Puritan theology.

Following this profound spiritual transformation, Ames quickly became the moral compass and conscience of the college. He viewed himself as Ezekiel's watchman (Ezek 33), with a duty to warn students about sin and to promote a deeper faith and purity among them. But this role was short-lived. With King James's edict of tolerance at the 1604 Hampton Court Conference, any Puritan activity at the colleges that involved criticism of the Church of England was suppressed.

The Puritan party at Cambridge, however, continued their unrelenting opposition to the Elizabethan settlement. This violation of the king's edict had serious consequences. Puritan spokesmen were soon stripped of their degrees and dismissed. The establishment's coup culminated in 1609 with the appointment of Valentine Cary to the mastership. Cary, who detested Puritanism, was far less qualified for the position than Ames, but he had more ecclesiastical clout. With his appointment, Christ College's approach to Puritanism became decidedly antagonistic. Ames's rebukes of the Church of England and his refusal to wear priestly vestments such as the surplice were increasingly resented. On December 21, 1609, when Ames preached a sermon that denounced gambling, the college authorities had him taken into custody and suspended his degrees.

In 1610, Ames decided to seek the freer academic and ecclesiastical climate of the Netherlands. He first went to Rotterdam where he met John Robinson, pastor of the English separatist congregation at Leiden.

Following a brief stay in Rotterdam and Leiden, Ames was employed by Sir Horace Vere as military chaplain of the English forces stationed at The Hague. Here Ames wrote prolifically against the Arminianism that would soon precipitate an ecclesiastical crisis. That crisis among the Dutch was eventually addressed at an international synod in the Dutch city of Dordrecht (1618-1619). Because of his expertise in addressing issues of the Arminian struggle, Ames, an Englishman and nonvoting member of the Synod of Dort, was called to be chief theological advisor and secretary to Johannes Bogerman, the presiding officer. Members of the Synod of Dort ruled in favor of the historic Calvinist position on all five points raised by the Arminians, much to Ames's joy.

To support his family Ames turned to private lecturing and tutoring university students for three years after the Synod of Dort. He ran a little private "house college." Theological students lived in Ames's home and he taught them Puritanism and systematic theology according to the logical method of Petrus Ramus. He later developed some of these lectures into his famous *Marrow of Theology*.[4]

In 1622, officials at Franeker University, a relatively new institution in the remote province of Friesland, appointed Ames as professor of theology. On May 7, 1622, Ames gave his inaugural address on the Urim and Thummim, based on Exodus 28:30. Four days after his inauguration as professor, he received the doctor of theology degree upon successfully defending thirty-eight theses and four corollaries on "the nature, theory, and practical working of Conscience." In 1626, he was appointed Rector Magnificus, the highest honorary academic office in the university.

During his eleven-year tenure at Franeker, Ames became known as the "Learned Doctor" who tried to "Puritanize" the entire university. Ames acknowledged that the university was orthodox in doctrine, but did not feel that a majority of the faculty and student body were sufficiently Reformed in practice. Their faith was not yet translated into proper Christian observance. The faculty, in particular, were, for Ames's thinking, too dependent on Aristotelian logic and inadequately emphasized human responsibility and the exercise of the human will in Christian living. Therefore, Ames again organized a kind of rooming house or "college" in his house, within the university where tutorial sessions, lectures, and numerous theological discussions took place.[5] As rector, Ames promoted piety, enforced sabbath observance, shortened Christmas and Easter holidays and tightened student discipline. His puritanical reforms produced what was called "the Reformation" of the 1620s.

Through lecturing and prolific writing during his Franeker years, Ames maintained a strong stance against Arminianism, but his greatest contribution was in theology and ethics, which he saw as a unified system that helped the Christian live a life of genuine piety. Here he wrote his two greatest works, *Medulla Theologie* (*The Marrow of Theology*) and *De Conscientia* ("Of the Conscience," translated in English as *Conscience with the Power and Cases Thereof*). In his system of theological and moral divinity, Ames incorporated the Ramist philosophy and method he had learned at Cambridge.

Ramism was a philosophy that sought to correct the artificial sophistry of the Aristotelianism of the day that was characterized by a breach between life and thought, between knowing and doing, and in the case of the religious life, between

---

[4]Horton, *Ames*, p. 13.

[5]See Sprunger, *The Learned Doctor Ames*, chap. 4; idem, "William Ames and the Franeker Link to English and American Puritanism," in *Universiteit te Franeker, 1585-1811*, ed. G. Th. Jensma, F. R. H. Smit and F. Westra (Leeuwarden: Fryske Academy, 1985), pp. 264-85.

theology and ethics. Ramism was developed by Petrus Ramus (1515-1572), a six-teenth-century French Reformed philosopher.[6] Ames incorporated the thought of this Huguenot into his own work, seamlessly weaving theology and ethics together into a program of obedient, covenant living.

Students came from all over Europe to study under Ames. His most famous pupil was Johannes Cocceius, who would later carry covenant theology well beyond Ames's thought. Yet Ames was not content, for some students and faculty members did not appreciate Ames's efforts to achieve deeper or further reformation. A clique of professors, led by Johannes Maccovius, sabotaged Ames's efforts.

In 1632, Ames accepted an invitation from his friend Hugh Peter to join him in copastoring the English-speaking Congregationalist church at Rotterdam. Ames was attracted to the invitation because of Peter's design for an independent, cove-nant-centered congregation that strove for a purged membership of regenerate be-lievers. Ames had long argued for such Congregationalist principles within and outside Puritan circles.[7]

In late summer of 1633, Ames finally headed south to Rotterdam. In the fall, the Maas River breached its banks, and Ames, who was already unwell, became even sicker after his house was flooded. He died of pneumonia on November 11 at the age of fifty-seven in the arms of his friend, Hugh Peter. To the end, he remained firm in faith and triumphant in hope.[8]

Shortly before his death, Ames had seriously considered joining his friend John Winthrop in New England, but God had another "New World" in mind for him. Though Ames had great influence on the theological and intellectual history of New England—particularly through the *Marrow*—he never arrived at its shores. Four years after Ames's death, his wife and children went to live in the Puritan set-tlement of Salem, Massachusetts. They brought Ames's library with them, which formed the nucleus of the original library for Harvard College, though fire later destroyed most of the books.

THE MARROW OF THEOLOGY

Although William Ames's *Marrow of Theology* was first published in Latin as *Medulla Theologiae* in 1627, its main ideas were expressed earlier than that. The theological

---

[6]Sprunger, *Learned Doctor Ames*, p. 107; Eusden, Introduction to Ames, *Marrow*, p. 37.

[7]Ames, *Marrow*, book I, chapter 32, paragraphs 6 and 15 (hereafter 1:32.6 and 15); cf. his *A Reply to Dr. Mortons Generall Defence of Three Nocent Ceremonies* (1622), *A Reply to Dr. Mortons Particular Defence of Three Nocent Ceremonies* (1623), and *A Fresh Suit Against Human Ceremonies in Gods Worship* (1633). Increase Mather said that Ames gave us "perfect Congregationalism" (*A Disquisition Concerning Ecclesiastical Councils* [Boston, n.p., 1716], pp. v-vi).

[8]Sprunger, *Learned Doctor Ames*, p. 247.

lectures that Ames gave from 1619 to 1622 as tutor to the students at Leiden were reworked while he stood, as he put it, "idle in the marketplace." They were first released in Latin (1623) in fragmentary form from Franeker. Four years later, after Ames found financial security within the scholarly environment of the university, he finally finished what would become his landmark publication.

The book was intended to serve as a useful compendium of theology for laypeople and theological students. It immediately earned recognition and acclaim in scholarly and ecclesiastical circles, and was quickly translated into many languages. The first English translations were published in 1642 and 1643.

Major Theme

The opening theme of *Marrow* is remarkably simple and terse. "Theology is the doctrine of living to God," Ames wrote. This statement, simple as it may appear, is loaded with meaning. Grounded in how Ames was raised, it found theological and scholarly articulation at Christ's College, and over time Ames developed it into a theological system.

The theology of this book is all about practical Christianity—a Christianity of the whole person, not just the intellect, will or affections. It demonstrates Ames's passion that thought and life should represent a single system of practical, vital Christianity. Ames tried to show that theology does not deal primarily with statements about God, but rather with knowledge of how to live to God, that is, "in accord with the will of God."

Ames centered theology more on *action* than on *knowledge*. For Calvin, theology focused on knowing God and knowing oneself, though active faith was never far behind knowledge. For Ames, knowing God was never the end or goal of theology; rather, the end was to bring the heart and will into subjection to God and his Word.[9] Practical Christianity was the centerpiece of theology.

In this regard Ames was moving in a direction established by his mentor Perkins and reflecting the influence of Petrus Ramus, who said, "Theology is the doctrine of living well." Perkins saw theology as "the science of living blessedly forever." This blessed life, according to Perkins, is obtained via knowledge of God and knowledge of self. In this respect, Perkins's theology was a combination of the theology of Calvin and the methodology of Ramus. Ames, however, sought to distance himself from this view because of his concern that living blessedly could promote self-indulgence. After all, what constitutes the blessed

---

[9]William Ames, *The Substance of Christian Religion: Or, a Plain and Easy Draft of the Christian Catechism, in LII Lectures* (London: T. Mabb for T. Davies, 1659), Q. 113.

life? What constitutes happiness? As John Dykstra Eusden put it: "For Ames the end of theology was never to produce blessedness, which he felt related chiefly to man's ultimate aspiration and desire. In search for his own blessedness, man could miss God, the very object of his living rightly."[10] For Ames, theology was the art of Christian living. This art does not exist in a vacuum; rather, it is informed and driven by a heartfelt desire to obey God. Theology prompts the exercise of Christianity.

Ames's emphasis on the will was one of the key points of the controversy between him and his Franeker colleague Maccovius. Maccovius emphasized the primacy of the intellect in the regenerate mind; that is, the will is renewed through the intellect. The intellect is the *terminus a quo* (the point of departure of a process); the will is the *terminus ad quem* (the final goal of a process). But Ames held to the primacy of volition. Faith involves "an act of the whole man—which is by no means a mere act of the intellect," he wrote, but the act of the will in believing the gospel is that which, by the Spirit's grace, makes knowledge saving. Saving knowledge, therefore, differs from mere knowledge by involving the wholehearted commitment of the will. Ames wrote, "Although faith always presupposes a knowledge of the gospel, there is nevertheless no saving knowledge in anyone . . . except the knowledge which follows this act of the will and depends upon it."[11]

This position differed from much of established orthodoxy in the early seventeenth century, which said that faith proceeded from knowledge. Consequently, Ames's position on faith and volition came under scrutiny by the orthodox Reformed. Interestingly, Gisbertus Voetius, a follower of Ames and a leader in developing the Reformed system of theology and piety in the post-Reformation Netherlands, declared that attributing salvation to the will was unheard of in Reformed theology, with the exception of Ames who was the only one he had known to defend that view publicly.[12]

By focusing on the will as the center of faith, Ames wanted to demonstrate that true piety takes place in a covenant relationship between the sinful creature and the redeeming Creator. Faith as an act of the will is a true mark of covenant obedience as the creature is asked to respond with faith and obedience to the covenant promises offered freely in Christ. Covenant theology is the heart of Ames's theological system.

---

[10]Eusden, introduction to Ames, *Marrow*, p. 47.

[11]Ames, *Marrow*, 1:3.3-4.

[12]Voetius, *Selectarum Theological* (Utrecht: Joannem à Waesberge, 1669), 5:289.

ORGANIZATION AND CONTENT

The Marrow is organized according to a Ramist system of dividing and subdividing truth into sets of categories.[13] Ames taught that theology, the doctrine of living to God, consists of, first, "faith" (book one, chapters one to forty-one, pages 77-216), or what one believes, and second, "observance" (book two, chapters one to twenty-two, pages 219-331), or how one practices faith and does good works in obedience to God. Such works flow from and add life and meaning to faith. Those two major categories—faith and observance—comprise the fountainhead from which Ames's entire theological system flows. The concept of faith in book one and its observance by way of the Calvinist call to good works in book two led Ames to explain his theological system through various marks and fruits of living to God.

After defining faith as "the resting of the heart on God" and setting forth faith as an act of the whole person, especially the will, Ames discussed the object of faith, which is God. Following his teaching on the knowledge and essence of God (book one, chapters four and five; hereafter, I:4, 5), Ames set forth God's "efficiency," which he defined as the "working power of God by which He works all things in all things (Eph I:11; Rom 11:36)" (1:6). He then discussed God's decree as the first exercise of God's efficiency (1:7). He established that everything happens because of God's eternal good pleasure as demonstrated in his creation and providence (1:8, 9). God's preserving grace extends over the created order, while the special government that God exercises toward humanity, the "intelligent creature," is the covenant of works (1:10). By violating this conditional covenant, humanity tragically fell into sin. That fall had serious and eternal consequences, including spiritual and physical death and the propagation of original sin (1:11-17).

But there is still hope. Condemnation is overturned by restorative grace through redemption. Through the person and work of Christ, fallen humanity can have renewed fellowship with God. All of this happens solely for God's good pleasure and out of his "merciful purpose" (1:18-23).

In chapter twenty-four, titled "The Application of Christ," Ames's covenant theology becomes more obvious. The means through which the covenant of redemption between God and Christ comes to fruition is the covenant of grace, which the Scriptures call the "new covenant." In other words, the "application of Christ" is administered covenantally. After explaining how the new covenant differs from the old, Ames asserted that the essence of the covenant of grace continues

---

[13]For an outline of the entire book in a Ramist fashion, see Ames, "Method and Chart of the *Marrow*" in *Marrow*, pp. 72-73.

through different historical eras until, finally, in the last day, believers will be swept up into glory, and the covenant of grace inaugurated at the fall will finally be consummated.

The covenant of grace is both *conditional*, for faith is required, and *absolute*, for "the condition of the covenant is also promised in the covenant." To Ames, as John von Rohr points out, "The promise of fulfillment of covenant conditions was itself covenant promise." Thus in the final analysis, grace does all and the believer learns to rest on a promising, decreeing God.[14]

It is noteworthy that in Ames's theology the decrees of election and reprobation are not discussed until chapter twenty-five. They do not appear in his earlier chapters on the decree of God (1:7) or on his government over intelligent creatures (1:10). Ames was satisfied to place the doctrine of predestination as part of the doctrine of assurance. For Ames, assuring grace belonged with his examination of the order of salvation, before moving through "union by calling," justification, adoption, sanctification, and glorification (1:26-30). This is the substance of his "application of the covenant of grace considered in itself."[15]

Ames then devoted two chapters to the subject of the application of redemption, which is the church. After considering the mystical, invisible church (1:31) and the instituted or visible church (1:32), he addressed the way or means of the application of redemption, devoting chapters to Holy Scripture (1:34), the ministry (1:33, 35), the sacraments (1:36, 41) and ecclesiastical discipline (1:37).

Finally, Ames explained the *administration* of the application of redemption, that is, how God administers the covenant of grace (1:38, 39, 41). He focused on the chronology of covenant administration by dividing history into time periods, showing how there has been progression from "the imperfect to the more perfect" and "from the general and obscure to the more specific and clear" (1:38.2, 3). From Adam to Abraham, the covenant of grace was administered by general promises, such as Genesis 3:15 (1:38.14). From Abraham to Moses, the covenant was administered chiefly along a family line to Abraham and his posterity (1:38.20). From Moses to Christ, the church was in its childhood under the covenant and the ministry was "almost always an extraordinary one conducted by prophets" (1:38.12). From Christ's coming in the flesh all the way to his return on the clouds, the church freely receives the application of the covenant as a spiritual heir through the spirit of adoption, rather than as an earthly child in the spirit of fear and bond-

---

[14]Ibid., 1:24; John von Rohr, "Covenant and Assurance in Early English Puritanism," *Church History* 34 (1965): 199-202.

[15]Ames, *Marrow*, 1:30.

age (I:38.8, 9; I:39.9). Upon Christ's return, "the application which has only been begun in this life will be perfected" (I:41.1).

Throughout Ames's explanation of covenant administration in various time periods, he uniquely configured two major doctrines—"redemption by Christ" and the "application of redemption"—that flow out of God's restorative grace at the Fall. He took each element of the order of salvation and applied it to some fact or event in each covenantal time period that he had enumerated. By placing predestination in the order of salvation, Ames dovetailed the eternal aspect of the life of the elect into the temporal and historical progression of redemptive history. The logical elements of the order of salvation were thus wrapped into the chronological periods of covenant administration through the history of salvation. Each period in salvation history was coordinated with a corresponding series of conditions or states of believers (I:30-39). In this way Ames avoided the apparent incongruity between covenant and decree that has often dogged Reformed theology. He offered an internally consistent system of covenant theology that does justice to both God's decretal activity and his covenantal commitment.

We have seen that Ames's theological teaching began with faith, which is explained in book one of *Marrow*, within a covenantal framework. Book two offers the second half of Ames's Ramist system of theology: the observance or obedience that accompanies faith. Obedience is accomplished through virtue and good works, and is manifested in religion (love to God) as well as justice and charity (love to neighbor). Here Ames explained how the first table of the law and its theological virtues are the foundation of religion and worship of God, while the second table of the law and its charitable virtues constitute the paradigm for interpersonal behavior. This blueprint for the Christian life is expressed by acting toward God and each other as the Ten Commandments prescribe (2:1-22). Ames developed this blueprint for practical Christian living in his *Marrow* and *Conscience with the Power and Cases Thereof* (1630 in Latin, 1639 in English), which became a landmark in moral theology, passing through nearly twenty editions in one generation.[16]

INFLUENCE

The Marrow of Theology was most influential in New England, where it was generally regarded as the best summary of Calvinistic theology ever written. It was required reading at Harvard and Yale well into the eighteenth century, when it was

---

[16]For Ames as a Puritan casuist, see George L. Mosse, *The Holy Pretence* (Oxford: Basil Blackwell, 1957), pp. 68-87.

supplanted by François Turrettini's *Institutes of Elenctic Theology.*[17] Thomas Hooker and Increase Mather recommended *Marrow* as the most important book beyond the Bible for making a sound theologian. Jonathan Edwards made copious marginal notes on his own copy of *Marrow*, and acknowledged his indebtedness to Ames.

Ames's influence in New England, however, went beyond his manual of theology. His ecclesiological writings laid the groundwork for nonseparating Congregationalism in New England, a movement that maintained that the Congregational churches of Massachusetts Bay Colony ought to be a model seeking the reform of the Church of England rather than separating from it. The Cambridge Platform of 1648 in particular reflects Ames's thought. Then, too, his Puritan Ramism was eagerly embraced and became characteristic of New England Puritanism.[18] New England Puritans such as John Cotton, Increase Mather and Cotton Mather quoted Ames more frequently than they quoted Calvin. Increase Mather said, "It is rare for a *scholastical wit* to be joined with an *heart warm in religion*, but in Ames it was so."[19] Cotton Mather called Ames "that profound, that sublime; that subtle, that irrefragable—yea, that angelic doctor."[20]

Ames and his *Marrow* had their second greatest impact in the Netherlands. According to Matthias Nethenus, Voetius's colleague at the University of Utrecht, "In England, the study of practical theology has flourished marvelously, and in the Dutch churches and schools, from the time of Willem Teellinck and Ames it has ever more widely spread, even though all do not take to it with equal interest."[21] Keith L. Sprunger notes that though Ames found the Dutch too intellectual and not sufficiently practical, he promoted Puritan piety with some considerable success in an effort to "make Dutchmen into Puritans."[22] In addition to Voetius, he greatly impacted Peter van Mastricht (a Dutch pietist whose systematic theology Jonathan Edwards thought even surpassed that of Turrettini's for usefulness), who drew heavily on Ames, especially in covenantal thinking and casuistry.

Nearly all of Ames's books were printed in the Netherlands, many in Latin for the international scholarly community. *The Marrow of Theology* and *Conscience with the*

---

[17]S. E. Morison, *Harvard College in the Seventeenth Century* (Cambridge, Mass.: Harvard University Press, 1936), p. 267.

[18]Keith L. Sprunger, "Ames, Ramus, and the Method of Puritan Theology," *Harvard Theological Review* 59 (1966): 133-51.

[19]Cotton Mather, *The Great Works of Christ in America: Magnalia Christi Americana*, 2 vols. (1701; reprint, Edinburgh: Banner of Truth Trust, 1979), 1:245.

[20]Ibid., 1:236.

[21]Horton, *Ames*, p. 15.

[22]Sprunger, *Learned Doctor Ames*, p. 260.

Power and Cases Thereof were soon both translated into Dutch and printed at least four times in the seventeenth century.[23] His ecclesiological writings, however, were not printed as often, suggesting that his theology and casuistry made more impact in the Netherlands than his Congregationalist views.

Ironically, Ames was least influential in his homeland of England, although there, too, he was considered Perkins's most influential disciple and true heir. Ames's major works were widely circulated, and influenced English Calvinistic theology throughout the seventeenth century. His *Marrow of Theology* was particularly highly esteemed by the Puritans. Thomas Goodwin said that "next to the Bible, he esteemed Dr. Ames's his Marrow of Divinity as the best book in the world."[24]

CONCLUSION: GRACE AND OBEDIENCE

Did Ames depart from the mainstream of Reformed theology, as Kuyper and Kendall contend? No. As we have seen, Ames was instrumental in contrasting Reformed thought with that of an orthodoxy that was beginning to lose its vitality. Covenantally based obedience is activism of a Christian sort. This sort of activism is not mere voluntarism. True, Ames's emphasis was on the will: "The true and proper subject of theology is the will."[25] But Ames, as a faithful son of the Reformation, continued to emphasize, "the final dependence of faith, as it designates the act of believing, is on the operation and inner persuasion of the Holy Spirit."[26]

Moreover, Ames's focus on the will should be seen for what it is: a combination of faith and observance in theological commitment. Ames worked this out in philosophical and theological battles with his Franeker colleagues, which demonstrates his attempts to reintroduce a vital piety to the stagnant church of the seventeenth-century Netherlands. Neither faith nor practice is adequate by itself. Faith divorced from practice leads to "cold orthodoxy," while an isolated emphasis on the will and on good works leads to Arminianism. The story of Ames's life— and the theme of his thought as evidenced in *Marrow of Theology, Conscience*, and other writings—shows that he strove for proper balance between the two.[27] Key to this balance was placing obedience within the covenant.

Ames legitimized this covenant obedience as characterizing the Christian life

[23]C. W. Schoneveld, *Intertraffic of the Mind: Studies in Seventeenth-Century Anglo-Dutch Translation with a Checklist* (Leiden: E. J. Brill, 1983).

[24]Increase Mather, "To the Reader," in James Fitch, *The First Principles of the Doctrine of Christ* (Boston: n.p., 1679).

[25]Ames, *Marrow*, I:1.9.

[26]Ibid., I:3.12.

[27]See William Ames, *An Analyticall Exposition of Both the Epistles of the Apostle Peter* (London: E.G. for Iohn Rothwell, 1641).

with his system of covenant theology. Without this foundation, Ames's system would surely have collapsed, for voluntarism on its own has no biblical content. Ames demonstrated the biblical truth that although justification is by grace alone through faith alone, and never by works and obedience, the believer's response of obedience is absolutely vital to authentic covenant life and to Christianity itself.

While tenaciously holding to the one-sided, unconditional character of the covenant of grace, Ames also stressed the responsibility of the covenant child. Because faith is known by its works, obedience underlies the experiential life of the covenant child. This obedience is an informed piety, the alignment of doctrine with life, the intersection of orthodoxy with orthopraxy. With his system of covenant theology, Ames demonstrated that there is harmony, not contradiction, between grace and obedience. The formal structure of this obedience was a Christian life whose direction and content were set by the Ten Commandments.

The Marrow of Theology more clearly and systematically set forth "the gist of Puritan thought about God, the church, and the world" than any other Puritan book.[28] It is essential for understanding the Puritan view of covenant, sanctification and activism, and is highly recommended for laypeople and theologians alike. It ought to be a part of every church and pastor's library, as it is still worth consulting today.

SELECT BIBLIOGRAPHY

Primary Sources

Ames, William. *An Analytical Exposition of Both the Epistles of the Apostle Peter.* London: E. G. for Iohn Rothwell, 1641.

————. *Conscience with the Power and Cases Thereof.* London: E. G. for Iohn Rothwell, 1639; reprint, Norwood, N.J.: Walter J. Johnson, 1975.

————. *A Fresh Suit Against Human Ceremonies in God's Worship.* Rotterdam: n.p., 1633; reprint in copy form, Edmonton: Still Waters Revival Books, 1998.

————. *The Marrow of Theology*, trans. from 3rd Latin edition (1629). Edited and introduced by John D. Eusden. Boston: Pilgrim, 1968; reprint, Grand Rapids: Baker, 1997.

————. *The Substance of Christian Religion: Or, a Plain and Easy Draft of the Christian Catechism, in LII Lectures.* London: T. Mabb for T. Davies, 1659.

————. *Technometry.* Edited and Introduced by Lee W. Gibbs. Philadelphia: University of Pennsylvania Press, 1979.

---

[28]Douglas Horton, foreword to Ames, *Marrow*, p. vii.

Quick, John. "The Life of William Ames, Dr. of Divinity." In "Icones Sacrae Anglica-pae," at Dr. Williams's Library in London.

Secondary Sources

Boerkoel, Benjamin J., Sr. "William Ames (1576-1633): Primogenitor of the *Theologia-Pietatis* in English-Dutch Puritanism." Th.M. thesis, Calvin Theological Seminary, 1990.

Horton, Douglas. "Let Us Not Forget the Mighty William Ames." *Religion in Life* 29 (1960): 434-42.

Horton, Douglas, trans. and ed. *William Ames by Matthew Nethenus, Hugo Visscher, and Karl Reuter.* Cambridge: Harvard Divinity School Library, 1965.

Pickell, Charles N. "The Freedom of the Will in William Ames and Jonathan Edwards." *Gordon Review* 5 (1959): 168-74.

Sprunger, Keith L. "Ames, Ramus, and the Method of Puritan Theology." *Harvard Theological Review* 59 (1966): 133-51.

———. *The Learned Doctor William Ames: Dutch Backgrounds of English and American Puritanism.* Chicago: University of Illinois Press, 1972.

———. "William Ames and the Franeker Link to English and American Puritanism." In *Universiteit te Franeker, 1585-1811,* edited by G. Th. Jensma, F. R. H. Smit and F. Westra, pp. 264-85. Leeuwarden: Fryske Academy, 1985.

Van't Spijker, Willem. "Guilielmus Amesius." In *De Nadere Reformatie en het Gereformeerde Piëtisme,* edited by T. Brienen, pp. 53-86. 's-Gravenhage: Boekencentrum, 1989.

Van Vliet, Jan. "William Ames: Marrow of the Theology and Piety of the Reformed Tradition." Ph.D. dissertation, Westminster Theological Seminary, 2002.

Visscher, Hugo. *Guilielmus Amesius, Zijn Leven en Werken.* Haarlem: J. M. Stap, 1894.

CHRIST THE FOUNTAINE OF LIFE

BY JOHN COTTON
(1584-1652)

Charles E. Hambrick-Stowe

JOHN COTTON PUBLISHED HIS CLASSIC EXPOSITION OF PURITAN SPIR-
itual life, *Christ the Fountaine of Life*, in London in 1651. The book appeared at the
very end of his life, after almost two decades of ministry in New England. But the
text harks back to his early career as perhaps the most dynamic among a new generation of Puritan preachers stepping into the pulpit during the 1610s and early
1620s. Cotton probably first delivered the material as a sermon series in old England well before 1630 when he and other leading Puritans were being forced from
their churches. *Christ the Fountaine of Life*, therefore, bridges early seventeenth-century
Puritanism with the experience of believers at mid-century, as well as underscores
the ongoing trans-Atlantic character of the movement.[1]

Cotton fixed on a single verse of Scripture for the first eleven of the sixteen sermons collected in the book: "Whoever has the Son has life; whoever does not have
the Son of God does not have life" (I Jn 5:12; the concluding sermons are on vv.
13-17). The sermons make plain that, in the Puritan experience of Christian faith,
true spirituality is rooted in the person and work of Jesus Christ. Puritans held that,
through the work of redemption in the human soul, God in Christ pours out his

---

[1] John Cotton, *Christ the Fountaine of Life: Or, Sundry Choyce Sermons on Part of the First Chapter of the First Epistle of St. John*
(London: Robert Ibbitson, 1651). While the original spelling is retained in the book's title, in quotations I have
modernized some spelling, capitalization and punctuation (e.g., by dropping the *e* in words like *fountaine*, *soule*,
signes, *onely*, or *wayes*, and by adding an apostrophe where appropriate, as in "God's grace"). Cotton's published
works are discussed in a bibliographical note at the end of Larzer Ziff, *The Career of John Cotton: Puritanism and the
American Experience* (Princeton, N.J.: Princeton University Press, 1962), pp. 261-68.

Holy Spirit so that believers personally experience salvation and see practical effects in their lives. As Cotton explained with side-references to the Gospel of John, "our sanctification and consolation . . . spring both from one fountain, and that is the Spirit of God's grace." While the Holy Spirit "is the comforter, that is, our sanctifier, and this springs in us to everlasting life . . . he that can give a spirit of sanctification and consolation, is only the Lord Jesus Christ." So "this life of consolation and sanctification spring[s] from the Spirit as from a fountain" and it is Jesus Christ who "sets open this fountain." Scripture, the preached Word, and prayer are the primary means by which believers come to "grounded knowledge, that Christ, and eternal life is theirs." As the final sermons in the book reiterate, "there is a mighty power in the Word" and the "mighty power of the name of Christ" becomes ours "whensoever we use his name in prayer." Puritanism in old and New England underwent many changes as the movement responded to political and social challenges throughout the century, but the themes Cotton set forth in his early preaching and published in book form the year before he died remained constant.[2]

COVENANTAL PIETY

John Cotton and his family sailed for New England in the summer of 1633. They were part of an emigration movement within English Puritanism which, beginning in the 1620s with settlement of Plymouth and Salem, by 1630 established its political, intellectual and spiritual hub in the town of Boston. The passenger list for the *Griffin* included two other leading pastors, Thomas Hooker and Samuel Stone. John Cotton had served for twenty years within the Church of England as vicar of St. Botolph's, a leading Puritan parish in Boston, Lincolnshire. Thomas Shepherd, who would soon make the journey himself, interpreted the significance of their joining the "Great Migration": "I saw the Lord departing from England when Mr. Hooker and Mr. Cotton were gone." Cotton received what he considered a very personal confirmation from God of the hard decision to emigrate—the birth of a son. Following the death of his wife Elizabeth, in April 1632 he had married Sarah Hawkridge Story, a widow with one daughter. While no children had issued from Cotton's first marriage, on board ship Sarah gave birth to their first child, a son whom the couple aptly named Seaborn. With their emerging congregational ecclesiology, they refrained from having him baptized until they were properly members of a gathered church. Cotton was approaching his forty-ninth birthday when,

---

[2]Cotton, *Fountaine*, pp. 1, 4, 181, 191, 202, 221.

shortly after their arrival in Massachusetts Bay Colony, the church in new Boston called him to serve as teacher alongside their pastor John Wilson.[3]

Puritanism found in New England an environment in which to manifest its version of Calvinist covenant theology and New Testament restorationism in both church and state. As John Cotton wrote in *Christ the Fountaine of Life*, by the covenant of grace God brings his elect into the church: "he calls them his people, and saints." There is also a "three-fold covenant" available to people generally, whether or not they have experienced God's saving grace in Christ. God establishes this social covenant "between prince and people" in "all well governed commonwealths," as well as in the marriage "covenant between man and wife" and in all relationships "between friend and friend." Massachusetts and Connecticut through the first two generations developed as a bold socio-political experiment, loosely coordinated by ministers and magistrates in their separate ecclesial and civil realms. However flawed by human error, the system was intended to operate under the sovereignty, and for the glory, of God.[4]

While New England Puritanism can be studied as a political or intellectual movement, above all it persisted as a movement for spiritual renewal with its core value as God's justification and sanctification of his people through the work of Christ. Personal religious experience was the cornerstone of the entire structure. Churches comprised redeemed "saints" gathered by God out of the world (but not separated from it) and the civil franchise was open to all male church members. Principles that defined church polity, family life and a just society were grounded in biblical standards of godliness and rooted in the belief that life's meaning was found only by individuals who personally received, through an experience of conversion, God's gift of salvation in Christ. As Cotton expressed it, "when we subject all the passages of our heart and life to his will . . . we do not any thing in our callings, but we do it in obedience to Christ, and according to the rules of Christ, and for the glory of Christ."[5]

New England orthodoxy's exploration of church and state issues in which John Cotton participated were especially important in the 1640s, during the English Civil War when Puritans of every stripe on both sides of the ocean sought to sway that nation's future. True to his tradition, all his publications on the social covenant

---

[3]Thomas Shepard, "Autobiography," in *God's Plot: The Paradoxes of Puritan Piety, Being the Autobiography and Journal of Thomas Shepard*, ed. Michael McGiffert (Amherst: University of Massachusetts Press, 1972), p. 55. For the details of Cotton's life, see Ziff, *Career of John Cotton* and Everett Emerson, *John Cotton* (Boston: Twayne, G. K. Hall & Co., 1990).

[4]Cotton, *Fountaine*, pp. 33-34.

[5]Ibid., pp. 12-13.

and ecclesiology revolved around Puritanism's vital center, God's grace in Jesus Christ. In seminal works like *The Keyes of the Kingdom of Heaven* (1644) and *The Way of Congregational Churches Cleared* (1648) he developed church polity on the basis of "believers making public confession of their faith before the Lord, and their brethren." He played a key role at the synod that produced the Cambridge Platform (1648), which defined the church as "a company of saints by calling, united in one body by a holy covenant, for the public worship of God and the mutual edification one of another in the fellowship of the Lord Jesus." In their exchange following Roger Williams's expulsion from Massachusetts and settlement in Rhode Island, Cotton upheld the partnership of church and state as the best means of extending the benefits of the gospel to all inhabitants. If history has favored Williams's *The Bloudy Tenent of Persecution* (1644) over Cotton's reply, *The Bloudy Tenent, Washed and Made White in the Bloud of the Lamb* (1647), Cotton's position that personal faith and public life are interconnected has also persisted in America. His involvement in the translation and publication of *The Whole Booke of Psalmes* (the *Bay Psalm Book,* 1640) and his monograph *Singing of Psalmes a Gospel-Ordinance* (1647) undergirded both public worship and personal devotion. His children's catechism, *Milk for Babes, Drawn Out of the Breasts of Both Testaments* (1646), was widely used for family devotions.[6]

The biblical text for *Christ the Fountaine of Life* could be said to lie at the heart of all Cotton's works on more public topics and of collections of lectures and sermons published after his death. He paraphrased it bluntly on the first page of the book: "So . . . find Christ, find life. Find him not, but be estranged from him, and find death." In personal, family, church, and civic life the stakes were high, a matter of life and death, with eternal consequences.

Puritanism's "Pith and Marrow"

John Cotton's childhood in Derbyshire (he was second of four children of Roland and Mary Hurlbert Cotton) was fertile soil for the seed of Puritanism's personal and social vision to germinate. The vicar at St. Alkmund's Church where the family attended, his teacher (also an ordained clergyman) in the Derby Grammar School, and his lawyer father were all men who, during those years of the late 1580s and the 1590s, were at least sympathetic to the kinds of reforms associated with the label "Puritan." Cotton was well prepared to enroll at Trinity College, Cambridge in 1598. Thirteen years old at matriculation, he would spend the next decade and a half at the university. As an undergraduate he was influenced, but not quite con-

---

[6]See Larzer Ziff, ed., *John Cotton on the Churches of New England* (Cambridge, Mass.: Harvard University Press, 1968). Williston Walker, *The Creeds and Platforms of Congregationalism* (1893; reprint, Boston: Pilgrim Press, 1960), p. 205.

verted, by the sermons of the premier Puritan theologian William Perkins. After receiving his B.A. in 1603, Cotton identified himself with the Puritan cause by accepting a fellowship at Emmanuel College, the intellectual center of the movement and hotbed of its spiritual life. He received his M.A. degree in 1606 and continued at Emmanuel as a tutor, lecturer and preacher, quickly developing as an eloquent and popular homiletician. But in 1609 the straightforwardly "plain" preaching of Richard Sibbes, a fellow at St. John's College, convicted Cotton that he was in fact without Christ. This spiritual crisis led to an agonizing conversion experience, which led to his abandonment of the literary sermon style for which he was admired.

Cotton's first sermon in the overtly Puritan manner and tone was greeted with reproach by many, but it sparked the conversion of John Preston (future master of Emmanuel College) and Cotton took this as God's sign of approval. Ordained in 1610, Cotton remained at Emmanuel until 1612 when the committee from St. Botolph's persuaded him it was time to shift into parish ministry. He received his Bachelor of Divinity and married Elizabeth Horrocks, who came from a clerical family, the following year.

St. Botolph's Church was a surprisingly prestigious pulpit for a young cleric still in his twenties. The magnificent stone edifice illustrates what Cotton sacrificed professionally in 1632 when, summoned to appear before the Church of England's High Court, he went underground for almost a year and then embarked for New England. For two full decades, from 1612 until the pressure of Bishop William Laud became insurmountable, St. Botolph's provided an ideal community within which to exercise a spiritually vital, gospel-oriented ministry. Thanks to influential lay leaders and his own ecclesiastical diplomacy, despite two brief suspensions by his bishop, Cotton largely got away with nonconformity , namely, refusing to wear vestments, make the sign of the cross or pray strictly from the *Book of Common Prayer*. While some radical Puritans argued that believers should abandon parish churches and form more spiritually pure congregations of the redeemed, those who were soon to settle Massachusetts and Connecticut repudiated separatism as too extreme. Hoping to reform from within, Cotton encouraged a more spiritual fellowship by gathering a covenanted "church within the church" at St. Botolph's.

An intense personal and corporate spiritual life was fostered by Cotton's Sunday sermons at St. Botolph's and his famous Thursday lectures. As he argued in *Christ the Fountaine of Life*, vital worship was itself one of the "signs the Holy Ghost hath given us of our having Christ." Describing worship as "the debasing of our selves" and the "prizing" of Christ "above all other things in the world," he preached that "when the soul esteems nothing more worth the knowing than Jesus Christ" the believer comes to "know and feel the virtue and power of Christ in his heart." Christ might also be known in other ways, but above all "the very worshipping of him, is the having of him." Puritans rejected priestly ritual, which is what they considered Church of England liturgy, in favor of free and faithful praise "performed to Christ, in mind, in heart, and in life" by God's people.[7]

A chief purpose of the New England enterprise was to create churches in which such worship would occur. In worship sinners might be converted, believers could be nurtured in faith, and society was firmly grounded on godliness through biblical preaching. Cotton would not have felt his manuscripts from the 1610s or 1620s needed updating on these topics when they were published in 1651.

Cotton began *Christ the Fountaine of Life* by identifying sin as the basic human problem. Simply, because of "the transgressions we have done . . . we had deserved death." Since "it is beyond the power of the creature to keep alive his own soul, no not so much as natural life," how much more is it "far beyond the capacity of the creature" to "translate himself from death to life." The spiritual and moral "insufficiency" in our lives is so great that even if we were to "die for our sins ourselves, our death would not free us from the punishment." The Christian answer is that God offers salvation by "the Son taking upon him our nature, that nature which had offended God . . . so that by his death [Christ] gave to God, not only the price of our redemption, but prevailed with the Father to bestow upon him the Spirit to give where, and to whom he will." The question before every individual is whether "we be alive or dead," to know "what it is to have a Christ" in whom God has channeled "all the springs of life." All else in private and public life build on this foundation. "This contains the pith and marrow of Christianity."[8]

The chasm between complete human depravity and God's holy sovereignty created a spiritual crisis for Puritan faith. The Reformed doctrine of God's inscrutable will in election, codified in the *Canons of Dort* (1619) and the *Westminster Confession* (1646), could lead to the assumption that one can never be sure of standing among the redeemed. Pastor-theologians like John Cotton insisted that the crisis can be resolved. Assurance "that we have the Lord for our God" and that he has "put new life in us" is available to believers. *Christ the Fountaine of Life* offered guidance on the practice of meditative self-examination (or "trial of our estates") according to biblically-sanctioned "signs the Holy Ghost hath given us of our having Christ." The first of these, already noted, was sincerity of worship.

---

[7]Cotton, *Fountaine*, pp. 5-6, 8-9.
[8]Ibid., pp. 1-5.

Those who are "yet doubtful whether [they] have Christ or no" may accept it as "evidence to the soul" that they are saved if they come "inquisitive to know all the virtue that is in Christ," believing that "there is nothing better worth the knowing." When a person worships "in the deep affection of his heart" by loving Christ above all else, and "loathes himself" for his own unworthiness, it is a sign of God's grace. Finally, if we worship in "hearty obedience" and "marvelous sub-jection" to God's will—if we "lay our hands upon our mouths and sit down and quiet our selves" in "patient submission to the heart of God"—we may believe that we belong to Christ. The alternative is to "grudge at this and that evil which befalls us," to "prefer ten thousand other things" before Christ, and to "look at ourselves as the great Omegas of the world."[9]

Cotton also held that "we are said to have Christ" in Scripture "by pur-chase." Since a historic criticism was that by the sale of indulgences the Catholic Church presumed to sell salvation, Cotton's warning that "without laying out of money, [Christ] cannot be had" is ironic. Citing the Song of Solomon and Acts chapter nine, he insisted that "should a man offer his house full of treasure for Christ, it would be despised" and "if the gift of the Holy Ghost cannot be bought for money, how can the Lord Jesus Christ be bought for money?" But, in what amounts to a stewardship sermon, he stated that anyone who holds fast to his money "lets go the Lord Jesus Christ." Under persecution, certainly, a believer must be willing to "hazard all his estate" for the sake of the gospel. When the Church of England ousted Puritan preachers from parishes, it be-came necessary for believers to "lay out liberally for the Gospel of Christ." Thus, "without the expense of money" to support the ministry, Christ "cannot be had." Understanding "cost" spiritually, Christ is "purchased, not so much by money" but by believers parting with "their honourable sins, their sweet and delightful sins, their profitable sins, and those wherewith they have been most captivated." Looking at people, God "knows that one may as well pull their hearts out of their bellies, as some sins out of them." So when we give up our "most darling delightful sins" and put them "out of our hearts and hands," God delights to "reveal himself" and "give us the Lord Jesus Christ, and life and healing in him."[10]

The concluding section on counting the cost of salvation as a means of assur-ance suddenly found Cotton on controversial ground, with painful echoes from the mid-1630s. He warned sternly against trusting religious practices, including

---

[9]Ibid., pp. 5-9, 11-14, 29.
[10]Ibid., pp. 15-21.

"the use of the blessed Ordinances of God" and signs of "growth of sanctification," as evidence of justification. Especially "when we cannot have the Ordinances without impure mixtures of human invention," we must "let them go, rather than defile our hearts and hands with sin against God." Sometimes we must "sit loose" and not "look for life in the Word or Sacraments, or communion with God's servants," but simply "look for it all in Christ." This direct connection between soul and Christ appears to denigrate ecclesial structures and practices otherwise revered as "means of grace." Cotton did qualify his rhetoric: "not that God would have us cast his Ordinances behind our backs, but therein to seek him." Elsewhere in the book he urged that there is a certain devotional "preparation we must make for Christ to come into us." And he cautioned that "the Holy Ghost would not have ministers nor any other to be wise above what is written" in Scripture. But flourishes like his comparison of "the Sacraments, Word, and Prayer" with "the golden calves at Dan and Bethel"—and his warning that we must "look at them all as loss, and dross, and dung, that you may win Christ"—more likely hit the mark with the hyperspiritual and those inclined toward separatism. This message from his lips in England made a deep impression on a zealous parishioner named Anne Hutchinson.[11]

ASSURANCE OF GRACE

Detecting "impure mixtures of human invention" in the clergy's conduct of worship was one thing in England with reference to the established liturgy, but quite another when Anne Hutchinson acted on Cotton's exhortations in new Boston. At her devotional gatherings for women (which men began to attend) she judged the sermons of New England ministers (except her beloved Cotton) tainted with works righteousness and promoting virtuous behavior as the way to salvation, a covenant of works rather than the covenant of grace. Cotton did differ from most New England ministers in his ambiguous view of sanctification's relation to justification. Many times in *Christ the Fountaine of Life* he voiced the majority teaching that believers may find comfort by discerning marks of holiness in daily life, encouraging the notion that sanctification offers some evidence of justification. But in heated passages he also contended that "if we would have Christ, and life in him" we must abandon our "confidence" and "trust upon a gift" of the Spirit. Virtuous deeds, even if God-empowered, are no sign of "sanctified grace" but merely of "common grace." Any reliance on hu-

---

[11] Ibid., pp. 21-30, 41, 180.

man behavior opens the door to hypocrisy and spiritual death.[12]

Anne Hutchinson sensed God speaking directly through Cotton's sermons. He taught that under the power of the Spirit some may "discern many secret hidden mysteries and meanings of the Holy Ghost in Scripture, more than ever [we] could by any reading or instruction" and receive "some special work of the Spirit of God . . . to foresee some special blessings." God calls such a saint then "to teach others also, to lead on others of their neighbors in the ways of God." Hutchinson acted on Cotton's view that when God "lift[s] us far beyond all our own apprehensions and gifts" it is possible to identify "much difference between one Christian and another." The Hutchinsonian faction within the church and town of Boston not only embraced a highly "spiritual" theology leaning toward gnosticism, but they also posed a political and military threat in the Commonwealth. Throughout a series of civil and ecclesiastical trials in which the insurgents were branded as "antinomian," John Cotton's ministerial colleagues begged him to repudiate his disciple. Prior to the excommunication and exile of Anne Hutchinson and others in 1637, a chastened John Cotton cast his lot with New England orthodoxy. The Antinomian Controversy was an anguished moment in Cotton's career. His stature was such, however, that he quickly resumed his influential position among the clergy.[13]

In *Christ the Fountaine of Life* Cotton taught that assurance of grace comes "by way of covenant." This affirmation centers him in the Calvinist tradition that New England Puritanism sought to vindicate. With reference to biblical sacrifices, he preached, "when we come to make a covenant with God, we profess our selves as guilty of death, and therefore look up to Christ, desiring that his death might be imputed to us, and we offer our selves, souls and bodies to be obedient to God to the death." We must confess not only committed sins but also "how little good we have done, and how little serviceable we are," and in humility "return and bewail our breach of covenant with God." Covenant renewal offers a further means of assurance of being among the elect—the experience of "receiving Christ by faith." Cotton invited believers "to receive him into our hearts as into his proper house," to become "temples of the living God." We are then "open hearted to God" in the ordinances of worship and prayer, having "brought down our high spirits, and raised up our too low, base and dejected spirits, and laid all level before him." With

---

[12]Cotton, *Christ the Fountaine*, pp. 24-27, 92. For the Anne Hutchinson crisis, see David D. Hall, ed., *The Antinomian Controversy, 1636-1638: A Documentary History*, 2nd ed. (Durham, N.C.: Duke University Press, 1990) and William K. B. Stover, *"A Faire and Easie Way to Heaven:" Covenant Theology and Antinomianism in Early Massachusetts* (Middletown, Conn.: Wesleyan University Press, 1978).

[13]Cotton, *Christ the Fountaine*, pp. 24-27, 62.

"all sinful and unclean" and even "common" matter removed, Christ will surely "come suddenly into his Temple." Evangelicalism's emphasis on personal faith, and especially asking Jesus into one's heart, is no recent innovation but is rooted in the Puritanism of John Cotton.[14]

If assurance rests in "having Christ," then the heart must fix only and always on Christ himself. Although blessings follow, to have the Son is to desire "not so much his benefits as himself." To be motivated by forgiveness or spiritual gifts, Cotton argued, is to be like a man who professes love for a woman but "chiefly aims at her estate, to provide for himself." Far better is the woman who "in true conjugal affection" wishes nothing more from her husband than the man himself. "Give me Christ, and I have enough. Who, or what, is there besides Christ?" Christ responds to such love by pouring out "the spirit of the Son" and binding us to himself with "a spirit of liberty" and "a spirit of prayer." Thus "knit to the Lord Jesus Christ," Cotton boldly stated, "we are made partakers of the divine nature" of Christ. Specifically, God establishes "conformity to Christ in his offices" of king, priest and prophet. As kings we can "rule over all our lusts," fulfill life's responsibilities, and with a "heroic noble spirit . . . over-look all earthly drudgery, and resist any enemy we meet with." As priests we are authorized "to offer up sacrifices of prayer and thanksgiving to God." And God "pours out his Spirit" upon us as prophets to proclaim to others the "secrets of God's counsel" and "meanings of the Holy Ghost in Scripture."[15]

Worldly people misunderstand the "strange kind of liberty which the children of God are advanced to by the spirit of the Son." Outward circumstances may not change as we wish. Still, believers are free from the fear of sin, hell, death, and "all the enemies of our salvation." Like a much later holiness preacher, Cotton promised that the Holy Spirit brings "liberty from all the power and dominion of sin." Everyone lapses occasionally, but a believer knows that "God hath freed me . . . from the law and trade of sin and of death." With forgiveness of our sins we are "saved from them, by turning from them." With Christ "not only for a Saviour, but for . . . Lord and Prince" we are "guided and governed by the Lord Jesus" through "many strong oppositions." Cotton explained this "life of righteousness" by connecting the experience of justification with "such effects of the life of sanctification as show themselves in the lives of Christians." Saved only by grace, God's "Spirit of grace" produces an "inclination, and disposition, and habit" along with assurance that "God hath given you a new life."[16]

---

[14]Ibid., pp. 31-45.
[15]Ibid., pp. 58-65.
[16]Ibid., pp. 65, 69, 79-81, 92, 127.

JUSTIFICATION AND SANCTIFICATION

Cotton identified three ways to "discern the life of God's grace": by "the *causes* of it . . . the *effects* of it . . . [and] the *qualities* and properties of it." God works by the Holy Spirit to "cause" salvation through the operation of his Word, usually through sound preaching. While some "cannot readily tell you what promise did first bring them on to God," he admitted, "yet a word of promise it was, and ordinarily a word of promise which the word preached did apply to thy soul, and caused thy heart to reach forth and to lay hold upon it." Further self-examination could help one "call to mind that such a promise" had in fact initiated the "renewal of the whole soul." In any case, a good testimony—"how you now find your heart is apt to speak, when you speak of that estate you are in"—is "a good sign to you" of salvation. Next, Cotton described the "effects of spiritual life" explicitly as the "fruits of your life of justification." Among these are an "inward peace of conscience" and a loathing of any behavior that would jeopardize salvation. "If we fly from sin, as from the grave or hell, then surely those sins are pardoned which we do abhor. And that peace and reconciliation is procured which we desire."[17]

Vigilant against works righteousness, Cotton nevertheless did connect justification and sanctification in his piety. Since "sanctification is found partly in the heart and partly in the life," certain "effects of the life of our sanctification" become clues that "we may know we have Christ and life in him." These include the blending of traits not juxtaposed in natural behavior, such as joy with "fear and trembling" before God, "modesty mixed with much magnanimity," "diligence in worldly business, and yet deadness to the world," and "love of enemies." Further, believers fulfill life's responsibilities as "spiritual duties," undertaking daily tasks not as "good works" but with a "sense of our own insufficiency without Christ," in a way that we have "the Word of God for our warrant," and for "the glory of God in all our performances." Cotton likened the life of faith to processes of natural growth and nourishment. Just as digested food is made "all one with our selves," by regularly ingesting "the Word and Ordinances" we are "fashioned and made conformable to Christ." In nature a creature "grows till it comes to its full maturity"; so "the life of sanctification is growth" in Christ. "We grow to the end of our days, and then are forthwith translated to immortality." If at times we seem to "grow backward" spiritually, just as with physical sickness, by repentance we must "purge . . . expel, and drive out of the body that which is noisome and hurtful . . . and sweat it out."[18]

Cotton also interpreted "the properties and qualities of this life" of faith with

---

[17]Ibid., pp. 95-104. Emphasis mine.
[18]Ibid., pp. 109-10, 113-15, 119-20, 127, 129-30, 138-41.

analogies from nature—warmth, movement, and a "sweet and savory" fragrance (comparing the unregenerate to "cold and stiff" corpses that "must be buried" when they "begin to smell"). In contrast to "empty speculation," faith involves knowledge that is "full of heat" but without dangerous emotionalism. Unbridled "zeal is but a wild-fire without knowledge." Nevertheless, "if Christians have a knowledge of God, but no zeal, there is no saving life in that knowledge." We must exhibit "some kind of warm breathing" in our prayers. Even when we cannot vocalize prayer because of "anguish . . . discouragement . . . temptations . . . [or] afflictions . . . the very sighs of such a soul come from some warmth of spirit within." For a cold faith Cotton offered the remedy of fellowship with other Christians. Fire dies when logs are scattered, but "if you lay two or three warm brands together, they will kindle one another." Just so, an individual believer, "if he meet with two or three like himself, they presently begin to kindle one another, and the breath of such Christians, is like bellows, to blow up sparks one in another, and so in the end they breathe forth many savory and sweet expressions in their hearts, and edify themselves by their mutual fellowship with one another." In a congregation, as with a stack of wood, all it takes is "two or three . . . that are well kindled, and they will set all a fire that comes nigh them." Puritanism was an intensely personal but never a private faith. Indeed, radical individualism is essentially sinful and inherently anti-Christian. "When Satan means to put out the light and life of religion, out of both church and commonwealth, he lays one Christian in a corner, and another in another." Finally "a lazy spirit shall come upon them, and so they lie, till they be dead in trespasses and sins."[19]

Assurance of grace, again, is available through self-examination: "Doest thou pray to God with some kind of panting after him, and thy spirit is to faint within thee, and thou canst sit down and bemoan thy self to God?" If so, "there is breath in thee." Similarly the ability to "bring out a word to edify thy brethren" signifies that "it is well" with the soul. Conversely, "if there be no breath in thee, it is an evident sign thou art dead, or at least in a deep sleep." Cotton warned in stark terms against "the dangerous and uncomfortable estate of every soul as hath not Christ." We would naturally cry out in horror if we were to discover the body of a family member, but is it not far worse to be dead in sin than just physically dead? "Weep for these children, and those friends, that husband, or wife, or brother, or sister; weep for every soul that is in an estate of sin and death, they are as so many dead corpses." Never stop praying for them and with them, Cotton urged, "till thou hast got some grace from Christ for them." There is neither comfort nor hope in "earthly blessings," but "if you have

---

[19]Ibid., pp. 144-49.

Christ you have enough."[20] As Cotton taught in one of the concluding sermons, if a believer prays "with fervency and heat of spirit," in humility, and in "some kind of childlike confidence" that the Father "knows what you want better than you can ask," then God will hear and "undoubtedly give." Prayer in the "mighty power of the name of Christ" becomes more than a matter of inner striving. It is "now the prayer of Christ" and "the Holy Ghost also" at the throne of grace. When prayers come before the Father "by this means, it is not possible that our prayers should be rejected." Cotton offered "confidence" and "comfort to every soul that hath given up itself to Christ, and do thus call upon his name."[21]

CONCLUSION

Christ the Fountaine of Life expresses Puritanism's evangelical and pastoral impulses as plainly as any of the widely used devotional manuals published in London and Boston during the seventeenth century. John Cotton issued the warning and invitation to his people on both sides of the Atlantic. Without Jesus Christ there is only eternal death, but by "the Spirit of God's grace" we may certainly know and forever enjoy "this life of consolation and sanctification springing from the Spirit as from a fountain" because Christ is "he that sets open this fountain."[22]

SELECT BIBLIOGRAPHY

Cotton, John. *Christ, the Fountaine of Life*. New York: Arno, 1972.
————. *The Correspondence of John Cotton*. Edited by Sargent Bush. Chapel Hill: University of North Carolina Press, 2001.
Emerson, Everett. *John Cotton*. Boston: Twayne, G. K. Hall & Co., 1990.
Hall, David D., ed. *The Antinomian Controversy, 1636-1638: A Documentary History*. 2nd ed. Durham, N.C.: Duke University Press, 1990.
Hambrick-Stowe, Charles E. *The Practice of Piety: Puritan Devotional Disciplines in Seventeenth-Century New England*. Chapel Hill: University of North Carolina Press, 1982.
Stoever, William K. B. *"A Faire and Easie Way to Heaven:" Covenant Theology and Antinomianism in Early Massachusetts*. Middletown, Conn.: Wesleyan University Press, 1978.
Ziff, Larzer. *The Career of John Cotton: Puritanism and the American Experience*. Princeton, N.J.: Princeton University Press, 1962.
————, ed. *John Cotton on the Churches of New England*. Cambridge, Mass.: Harvard University Press, 1968.

---

[20]Ibid., pp. 156, 169-70, 176.
[21]Ibid., pp. 210, 212-14.
[22]Ibid., p. 4.

❧ 5 ❧

THE BRUISED REED

BY RICHARD SIBBES
(1577-1635)

Ronald N. Frost

THE "HEAVENLY" RICHARD SIBBES—THE ADJECTIVE SERVING AS A
virtual title for him in Puritan circles—was famous for his affective spirituality.[1]
During the reigns of James I and Charles I, Sibbes flourished as an educator and
preacher at both Cambridge and London until his death. His sermon series *The
Bruised Reed and Smoking Flax* (in print from 1630 to 1658) was highly regarded for
its distinctive voice among the pastoral books of the era. Richard Baxter, for instance, remembered receiving a copy of the book as a youth. It "opened more the
love of God to me, and gave me a livelier apprehension of the mystery of redemption, and how much I was beholden to Jesus Christ."[2] That Sibbes, who regularly
left his works unpublished, took time to edit and publish the *Bruised Reed* suggests
its importance to him.[3] The book, published when he was fifty-three, also offered
his mature thought and epitomized his main theological concerns.

INTRODUCTION TO SIBBES'S MINISTRY
Baxter's testimony to the impact of Sibbes's ministry was similar to many others

---

[1] Alexander B. Grosart, "Memoir of Richard Sibbes, D.D.," in Richard Sibbes, *Works of Richard Sibbes*, ed. Alexander
B. Grosart, 7 vols. (1862-1864; reprint, Carlisle, Penn.: Banner of Truth Trust, 1973-1982), I:xix. Grosart's edition serves as the standard source for Sibbes studies.

[2] Baxter, *Reliquiæ Baxterianæ*, pp. 8, 4, lib. i., pt. I, 1696, folio. Cited by Grosart, "Memoir," I:xxi.

[3] He notes in his foreword ("To the General Reader") that he was aware of a plan for the works to be published
by an auditor, thus he wanted to offer a reliable edition and to include "some fresh thoughts." (Sibbes, *Works*,
1:38). The dates for the sermons are unknown, thus this relative sense of urgency to preclude an unauthorized
publication suggests that the sermons were close in time to the 1630 publication. Most of Sibbes's sermons (i.e.,
those beyond volume one of his *Works*) were published posthumously.

who expressed a distinct sense of God's love after hearing him speak or by reading his sermons. A layman, Humphrey Mills, also expressed his relief at hearing Sibbes's unique message of grace:

> I was for three years together wounded for sins, and under a sense of my corruptions, which were many; and I followed sermons, pursuing the means, and was constant in duties and doing; looking for Heaven that way. And then I was so precise for outward formalities, that I censured all to be reprobates, that wore their hair anything long, and not short above their ears; or that wore great ruffs, and gorgets, or fashions, and follies. But yet I was distracted in my mind, wounded in conscience, and wept often and bitterly, and prayed earnestly, but yet had no comfort, till I heard that sweet saint . . . Doctor Sibbs, by whose means and ministry I was brought to peace and joy in my spirit. His sweet soul-melting Gospel-sermons won my heart and refreshed me much, for by him I saw and had much of God and was confident in Christ, and could overlook the world. . . . My heart held firm and resolved and my desires all heaven-ward.[4]

This gracious quality in Sibbes's sermons has been seen by some historians to be a matter of personal disposition—a warm-hearted pastoral orientation, but without offering a distinctive theology.[5] Such a view fails to capture the theological impact Sibbes had among an important group of theologians. He was certainly irenic and politically astute as he engaged the diverse views held by other Puritans and was alert to the challenges of preaching virtually under William Laud's nose, but he was scarcely a modest or merely derivative theologian. Rather, he was a persistent but careful advocate of a distinctively affective theology that he recovered and developed from some of the earlier reformers, including Martin Luther and John Calvin.[6] In particular he emphasized the inherent community of the Trinity, rather than follow the more common Reformed emphasis on God's simplicity and essential unity.[7] This distinctive orientation was translated into an applied theology of sanctification

---

[4]John Rogers, *Ohel or Bethshemesh, A Tabernacle for the Sun* (London, n.p., 1653), p. 410; this work is a collection of Puritan testimonials. The particular sermons that affected Mills are not cited in the testimony. Susan Hardman Moore alerted me to this source.

[5]E.g., Mark Dever, *Richard Sibbes: Puritanism and Calvinism in Late Elizabethan and Early Stuart England* (Macon, Ga.: Mercer University Press, 2000), chap. 6. Dever evaluates Sibbes's works by finding excerpts that affirm certain touchstone Reformed doctrines and endorses Sibbes as "one of the last of the great Reformed preachers in England" (p. 134). The reader is left to infer that Sibbes was merely a subsidiary rather than a seminal theologian. For an alternative interpretation that informs this chapter, see R. N. Frost, "Richard Sibbes' Theology of Grace and the Division of English Reformed Theology" (Ph.D. dissertation, University of London, 1997).

[6]Frost, "Richard Sibbes," pp. 50-58.

[7]See Amy Plantinga Pauw, *The Supreme Harmony of All: The Trinitarian Theology of Jonathan Edwards* (Grand Rapids: Eerdmans, 2002), who discusses (a) Jonathan Edwards's substantial engagement of Sibbes's trinitarian and affective theology, and (b) Edwards's mere affirmation of God's simplicity and his strong development of God's trinitarian nature (Edwards's "Triplicity").

and personal assurance in *The Bruised Reed*.

In *The Bruised Reed* Sibbes portrayed God as reaching out to his elect people on the basis of his fatherly love for Christ, in whom the elect are united by the Spirit's work. In taking this stance Sibbes also meant to challenge the tendencies toward destructive self-absorption—illustrated by Humphrey Mills' testimony—that came from examining one's own behaviors for signs of grace in order to gain assurance of salvation. This theology of "preparationism" held that a person who is uncertain of his status with God could presume that any significant evidences of godly conduct can be used as evidence that God's grace is at work in him, something that pointed to a higher likelihood of election. This moralistic premise was being used rather widely in Puritan circles. But it amounted, Sibbes charged, to adopting "the fig leaves of morality" as the grounds for assurance.[8] In a typical strategy of indirect confrontation Sibbes linked this error to the Roman Catholics rather than to his Puritan colleagues. Yet, in case the point was missed, he also warned that such emphases on human-initiated morality offers "too much respect to man [which is] one of the inlets of popery."[9]

The need for Sibbes to include such nudges pointed to a growing divide among the Puritans. William Erbery (1604-1654), a younger contemporary of Sibbes, saw that divide and held Sibbes to be a leader of the "free-grace" movement, the party of Puritans who opposed any idea that grace is conditioned by human cooperation.

> I observed four great steps of God's glorious appearance in men's preaching. First, how low and legal were their teachings as they learned the way of preaching from Mr. Perkins, Bolton, Byfield and Dod and Dike. . . . Next the doctrine of free grace came forth, but with less success or fruit of conversion by Doctor Preston, Sibs [Sibbes], [and] Crisp. . . . Thirdly the letter of scripture, and flesh of Christ hath been highly set up by both the famous Goodwins: . . . [Thomas] excels in spiritual discourses of Christ's death, resurrection, ascension, and intercession, yet much according to the flesh, for he meddles not with the mystery of Christ in us. . . . [The fourth step] is the knowledge of Christ in the Spirit.[10]

---

[8]"Moralism" in this context indicates the reliance of some Puritans on the Bible's "Moral Law" to define behavioral duties in spirituality. Sibbes's heart-based anthropology, by contrast, held that spirituality is the fruit of supernaturally transformed affections that would always satisfy the demands of morality but never rely on them as guideposts. Sibbes's challenge to "the fig leaves of morality" thus raised a basic question about the form of anthropology that should be applied in matters of spirituality. This distinction will be discussed later in the chapter.

[9]Sibbes, *Works*, 1:44, 53; cf. 1:55, 59.

[10]William Erbery, *The Testimony of William Erbery* (London: n.p., 1658), pp. 67-69; cited in Stanley P. Fienberg, "Thomas Goodwin's Scriptural Hermeneutics and the Dissolution of Puritan Unity," *Journal of Religious History* 10 (1978): 36.

Erbery's contemporary assessment was accurate. While Sibbes acknowledged some biblical support in calling Christians to obedience as a duty (Erbery's category of "low and legal" preaching) Sibbes clearly understood that duty can only be sustained if it is supported by the motivation of desire. Thus Sibbes featured God's winsome love more than his power: the Spirit accomplishes both conversion and sanctification by a single means: through the revelation of God's attractiveness by an immediate, personal disclosure. This unmediated initiative was seen to be the means by which God draws a response of heartfelt devotion from the elect.

In this framework some additional theological assumptions were revised. For instance, Sibbes understood grace to be God's love offered immediately (rather than mediately) by the Spirit to the elect.[11] By identifying grace primarily as a relational characteristic of God—the expression of his goodness—instead of a created quality or an empowerment of the will, Sibbes insisted that God transforms human desires by the Spirit's immediate love and communion. Faith, for Sibbes, was not a human act-of-the-will but a response to God's divine wooing. God's laws, Sibbes argued, must be "sweetened by the gospel" and offered within a framework of "free grace."[12] He also held a moderately developed form of affective anthropology.[13]

Others after Sibbes became sharper in their views, but he was the senior figure among them and their basic assumptions were the same. Thus, when Sibbes's views are placed in the context of debates over nature and grace in his era—including the continued Calvinist-Arminian struggles, the Antinomian Controversy of New England (1636-1638) and the doctrinal upheavals of the English Civil War—Sibbes emerges as a seminal figure among a small but energetic band

---

[11]E.g., Geoffrey Nuttall, *The Holy Spirit in Puritan Faith and Experience* (1946; reprint, Chicago: University of Chicago Press, 1992), p. 14, for Sibbes's role in promoting the Spirit. Additionally, a number of recent studies have pointed to Sibbes's role in leading a more affective theology. See, for instance, Michael Schuldiner, *Gifts and Works: The Post-Conversion Paradigm and Spiritual Controversy in Seventeenth-Century Massachusetts* (Macon, Ga.: Mercer University Press, 1991); Stephen Strehle, *The Catholic Roots of the Protestant Gospel: Encounter Between the Middle Ages and the Reformation* (Leiden: E. J. Brill, 1995); Janice Knight, *Orthodoxies in Massachusetts: Rereading American Puritanism* (Cambridge, Mass.: Harvard University Press, 1994); Frost, "Richard Sibbes."

[12]Sibbes, *Works*, 1:59; 1:39.

[13]Augustine's affective position emerged in the Pelagian debate. Augustine held sin to be concupiscence of the heart—an enslavement to a love of self rather than God. In Augustine's anthropology the heart is held to generate values; the mind uses the heart's values to consider its options and to offer its best judgments; the will uses those judgments to engage in action. Sibbes's familiarity with Augustine's views is evident in the *Bruised Reed*, including at least four citations or allusions to the Latin father (pp. 57, 58, 68, 70). For a summary of this tradition see R. N. Frost, "Aristotle's *Ethics*: The *Real* Reason for Luther's Reformation?" *Trinity Journal* 18 NS (1997): 223-41.

of Puritan ministers who pressed for a more trinitarian and relational version of Reformed theology.[14]

BIOGRAPHICAL NOTES

Richard Sibbes was born in 1577 to a wheelwright of moderate means in the village of Tostock, England.[15] An able student, Sibbes received the patronage he needed to gain a place at St. John's College, Cambridge, in 1595, where he completed his sequence of Bachelor's and Master's degrees in 1602. He began tutoring as a fellow of St. John's in 1601 and was soon rewarded with positions of increasing responsibility and status.[16] In 1610 he was granted the Bachelor of Divinity degree and received a Doctor of Divinity in 1627.[17] Along with his educational advancements Sibbes's emerging skills as a preacher flourished when he was appointed lecturer at Holy Trinity Church, Cambridge, in 1610 (continuing until 1615), and then in 1617 as preacher at Gray's Inn—one of the prestigious London Inns of Court. There he had a significant platform to speak to London's sympathetic politicians. The dedication of Sibbes's *Bruised Reed*, for instance, was to Sir Henry and Lady Mary Vere.[18] He also took the opportunity to engage with other Puritan ministers in the city to promote their common ambitions.

Sibbes was a moderate Puritan, one who would still conform to the requirements of ecclesiastical uniformity.[19] Yet on two occasions he drew the unhappy attention of William Laud, later archbishop of Canterbury. The first was for his part in trying to raise financial support for Protestant refugees in Germany and Bohemia (1627), and the second for his part in leading a fundraising project to place Puritan preachers in teaching posts ("lectureships") among parish churches

---

[14]Sibbes was linked to the Antinomian Controversy, for instance, through John Cotton who had been converted under Sibbes's preaching. Both men defined saving grace in relational terms, as the believer's response to God's love disclosed to the elect through Scripture, by the Spirit. See David D. Hall, *The Antinomian Controversy, 1636-1638: A Documentary History*, 2nd ed. (1968; reprint, Durham, N.C.: Duke University Press, 1990), e.g., p. 197, n. 46.

[15]For Sibbes's biographical data, see Dever, *Richard Sibbes*, chap. 1. A contemporary memoir by Zachary Catlin is available in Sibbes's *Works*, I:cxxxiii-cxli, appended to A. B. Grosart's biographical summary, p. xix.

[16]See Dever, *Richard Sibbes*, pp. 30-33. Sibbes was elected both Senior Dean and Lector Domesticus of the college in 1615. In 1619, after Sibbes had begun spending substantial time at his new post at Gray's Inn, he was made a senior fellow at Cambridge.

[17]Dever, *Richard Sibbes*, p. 37; Grosart, "Memoir," I:cxi.

[18]Sir Henry Vere served in the army for King James and was the first peer created by Charles I. Sibbes, *Works*, 1.35 (notes).

[19]Mark E. Dever, "Moderation and Deprivation: A Reappraisal of Richard Sibbes," *Journal of Ecclesiastical History* 43 (1992): 396-413.

(1632). Sibbes submitted in both cases and neither event diminished his freedom to minister.[20] In 1626 he was appointed master of Katharine Hall, Cambridge University, a post he held together with his role as preacher at Gray's Inn to the end of his life.[21] For more than a decade he shared his unique beliefs from these twin platforms with an impact that is still being measured by Puritan specialists. Sibbes's book thus unfolds the substance of his unique insights in early Stuart England.

THE BRUISED REED AND SMOKING FLAX

The Bruised Reed title came from Matthew 12:20: "A bruised reed shall he not break, and smoking flax shall he not quench, till he send forth judgment unto victory" (*Geneva Bible*, 1599). Sibbes's ambition was to lead his readers to a profound assurance of their salvation.[22] He intended to show how God's "free offer of grace" was able to bring such comfort.[23] In his foreword to the book he took immediate aim at the "false representations of Christ," against which he meant to offer the true Christ, "all whose ways to such being ways of mercy, and all his thoughts, thoughts of love."[24] The distinction of God's love in Christ as "affectionate" marked a trinitarian distinction for Sibbes. William Perkins, whose preaching Sibbes would have heard as a student, offered an alternative view of God by starting with an anthropopathic premise. That is, the "affections of the creature are not properly incident unto God, because they make many changes, and God is without change. And therefore all affections and the love that is in man and beast is ascribed to God by figure."[25] Perkins, then, would preach about God's love to laymen; but in works meant for scholars—those initially published in Latin—he was careful to define all of God's works as functions of his self-concerned will. Sibbes, by contrast, believed

---

[20]On both occasions Sibbes was called to testify before the High Commission, which led to a reprimand in the first case and dissolution of the fundraising organization in the second. However no further consequences can be traced in Sibbes's career. See Grosart, "Memoir," I:lx-lxxv.

[21]Grosart notes that a variance would have been necessary for Sibbes to retain both posts. The special arrangement points to Sibbes's standing. Grosart, "Memoir," I:xlviii-xlix.

[22]Michael P. Winship, *Making Heretics: Militant Protestantism and Free Grace in Massachusetts, 1636-1641* (Princeton, N. J.: Princeton University Press, 2002), miscasts Sibbes's view of assurance by suggesting that Sibbes believed "the immediate witness of the Spirit [was] . . . a rare and special experience and a supplement to the assurance derived from faith and sanctification" (p. 36). Sibbes's pneumatology and spiritual anthropology were actually very distinct from assurance-by-sanctification views held by William Perkins and others (contra Winship's assertion, pp. 16-17). Sibbes's optimistic version of assurance relied on the Spirit's continuing disclosures of his love, which then elicit responsive affections from the saint. Transformed affections then generate transformed behaviors.

[23]Sibbes, "To the General Reader," *Works*, I:39. Most spellings are modernized.

[24]Sibbes, *Works*, I:38.

[25]William Perkins, *The Workes of . . . William Perkins*, 3 vols. (London, n.p., 1626), I:742. See Frost, "Richard Sibbes," p. 61; cf. Bryan D. Spinks, *Two Faces of Elizabethan Anglican Theology: Sacraments and Salvation in the Thought of William Perkins and Richard Hooker* (Lanham, Md.: Scarecrow, 1999), pp. 58-59.

that God's imminent, intratrinitarian communion consisted of an eternally active love. This love overflowed to the creation as God's centrifugal self-giving.

The Bruised Reed sermons were gathered, thematically, around the section of Matthew's gospel (Mt 12:15-21) that applied segments of Isaiah 42 to the ministry of Jesus. The narrative of the gospel engaged two features of the messianic servant from the Isaiah text: (a) Jesus refused to draw attention to himself, and (b) he was sensitive to the fragile spiritual state of his followers. It was the second point that Sibbes pressed home as the main thrust of his sermons concerning Christ: "He is a physician good at all diseases, especially at the binding up of a broken heart."[26] The problem of sin and God's solution to sin, Sibbes regularly proclaimed, are both matters of the heart. The solution to sin is a believer's entry into God's eternal love for Christ through the real but mystical union of Christ to the church, his body. His consciously trinitarian framework ensured God's love for his saints, not on the basis of their behaviors, nor strictly on juridical grounds, but in a relationship motivated by filial affection.

> And what a comfort is this, that seeing God's love rests on Christ, as well pleased in him, we may gather that he is as well pleased with us, if we be in Christ! For his love rests in whole Christ, in Christ mystical, as well as Christ natural, because he loves him and us with one love. Let us, therefore, embrace Christ, and in him God's love, and build our faith safely on such a Saviour, that is furnished with so high a commission. See here, for our comfort, a sweet agreement of all three persons: the Father gives a commission to Christ; the Spirit furnishes and sanctifies to it; Christ himself executes the office of a Mediator. Our redemption is founded upon the joint agreement of all three persons of the Trinity.[27]

Three themes emerge in *The Bruised Reed*. Sibbes began with a call for moderation in applying the moral demands of the Bible on young Christians and nonbelievers. Most parishioners, he believed, were already insecure enough about their standing with God. Ministers, instead, should point to God's attractiveness. The second theme followed logically from the first. Since God's plan is to redeem people by his own working, not by their efforts, the role of the Spirit in the covenant of grace needed to be unfolded. The final movement explored the nature of life lived under Christ's rule and with the Spirit's presence, what Sibbes called Christ's "government" of the soul.

Bruising souls for conversion. The first nine chapters of the book unfold what it

---

[26]Sibbes, *Works*, 1:45.
[27]Ibid., 1:42-43.

means to be a "bruised reed" and "smoking flax." Sibbes began by acknowledging the premise, shared by most of his Puritan colleagues, that God uses the moral laws of the Bible to illuminate human immorality. Thus the moral grief felt by Humphrey Mills, noted already, would not have been uncommon. Mills's three years of feeling "wounded for sins, and under a sense of my corruptions" represented the bruising felt by many parishioners as their preachers pounded home the demands of God's holiness.[28] Where Sibbes differed from many colleagues, however, is in his disease-and-cure solution. The solution to an unholy heart is the good news of the gospel rather than "the fig leaves of morality." His implicit audience at many points of this section would have been his ministerial colleagues. Without naming names, Sibbes made it clear that he knew not all would agree with him.

> Profane spirits, ignorant of God's ways in bringing his children to heaven, censure broken-hearted Christians [as] desperate persons, whenas God is about a gracious work with them. It is no easy matter to bring a man from nature to grace, and from grace to glory, so unyielding and untractable are our hearts.[29]

The challenge is to find a balance between confronting sin and offering the comfort of promised mercy: to "preserve just bounds of mercy and severity" which is only achieved by having "a spirit above our own."[30] It was the parish pastor who bore the burden of bruising saints—and prospective saints—by using the law to call for godly obedience. But where should a minister look to find the Spirit's just bounds in the work of confronting sin? Sibbes looked to Christ and his original choice of leaders to build the church. Mercy was his measure. "Christ chose those to preach mercy, which had felt most mercy, as St. Peter and St. Paul; that they might be examples of what they taught." And even Christ himself came to earth emptying himself of majesty "in tender love to souls." Thus Sibbes insisted that it is incumbent on ministers to show similar humility and care: "Shall man be proud after God hath been humble?" Failure to apply this truth would be to engage in the proselytizing efforts of the "ministers of Satan" and to be like the Jesuits.[31] Indeed, the perceived misuse of the moral law by Roman Catholics gave Sibbes one of his sharpest rhetorical points in warning overly-moralistic Puritans:

> Those fiery, tempestuous, and destructive spirits in popery, that seek to promote

---

[28]For one Puritan's sense of moral distress in Sibbes's era, see Paul S. Seaver, *Wallington's World: A Puritan Artisan in Seventeenth-Century London* (Stanford, Calif.: Stanford University Press, 1985).

[29]Sibbes, *Works*, 1:44-45.

[30]Ibid., 1:55.

[31]Ibid., 1:54.

their religion by cruelty, show that they are strangers to that wisdom which is from above, which makes men gentle, peaceable, and ready to show that mercy [which] they have felt before themselves.[32]

His point was not to avoid confronting sin, including the generic "looseness of life" which "is cruelty to ourselves, and to the souls of others," but to avoid damaging other believers "by hasty censures, especially in things of an indifferent nature." The question of motives, more than behaviors, was crucial both in confronting the sin and in offering restoration. Sibbes's advice was that love should cover leaders like a "mantle" when making judgments on "lesser errors."[33] The proper analogy for ministry is a "common hospital," with believers considering "what affection Christ" the "great physician" would apply to the spiritual disease being addressed. Thus the law may be used to display and confront sin, but the basic motive of ministry must be Christ's love and mercy being used to draw—rather than to coerce by threats or force—bruised souls to embrace holiness.

A Spirit-centered covenant of grace. In chapters ten through seventeen Sibbes offered the covenantal structure of his affective vision of faith, as well as some advice on how to be assured of God's saving work. His covenantal language sounded similar to the emerging federal theology of his day if treated superficially. The federal model, suggested in the *Golden Chaine* of William Perkins, and later developed in the *Westminster Confession of Faith*, held that God offers two fundamental covenants, one of works and another of grace. Where Adam failed to maintain the covenant of works, Christ succeeded. Those who recognized their own Adamic failure to achieve righteousness through works and who took Christ in faith were given a better covenant in Christ, the covenant of grace. These parallel covenants were held to be in operation from Adam onward, with a proleptic certainty from Adam to the coming of Christ that the guilt of sin would be cared for; after the cross all believers could look back to the cross for their confidence.

Sibbes used the language of two covenants in *The Bruised Reed*—one of works and the other of grace—but he actually adopted Luther's polarity between the two chronological covenants of the Bible. That is, he held the Mosaic law of the Old Testament to be a covenant of works because of its conditional features. By contrast the coming of Christ and the Spirit brought a new era. Thus a believer must know how to distinguish "between the covenant of works and the covenant of grace, be-

---

[32]Ibid., 1:55.
[33]Ibid., 1:56.

tween Moses and Christ."[34] And all those who were saved in the Old Testament era were saved not by works but by transformed hearts, a change that reflected an "evangelical mitigation."[35] The fundamental requirement of both covenants is the same—the Shema call in Deuteronomy 6:5 to love God. But in the Mosaic era it "must be taken in the rigour," that is, by human effort, while under grace it becomes "delightful to the inner man."[36]

In distinguishing the two covenants Sibbes warned that it is the error of the Roman Church to collapse the Mosaic law and the gospel of Christ's grace into one covenant. Sibbes's law-gospel polarity was, in fact, much more Lutheran than Reformed, which helps account for the charges by John Cotton and others of Sibbes's offspring in the New England antinomian debate that their opponents had, indeed, collapsed the two covenants into one.

The pastoral benefits of the covenant of grace were unfolded throughout this section of *The Bruised Reed*. Because the "duty" to love God is actually kindled in the soul by the gracious presence of the Spirit, believers could relax with the assurance that their appetite for spiritual matters would grow because "holy truths are conveyed by way of a taste" and "grace alters the relish." Or, in a separate analogy, just as fire carries sparks upward, "so the Spirit of Grace carries the soul heavenward."[37] The latter analogy captured the second phrase of Sibbes's title "*and Smoking Flax*" that he believed to be God's assurance to weak Christians that even the faintest desire for God displayed a work of his grace in them—promising to take believers beyond the stage of merely smoking into the status of the fully enflamed.

Christ's government of the soul. In the final section of *The Bruised Reed*, chapters eighteen to twenty-eight, Sibbes invited readers to a vision of life under Christ's "government." This unveiled the main assumptions of Sibbes's spiritual anthropology, which, in turn, represented the most distinctive features of his applied theology. Some context is needed to understand how his approach set him apart from many of his Puritan colleagues.

While Sibbes was a student at Cambridge, William Perkins was answering the question of how God reaches humanity—the relation of grace to nature—by reengaging Thomas Aquinas's thirteenth-century cooperative approach to salvation.[38] Aquinas, with Aristotle, believed that morality is determined by the will,

---

[34]Ibid., 1:58.
[35]Ibid., 1:59.
[36]Ibid.
[37]Ibid., 1:60, 62.

so that virtue is gained by making the virtuous choice. In its Christian expression the human will must be engaged in a saving choice to believe. But Aquinas also held, with Augustine, that the will is crippled by sin. Aquinas's solution was to synthesize the moral axiom of Aristotle and Augustine's axiom of disability: God places a newly created gift of grace in the souls of the elect that enables the will to operate once again. By this means of gracious enabling the will receives the necessary power to embrace salvation by an act of faith. This enabling "habit of grace" allows a person to make the saving decision, a decision God crowns with merit.

This cooperative scheme featured the human and divine wills working together, with the mind using information offered by God. When the will has a set of options set before it, its challenge is to overcome distracting affections. The greater the power of the properly informed will, the greater its ability to defeat faulty passions. The act of believing is thus the premier work of the will, and is only accomplished by the prevenient enabling grace God provides.

Sibbes's anthropology, by contrast, held that the mind and will are merely instruments of the affections. This offered the compatibilistic solution to the question of how nature and grace are engaged in conversion: God works through the affections of the elect, drawing them to share his values by transforming their hearts. The fallen will, then, is not disabled and in need of more power, but disaffected—that is, morally opposed to God's rule because of distorted passions—and thus in need of God's love. In salvation the Spirit comes to the elect to disclose God's love to them, which then moves their wills to embrace God's ways.

> Christ and we are of one judgment, and of one will. He hath his will in us; and his judgments are so invested into us, as that they are turned into our judgment, we carrying "his law in our hearts, written by his Spirit" (Jer 31:33).[39]

If believers' "affections and duty" decline, the solution is "to warm ourselves at this fire of his love and mercy in giving himself for us."[40] But even in this apparent initiative of the believer it is actually the Spirit's work by which "he draws us strongly" and must "subdue our hearts, and sanctify them to love him, without which all motives would be ineffectual."[41]

---

[38]Perkins drew heavily from Geneva, incorporating many elements of Theodore Beza's synthesis into his own theology. See Strehle, *Catholic Roots*, on the Protestant use of the late medieval voluntarist tradition. Also, Richard A. Muller, *Christ and the Decree: Christology and Predestination in Reformed Theology from Calvin to Perkins* (Durham, N.C.: Labyrinth, 1986).

[39]Sibbes, *Works*, I:78.

[40]Ibid., I:79.

This assertiveness by the Spirit was critical to Sibbes's concept of Christ's spiritual government, a belief that Christ, in his humanity, relied on the Spirit for his own spiritual conduct. The kenosis represented Christ's purpose to demonstrate to all believers how life in the Spirit is accomplished. The common reliance of both Christ and his body on the Spirit's presence and guidance in their daily conduct served as their bond of union, making the language of "one body" more than a metaphor.

Yet for believers, unlike Christ, the need for the Spirit's immediate work is based, prior to grace, on a fundamental disaffection: "God finds nothing in us but enmity" which then must be transformed.[42] Thus Sibbes looked for the Spirit to function as an active presence in believers' lives. "The same Spirit that enlightens the mind, inspires gracious inclinations into the will and affections, and infuses strength into the whole man."[43] Judgments are thus born of a "soft and pliable heart" rather than vice versa.

> For without a work upon the heart by the Spirit of God, it will follow its own inclination to that which it affects. . . . For the heart unaltered will not give [freedom] to the judgment coldly and soberly to conclude what is best. . . . Judgment hath not power over itself where the will is unsubdued, for the will and affections bribe it to give sentence for them.[44]

Thus it is only in union with Christ, through the transforming work of his Spirit, that "Christ prevails" and then "he backs his own graces in us." Sibbes treated this relational theology of grace as a virtual formula: "Grace conquers us first, and we by it conquer all things else; whether it be corruptions within us, or temptations without us." By this "government of Christ's Spirit . . . our wills are brought to his will."[45]

CONCLUSION

In the penultimate paragraph of *The Bruised Reed* Sibbes recalled Luther's role as God's man by whom he "kindled that fire by which all the world shall never be able to quench."[46] The parallels between Luther's views and those held by Sibbes are intriguing, including the polarity of law and grace, an affective anthropology and a

---

[41]Ibid., 1:80.
[42]Ibid., 1:82.
[43]Ibid.
[44]Ibid., 1:83.
[45]Ibid., 1:87.
[46]Ibid., 1:100.

strong emphasis on the Spirit's immediate work in believers. It points to Sibbes' role in offering a bold but irenic counterpoint to the moralistic Puritanism of his era. He perceived a shift within the English Protestant Reformation away from its roots in the century since Luther shook the world. In particular, Sibbes resisted the themes of cooperative theology that were emerging in federal theology. His goals, however, were mainly pastoral, seeking to free his listeners from what he saw as a bruising use of the law in his day. The message of the gospel is freedom, the freedom and assurance of being loved by God while being unlovely. This message had a significant impact on other Christian leaders of his day, and beyond. Jonathan Edwards, for one, found great support in Sibbes for his own emphasis on the place of the transformed affections in explaining spiritual motivations.

Finally, Sibbes's focus in *The Bruised Reed and Smoking Flax* expressed a refreshing confidence in God's gracious love offered in Christ and communicated by the Spirit to growing Christians. His last sentence of the work captured this as he called upon Christ "to let the prevailing power of his Spirit in us be an evidence of the truth of grace begun, and the pledge of final victory, at that time when he will be all in all, in all his, for all eternity. Amen. Finis."[47]

Select Bibliography

Primary Source

Sibbes, Richard. *The Works of Richard Sibbes*. 7 vols. Edited by Alexander B. Grosart. Edinburgh: Banner of Truth Trust, 1973-1982.

Secondary Sources

Dever, Mark. *Richard Sibbes: Puritanism and Calvinism in Late Elizabethan and Early Stuart England*. Macon, Ga.: Mercer University Press, 2000.

Knight, Janice. *Orthodoxies in Massachusetts: Rereading American Puritanism*. Cambridge, Mass.: Harvard University Press, 1994.

Nuttall, Geoffrey F. *The Holy Spirit in Puritan Faith and Experience*. Reissue with introduction by Peter Lake. Chicago: University of Chicago Press, 1992; first published by Basil Blackwell, 1946; 2nd ed., 1947.

Pauw, Amy Plantinga. *The Supreme Harmony of All: The Trinitarian Theology of Jonathan Edwards*. Grand Rapids: Eerdmans, 2002.

Schuldiner, Michael. *Gifts and Works: The Post-Conversion Paradigm and Spiritual Controversy in Seventeenth-Century Massachusetts*. Macon, Ga.: Mercer University Press, 1991.

---

[47]Ibid., I:101.

⚜ 6 ⚜

LETTERS

BY SAMUEL RUTHERFORD

(1600-1661)

John Coffey

BY ANY STANDARD, THE *LETTERS OF SAMUEL RUTHERFORD* IS A CLASSIC OF Protestant devotional literature. The first edition (containing 286 letters) was published in 1664, under the title *Joshua Redivivus, or Mr Rutherfoord's Letters*. By the year 2000 almost eighty editions had been published in Britain and America. "In Scottish homes for some two centuries," writes Stuart Louden, "the most widely read devotional classic, apart from the Bible, was Rutherford's *Letters.*"[1] The *Letters* were endlessly quoted, collected, selected, anthologized and even versified. Images from them were woven into a well-known hymn, "The Sands of Time Are Sinking."[2] Their author became renowned as a kind of Protestant saint. Both his former parish of Anwoth and his tomb in the cathedral graveyard at St. Andrews became places of evangelical pilgrimage. The *Letters* were also translated into German, French and Gaelic, and there have been at least fifteen editions in Dutch. In English, an abridged version is still in print today, as is Andrew Bonar's complete edition, containing 365 letters. And like other classics discussed in this book, Rutherford's *Letters* can be found on the World Wide Web.[3]

The irony is that according to Robert McWard, their first editor, Rutherford

---

[1] R. S. Louden, "Samuel Rutherford," in *The Westminster Dictionary of Christian Spirituality*, ed. G. Wakefield (Philadelphia: John Knox Press, 1983), p. 345.

[2] See also F. Cook, *Grace in Winter: Rutherford in Verse* (Edinburgh: Banner of Truth Trust, 1989).

[3] For a list of the various editions and a thorough discussion of Rutherford's life, thought and reputation see J. Coffey, *Politics, Religion and the British Revolutions: The Mind of Samuel Rutherford* (Cambridge: Cambridge University Press, 1997). Many of the themes of this essay are explored more fully in my book.

"did not at all intend" them for publication and "did violence to the desires of many in refusing to publish them."[4] Copies of the letters had been circulating in manuscript among "the godly" (as they called themselves) since the 1630s. As one contemporary explained, various people "began to gather them together, and have whole books full of them."[5] Several of these small books of transcribed letters still survive in Scottish archives, though most of the originals have long since disappeared. The care that individuals took to copy the letters from the originals and then from notebook to notebook shows how quickly they acquired classic status. The lawyer Sir Archibald Johnston of Wariston, principal drafter of the Scottish National Covenant, explained why they were so valued when he wrote in his diary in 1652: "I found much life and love in Mr. Samuel Rutherford's letters."[6]

Many readers have subsequently shared Wariston's experience. The English Puritan Richard Baxter, who disagreed strongly with Rutherford on some matters, was nevertheless reported as saying, "But for that book of letters, hold off the Bible, such a book the world never saw the like!"[7] John Wesley, who had little sympathy for Rutherford's Calvinism, was also won over by his spirituality. He included a section from the *Letters* in volume 28 of his *Christian Library* (1753). "These letters," he commented in his preface, "have been generally admired by all the children of God for the vein of piety, trust in God and holy zeal which runs through them." The great Victorian Baptist, C. H. Spurgeon, wrote: "When we are dead and gone let the world know that Spurgeon held Rutherford's *Letters* to be the nearest thing to inspiration which can be found in all the writings of mere men."[8] Hudson Taylor, founder of the China Inland Mission, often meditated on the *Letters*. Inspired by Rutherford's love of the Song of Songs, he wrote a devotional study of the book entitled *Union and Communion* (1914).[9]

With testimonials like this, the classic status of Rutherford's *Letters* is hardly in doubt. Yet some may question whether a Scottish work could really be a *Puritan* classic. Puritanism, after all, is traditionally seen as a movement that began within the Church of England and was exported to New England in the 1620s and 1630s. Scotland, by contrast, was the heartland of Presbyterianism, and Rutherford is usu-

---

[4]Preface to *Joshua Redivivus, or Mr Rutherfoord's Letters* (1664).

[5]John Row, *The History of the Kirk of Scotland* (Edinburgh, n.p., 1842), pp. 396-97.

[6]*Diary of Sir Archibald Johnston of Wariston*, ed. D. H. Fleming (Edinburgh: Scottish Historical Society, 1919), 2:167.

[7]Robert Wodrow, *Analecta*, 4 vols. (Edinburgh: n.p., 1842-1843), 3:89.

[8]C. H. Spurgeon in *The Sword and the Trowel* (June 1891).

[9]Hudson Taylor and G. Taylor, *Hudson Taylor and the China Inland Mission: The Growth of a Work of God* (London: China Inland Mission, 1918), p. 163.

ally referred to as a Scottish Presbyterian, not a Puritan. However plausible this sounds, it sets up an artificial separation between zealous Protestants in the north and the south of Britain. The term *Puritan* was originally used as a term of abuse, and it is to be found in Scotland as well as England. In several letters, Rutherford warned his correspondents not to be intimidated when they are "nicknamed Puritans."[10] As the leading historian of Puritanism, Patrick Collinson, has shown, "the hotter sort of Protestant" attracted abuse from both their neighbors and the authorities (including monarchs and bishops). Zealous Protestants created controversy and divided communities because of their fervent pursuit of godliness and further reformation in church and society.[11] If the abusive term *Puritan* was rare in Scotland, this is because "hot Protestants" were more dominant in the land of John Knox than in England. As Rutherford explained, England was "a country where the Sun of righteousness, in the Gospel, shineth not so clearly as in this kingdom."[12] But in both nations, "the godly" formed a distinctive subculture, marked out by avid sermon consumption, sabbatarianism, public fasts, family prayer, psalm singing, diary keeping, covenanting and intense preoccupation with personal salvation.[13] It was within this subculture that Rutherford's letters first began to circulate.

LIFE AND LETTERS

Before exploring why the *Letters* had such appeal, we need to understand something of Rutherford's life. He was born around 1600 in the southeast of Scotland, and educated at Edinburgh University. His first pastor was a leading Presbyterian controversialist, David Calderwood, and as a college student Rutherford probably attended radical Presbyterian conventicles. In 1623 he became a teacher at the university, but his glittering academic career was catastrophically derailed by scandal in 1626. He was removed from his post due to the premarital pregnancy of his future wife, Eupham Hamilton. Chastened and humiliated, his thoughts turned toward the parish ministry.

In 1627 he became the minister of the tiny village of Anwoth in the southwest of Scotland. The parish had been suffering a "miserable extreme famine of the

---

[10]Rutherford, *Letters*, p. 512; also pp. 53, 134. All references to the *Letters* will be taken from *The Letters of Samuel Rutherford*, ed. A. Bonar (Edinburgh: Banner of Truth Trust, 1984). I have taken the liberty of modernizing some of the spelling.

[11]P. Collinson, *The Puritan Character* (Los Angeles: Clark Memorial Library, 1989).

[12]Rutherford, *Letters*, p. 42.

[13]See P. Collinson, "Elizabethan and Jacobean Puritanism as Forms of Popular Religious Culture," in *The Culture of English Puritanism*, ed. C. Durston and J. Eales (London: MacMillan, 1996); D. Mullan, *Scottish Puritanism* (Oxford: Oxford University Press, 2000).

word," with only one sermon every fortnight. Rutherford, eager to demonstrate his repentance by good works, transformed the situation. He was a whirlwind of passionate energy, a model Reformed pastor. As one contemporary commented, "he seemed to be always praying, always preaching, always visiting families, always visiting the sick, always catechising, always teaching in the schools, always writing treatises, always reading and studying."[14] "He used ordinarily to rise by three o'clock in the morning," wrote John Livingstone, and "was the instrument of much good among a poor ignorant people, many of which he brought to the knowledge and practice of religion."[15] It was at Anwoth that Rutherford began his famous correspondence—the first surviving letter dates to 1627. He had established a network of connections with the gentry of southwest Scotland, and his letters were written to inspire the godly to stand up to the pressure of the bishops who were trying to enforce conformity within the Church of Scotland.

Rutherford's subversive influence soon came to the attention of the authorities, and in 1636 he was deprived of his charge and placed under house arrest in the Episcopalian stronghold of Aberdeen, in the far northeast of Scotland. Frustrated at his exile, he released a torrent of letters in 1636 and 1637 to godly women, nobles, gentry, merchants and ministers all across the land. Indeed, 219 of Rutherford's surviving letters were written from Aberdeen, two-thirds of the total. These were the letters copied and circulated among the godly. They display a dark sense of foreboding over the nation's future, together with the hope that the cause of Christ would revive.

Rutherford's hopes were to be realized sooner than he expected. When King Charles I attempted to impose a new service book on the Scottish church, there was a dramatic riot in St. Giles Cathedral in Edinburgh. Rutherford's fellow Presbyterians spearheaded a movement of protest that culminated in the signing of a National Covenant in February 1638, when the political and religious leaders of Scotland vowed to defend the true Reformed religion against its foes. Rutherford returned triumphantly from Aberdeen, and played an active role in the General Assembly of 1638, which abolished bishops in the Kirk. He was now one of the most influential ministers in Scotland. In 1639, he was appointed professor of divinity at New College, St. Andrews, a post he held until 1660. Over the next few years, the British Isles became engulfed in military conflict, as first the Scottish Covenanters and then the English Parliamentarians went to war with the king.

The Covenanters and Parliamentarians formed an alliance in 1643, and Ruth-

---

[14]Wodrow, *Analecta*, 3:88.

[15]*Select Biographies*, ed. W. K. Tweedie, 2 vols. (Edinburgh: Woodrow Society, 1845-1847), 1:320.

erford was sent to London as one of the Scottish commissioners to the Westminster Assembly of Divines. In these four years he participated in the Assembly's debates over church government and the drafting of its great documents: the Westminster Confession of Faith and the Larger and Shorter Catechisms. He also published major books, including *Lex, Rex: or the Law and the Prince* (1644), an erudite defense of armed resistance to Charles I. He wrote extensively against Independency, Erastianism and religious toleration, and his calls for the suppression of dissent earned him a place in John Milton's sonnet "On the New Forcers of Conscience under the Long Parliament." In *A Free Disputation against Pretended Liberty of Conscience* (1649), Rutherford condemned radical Puritan tolerationists and defended religious coercion.

By the time he prepared to return to Scotland in November 1647, Rutherford was aware that the Assembly's achievements were jeopardized by the rising strength of the Independent party backed by the army. He was about to see his dreams of a Presbyterian Britain shattered. When Charles I launched another civil war, the king was defeated, placed on trial and executed by the English Independents in 1649, led by Oliver Cromwell. The Covenanters refused to acknowledge the legitimacy of the English regime and were quickly invaded and crushed by Cromwell. Divided over how they should respond to this calamity, the ministers of the Kirk split into two warring factions for the rest of the 1650s. Although Rutherford continued to preach and to publish major theological works, he was alienated from many of his former friends.

When King Charles II was restored to the throne in 1660 after the death of Cromwell, copies of *Lex, Rex* were publicly burned and Rutherford was removed from his position in the university and his charge in the church. His friends feared that he might face execution for treason. However, early in 1661, Rutherford fell seriously ill. On March 8, he issued a last will and testimony, and near the end of the month, he died. His life had ended in bitter disillusionment; the causes for which he had fought lay in ruins. But on his deathbed he spoke rapturously of heaven: "I shall live and adore Him. Glory, glory to my Creator and to my Redeemer for ever. Glory shines in Emmanuel's land."[16]

The fervent piety expressed in Rutherford's dying words was to be his lasting legacy. If his reputation had rested on the works he published in his lifetime, he would never have become a famous name among evangelical Protestants. For with the partial exception of *Lex, Rex*, and some of his sermons, the books he had pub-

---

[16]Samuel Rutherford, *A Testimony Left by M. Rutherford to the Work of Reformation in Britaine and Ireland* (Lanark, U.K.: n.p., 1739), p. 15.

lished in his lifetime were largely forgotten. His bulky volumes of Presbyterian ec-clesiology, his Latin treatises in defense of Calvinist orthodoxy, and his major works against heresy and toleration were soon gathering dust. But the letters he had never intended for publication were to make him famous for centuries to come. Their author would become known as "the Saint of the Covenant," "the seraphic Rutherford."

THE ATTRACTIONS OF THE *LETTERS*

In some ways the subsequent popularity of the *Letters* is a puzzling phenomenon. The language in which they are written is often archaic, and the vocabulary is so distinctively Scottish that Bonar's edition includes a lengthy glossary to help the reader. Indeed, the *Oxford English Dictionary* uses hundreds of quotations from the *Letters* to illustrate the use of obscure, colloquial or obsolete words. Yet Rutherford's prose was characterized as much by vivid images as by quaint vocabulary. He drew deeply on the apocalyptic visions of Revelation and the poetic literature of Scrip-ture, especially the Song of Songs, the Psalms, and the prophets Isaiah, Jeremiah and Ezekiel. Throughout the letters, biblical imagery and Hebraic language jostled alongside familiar domestic scenes: smoky inns, silly children, ships at sea, sandcas-tles on the shore, the sparrows and swallows of Anwoth, the wet and stormy Scot-tish weather. Reading the *Letters* could be an aesthetic pleasure, a literary delight, and the sheer force of Rutherford's expression was legendary. With their riot of im-agery, his letters were not a model of disciplined prose, but they were powerfully imaginative.

The *Letters* also became renowned for their words of wisdom. Rutherford's say-ings had a proverbial quality about them, which explains why they have been quoted from evangelical pulpits for generations. Almost casually, Rutherford could encapsulate profound spiritual insight in a single phrase:[17]

> Grace groweth best in winter.
> How soon would faith freeze without a cross!
> If ye would be a deep divine, I recommend to you sanctification.
> Be greedy of grace.
> I may be a book-man, and yet be an idiot and stark fool in Christ's way.
> Learning will not beguile Christ.
> Providence hath a thousand keys.
> Christ hath fastened heaven to the far end of the cross.

---

[17]These phrases, in the above order, are found on the following pages in Rutherford's *Letters*, pp. 157, 161, 170, 208, 219, 238, 247, 354, 455, 468, 536, 591.

Faith may dance, because Christ singeth.
There cannot be a more humble soul than a believer; it is no pride for a drowning
man to catch hold of a rock.
Faith is ever a neighbour to a contrite spirit.
All our songs should be of His free grace.
God forbid that this were good reasoning, "No feeling, no grace."

Such sayings, pithy and direct, but also gnomic and thought provoking, stick in
the mind. As one Scottish reader, Jock Purves, testified near the end of his life:
"And oh! that quotation from Rutherford, 'My faith hath no bed to sleep on but
omnipotency,' Marvellous! Wonderful! I think about it all the time."[18]

The accessibility of the epistolary genre also contributed to the popularity of
the *Letters*. The Puritans are renowned for their wordiness, and Rutherford was no
exception. But most of his letters are between one and four pages in length, and can
be read in a matter of minutes. Indeed, some have used them for daily meditation,
a practice facilitated by the fact that Andrew Bonar's edition contains precisely 365
letters, one for every day of the year. Readers can dip in and out of Rutherford's
Letters in a way that is not possible with other Puritan classics.

The *Letters* also allow us to get to know Rutherford's correspondents. Bonar's
edition provides biographical notices of recipients before each letter, and readers
quickly get to know the key figures in Rutherford's godly network. Rutherford did
not merely write to famous people, learned ministers and powerful politicians.
Many of his correspondents were ordinary and otherwise obscure, and they included godly women, unconverted young men, the recently bereaved and other
troubled souls. The variety of their situations and experiences means that readers
can usually find someone with whom to identify.[19] Remarkably, almost half of the
correspondence (171 letters) is addressed to women, much of it to two women in
particular: Lady Kenmure (56 letters) and Marion McNaught (44 letters). None
of Rutherford's male correspondents received anywhere near this number of letters,
and the seriousness with which he treated these women goes a long way toward explaining the appeal of the book among female readers.

For others, the *Letters* have been a window into history. Arranged chronologi-
cally, as they are in Bonar's edition, they allow us to follow Rutherford's fortunes
from 1627 to 1661. We see his early despair at the state of the Kirk, his initial rejoicing at the National Covenant and the Westminster Assembly and then his ulti-

---

[18]Quoted in F. Cook, *Samuel Rutherford and His Friends* (Edinburgh: Banner of Truth Trust, 1992), p. 146.
[19]See Alexander Whyte, *Samuel Rutherford and Some of His Correspondents* (Edinburgh: Oliphant, Anderson & Ferrier,
1894); Cook, *Samuel Rutherford and his Friends*.

mate disappointment. In his conspiratorial letters to Marion McNaught and Lady Kenmure, we catch the drama of political conflict as he passes on confidential information and describes his clashes with the bishops. For Presbyterians, in particular, this is a vivid firsthand account of a critical chapter in the history of their tradition.

"THE FURNACE OF AFFLICTION"

Yet for all these varied attractions, the *Letters* also have a dark side. Rutherford's classic can make bleak reading. The letters were products of a specific era of European history, the age of the Wars of Religion, when Catholics and Protestants were pitted against each other in a bitter struggle. Although Catholicism was weak in Britain, Puritans were convinced that the rise of High Church Anglicanism under Archbishop Laud was a crypto-Catholic plot to subvert the true Reformed religion. Rutherford was in open conflict with the new Laudian bishops, and he placed Scottish events into a European context, closely following the course of the Thirty Years War in Germany. His letters during the 1630s are shot through with a dark apocalypticism drawn from the book of Revelation. In the early 1630s, when the Swedish King Gustavus Adolphus was winning a series of Protestant military victories in Germany, Rutherford was hopeful that the destruction of the popish Babylon was nigh. He was distraught by news of Gustavus's death in 1632, but continued to believe that the Lamb would soon destroy the Beast and the Dragon. He also longed for the conversion of the Jews, which he believed was imminent and would usher in "the fullness of the Gentiles."[20] But although he foresaw the ultimate salvation of the nations, Rutherford was pessimistic about the near future, believing that God's wrath was coming on "apostate Scotland" for its "broken covenant."[21] He was vehement in his vituperation of the bishops, calling them "bastard prelates," "idol-shepherds," "lovers of Babel."[22] Like "Baal's priests" they were introducing "idols," "gross heresies," "bastard canons" and ceremonies from "Antichrist's foul womb."[23] The Kirk, he declared, had become a "whore," a "harlot-mother" on her way to "Rome's brothel-house."[24]

The darkness of Rutherford's apocalyptic vision and the bitterness of his rhet-

[20]Rutherford, *Letters*, pp. 122-23, 570-71.
[21]Ibid., pp. 333, 348.
[22]Ibid., pp. 53, 300.
[23]Ibid., p. 400.
[24]Ibid., pp. 87, 410.

oric was characteristic of the age of religious war, but it grated on post-Enlighten-ment ears. The great Scottish preacher Alexander Whyte, a leading commentator on the *Letters*, lamented Rutherford's "ecclesiastical hardness and narrowness" and testified to the "distress" he experienced when reading "the polemical parts of his heavenly *Letters*."[25] But he still believed that the piety of the *Letters* placed Rutherford among the great mystics of church history. Whyte's view was widely shared by other evangelicals. For many readers, the *Letters* could be read with great spiritual profit, despite being marred by their vitriol.

But the bleakness of the *Letters* did not simply arise from Rutherford's immersion in ecclesiastical conflict. It also reflected his experience of personal affliction. Within three years of coming to Anwoth, Eupham and Samuel's young children had died. Eupham herself was terribly ill:

> My wife's disease increaseth daily, to her great torment and pain night and day, she
> has not been in God's house since our communion, neither out of her bed. I have
> hired a man to Edinburgh to Doctor Jeally and to John Hamilton. I can hardly be-
> lieve her disease is ordinary, for her life is bitter to her; she sleeps none, but cries as
> a woman travailing in birth.[26]

In 1630, "after long disease and torment," Eupham "departed this life." Ruth-erford's response was that of Job: "The Lord hath done it; blessed be His name."[27] He himself had been in his sick bed for thirteen weeks with fever while Eupham lay dying. He was to live as a widower for the rest of the 1630s, deprived of "the delight of mine eyes." Even in 1634 the "wound" caused by his wife's death had "not yet fully healed and cured."[28]

Rutherford's bitter personal loss enabled him to counsel and comfort the be-reaved. No fewer than seventeen of his letters were written to those who had lost loved ones. As he struggled to come to terms with suffering, Rutherford developed a theology of affliction.[29] One of his key emphases was on the sovereignty of God. Lady Kenmure, to whom he wrote three times on the death of her children, was told that "faith will teach you to kiss a striking Lord; and so acknowledge the sov-ereignty of God (in the death of a child) to be above the power of us mortal men. . . . If our dear Lord pluck up one of His roses, and pull down sour and green fruit

---

[25]Whyte, *Samuel Rutherford*, p. 11.

[26]Rutherford, *Letters*, p. 49.

[27]Ibid., p. 53.

[28]Ibid., pp. 122-23, 570-71.

[29]See *The Refiner's Fire: Thoughts on Affliction Selected from the Works of Archbishop Leighton, Rutherford, Hooker, Newton, Cecil and Other Eminent Writers* (London: n.p., 1875), pp. 104-62.

before harvest, who can challenge him?"[30] Like Job, the Christian must resign herself to God, secure in the knowledge that the puny human intellect could not comprehend the Almighty's purposes.

Rutherford also taught that afflictions were God's way of sanctifying us. His advice to one bereaved woman is striking: "You must learn to make your evils your great good; and to spin comforts, peace, joy, communion with Christ, out of your troubles, which are Christ's wooers, sent to speak for you from Himself."[31] Speaking of himself he wrote, "Oh, what owe I to the file, to the hammer, to the furnace of my Lord Jesus! Who hath now let me see how good the wheat of Christ is, that goeth through His mill."[32] As he was fond of saying, Christ woos his bride "in the furnace of affliction."[33] Troubles had soul-making potential. "Is it not great art and incomparable wisdom in my Lord, who can bring forth such fair apples out of this crabbed tree of the cross?"[34]

As well as sending afflictions, Christ could also remove his presence for a time, leaving the believer feeling empty and alone. Rutherford drew this conclusion from his reading of the Song of Songs, and his letters and sermons depicted Christ as a lover who temporarily withdrew from his beloved.[35] In one letter he wrote, "He hath fettered me with His love, and run away, and left me a chained man. . . . My ebbings are very low, and the tide is far out when my Beloved goeth away."[36] The *Letters* reveal that Rutherford was intimately acquainted with the highs and lows of spiritual experience. He could swing from rapture to "great heaviness." As he himself admitted, "I am made of extremes."[37] In one letter he confessed, "I have not now, of a long time, found such high spring-tides as formerly. The sea is out, the wind of His Spirit is calm."[38] At such times Christ seemed like a *Deus absconditus*, an absent God.

But Christ had good reasons for such "desertions." Rutherford believed that the frail vessel of the human soul would burst if it took in "a sea of His love."[39] "Full manifestations" would simply overwhelm us. As he wrote to Lady Gaitgirth, "it is

---

[30] Rutherford, *Letters*, p. 98.

[31] Ibid., p. 246.

[32] Ibid., p. 161

[33] Ibid., p. 122.

[34] Ibid., p. 355.

[35] See M. Roberts, "Samuel Rutherford: the Comings and Goings of the Heavenly Bridegroom," in *The Trials of Puritanism: Papers Read at the 1993 Westminster Conference* (London: The Westminster Conference, 1994), pp. 119-34.

[36] Rutherford, *Letters*, p. 432.

[37] Ibid., pp. 79, 114, 315.

[38] Ibid., p. 537

[39] Ibid., p. 504.

good for you that He hideth Himself sometimes. . . . He knoweth that ye could not bear . . . a fair gale, a full moon, and a high spring-tide of His felt love. . . . His kisses and His visits to His dearest ones are thin-sown."[40] But by withdrawing for a time, Christ also achieved certain things: he guarded against spiritual pride in the believer, intensified his longing and taught him to live by faith, not by feelings. Christ's absence, wrote Rutherford, "giveth sap to humility, and putteth an edge on hunger, and furnisheth a fair field to faith to put forth itself, and to exercise its fingers in gripping it seeth not what."[41] The silence of God did not mean that he had changed, and the eye of faith could discern his constancy. Even low tides had their spiritual value. Alexander Whyte observed, "Rutherford is never more helpful to his correspondents than when they consult him about their ebb tides." Since Rutherford himself experienced both spiritual exaltation and spiritual depression, he could comfort and counsel those who worry "when the tide is low."[42]

But for all his Calvinist stress on divine sovereignty, Rutherford did not wish to encourage passivity and resignation in Christians. He was fond of repeating the adage: "Duties are ours; events are the Lord's."[43] Providence should not be used as an excuse for inaction. In Pauline tones he insisted that effort was essential to the Christian life: "Take pains, above all things, for salvation; for without running, fighting, sweating, wrestling, heaven is not taken."[44] As he wrote to one correspondent:

> bend yourself to the utmost of your strength and breath in running fast for salvation; and in taking Christ's kingdom, use violence. It cost Christ and all His followers sharp showers and hot sweats, ere they won to the top of the mountain; but still our soft nature would have heaven coming to our bedside when we are sleeping, and lying down with us that we might go to heaven in warm clothes.[45]

Christ's disciples, Rutherford believed, should not expect a comfortable life. The theme of taking up the cross reverberates throughout the *Letters*. "Crosses are proclaimed as common accidents to all the saints, and in them standeth a part of our communion with Christ."[46] Yet those who embraced the cross would discover that Christ "hath overgilded that black tree, and hath perfumed it, and oiled it with

---

[40]Ibid., p. 367.
[41]Ibid., p. 467.
[42]Whyte, *Samuel Rutherford*, p. 17.
[43]Rutherford, *Letters*, pp. 226, 235, 238.
[44]Ibid., p. 399.
[45]Ibid., p. 389.
[46]Ibid., p. 477.

joy and consolation."[47] "Those who can take that crabbed tree handsomely upon their back, and fasten it on cannily, shall find it such a burden as wings unto a bird, or sails to a ship."[48]

Despite this, the troubles of life made Rutherford long for heaven. Throughout the *Letters* he reminded his readers of the brevity of this life and the reality of eternity. This world, he insisted, is "a fool's idol, a clay prison," a "worm-eaten apple."[49] Those who chase after wealth, fame and pleasure are forgetting that their days are short. In urging one correspondent to forsake whoring, drunkenness, sabbath-breaking and godlessness, Rutherford wrote: "Ye know that this world is but a shadow, a short-living creature, under the law of time. Within less than fifty years, when ye look back to it, ye shall laugh at the evanishing vanities thereof, as feathers flying in the air, and as the houses of sand within the sea-mark, which the children of men are building."[50] The saints who had endured earth's winter would then experience "their eternal summer." Christ and his cross would "part at heaven's door, for there is no houseroom for crosses in heaven."[51]

The tough quality of Rutherford's *Letters* must not be overlooked. Written in the age of religious wars, they bear the marks of bitter polemical dispute. Written in the midst of spiritual affliction, they provide an antidote to glib triumphalism. Written at times of spiritual depression, they face up to the low tides of Christian experience. It is impossible to read the *Letters* and come away with the idea that the life of faith is a pleasure cruise. Rutherford reminds us that it is more like a seventeenth-century sea voyage, in which our small ship is tossed and battered by many storms. People "love to go to heaven by dry land," he remarked, "and love not sea-storms." "We live in a sea where many have suffered shipwreck, and have need that Christ sit at the helm of the ship."[52]

"The Love-Kisses of Sweet, Sweet Jesus"

We have covered a good deal of ground, but only now do we come to the primary reason for the *Letters*' appeal. Rutherford's favorite theme was the beauty of Christ. Jesus was "that Flower of Jesse," "the sweetest apple in all God's heavenly paradise," "the fairest, the sweetest, the most delicious Rose of all His Father's great field."[53]

---

[47] Ibid., p. 153.
[48] Ibid., p. 148.
[49] Ibid., pp. 527, 227.
[50] Ibid., p. 325.
[51] Ibid., pp. 485, 479.
[52] Ibid., pp. 329, 129.
[53] Ibid., pp. 80, 79, 89.

Rutherford's admirers have agreed that the *Letters* are a Christian classic because of their vision of Christ.

Rutherford constantly depicted Christ as the lover from the Song of Songs, and the *Letters* are full of extraordinary metaphors drawn from that unique work of Old Testament literature. He wrote breathlessly of "love letters," "love-tokens," "love banquets," "love-looks," "love-blinks," "love-sickness," "love-beds" and even "love-grips." He sulked at Christ's "glooms" and "frownings" and sang of his "soft and sweet kisses to me"; he waxed lyrical about Christ's "soul-ravishing countenance"; he longed to take Christ in his arms, to experience "everlasting huggings, and embracings."[54] For Rutherford, Christ delighted all the spiritual senses, just as the lover in the Song of Songs was beautiful to see, hear, smell, taste, and touch.

> Oh, what a sight to be up in heaven in that fair orchard of the new paradise; and to see, and smell, and touch, and kiss that fair field-flower, that evergreen Tree of life!
> . . . Christ, Christ, nothing but Christ can cool our love's burning languor. O thirsty love! Wilt thou set Christ, the well of life, to thy head, and drink thy fill? Drink, and spare not; drink love, and be drunken with Christ! Nay alas! The distance between us and Christ is a death. Oh, if we were clasped in each other's arms.[55]

The lushness of this spirituality has not been to everyone's taste, and Victorian commentators often expressed concerns over the wisdom and propriety of the sensual language. As one writer remarked, "There are some to whom the unpruned lusciousness of Rutherford's preaching, its gush of emotion, and frequent tone of rapture, are not acceptable."[56] In reality, the devotional use of the Song of Songs was thoroughly conventional among Puritans, and Rutherford only stands out because he employs its imagery with such abandon. His exuberant piety explodes the stereotype of the dour and formal Scottish Presbyterian. And it fits with a major recent study claiming that the post-Reformation Scottish clergy combined "rational, text-based discourse in the new mode, with fervent homiletics, and visions, prophecies and miracle-working."[57] It also reminds us that for all his fierce antipopery, Rutherford could draw appreciatively on medieval sources. Christocentric interpretations of the Song of Songs had been a staple of Christian spirituality throughout the Middle Ages and it is quite likely that Rutherford was inspired by

---

[54]The final phrase is taken from Rutherford's *Christ Dying* (London: n.p., 1647), p. 83. Of all Rutherford's books, this collection of sermons is perhaps closest in style to the *Letters*.

[55]Rutherford, *Letters*, p. 173.

[56]W. G. Blaikie, *Preachers of Scotland* (Edinburgh: n.p., 1888), p. 116.

[57]Margo Todd, *The Culture of Protestantism in Early Modern Scotland* (New Haven, Conn.: Yale University Press, 2002), p. 400.

Bernard of Clairvaux's famous sermons on the Song. As in his political and theological writings, Rutherford displays a surprising openness to Catholic influences.

Indeed, the intensity of Rutherford's vision has led many readers to describe him as a "mystic." The term needs to be used with care. If by mystic we mean someone with an intense desire for immediacy of communion with God, then Rutherford certainly was one. But if we are thinking of a person who seeks the absorption of their human personality into the divine, or direct access to personal revelation that bypasses Scripture, then he most definitely was not. Indeed, Rutherford has been described as an "anti-mystic," because in other works he condemned contemporary sects that spoke of being divinized, or "Godded with God." So instead of describing Rutherford and other Puritans as mystics (implying a rather vague and nondoctrinal spirituality), we should use their own term and call them "affectionate theologians" (highlighting their belief that doctrine must be internally appropriated and felt).[58]

Rutherford was aware of his tendency to make "an idol of Christ's kisses." "I would fain learn not to idolise comfort, sense, joy and sweet, felt presence," he wrote. "All these are but creatures . . . the Bridegroom Himself is better than all the ornaments that are about him."[59] His desire for Christ's presence was also balanced by a sense of his transcendence. Even "the highest angels who see Him face to face, seeth not the borders of His infiniteness. They *apprehend* God near hand; but they cannot *comprehend* Him."[60] For how could a mere creature comprehend an omnipresent God?

> For the Lord is before me, and I am so bemisted that I cannot follow Him; He is behind me, and following at the heels, and I am not aware of Him; He is above me, but His glory so dazzleth my twilight of short knowledge, that I cannot look up to Him. He is upon my right hand, and I see Him not; He is upon my left hand, and within me, and goeth and cometh, and His going and coming are a dream to me; He is round about me, and compasseth all my goings, and still I have Him to seek. He is every way higher, and deeper, and broader than the shallow and ebb handbreadth of my short and dim light can take up; and therefore, I would that my heart could be silent, and sit down in the learnedly-ignorant wondering at the Lord, whom men and angels cannot comprehend.[61]

---

[58] I owe this suggestion to Mark Dever, *Richard Sibbes* (Macon, Ga.: Mercer University Press, 2000), chap. 6: "An 'affectionate' theologian."

[59] Rutherford, *Letters*, pp. 503, 316.

[60] Ibid., pp. 317-18.

[61] Ibid., p. 317.

CONCLUSION

In a perceptive essay on Rutherford, A. T. Innes recounted a story told by Robert Wodrow. Rutherford, preaching on contemporary disputes, was suddenly distracted from his theme and caught up with praising Christ. A bystander whispered, "Ay, now you are right—hold you there!" "And undoubtedly," Innes concluded, "that has been the verdict of posterity." Eighteenth- and nineteenth-century evangelicals, repelled by what they saw as the aridity of Rutherford argumentation, and disturbed by his uncharitable acrimony, often regarded his writings as "a harsh and astringent cup, with a lump of sugar at the bottom."[62] Editions of selected letters bore revealing titles: *Gleanings from Rutherford* (1854), *Christ's Cross* (1855), *Manna: Crumbs for Hungry Souls* (1865), *A Garden of Spices* (1869), *Rubies from Rutherford* (1892), *The Loveliness of Christ* (1893), *The Upward Way* (1903), *The King in His Beauty* (1955). The *Letters* were valued because they emphasized themes dear to the evangelical holiness movement: the way of the cross, sanctification and affection for Christ. They provided spiritual nourishment (*Gleanings* and *Manna*) and spiritual delight (*Spices* and *Rubies*). Captivated by the religion of the heart, pietist evangelicals bypassed polemical treatises and focused on Rutherford the pastor, preacher and correspondent.

The pietist tendency to deprecate erudition has come at a cost—"the scandal of the evangelical mind"—and we can be thankful that in recent years scholars have begun to rediscover the theological and political thought of early modern Protestants.[63] But we should remember why evangelical pietists reacted against seventeenth-century scholasticism while preserving seventeenth-century devotion. Rutherford's career demonstrates that doctrinal and ecclesiastical disputes often degenerated into bitter wrangling, and left a legacy of hatred and spiritual dryness. As he himself confessed near the end of his life:

> When the head is filled with topics, and none of the flamings of Christ's love in the heart, how dry are all disputes? For too often, fervour of dispute in the head weakens love in the heart. And what can our Paper-industry add to the spotless truth of our Lord Jesus?[64]

This passage could almost serve as a pietist motto. It reminds us that if we have not love, we are nothing.

---

[62]A. T. Innes, "Samuel Rutherford," in his *Representative Nonconformists* (London: n.p., 874), p. 50.

[63]See Mark Noll, *The Scandal of the Evangelical Mind* (Grand Rapids: Eerdmans, 1994); C. R. Trueman and R. S. Clark, eds., *Protestant Scholasticism: Essays in Reassessment* (Carlisle, U.K.: Paternoster, 1999); Q. Skinner, *The Foundations of Modern Political Thought*, vol. I, *The Reformation* (Cambridge: Cambridge University Press, 1978).

[64]Samuel Rutherford, *A Survey of Thomas Hooker* (London: n.p., 1658), sig A2.

SELECT BIBLIOGRAPHY

Primary Sources

Barnes, Sidney, ed. *Inspirational Treasury on Samuel Rutherford.* Belfast: Ambassador, 2001.

Rutherford, Samuel. *The Letters of Samuel Rutherford.* Edited by Andrew Bonar. Edinburgh: Banner of Truth Trust, 1984.

————. *The Letters of Samuel Rutherford.* Abridged edition. Edinburgh: Banner of Truth Trust, 1997.

————. *Quaint Sermons of Samuel Rutherford.* Edited by Andrew Bonar. Morgan, Penn.: Soli Deo Gloria, 1999.

————. *The Trial and Triumph of Faith.* Edinburgh: Banner of Truth Trust, 2001.

Secondary Source

Coffey, John. *Politics, Religion and the British Revolutions: The Mind of Samuel Rutherford.* Cambridge: Cambridge University Press, 1997.

OF THE OBJECT AND ACTS OF JUSTIFYING FAITH

BY THOMAS GOODWIN (1600-1680)

Michael S. Horton

HEIR TO THE MANTLE OF CAMBRIDGE PURITANISM, THOMAS GOODWIN (1600-1680) appeared at the end of that notable line of the so-called spiritual brotherhood, including William Perkins, Paul Baynes, Richard Sibbes and John Preston. In his own right, Goodwin became a seminal figure in the consolidation and further development of English Calvinism. Given his unusual longevity, Goodwin was able to leave his mark as leader of the "dissenting brethren" at the Westminster Assembly, later serving as coauthor of the Savoy Declaration along with John Owen. Also with Owen, who was vice chancellor of Oxford University, Goodwin oversaw the reform of this institution in his capacity as president of Magdalen College. In addition, Goodwin was a Dutch exile during the reign of Charles I after which he was a chaplain to Oliver Cromwell. Later, as a London pastor he died just before he could board ship for New England.

Converted out of a spiritual lethargy that leaned toward the rhetorical flourishes of the famous moralizing preachers of the day whom he identified as Arminian, Goodwin was advised by Richard Sibbes, "Young man, if you ever would do good, you must preach the gospel and the free grace of God in Christ Jesus."[1]

Increasingly, however, Goodwin came to conclude that Sibbes's concern was in the minority. In the preface to his *Christ Set Forth*, Goodwin relates:

I have by long experience observed many holy and precious souls, who have clearly

---

[1] Cited by Brian Freer, "Thomas Goodwin the Peaceable Puritan," in *Diversities of Gifts: The Westminster Conference Papers* (London: Westminster Chapel, 1980), p. 12.

and wholly given up themselves to Christ, to be saved by him his own way, and who at their first conversion (as also at times of desertion) have made an entire and immediate close with Christ alone for their justification, who yet in the ordinary course and way of the spirits have been too much carried away with the rudiments of Christ in their own hearts, and not after Christ himself.[2]

These troubled souls were more concentrated upon "searching into the gracious dispositions of their own hearts, so to bring down, or to raise up (as the apostle's words are, Rom. x. 8), and so get a sight of Christ by them. Whereas Christ himself is 'nigh them' (as the apostle there speaks), if they would but nakedly look upon himself through thought of pure and single faith."[3] The people seemed more interested in graces within their own hearts than with the grace of God in Jesus Christ and therefore rested in the former rather than the latter.[4] John Owen shared Goodwin's concerns, complaining of "superstition, self-righteousness, and anxiety of conscience in them who take up the burden which is so bound for them," warning that such preaching has abandoned the "covenant of grace" for the "covenant of works."[5]

Every generation faces its own challenges with respect to preserving the clarity of the gospel, and Goodwin's approach exhibits the Puritans at their best: doctrinal precision in the interest of practical piety. It will be the purpose of this chapter to focus on Goodwin's understanding of the object and acts of justifying faith.

While some recent scholars have too sharply contrasted Calvin and later Calvinism, it is undeniable that the Continental Reformed tradition, following Calvin and his contemporaries, differs from the Puritan (Westminster) tradition in its precise understanding of the nature of faith in relation to assurance. According to the former, assurance is directly related to the essence of faith; in other words, to believe is to be assured. The latter argue that faith and assurance are distinct: there is the faith that looks to Christ alone for salvation (the *actus fidei* or act of faith, also known as the *faith of recumbency*) and the faith by which the believer knows that he or she is the recipient of that salvation (*fides reflexa* or reflexive faith, also known as *assurance*). Although this difference is real and not without some significant theological and pastoral implications, advocates of discontinuity between Calvin and

---

[2] Thomas Goodwin, preface to "Christ Set Forth in His Death, Resurrection, Ascension, Sitting at God's Right Hand, Intercession, As the Cause of Justification, and Object of Justifying Faith. Upon Rom. 8. Ver. 34," in *The Works of Thomas Goodwin, D.D.* (London: James Nichol, 1862), 4:3-10.

[3] Ibid., p. 3.

[4] Ibid., 4:3-6.

[5] John Owen, preface to "Of the Mortification of Sin in Believers, Etc.," *The Works of John Owen*, ed. William H. Goold (Edinburgh: Banner of Truth Trust, 1967), 6:3.

later Calvinists (i.e., the Puritans) have reduced it to a fundamental difference between the grace-oriented theology of the former and the works-oriented theology of the latter. In what follows we will see in Goodwin an example of how this thesis simply cannot stand up under closer scrutiny.

If the distinction between faith and assurance is itself evidence of a creeping legalism and "Arminian" voluntarism (i.e., emphasizing the will rather than the intellect as the dominant human faculty), surely Goodwin would serve as an example. He certainly separated faith and assurance not only beyond what Calvin articulated but more radically than most Puritans. As we shall see, however, his understanding of the object and act of justifying faith is antithetical to the caricature proposed by R. T. Kendall, J. B. Torrance and other proponents of the discontinuity thesis.[6] The following corresponds to Goodwin's own outline, as he divides his discussion of justification into faith's object and its acts.

PART ONE: THE OBJECT OF JUSTIFYING FAITH

God's merciful nature. Goodwin began his discussion of justification by relating it to the general revelation of God's nature. While God is partially revealed in general revelation, the gospel is not: "the way of faith, and of being saved by Christ, is a new way, whereof there are no footsteps in nature, neither corrupt nature nor pure nature."[7] In the vein of the magisterial reformers, Goodwin began with the divine nature—not God's nature in general, but specifically his nature as it is disposed toward mercy.[8]

Because faith is difficult, "the consideration of the mercies in God's heart and nature is the strongest, the most winning and obliging" of all of the divine attributes.[9] However, Goodwin was not even content to allow faith's gaze to rest upon an abstract attribute of mercy in God, but took it yet a step further: "And God hath minted his mercies forth from out of his purposes into promises where

---

[6]Goodwin represents the tendency within federalism to emphasize the objective (justification) and unconditional (absolute) side of the covenant, especially against other covenant theologians who seem to be emphasizing the subjective and conditional side excessively. For examples of the discontinuity thesis, see Brian Armstrong, *Calvinism and the Amyraut Heresy* (Madison: University of Wisconsin Press, 1969); Holmes Rolston III, "Responsible Man in Reformed Theology: Calvin vs. the Westminster Confession," *Scottish Journal of Theology* 23 (1970): 2; Alan Clifford, *The Atonement and Justification* (Oxford: Oxford University Press, 1990); J. B. Torrance, "Contract or Covenant," *Scottish Journal of Theology* 23 (1970): 1; and especially R. T. Kendall, *Calvin and English Calvinism to 1649* (Oxford: Oxford University Press, 1979). Among the many ever-growing lists of critics of this thesis see especially Richard Muller, *Christ and the Decree: Christology and Predestination in Reformed Theology from Calvin to Perkins* (Grand Rapids: Baker, 1986); Joel Beeke, *The Assurance of Faith* (Amsterdam: Peter Lang, 1991).

[7]Goodwin, *Justifying Faith*, 8:329

[8]Ibid., p. 3.

[9]Ibid.

they lie exposed, and to be given forth to every one that will come in for grace, and take them from mercy's hands, even 'redemption from all iniquity.'"[10] In short, the mercy of God is evident in his revealed promises.

God's merciful will. Because God has expressed his merciful nature in his merciful will and through a merciful promise, faith is given sufficient reason to hope in God's mercy.[11] Therefore, we must turn to special revelation, and to the free offer of the gospel in particular, where God's mercy is given concrete expression in the form of promises. The gospel of salvation by Christ, through grace alone, is taught in both testaments: "This proclamation of grace being a magna charta of the Old Testament."[12]

Goodwin combed the Scriptures for references to other divine attributes and discovered, for instance, that even the title Alpha and Omega "is spoken in relation unto grace and salvation. . . . Thus it is in his loving us, and thus it is in his saving us; he is the first and last in both."

> It is not as the Papists say, who acknowledge God to be the first in the benefits of salvation, as that at the first mercy doth all in justification (and they call it therefore the first justification), which they ascribe to God's grace wholly; but then they feign a second justification, as that which saves us, and makes us heirs of eternal life through the merits of works. Oh, but Jehovah merciful and gracious is the first and the last, and all and everything of grace depends upon him, and it is wholly grace and mercy from first to last.[13]

Because God is merciful from first to last, one should come to him in faith, especially when one has sinned:

> "Trust in him at all times"; for he that was, and is to come, is your Jehovah merciful. . . . You are not to imagine that indeed when we have walked holily, and only then, we may come with expectation of mercy and pardon from him: no, but trust in him "at all times," only come humbling yourselves, and turning unto him; draw near to him and he will draw near to you. God is not as man, to be merciful by fits, when the good humour comes on him.[14]

Goodwin insisted on a trinitarian scheme for appreciating mercy as a divine attribute, which was considered in the context of the eternal covenant of redemption

---

[10]Ibid., pp. 5-6.
[11]Ibid.
[12]Ibid., p. 19.
[13]Ibid., p. 39.
[14]Ibid., p. 41.

(*pactum salutis*): "The Father had the decreeing part of all mercy, the Son the pur-
chasing part, and the Holy Ghost the operative part, which requires power and
strength."[15] Power and strength are necessary, because mercy without power produces pity, but it is not helpful.[16] In his covenantal mercy God not only has the
nature and will to save, but he also has the power to save to the end, and a sovereignty which, far from challenging God's goodness, is indispensable to its achieving
the divine ambition to save. A simplistic understanding that "God is love," or
"God is mercy," is not enough. Goodwin wrote:

> He presents himself to sinners; and if to them he had said at first dash, God is good,
> or God is gracious, or God is love, sinners would have said, This speaks short to us,
> and why? Because he is good to all his creatures that never sinned; ay, but merciful,
> with that proper effect, "pardoning iniquity, transgression, and sin," that is a wel-
> come saying to sinners, and speaks home to their case.[17]

While some would say that mercy is arbitrary in God, Goodwin countered with the
assertion that divine action depends on the divine nature in which arbitrariness does
not reside, and that nature is mercy.[18] Others maintained that mercy is a sign of weak-
ness, but Goodwin argued that God's display of mercy, not raw power, is his crowning
glory.[19] If mercy is God's chief attribute, forgiveness is mercy's chief expression.

Goodwin saw faith primarily as persuasion, with God's forgiving mercy as the
object. He reaffirmed the traditional definition of faith: knowledge, assent, trust.[20]
God's mercy moves him to forgiveness and forgiving mercy moves us to faith.[21]
"We cannot want the knowledge of any of his attributes, but our faith will be the
weaker for it," so knowledge is an indispensable part of faith. Faith is a gift, as
mercy not only *promises* but *performs*. Unlike his other attributes, which are "to himself and for himself," mercy is the attribute that has no other use "but to be given
all forth unto sinners for his glory."[22]

God as revealed in Christ. It is as if Goodwin saw the object of faith—God's forgiving mercy—in terms of concentric circles. The outside ring is God as he is merciful naturally. The next ring inside is God as he is considered as having a merciful
will towards us. The third circle is God as revealed in Christ. We must not believe

---

[15] Ibid., p. 46. This is fleshed out more fully in pp. 144ff.
[16] Ibid., p. 50.
[17] Ibid., p. 56.
[18] Ibid., pp. 109-10.
[19] Ibid.
[20] Ibid., pp. 114-21.
[21] Ibid., pp. 117.
[22] Ibid., pp. 125.

in God abstractly considered, but rather, "under the apprehension of his person, Son of God and God-man (which properly is called his person), not God simply in his divine nature singly considered but God manifest in flesh, or the Son of God made flesh."[23] Since no one has seen God but the Son, we must look to the Son as the reliable expression of the Father's merciful nature and will.

In Puritan fashion, Goodwin encouraged his readers to move beyond speculation and mere assent concerning Christ the Mediator.[24] Knowledge, as we have already seen, was essential in Goodwin's understanding of justifying faith; nevertheless, knowledge must be combined with a childlike assent and embrace.[25] In most occasions, Goodwin's favorite definition of faith was the image of "looking unto Christ." Even when we are impotent, the Spirit creates hands to "lay hold upon Christ."[26]

Christ as offered in the covenant of grace. Faith does not merely eye God as merciful in nature and in will, nor stop at the sight of Christ himself as the God-man, but it also takes hold of Christ specifically as he is offered in the covenant of grace. Here, we reach the target within these concentric circles: "Yea, let me add this farther, that God justifying is the main and ultimate object of your faith."[27]

> Christ's merits have their efficacy to justify us *ex compacto*, from agreement between
> the Father and the Son. . . . There are two things in justification. 1. The righteousness
> imputed; and that is Christ's, and to him we go for it. 2. The act of imputation, the
> accounting it mine or thine; and that is the act of God primarily. . . . In a word, God's
> free grace is the original, Christ's righteousness is instrumental to the manifestation
> of free grace, and faith is the instrument of apprehending all. . . . And faith, as it is
> our act, is nothing at all in our justification, but only as it apprehends all. . . . God
> pardons not the debt by halves, nor bestows Christ's righteousness by parcels, but
> entitles us to the whole in every of those moments of justification.[28]

Furthermore, the object of faith is not the work of Christ *within* the believer, but the work of Christ *without* and *for* the believer *extra nos* (outside of us). Because the work of Christ was performed in history apart from our participation, we can be confident in its efficacy to satisfy God's judgment. Here, Goodwin returned to the covenantal theme of absolute promises. Siding with the Lutheran Paul Gerhard and

---

[23]Ibid., p. 184.
[24]Ibid., p. 187.
[25]Ibid.
[26]Ibid., p. 147.
[27]Ibid., p. 133.
[28]Ibid., p. 134.

arguing against the skillful apologist for Trent, Robert Bellarmine, Goodwin pointed out his suspicion of regarding faith as a "condition," in the sense most likely intended by Bellarmine:

> By absolute declarations, &c., I mean such as are not made unto conditions or qual-ifications, which first should be viewed by the soul to be in itself as a ground to be-lieve upon God and Christ for justification. Gerard, in his controversy with Bellarmine, puts this meaning upon the terms absolute promises and conditional. The promises (says he, speaking of the gospel-promises) may be called absolute in opposition unto our works and merit, and yet conditional in that God requireth faith, and so no works being required to justification, they are in that respect not conditional. But granting, as well as he, that faith is requisite, and faith alone, I do withal affirm that there are promises that are absolute, holding forth no condition, as they are the object of faith. And faith, viewing merely what is in those promises, which specify no condition of faith itself, lays hold on God's grace, and Christ as therein manifested. And thus absolute promises stand in full opposition unto all conditional promises.[29]

Such passages, replete throughout Goodwin's discussions of the covenant, dem-onstrate his concern for keeping the objectivity of "Christ set forth" before the be-liever's spiritual sight. Goodwin hesitated to say with Gerhard that faith alone is the condition for justification, because of the possibility that "conditional" might lead one to believe that there is something left to do in order to make the work of Christ complete. The promise is not, "Come unto me if you will do thus and so," and likewise Goodwin was worried that even seeing faith as a "condition" will open the floodgate for a covenantal conditionality that he and Owen regarded as dangerously widespread in both conformist and nonconformist circles.[30]

Goodwin insisted on such phrases as "believing on that object requires no con-ditions"; "the naked object for faith to look at"; "bare proposal of him"; "nakedly declared."[31] Furthermore, he insisted that the unconditional nature of faith is ulti-mately grounded in God's unconditional election:

> God looks on him as ungodly, as one without any work, or disposition, or qualifica-tion which he respects in justifying. . . . Yea, he is one who views nothing but the contrary, viz., mere ungodliness in himself, for which he should be condemned. . . . For look, as God doth not choose him unto salvation upon faith foreseen, or good works foreseen, so nor doth the soul believe in God upon works foreseen, or faith

---

[29]Ibid., p. 205.
[30]Ibid.
[31]Ibid.

foreseen. . . . God then looks into his own heart only for that which should move him to do this.[32]

Moreover, Goodwin was neither an antinomian (opposed to the law) nor a mystic, but insisted that the believer look not to his faith but to Christ; thus the object of faith is an absolute, not a conditional, promise. Goodwin desired to avoid confusing faith with obedience, so he excluded any introspection in the exercise of faith.[33]

Consequently, Goodwin was concerned that people may mistakenly view faith as justifying because it is regarded as a work or virtue, just as they formerly viewed charity, penance and other works. Justification is not pronounced on the basis of inward changes, but on the basis of an external righteousness, and Goodwin was clearly concerned that works and grace had not only been confused by the Arminians, but perhaps even by some of his own brethren. Goodwin was worried that some, by emphasizing the conditional side of the covenant, came perilously close to making that same mistake.

But we must once again notice that Goodwin was not alone here in insisting on such sharp distinctions when this question is at stake. In fact, Richard Sibbes warned that confusing justification with sanctification or even with regeneration was tantamount to deserting the faith.[34] For Sibbes, as for Goodwin, to exercise justifying faith was not to look upon faith, but upon Christ.

There is nothing that should move one to believe except "merely God as justifying"—not God as good and kind; not God as Creator and provider, nor as judge and friend. Nor is one to look to one's own faith as justifying; this accounts, at least in part, for the removal of assurance (*fides reflexa*) beyond the reaches of the direct act of faith itself (*actus fidei*). Goodwin feared that if believing contains, in its very essence, the experience of "full assurance," one who lacks such an experience will undoubtedly concentrate on faith subjectively considered (*fides qua creditor*) rather than on faith objectively considered (*fides quae creditor*). Archbishop Ussher shared the same concern to make this point clear: it is faith alone (*sola fide*), "and that not considered as a virtue inherent in us, working by love; but onely as an instrument or hand of the soule stretched forth to lay hold on the Lord our righteousnesse."[35]

The covenantal scheme, far from introducing a scholastic legalism into the Reformed tradition, provides the basis for what is arguably the clearest defense of fo-

---

[32]Ibid., p. 217.
[33]Ibid.
[34]Richard Sibbes, *The Complete Works of Richard Sibbes* (Edinburgh: James Nichol, 1863), 1:388.
[35]Archbishop James Ussher, *A Body of Divinity* (London: n.p., 1658), pp. 193, 196.

rensic justification in the whole Protestant confessional tradition. Far from any
"voluntarism" that would prepare the way for an Arminian view of faith, the Westminster Larger Catechism declares,

> Faith justifieth a sinner in the sight of God, not because of those other graces which
> doth always accompany it, or of good works that are the fruits of it, nor as if the
> grace of faith, or any act thereof, were imputed to him for his justification; but only
> as it is an instrument by which he receiveth and applieth Christ and his right-
> eousness.[36]

In God's work of justification, one must recognize Christ as the one who fulfilled all obedience owed by each one of the elect to the covenant of works. In effect
the believers are only saved by grace because Christ merited their salvation by
works.[37] Following the Reformation tradition, Goodwin recognized that everything in the Bible can be divided into the two categories of law and gospel. When
speaking of the Christian faith in general, the entire content of the Bible is the object of faith, but when speaking of justification, "the grounds of justifying faith are
accordingly the promises of justification and salvation by Christ contained in the
word."[38] He added elsewhere,

> You know that there is a special part of God's word, which is the gospel. . . . Now
> what is the gospel? Truly it is nothing else (take it strictly in the special sense and
> meaning of it) but that doctrine which holds forth the grace of God justifying, par-
> doning, and saving sinners, and which holds forth Jesus Christ made righteousness
> to us. . . . The apostle in Rom.x.8, speaking of the gospel in distinction from the law,
> and from all else in the Scripture, saith, "This is the word of faith which we
> preach."[39]

Goodwin insisted upon this understanding of faith especially because it supported his appeal to the gospel as an unconditional promise. The believer who rests
on conditions simply does not have any hope. While evidences and graces may be
useful in the reflex act, they cannot provide any security and will inevitably lead
from a covenant of grace to a covenant of works (i.e., "Do this and ye shall live").

> He [the one coming to faith] cannot rest on promises conditional, for he sees no
> qualifications of faith or any grace in himself. It is true, says that soul, "he that be-

---

[36] The Westminster Larger Catechism, Q.73, in *The Westminster Confession and Catechisms* (Glasgow: Free Presbyterian
Publications, 1973).
[37] Goodwin, *Justifying Faith*, 8:237.
[38] Ibid., p. 244.
[39] Ibid., p. 286.

lieveth shall be saved," but I am now to begin to believe, and have not faith yet; and
what ground will you give me of believing? For this there is no answer, but to lay such
promises before him: "God so loved the world that he gave his only Son," "Christ
came into the world to save sinners," &c. But how, will the soul say, should I know I
am one? That, I say, all the world cannot yet assure thee of; no promise is so general
as certainly to include thee, none so certain as to design thee. How then? says the
soul. Say I, they are all indefinite, and exclude thee not; they leave thee with an "it
may be thou mayest be the man"; and it is certain some shall be saved, and there is
nothing in thee shuts thee out, for God hath and will save such as thou art, and he
may intend thee. As therefore there is in such promises a certainty of the thing promised, that it shall be made good to some, so there is an indefiniteness to whom, with
a full liberty that it may be to thee. Now if the heart answer but the promise, two
things are begotten in it.[40]

Those two things are the faith of recumbency (direct act of faith) and assurance.[41] Hence the motive for making such a sharp distinction between faith and
assurance, at least for Goodwin, was not to throw people back on themselves to
secure their confidence by inward evidences; if anything, Goodwin demonstrated a
concern that the other view drives people to find faith within themselves, confusing
the experience of faith with the object of faith.

But is not the "indefiniteness" of faith too skeptical? Goodwin asked, "Is not
the purest and greatest trust strewn in putting one's self into the hands of a spirit
whom we know to be noble, though we certainly know not how he will deal with
us?"[42] But then, is trust anything more than assent? This is a fair question and reveals the Achilles' heel of Goodwin's sharp distinction between faith and assurance.
Goodwin countered that the issue is not how one can be sure of God's mercy and
promises toward sinners (we have seen how earnestly he sets out to display these).
This "indefiniteness" is determined by the covenantal, trinitarian scheme in which
the Father elects, the Son redeems the elect and the Holy Spirit brings the elect to
faith, and "Neither are any other redeemed by Christ, effectually called, justified,
adopted, sanctified, and saved, but the elect only."[43]

Goodwin maintained that the particularism of the covenant of grace and the
corresponding "indefiniteness" of the promises found in Scripture ought not to
lead one to despair of salvation. "It is as if men should say, We will not go to
church, for there is not room for all; and unless a church be built into which all may

---

[40]Ibid., p. 245.
[41]Ibid.
[42]Ibid., p. 246.
[43]*Westminster Confession of Faith*, chap. 3, sec. 6.

come, we will not stir."[44] Christ as he is presented in the universal offer of the gospel is sufficient as an object of faith, apart from having to say: This promise is made to you, Frank, and to you, Jane. The promises are general and indefinite in Scripture, Goodwin pointed out ("Come to me, all you who are weary"; "Christ Jesus came into the world to save sinners"; "everyone who believes," etc.), so we should admit the sufficiency of a general promise.[45] This is far from the Reformers' insistence on the particular application of the word of the gospel to all individuals within the covenant of grace. And no doubt this has a lot to do with the difference between their Augustinian ecclesiology (the church as a "mixed assembly") in contrast to the "gathered" or "pure church" idealism of the Independents. Nevertheless, it is inappropriate to conclude immediately that the differences between Calvin and Goodwin are directly soteriological.

Goodwin was also aware of the distinction, often useful, between *merit* and *works*. Many might say that merit has no place in the matter of justifying faith, but that works are conditions. However, Goodwin was resolutely opposed to such a confusion of the law and the gospel. "It is not the proud notion of merit only, . . . but of works too, [which] must be exploded. God loves not faith as a work, though it saves his children whom he loves," but as that which weds us to Christ's person.[46]

In the absence of the typical and more obvious "works of righteousness," the danger is that human nature will even turn faith into a work. Faith, then, was *possessing* Christ in all of his righteousness, not the *condition* of possessing, according to Goodwin.[47]

One may accuse Goodwin of being a bit pedantic in making such fine distinctions; certainly the Lutheran Gerhard, as Goodwin admitted above, as well as other Protestant scholastics did not consider it odd or inadmissible to call faith a condition.[48] Yet Goodwin's wariness on this point underscored his (and Owen's) concern to guard against the creeping moralism of their day.

Therefore, justification is a declaration that we are righteous while we are still sinners, *simul iustus et peccator*, the phrase Goodwin borrowed from Luther quite often throughout the treatise. Justification is purely forensic, while regeneration and sanctification are additional blessings flowing out of justification that yield inward transformation. "If therefore a man were justified by any other faith than by faith

[44]Goodwin, *Justifying Faith*, 8:247.

[45]Ibid., pp. 247-8.

[46]Ibid., p. 252.

[47]Ibid.

[48]Zacharius Ursinus, *The Commentary on the Heidelberg Catechism* (1852; reprint, Phillipsburg, N.J.: Presbyterian & Reformed), p. 113.

throwing himself upon Christ for justification, he should be justified by sanctification."[49]

At this point a summary statement of Goodwin's view of faith's object is in order. God's merciful nature and will, minted into promises in the form of a covenant of grace, with Christ the mediator and justification as the chief benefits, form the concentric circles which are more than sufficient to focus the direct act of faith looking to "Christ set forth."

PART TWO: THE ACTS OF FAITH

As we have seen, Goodwin would rather describe faith in its actions than define faith in its essence. Here we gain a better insight into Goodwin's notion of faith, as it is particularly related to justification, first according to its object and now according to its acts.

Faith as instrument, not object or basis. Goodwin was very much aware of and involved with John Owen's controversies with Arminians not only in the Netherlands but among the English Puritans themselves: men such as John Goodwin and Richard Baxter, and a number of other Puritan divines for whom high Calvinism equaled "Antinomianism."[50] Therefore, this was not merely a distant affair, but very much a controversy within the Puritan camp. The threat of Arminianism is also why Goodwin was so concerned to get the point across that people are saved through faith (*per fidei*) not on the basis of faith (*propter fidem*). "My brethren," Goodwin declared, "we are not made righteous by the act of believing; no, we are constituted and made righteous by that obedience of Christ on which we believe."[51]

Special faith. Even faith, if not directed toward God's special act of justifying sinners through the righteousness of Christ, cannot save. The special object of faith is not God *in se* (in himself), but is God in Christ justifying. Goodwin stated, as did John Calvin:

> that God in Christ, God as justifying, God as rewarding and pardoning sin, as he is thus, is the special object of faith [but] faith cannot see God as in himself, none can see God and live; that is appointed indeed for vision in the world to come.[52]

---

[49]Goodwin, *Justifying Faith*, 8:360.

[50]Cf. Beeke's discussion of the polemical response to John Goodwin by Owen, *The Assurance of Faith*, pp. 214-15, and for Edward Dowden's comment that Baxter was "too Arminian for the high Calvinists and too Calvinistic for the Arminians" (p. 312 n. 15). Daniel Williams was among the Puritans accused of neonomianism (ibid., p. 290).

[51]Goodwin, *Justifying Faith*, 8:290.

[52]Ibid., p. 292.

In fact, knowing God as he is, apart from Christ, "will drive a sinner off from God because all that they know and apprehend of God hath no special promise of mercy to them as sinners from that God."[53] According to Goodwin, Arminians assumed that human nature is either not so severely dominated by sin or that it has been so sufficiently healed by the universal work of Christ and the Holy Spirit that, like the "papists," they mistakenly believe that a man or woman can desire to be reconciled to God as a friend and father, even before he reveals himself as the one who justifies the wicked.

> Go, take a man that is ungodly, and how will this man ever come to believe in God, unless under this notion, that he is one that justifies the ungodly? . . . It is not believing that God is true, or holy, or just, simply considered in himself, if a man believe these never so strongly, that will justify him not; but to believe on God under this notion, that he is a justifier of the ungodly, this is a man's faith which is accounted to him for righteousness. . . . Now go, take a sinner, he would never have any boldness, never have any confidence, so much as to come to God; he would have no heart to do it; he would be driven off from him, if he did not first look on God as in Christ.[54]

Providing a precedent for such views, William Perkins himself argued against Rome, "But we hold that the faith which justified is a particular faith whereby we apply to ourselves the promises of righteousness and life everlasting by Christ," and not merely "a general or catholic faith" in articles of religion.[55] In light of these statements, it is not accurate to view the Puritans as speculative rationalists who deduced everything from the being of God. Otherwise:

> if we consider ourselves under the first covenant [since all of the unconverted are under the covenant of works or nature], all the attributes of God come in upon us with terror. . . . And therefore, let popish spirits say what they will, yet still unto us as sinners it is God as gracious, God as justifying, it is God as in Christ revealed, which is the proper and special object of justifying faith.[56]

Only this kind of faith can pacify the troubled heart: "faith only as pitched upon these objects nakedly, and barely, and singly, will quiet the heart, and bring peace with God; nothing else will do it."[57] These comments served to reiterate the

---

[53]Ibid.

[54]Ibid.

[55]William Perkins, *The Work of William Perkins*, ed. Ian Breward (Appleford, England: Sutton Courtenay, 1970), p. 535.

[56]Goodwin, *Justifying Faith*, 8:293.

[57]Ibid., p. 295.

concern of some Puritans to explain justifying faith as a matter of simply looking to Christ for righteousness "nakedly, barely, and singly," apart from repentance, eyeing Christ as sanctifier, and strenuous preparation and energetic activism, all of which are nevertheless affirmed and described in detail as ancillary acts of faith.

As we have seen in relation to the *object of faith*, the believer must come to God as the justifier of sinners even to obtain temporal blessings. The corollary *act of faith* is obvious; it does not justify "as a quality or act, but only as apprehending these [viz., God's grace and Christ's righteousness], and by no other act, is said to justify."[58]

Although, as we have seen, Goodwin viewed faith as active and as an act of the will, he admitted no other view of justifying faith than the sinner "throwing himself upon Christ."[59] Goodwin pointed out that for Rome faith is an inherent quality that justifies, and this was embraced by "others," presumably with Arminians on his mind, "who hold that faith justifies as an *act*," but this would simply mean that one is "clearly justified by sanctification."[60]

Very often after conversion, people will suppose that they can move beyond eyeing Christ for their justification, since they did that at conversion. Goodwin said that even if one wants to grow in sanctification, it is not to Christ as sanctifier where one will find his or her faith and charity improved, but as one looks upon Christ as justifier. Faith in God as justifying in Christ becomes the act of faith that grounds all other acts of faith, which have as their object God as Creator, provider and sanctifier.[61]

CONCLUSION

It is quite clear that Goodwin was a high Calvinist within a Puritan movement that, by the mid-seventeenth century, was a diverse collection of high Calvinists, moderate Calvinists and outright Arminians.

If Calvin and the Continental Reformed tradition on one side insist that assurance is of the essence of faith, while the Puritans and the Presbyterian (Westminster) tradition distinguish assurance from faith itself, one must not simplistically conclude (as the discontinuity thesis does) that this is due to a shift from a theology of justification by grace alone through faith alone to a voluntaristic combination of works and grace, but rather recognize the diverse ways in which this distinction was put to use by the Puritans themselves. While it is true that some

---

[58]Ibid.
[59]Ibid.
[60]Ibid. Emphasis added.
[61]Ibid.

emphasized the graciousness of justification by a "mere receiving" of Christ along with a severely introspective search for assurance, it is just as true that other Puritans challenged this severity at least in part by appealing to precisely this same distinction and in fact drawing the distinction in darker lines. Goodwin illustrates that one can separate faith from assurance—even more aggressively than some of his Puritan colleagues—with precisely the same pastoral and theological intentions as Calvin: to encourage a direct act of looking to Christ. Goodwin's method may be different than Calvin's, but the general instinct and concerns are the same.

SELECT BIBLIOGRAPHY

Primary Source

Goodwin, Thomas. *The Works of Thomas Goodwin.* 11 volumes. Edinburgh: James Nichol, 1855. The original edition, published in three large folio volumes: London: J. Darby and S. Roycroft, 1683-1692.

Secondary Sources

Beeke, Joel. *Assurance of Faith: Calvin, English Puritanism, and the Dutch Second Reformation.* New York: Peter Lang, 1991.

Clifford, Alan C. *Atonement and Justification: English Evangelical Theology 1640-1790.* Oxford: Oxford University Press, 1990.

Kendall, R. T. *Calvin and English Calvinism to 1649.* Oxford: Oxford University Press, 1977.

McGrath, Alister E. *Iustitia Dei: A History of the Christian Doctrine of Justification.* New York: Cambridge University Press, 1986.

Muller, Richard. *Christ and the Decree: Christology and Predestination in Reformed Theology from Calvin to Perkins.* Grand Rapids: Baker, 1986.

❦ 8 ❧

THE PARABLE OF
THE TEN VIRGINS

BY THOMAS SHEPARD (1605-1649)

Randall C. Gleason

TWO YEARS AFTER THE CONNECTICUT VALLEY REVIVAL (1734-1735) the spiritual fervor in Northhampton, Massachusetts had grown cold. Troubled by the spiritual decline in his congregation, Jonathan Edwards sought help from a book titled *The Parable of the Ten Virgins Opened and Applied* by Thomas Shepard.[1] Inspired by Shepard's passion to promote genuine conversions in his own New England church nearly a hundred years earlier, Edwards began preaching his own sermon series on the parable during the winter of 1737-1738.[2] Edwards soon realized the impact of Shepard's pastoral insights on his own congregation when revival broke during George Whitefield's visit to Northampton two years later in 1740. For Shepard's voice echoes through nearly every page of Edwards's defense of the Great Awakening in his celebrated *Discourse on Religious Affections* (1746).[3] Edwards's dependence on Shepard illustrates why *The Parable of the Ten Virgins* became an early classic among Puritan divines. After its publication in 1659, ser-

---

[1] The most recent edition is reprinted from *The Works of Thomas Shepard*, ed. John A. Albro. vol. 2 (Boston: Doctrinal Tract & Book Society, 1853) under the title *The Parable of the Ten Virgins* (Morgan, Penn.: Soli Deo Gloria, 1990).

[2] Edwards's nineteen sermons on the *Ten Virgins* remain unpublished in the Manuscript Library at Yale University. See Ava Chamberlain, "Brides of Christ and Signs of Grace: Edwards's Sermon Series on the Parable of the Wise and Foolish Virgins," in *Jonathan Edwards's Writings: Text, Context, Interpretation*, ed. Stephen J. Stein (Bloomington: Indiana University Press, 1996), pp. 3-18.

[3] William K. B. Stoever demonstrates that "virtually all of Edwards's characteristic vocabulary in *Affections*" is drawn from Shepard in his article entitled "The Godly Will's Discerning: Shepard, Edwards, and the Identification of True Godliness," in *Jonathan Edwards's Writings: Text, Context, Interpretation*, ed. Stephen J. Stein (Bloomington: Indiana University Press, 1996), pp. 85-99.

mons on the parable became the standard remedy for religious apathy throughout Puritan circles.[4] Yet surprisingly few today know much about the Puritan
pastor who inspired America's greatest theologian on the nature of authentic
Christian conversion.

"PASTOR EVANGELICUS" OF CAMBRIDGE, MASSACHUSETTS

The popularity of Shepard's *Ten Virgins* is due in part to his renown as a preacher
and example of personal piety among the early ministers of Massachusetts.[5] After graduating from Cambridge in 1627, the young man soon gained a reputation as a powerful preacher in Earles Colne, Essex. However, due to increasing
pressures from Bishop William Laud, he was expelled from his pulpit for nonconformity in 1630. Growing weary of hiding after narrowly escaping from
Laud's agents, Shepard decided to join the great Puritan migration to New England. Arriving in Boston with his wife and child on October 3, 1635, Shepard
wasted little time founding a new church among the recent immigrants in Newtown, Massachusetts. Believing like most New England ministers that church
membership should be limited to "visible saints,"[6] he required all new members
to make a public confession of their experiences of saving grace.[7] To encourage
them he immediately began a series of sermons on the characteristics of grace
that distinguished genuine conversion from the religious pretense common
within the Church of England. This series, based on an extended exposition of
Jesus' parable on the ten virgins (Mt 25:1-13), lasted from June 1636 to May
1640.

Due to Shepard's success as a pastor and leader in the colony, Newtown was
chosen as the location for New England's first institution of higher learning and
renamed Cambridge in honor of the university where most of the earlier ministers

---

[4]Selected examples include Samuel Loveday, *An alarm to slumbering Christians, or the parable of the wise and foolish virgins*
(London: Francis Smith, 1675); Benjamin Stonham, *The Parable of the Ten Virgins Opened* (London: n.p., 1676);
Thomas Manton's sermons on Matthew 25 first published in 1684 and reprinted in *The complete works of Thomas
Manton* (London: James Nisbet, 1870-1875), 9:319-423; and George Whitefield, "The Wise and Foolish Vir-
gins" in *Memoirs of George Whitefield*, ed. John Gillies (New Haven, Conn.: n.p., 1834), pp. 489-505.

[5]"Pastor Evangelicus" is Cotton Mather's tribute to Shepard as the great soul-winner in *The Great Works of Christ in
America: Magnalia Christi Americana*, 2 vols. (1701; reprint, Edinburgh: Banner of Truth Trust, 1979), I:380-94. Biographies on Shepard include John A. Albro, *The Life of Thomas Shepard* (Boston: Massachusetts Sabbath School Society, 1847), reprinted in *The Sincere Convert and the Sound Believer* (Morgan, Penn.: Soli Deo Gloria, 1999), pp. vii-
cxcii; and Thomas Werge, *Thomas Shepard* (Boston: Twayne, 1987).

[6]See Edmund S. Morgan, *Visible Saints: The History of a Puritan Idea* (Ithaca, N.Y.: Cornell University Press, 1963), pp.
80-112.

[7]For examples of confessions by Shepard's members see Michael McGiffert, ed., *God's Plot: Puritan Spirituality in
Thomas Shepard's Cambridge*, rev. ed. (Amherst: University of Massachusetts Press, 1994), pp. 149-225.

had studied.[8] Shepard's pivotal role in founding Harvard College as unofficial chaplain, lecturer and fundraiser is well known. Less known is his pioneering work with John Eliot (1604-1690) among the local Indians that helped to establish the first Protestant mission near Cambridge (1646).[9] Shepard also spearheaded the local synod that ratified the *Cambridge Platform* (1648),[10] a code of church discipline that defined congregational principles of self-government. He accomplished all this during his thirteen-year ministry in Cambridge that ended with his death from a severe cold at the age of forty-four. His exemplary ministry was carried on by his successor at Cambridge, Jonathan Mitchell (who later married Shepard's third wife Margaret), and by each of his three surviving sons who went on to pastor their own congregations after graduating from Harvard.

Among the first generation of ministers in New England, none have left behind a more complete record of both their public service and private devotion than Thomas Shepard. All of his major treatises remain in print today, including *The Sincere Convert* (1641), *The Sound Believer* (1645) and his *Theses Sabbaticae* (1649).[11] Shepard's autobiography and personal diary demonstrates how his major theological themes were worked out in his personal piety.[12] Of first importance is Shepard's vivid account of his own spiritual awakening that illustrates his belief that true conversion requires a total change of heart, mind and affections. After two years of study at Cambridge University "in much neglect of God and private prayer," Shepard confessed how he fell away from God into "loose and lewd company." Following one dreadful night of drunkenness, he heard John Preston (1587-1628), Emmanuel College's new headmaster, preach on "the change of heart" in a Christian, from Paul's words "Be transformed by the renewing of your minds" (Rom 12:2). The young student thought Preston to be "the most searching preacher in the world" and resolved to begin daily meditating upon "the evil of sin, . . . beauty of Christ, [and] the deceitfulness of the heart." For nearly a year Shepard wrestled through his doubts about God's existence and the truthfulness of Scripture. When "the terrors of the Lord began to break in

---

[8]Of the 140 university graduates who immigrated to New England before 1645, no less than 104 came from Cambridge, 35 of them from Emmanuel College.

[9]See the eyewitness reports in *The Day-Breaking, If Not the Sun-Rising of the Gospel with the Indians in New England* (London: n.p., 1647), probably written by Shepard along with *The Clear Sun-shine of the Gospel Breaking Forth upon the Indians in New-England* (London: J. Bellamy, 1648), that bears his name.

[10]See John H. Leith, ed., *Creeds of the Churches*, 3rd ed. (Louisville: John Knox Press, 1982), pp. 385-399.

[11]*The Sincere Convert* and *The Sound Believer* were reprinted together in *The Works of Thomas Shepard*, vol. 2, ed. T. Albro, (Boston: Doctrinal Tract & Book Society, 1853), now available under the title *The Sincere Convert and the Sound Believer* (Morgan, Penn.: Soli Deo Gloria, 1999). For the most recent edition of *Theses Sabbaticae* see *The Works of Thomas Shepard*, vol. 3, ed. John A. Albro (1853; reprint, Morgan, Penn.: Soli Deo Gloria, 1992).

[12]For an excellent edition of Shepard's autobiography and journal, see McGiffert, *God's Plot.*

like floods of fire," he was tempted with thoughts of suicide. Yet he recounted how the Lord "began to assuage sweetly" those terrors through the preaching of Preston until Christ finally "enabled me to believe" and "receive him as Lord and Savior and Husband."[13] Shepard's own experience confirmed his belief that no one can come to a saving faith in Christ "unless he first see, be convicted of and loaded with" the evilness of his sins. His preparation for conversion through the illumination of the Spirit and the preaching of the word is a dominant theme throughout his sermons.[14]

Shepard's journal illustrates how the conversion of the heart that secures our *union* with Christ must be followed by a lifelong process of meditation to prepare us for our *communion* with Christ in glory.[15] Shepard's rigorous practice of self-examination during the height of his ministry in Cambridge, Massachusetts, may appear morbid to modern views of spiritual maturity until we understand its importance to the practice of Puritan piety.[16] Puritans took seriously Paul's admonition to "Examine yourselves to see whether you are living in the faith" (2 Cor 13:5). Shepard was concerned not to foster the religious despair he experienced prior to his conversion, and his journal reveals how his daily self-examination and confession was meant to purge his soul of any hint of unbelief, sinful practices or selfish motives that would hinder communion with God. Once his conscience was cleared, his affections for Christ were quickly rekindled through meditation upon the wonder of his grace, goodness and glory. For example, on December 4, 1641, he began his daily examination in a "cloud of darkness and atheism," only to conclude with a sense of "having been ravished" by "God himself." Again on December 10 after "musing on . . . how many sins I had still to repent of," he closed his entry in celebration of God's goodness, sensing divine "hands and fingers . . . [taking] hold of me." He often spent his Saturdays meditating upon his sermons until his "heart was sweetly ravished."[17] This led to his reputation among the colonists as the "soul-ravishing minister" through whom "the Lord shed abroad his love so abundantly, that thousands of souls have cause to bless God for him."[18] Hence

---

[13]Ibid., pp. 43-44, 47.

[14]Shepard, *The Sincere Convert and the Sound Believer*, pp. 117, 237. Regarding Puritan views on preparation for conversion see Norman Pettit, *The Prepared Heart: Grace and Conversion in Puritan Spiritual Life*, 2nd ed. (Middleton, Conn.: Wesleyan University Press, 1989), pp. 61-83.

[15]McGiffert, *God's Plot*, pp. 82-134.

[16]On the Puritan practice of meditation, see Charles Hambrick-Stowe, *The Practice of Piety: Puritan Devotional Disciplines in Seventeenth-Century New England* (Chapel Hill: University of North Carolina Press, 1982), pp. 161-75; 278-87.

[17]McGiffert, *God's Plot*, pp. 103, 105, 84.

[18]Edward Johnson, *Wonder-Working Providence: 1628-1651*, ed. J. Franklin Jameson (1654; reprint, New York: Scribner's, 1910), pp. 94, 107.

Shepard's repeated appeals for self-examination and mediation on Christ through-out his sermons were firmly rooted in his own daily practice.

THE ANTINOMIAN CONTROVERSY (1636-1638) AND SHEPARD'S *TEN VIRGINS* (1636-1640)

Shepard's sermons on the *Ten Virgins* are also important for their effectiveness in preserving his congregation from the Antinomian Controversy that threatened to divide the churches of Massachusetts from 1636 to 1638.[19] Shepard re-counted how, in the months following the founding of the Cambridge church, "The Lord exercised us and the whole country with the opinions of the Famil-ists, begun by Mistress Hutchinson . . . and propagated . . . by members of [the] Boston church."[20] Shepard first warned the distinguished preacher of Boston, John Cotton, that his mention of "further revelations" and the possibility of "gross and scandalous sins" in true saints could lend support to the errors of the "Familists."[21] Soon Shepard was joined by others alarmed over the teachings of Anne Hutchinson and her links to John Cotton. When Hutchinson and her sup-porters accused all the ministers of the colony *except* Cotton of preaching "a cov-enant of works," Shepard and his colleagues called for a conference to expose their errors and to clarify Cotton's views. Shepard was especially troubled by Hutchinson's claim that a Christian could *not* be assured of salvation by "any graces, . . . or special change" of character but *solely* by the unconditional and ab-solute promises of the gospel confirmed "by immediate revelation" from the Holy Spirit.[22] Her further admission "that we are not bound to the Law . . . as a rule of life" confirmed growing fears of Antinomianism. Although the doctri-nal differences between Cotton and his fellow ministers were complex, Cotton eventually came to recognize the errors of Hutchinson and joined the others in condemning her. During her public trial Shepard specifically faulted her for de-nying any "inherent graces" within true saints that could serve as signs of true conversion. But for Shepard and the others it was her "revelations" of coming destruction upon the leaders of New England who brought her to trial that jus-

---

[19]On Puritan fears against Antinomianism, see Tim Cooper, *Fear and Polemic in Seventeenth-Century England: Richard Baxter and Antinomianism* (Aldershot, England: Ashgate, 2001), pp. 15-45.

[20]McGiffert, *God's Plot*, p. 67.

[21]For Shepard's letter and Cotton's response see David D. Hall's excellent collection of original documents in *The Antinomian Controversy, 1636-1638: A Documentary History*, 2nd ed. (Durham, N.C.: Duke University Press, 1990), pp. 24-33. The term *Familists* refers to a sect started by the Dutch mystic Hendrick Niclaes (c. 1502-1580) who claimed he received direct revelations from God.

[22]McGiffert, *God's Plot*, p. 67.

tified the court in banishing her.[23] Although Cotton's role in her prosecution restored public confidence in his ministry, Shepard remained troubled by his views
on grace and justification.[24] These events underlie Shepard's concern to clarify
the true nature of saving grace throughout his sermons.[25]

THE PARABLE OF THE TEN VIRGINS

Shepard divided his exposition of Jesus' parable into two major parts. The first focused on Matthew 25:1-5 that describes the church's need to prepare to meet
Christ. The second explained Matthew 25:5-12 that announces the coming of
Christ as bridegroom. He began his exposition by identifying "the kingdom of
heaven" as "the external kingdom of Christ in this world, that is the visible church."
He applied this specifically to the congregational churches of Massachusetts where
the members were recognized as "visible saints" by public profession. While a mix
of "wise and foolish virgins" was expected within the national Church of England,
Shepard went on to declare that even the purest of churches contain both wise-
hearted believers and foolish-hearted hypocrites. Therefore, even though the parable refers to the days immediately before the second coming of Christ (Mt 25:1),
Shepard believed its message had direct application to the "virgin churches" pros-
pering in New England. He warned them, "You have the pillow of peace to lie on,
and the cares of the world to make you dream away your time, and you have no
pinching persecutions to awaken you." As they awaited the return of their heavenly
bridegroom, he called them all to make "themselves ready for the marriage of the
Lamb" (cf. Rev 19:7).[26]

THE DIVINE ROMANCE

Although medieval ascetics had long used marriage imagery to describe their union
with God, the Puritans were the first to unite it with a wholehearted appreciation for
the joys of marital romance.[27] Like many Puritan preachers, Shepard drew a close

---

[23]Hall, *The Antinomian Controversy*, pp. 323-24, 352, 365, 374-78, 383-84. For Shepard's biblical justification for
Hutchinson's separation from the community, see his *Ten Virgins*, pp. 621-29.

[24]In his last entry of his autobiography (1639), Shepard claims, "Mr. Cotton repents not, but is hid only. . . . He
doth stiffly hold the revelation of our good estate still, without any sight of word or work" (McGiffert, *God's
Plot*, p. 77).

[25]Concerning Shepard's role in defending grace and assurance as commonly understood within the Puritan Covenant tradition, see William K. B. Stoever, *"A Faire and Easie Way to Heaven": Covenant Theology and Antinomianism in
Early Massachusetts* (Middleton, Conn.: Wesleyan University Press, 1978), pp. 58-80, 147-50, 177-78, 189-99.

[26]Shepard, *Ten Virgins*, pp. 16, 25-26.

[27]On the Puritan view of love and romantic marriage, see Leland Ryken, *Worldly Saints: The Puritans as They Really Were*
(Grand Rapids: Zondervan, 1986), pp. 39-51.

connection between God's love for the saints and the love between husband and wife. Of his first wife, Margaret Touteville, he recounted how "the Lord taught me much of his goodness and sweetness . . . when he had fitted a wife for me, . . . who was most incomparably loving to me." His fondness for her grew so strong within their first year of marriage (1632) that he found himself in danger of "delighting my soul in my dear wife more than in my God." After Margaret's death, he shared similar affections for his second wife, Johanna, the eldest daughter of Thomas Hooker. In his grief over her failing health, Shepard found comfort in Johanna's wish "that we should love exceedingly together because we should not live long together."[28] Drawing on the strength of these marital affections and the imagery of the parable, Shepard portrayed God's redemptive plan in terms of an epic romance between lovers.

Shepard viewed his work as a minister "to woo" the "chaste virgins" of his congregation into intimate communion with Christ. This metaphor served his pastoral objectives in several ways. First, the joys of marriage illustrate how Christ as an exuberant bridegroom passionately calls his beloved into daily communion with himself. Shepard urged his people to consider how Christ "makes love to thee." His love includes not only a share in "all his glory, his God, his Father, [and] his kingdom," but most importantly "himself." Second, the permanence of the marriage covenant assures true saints of Christ's unending love. As a faithful husband Christ pledges to put up with "all wrongs" and "never part" (cf. Hos 2:19) because our union with him is unbreakable.[29] "For Christ, when he enters into marriage covenant, does not suspend his love on our grace or holiness, . . . but on his own grace to wash away our filthiness" (cf. Eph 5:25-26).[30] Furthermore, his love is so strong that it creates in us a love that unites our hearts inseparably to his.

Third, since marriage demands exclusive devotion, we should be "divorced from all other lovers," seeking comfort and satisfaction only in Christ. Drawing on the language of the prophet Hosea (e.g., Hos 2:2; 4:11), Shepard spoke of "spiritual whoredom" that seeks consolation in the creature rather than the Creator. He warned that the neglect of private prayer, meditation and daily examination often produces a "whorish heart" divided between its love for Christ and the things of the world.[31] Fourth, the mutuality of marriage illustrates how Christ's perfect love for us demands that we love him in return. "It is not enough to be espoused unto Christ, . . . you ought to be in a continual readiness to clasp

---

[28]McGiffert, *God's Plot*, pp. 57, 73.

[29]All biblical references are made by Shepard.

[30]Shepard, *Ten Virgins*, pp. 41-49.

[31]Ibid., pp. 27-29, 65-67.

the Lord in your arms, and to lay your heads in his bosom in heaven."[32] Here Shepard echoed the Puritan belief that full enjoyment of communion with Christ required continuous preparation.[33] This was especially important in preparation for the Lord's Table and the sabbath. Although each begins with self-examination and confession, they should culminate in meditation upon Christ's immeasurable love for the saints (cf. Eph 3:18-19). The mere observance of the ordinances apart from a fresh vision of the love of Christ does little to rekindle the divine romance. But if we seek Christ in his ordinances, we will taste the sweetness of his grace and be ravished by his love. Finally, Shepard used the delay of the wedding day to illustrate how the physical absence of Christ makes the hearts of true believers grow fonder and their longings grow deeper. For since the "consummation of our marriage" is yet future, as faithful lovers our affections will only increase as our hope remains fixed upon our everlasting communion with the Lord.[34]

GOSPEL HYPOCRITES

After reassuring genuine saints of the joys of their heavenly romance, Shepard shifted his attention to the presence of hypocrites within the church. "Five of them were foolish, and five were wise" (Mt 25:2). He reasoned from this division that we should expect "a number of hypocrites mingling themselves with the purest of churches." Their "evangelical" outward appearance allows their hypocrisy to remain hidden for a while. With their lamps ready, they "appear and seem to be under grace," and seek earnestly for Christ's coming even though their wills and hearts remain unchanged. Shepard called them "gospel hypocrites" because common grace provides an outer semblance of sanctification, yet they never experience the "great change of the heart" wrought by the Spirit that grants genuine power over sin and Satan. True saints are assured by the "threefold light . . . of the Word, . . . of the Spirit, . . .[and] of experience." Each gives the unmistakable evidence of genuine transformation of heart "as by feeling heat, we know it is hot; by tasting honey, we know it is sweet." But the foolish virgins "see and hear by natural and acquired knowledge, but not by a divine, created, infused knowledge" that grants them wisdom unto salvation. In their folly they "fly from the light" of the Spirit

---

[32]Ibid., pp. 61-69.

[33]Regarding the Puritan distinction between the initial preparation for conversion and the ongoing preparation for glory see Stoever, "Faire and Easie Way to Heaven," pp. 192-99, and Hambrick-Stowe, Practice of Piety, pp. 166, 195-203.

[34]Shepard, Ten Virgins, pp. 143-61.

that would expose their unchanged hearts. Though they took lamps, "they took no oil with them" (Mt 25:3). They contented themselves with the temporary "blaze of outward profession" (i.e., the lamp) but they neglected the inward illumination of the Spirit (i.e., the oil). Without this oil of the Spirit their hearts lacked the humiliation of sin and understanding of Scripture necessary to effectively cure their hypocrisy. Though they longed for the bridegroom, fellowship with him was never their "last and utmost end."[35] Other appetites eventually crowded out their superficial desire for him. Likewise, in the church "gospel hypocrites" prove their folly by their neglect of the means of prayer, meditation, the ordinances and sabbath rest.

TRANSFORMED BY GRACE

The wise virgins took vessels of oil with their lamps (Mt 25:4). Shepard explained that the oil includes not only the Spirit of Christ but also the graces that inevitability flow forth from him. As vessels filled with the Spirit, the saints receive a "new nature" consisting of "created graces" that fuel their lamps to shine forth with acts of obedience. This new ability does not operate independently from the Spirit but "stands in daily need of the Lord Jesus." Yet the Christian has received these graces from Jesus Christ, otherwise the Christian would not be called to add one upon another (cf. 2 Pet 1:5-8). The denial of created graces in the saints is a delusion "hatched out of the steam of the lowest sink of hell," said Shepard, for it blurs the promise of being transformed into the glory of the Lord (cf. 2 Cor 3:18; Col 1:27). Christ is both "our righteousness by imputation of his holiness, and our sanctification by infusing" a new power of holiness within us. The saint is likened to a grain of corn that has the power of growth, yet it only bears fruit after the rain and sun have nourished it. Hence, Shepard exhorted the saints, "I know all strength is from Christ, but there is a permanent strength in you. You are not dead to act; you wrong the Lord and his grace if you think so. . . . [For] it is a heavy sin to shut up and imprison . . . the power of grace."[36]

Though the foolish virgins dipped their wick in the oil of the Spirit to light their lamps for a time, they lacked the fullness of the Spirit that results in a change of nature. They lacked the spiritual illumination that granted the wise virgins humiliation of sin and a saving knowledge of Christ as their "present, greatest and only good." Only this spiritual insight could take them beyond a mere historical

---

[35]Ibid., pp. 184, 192, 206, 222, 230, 241.
[36]Ibid., pp. 269-73, 275-76, 293.

faith that seeks something from Christ to a truly justifying faith that embraces Christ for himself, not for what benefits they can receive from him. In response to such faith the Lord provides the wise virgins the constant assistance of the Spirit that will never allow them to fall from Christ. This does not exclude temporary lapses into sin or unbelief, but rather guarantees that they will never depart from the Lord with their whole hearts, for their hearts are forever bent toward Christ by their new nature. Once their faith has united them securely to Christ, his sanctifying work begins to root out their self-seeking desires. As they behold the glory of Christ, their self-love is consumed by the heat of his love and replaced by new passions to please him. Ultimately those who are truly sanctified "make the Lord their last end and happiness" (cf. Gal 2:10). The reformation of their minds, wills and affections serve as indisputable proof that the wise virgins have received grace "of an eternal nature, . . . constantly preserved in them."[37]

THE DANGER OF CARNAL SECURITY

In spite of vast differences between the virgins, the parable warns that "the spirit of sloth and security" will overcome both wise and foolish virgins in the last days. "As the bridegroom was delayed, all of them became drowsy and slept" (Mt 25:5). Shepard explained that their sleep signifies a carnal security that posed a great threat to the health and vitality of the "virgin churches" of New England. Their lack of persecution and abundance of "spiritual gifts and graces" had produced an unexpected result. Rather than usher in the godly society of "visible saints" as Shepard had hoped, their religious freedom had led to spiritual indifference and decadence. Those who had escaped the persecutions in England had now succumbed to a "carnal security" that dulled their conscience toward sin and their passions for Christ's return. The "virgin churches" of Massachusetts faced a great temptation to slumber and sleep because "their beds [were] made soft" and "the storms" of persecution were "past."[38] Shepard pointed to the divisions among them and their wars with the Pequot Indians (1636-1637) as works of God's providence to awaken them out of their spiritual indifference. He warned them especially against settling for a "peace with their sin," a "peace that . . . gives up the fight against sin and Satan." Rather, they must rest in the Lord, "a rest which faith gives" only after it has conquered sin. For peace with Christ is not experienced through "sloth" but by waging war "against every temptation." The peace of faith often "finds and feels its rest most in the midst of trouble" because it is "in times of per-

---

[37]Ibid., pp. 313, 337, 351.
[38]Ibid., pp. 371-79.

secution" and hardship that "grace is most exercised" through prayer and watchfulness.[39] The danger of "carnal security" is its presumption of grace that refuses to be disturbed by secret sins and selfish motives.

Shepard spoke against the Antinomians who with their "golden dreams of grace," made "the Law no rule to a Christian's life." Denying the "activity of grace" in the heart of the Christian, they claimed "they could do nothing." By leaving "all to Christ," the Antinomians were making the Lord "a pillow for a slothful heart." According to Shepard, they failed to consider the "immutable assistance of the Spirit" that empowers believers to act in obedience to Christ. Furthermore they accused some ministers of promoting a "covenant of works" by exhorting their congregation to obedience. Shepard faulted the Antinomians because rather than looking to sanctification for evidence of grace, they sought a "peace and confidence" revealed directly by the Spirit that even the "sluggish" of heart may "keep . . . though he never grow better."[40] Shepard insisted that God's saving grace results in not merely the passive imputation of righteousness but also an active righteous disposition that should be exercised by all truly regenerated saints.

A WAKEUP CALL

Shepard called his congregation to resist the temptation of carnal security by making "the coming of the Lord real."[41] The Lord promised in the parable to help them in this by sending forth a "midnight cry" to awaken the sleeping virgins (cf. Mt 25:6). If the "cry of the word" would not rouse them, he would send the "cry of the rod" that would inflict "great extremities and distress" upon the saints, even "scattering them one from another in [the] woods." Shepard's allusion to those banished to the wilderness for their part in the Antinomian controversy is hard to miss here. In order to awaken the unrepentant, he claimed that God may even permit "captivity and plagues to destroy families." For the "sin of security," Shepard predicted, "the Lord will bring seven plagues more, and drive you into a wilderness, . . . and if this will not do, God will send spoilers that . . . shall carry you away [as] captives."[42] Yet the bridegroom of the parable proved compassionate toward all who slept in his absence. His voice was "not a cry of terror or wrath" but an invi-

---

[39]Ibid., pp. 394-99.
[40]Ibid., pp. 377-78, 401-2.
[41]Ibid., p. 406.
[42]Ibid., pp. 409-15. His allusions to the banishment of Anne Hutchinson no doubt fueled the popular consensus that the later massacre of her family in the wilderness by the Indians was an act of God's punishment.

tation for all to "come out and meet" him. To those foolish virgins, it was an invitation to come while there was still time and to "receive the eternal anointing of his Spirit of grace . . . in [their] hearts." To the wise virgins who also slept, the bridegroom's call served as a reminder that no sin of "security [or] carelessness, though deep [and] long" could "quench his love" for them or "break [their] marriage bond" to him. His call to them is certain because in the end there will be "no evil in them," for the "marriage covenant" promises he will "heal them of it" (cf. Eph 5:25).[43]

While the virgins slept in their security, the "glory" of their lamps grew dim from neglect. Now awakened by the cry, they all immediately "cleaned" their wicks in preparation for the bridegroom's coming (cf. Mt 25:7). The shining glory of the wise virgins' lamps was quickly restored by the rich supply of oil from the Spirit of holiness abiding in their hearts. In contrast, though the foolish virgins had a "profession of holiness," their outward glory faded away because they lacked "the fullness of the Spirit of Grace within." Though the Spirit of God supplied them a "plentiful measure of awakening grace," he had not granted them the "renewing grace to change their nature." In the end, the "common grace of the foolish virgins" proved to be a "counterfeit" because it did not last. When they realized their lamps were going out, "the foolish said to the wise, 'Give us some of your oil'" (Mt 25:8). Yet their request proved superficial because they did not seek the oil of holiness "without measure" but only enough to "beautify" themselves before others and quiet their consciences so they "may live more peaceably with [their] sin." In summary, Shepard warned against holding to "the outward form of godliness but denying its power" (2 Tim 3:5), because, once satisfied by such "false comforts," their desires would soon fade and their lamps would soon flicker out. [44]

PREPARED FOR GLORY

While the foolish went off to find oil for their lamps, the wise virgins that were ready (Mt 25:10) entered immediately into everlasting communion with Christ. Again Shepard stressed that they were "prepared beforehand for glory" (Rom 9:23) not by their own merits but by a "divine and glorious" preparation "wrought by the power of Christ, out of his eternal love." This preparation required first a change of heart to make the wise virgins fit "to enjoy communion with Christ." For if anyone was permitted to enter heaven "without a prepared heart . . . he would not stay there if he could escape." Therefore the Lord Jesus makes every effort to

---

[43]Ibid., pp. 423-25.
[44]Ibid., pp. 437-38, 451-58, 472-76.

prepare them to enjoy communion with him in glory. This includes clothing them with the "wedding garment . . . of his own righteousness" that truly makes them lovely and glorious (cf. Eph 5:25-26). For without this righteousness, "there is nothing but shameful nakedness" for all who stand in his holy presence. Christ also grants them the "the Spirit as a guarantee" (2 Cor 5:5) who so satisfies and purifies their hearts that their happiness and comfort can now be found only in Christ.[45] Final preparation for glory is not complete until the bridegroom has awakened those sincere believers who have fallen into a carnal security. Though some may continue to sleep and yet still receive their "garment of gladness in heaven," Shepard warned that they prove to be exceptions to the rule, for ordinarily the Lord does not permit "his dear servants [to] die in a secure state." Therefore, those who remained unprepared are called to examine themselves to see "if ever you had grace." If they were found wanting, Shepard exhorted them to "Pray unto the Lord that he would prepare you," for only God is able to prepare sinners to enjoy his presence. Once "prepared for glory," those sinners who are now saints should remain "watchful over [their] hearts" and vigilant against sin, constantly "refreshing [their] soul with the good will and commands of Christ." Yet even among those prepared, some remain "in many respects unready" for heaven by putting off church membership, neglecting the spiritual leadership of their families, and failing to grieve over their former sins.[46] Hence, Shepard called all saints to meditate daily on the love of Christ, because only the heat of Christ's love will consume their worldly passions. Only then will their hearts be fully prepared for the ravishing delights of Christ's love at his coming.

The announcement that "the door was shut" (Mt 25:10) signaled the exclusion of the foolish virgins from the wedding and awakened them to their miserable state. Because they "despised God's grace" by their failure to receive it in time, they were refused entrance by the Bridegroom's own words, "I do not know you" (Mt 25:12). Shepard laid out the magnitude of their misery in staggering terms. Since Christ had no thoughts of them, he made no promises to them. Therefore, he did not shed "one drop of blood for their lives." And since he finds no pleasure in them (cf. Mal 1:10), he cannot accept anything they do for him. Yet Shepard concluded on a hopeful note. Until either physical death or future judgment shuts the door, Christ's offer remains open to all who will receive him by grace. In the strongest of terms Shepard declared the universal offer of Christ's love "personally to every man" (cf. Mk 16:15). Though "his soul be stained with the most crying guilt of

---

[45]Ibid., pp. 549-57.
[46]Ibid., pp. 559-67.

the most hideous sins that ever the earth bore, or sun saw, yet the Lord makes love to him; the price is paid for him, if he will accept it." Shepard was quick to deny that this infers universal redemption, but his point was clear to all in his congregation. The love of Christ is "for thee, if the Lord gives thee a heart to receive" it, for "there is not one here present, but the Lord would have you receive his love."[47]

CONCLUDING REFLECTIONS

Those seeking a cure for spiritual apathy in their church or perhaps in their own lives would do well to follow the example of Jonathan Edwards and read Shepard's *Parable of the Ten Virgins*. As I think back over my time spent reading and reflecting on his sermons I am struck by a greater awareness of my own thoughts and motivations that draw me away from Christ to other things for heart satisfaction. *Ten Virgins* has renewed my vigilance against peace with sin and rekindled my passion to commune with Christ. Shepard has also reminded me that faithful pastors must always maintain the balance between their responsibilities to warn and evangelize the "foolish" pretenders as well as to comfort and exhort the "wise" saints mixed among their congregations. But most importantly, Shepard has taught me how to make sure that I am like the wise virgins. He concludes, "Be always converting, more humble, more sensible of sin, more near to Christ Jesus; and then you that are sure may be more sure; and you that are not may be sure indeed!"[48]

SELECT BIBLIOGRAPHY

Primary Sources
Hall, David D., ed. *The Antinomian Controversy, 1636-1638: A Documentary History*, 2nd ed. Durham, N.C.: Duke University Press, 1990.
McGiffert, Michael, ed. *God's Plot: Puritan Spirituality in Thomas Shepard's Cambridge*. Revised edition. Amherst: University of Massachusetts Press, 1994.
Shepard, Thomas. *The Parable of the Ten Virgins*. 1659. Reprint, Morgan, Penn.: Soli Deo Gloria, 1990.
————. *The Sincere Convert and the Sound Believer*. Morgan, Penn.: Soli Deo Gloria, 1999.
————. *The Works of Thomas Shepard*. 3 vols. Edited by John A. Albro. 1853. Reprinted; Morgan, Penn.: Soli Deo Gloria, 1992.

Secondary Sources
Johnston, O. R. "Thomas Shepard's 'Parable of the Ten Virgins.'" In *Puritan Papers Volume*

---

[47]Ibid., pp. 588-96.
[48]Ibid., p. 632.

One 1956-59, edited by D. Martyn Lloyd-Jones. Phillipsburg, Penn.: P & R, 2000.

Pettit, Norman. *The Prepared Heart: Grace and Conversion in Puritan Spiritual Life*. 2nd ed. Middleton, Conn.: Wesleyan University Press, 1989.

Stoever, William K. B. *"A Faire and Easie Way to Heaven": Covenant Theology and Antinomianism in Early Massachusetts*. Middleton, Conn.: Wesleyan University Press, 1978.

Werge, Thomas. *Thomas Shepard*. Boston: Twayne, 1987

PARADISE LOST

BY JOHN MILTON (1608-1674)

Leland Ryken

JOHN MILTON, STILL REGARDED AS THE SECOND GREATEST ENGLISH writer (behind Shakespeare), is as theologian Augustus Strong called him, "a Puritan of the Puritans" and the one in whom "the English Reformation finds . . . its poetical embodiment and expression."[1] Milton is also the prototypical Christian poet of the English language—the Christian poet who looms largest in the academic study of English literature. But even if Milton had not written any poetry, he would be considered an important Puritan because of the public role he played in the Puritan revolution of the seventeenth century.

A PURITAN LIFE

Milton was born into a prosperous middle-class London family in 1608. Something of the Puritan stock from which he sprang is suggested by a landmark event in the youth of Milton's father John. When John Sr. was found reading an English Bible in his room, his father disinherited him and exiled him from his parental home.

Milton himself received a Puritan upbringing. Raised on Bread Street within a stone's throw of St. Paul's Cathedral (adjacent to which most of the booksellers had their shops in Milton's day), Milton was baptized and catechized at All Hallows Church (today called St. Mary le Bow), which stood at the end of Bread Street. The pastor was the Puritan Richard Stock. For his grade school education, Milton attended one of the most prestigious grammar schools in England, St. Paul's School, which had been famous as a citadel of Christian humanism for a century by the

---

[1] Augustus Hopkins Strong, *The Great Poets and Their Theology* (Philadelphia: American Baptist Publication Society, 1897), p. 231.

time Milton attended it. While Milton's grammar school education was broadly Protestant, his college education was staunchly Puritan. Milton earned both a B.A. and M.A. at Christ's College, one of the two or three most thoroughly Puritan of the Cambridge University colleges in the early seventeenth century.

Theoretically headed for the ministry during his college years (as were most of the three thousand young men attending the university), Milton's Puritan convictions made him unwelcome in the Anglican Church when he left Cambridge in 1632, a year before William Laud became archbishop of Canterbury. Milton himself later described the situation in terms of his having been "church-outed by the prelates," even though "by the intentions of my parents and friends I was destin'd of a child, and in mine own resolutions" to become a minister.[2] Milton turned to poetry as his alternate calling. In fact, someone has recently made an excellent case for the view that Milton never did abandon ministry as a vocation; he simply chose poetry rather than the pulpit as his vehicle.[3]

While Milton's poetry has been his greatest legacy to the world, in his own day it was his political involvement that made him famous. During the middle phase of his life (1640-1660), Milton consciously laid aside his poetic ambitions in order to support the Puritan cause. Midway through this twenty-year hiatus in Milton's poetic career, he became totally blind, which was also the occasion for Milton's writing what to me is the greatest sonnet in the English language, "When I Consider How My Light Is Spent." During much of the twenty-year era, Milton was Latin Secretary to Oliver Cromwell, in the process becoming a famous international figure. Milton wrote volumes of polemical prose for the Puritan cause, some of it defending the regicide of Charles I but some devoted to more general Puritan issues such as the nature and government of the church.

Upon the restoration of the monarchy in 1660, Milton underwent the fate of other prominent Puritans. He lived in hiding while working on *Paradise Lost* and was briefly imprisoned in the Tower of London. Milton's final years, though, were spent in relative serenity and literary accomplishment. He was buried in the church of St. Giles Cripplegate, which had deep nonconformist roots dating back to the Reformation era and which to this day exhibits busts of Cromwell and Bunyan in addition to Milton.

---

[2]Milton's account occurs in a famous autobiographical passage appearing in his prose treatise *The Reason of Church-government Urg'd Against Prelaty* (1642), which I have quoted from *The Portable Milton*, ed. Douglas Bush (New York: Penguin Classics, 1976), pp. 130-31.

[3]Jameela Lares, *Milton and the Preaching Arts* (Pittsburgh: Duquesne University Press, 2001). This book places Milton's poetry into a context of (largely Puritan) preaching manuals of the sixteenth and seventeenth centuries.

PARADISE LOST: GETTING THE BIG PICTURE

First published in 1667, *Paradise Lost* is in every way a Puritan classic. Taking the story of the Fall as its basic material, this epic actually reaches out to encompass all of human history, bounded on each side by eternity.

The epic genre requires a poet to begin *in medias res* ("in the middle of things"), rather than at the beginning, but if for a moment we disregard the rearrangement of narrative chronology that the epic genre required, we can see that the Puritan work that *Paradise Lost* most resembles in the inherent structure of its content is Thomas Boston's *Human Nature in Its Fourfold State* (1720). The basic outline of the story is this: (1) life in heaven before the fall of Satan and before the creation of the world; (2) the fall of Satan and the rebellious angels; (3) creation of the world; (4) humankind's prelapsarian existence in paradise; (5) the fall of Adam and Eve; (6) fallen human history with its dual potential for depravity and redemption; (7) the end of history; (8) eternity. For the redeemed (represented in the story by Adam and Eve), the stages of development are perfection, fall, redemption, and consummation—human nature in its fourfold state.

For purposes of his epic, Milton rearranged this inherent chronology. Here is the main outline of the plot, the order of events as the action unfolds: (1) Satan and his fallen angels rouse themselves in hell and hold a council to determine how to get back at God for their expulsion from heaven; the plan is to send Satan to paradise to effect the fall of the human race; (2) in a corresponding council in heaven, the Father and Son contemplate the impending fall of the human race, and the Son offers to undertake the redemption of the human race; (3) upon Satan's arrival in paradise, humanity vicariously lives life as God intended it to be lived, in the form of Adam and Eve's pastoral life in a garden of perfection; (4) God sends Raphael to warn Adam and Eve of the threat of Satan's temptation, and during the visit provides two major flashbacks—the story of the rebellion of the sinful angels in heaven and the story of God's creation of the world; (5) Satan tempts Eve, and Adam and Eve lose the garden by eating the forbidden fruit; (6) God dispatches Michael to give Adam a vision of the future history of the human race, a vision that comes to focus on the atonement of Christ; (7) Adam and Eve are expelled from the garden as redeemed people.

That is the *descriptive* account of how the story unfolds. At a more *interpretive* level, several organizing schemes for the poem are helpful. One version arranges the poem in the form of what literary scholars call ring composition and what biblical scholars call chiasm (the essential feature of which is that similar material is covered in the two halves of the work, but in reverse order in the second half):

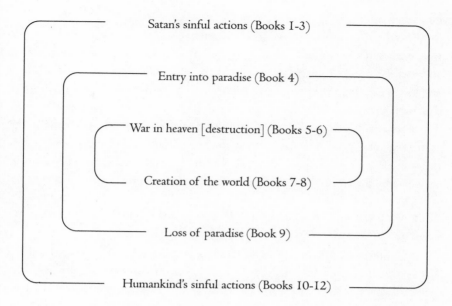

Satan's sinful actions (Books 1-3)

Entry into paradise (Book 4)

War in heaven [destruction] (Books 5-6)

Creation of the world (Books 7-8)

Loss of paradise (Book 9)

Humankind's sinful actions (Books 10-12)

Figure 9.1. Ring composition in *Paradise Lost*

Complementing this, we can also view the poem as proceeding by pairs of books: 1-2: Satan and hell; 3-4: heaven and paradise; 5-6: war in heaven; 7-8: creation of the world; 9-10: the Fall; 11-12: vision of future history. An additional organizing scheme that works wonders is to realize that the story's action takes place on four cosmic settings—heaven, hell, paradise before the Fall and ordinary fallen history.

We need to understand from the outset that Milton is a poet and storyteller rather than a writer of formal theology. We can, indeed, extract the doctrinal outline of big ideas in Milton's poem, but it is much closer to the actual texture of the poem to realize that a poet thinks in *images*. In keeping with his poetic instincts, Milton's primary intention is to make his reader live with the great images of the Christian faith. Correspondingly we will benefit most from reading *Paradise Lost* if we go to it not expecting to find yet another exposition of Puritan ideas but as an occasion to exercise our imaginations in contemplating the images of our faith. The specific images (broadly defined to include narrative scenes, characters and events as well as images) are in large part fictional, though they are rooted in the Bible wherever possible. The purpose of the fictions is to make the spiritual realities that they picture vivid to us. Certainly Milton did not envision himself as adding to the revelation of Scripture.[4]

Viewed thus, it is easy to see Milton's general strategy. For two books we live with images of evil and hell. Then we contemplate images of perfection in heaven and paradise. Next we imaginatively experience spiritual warfare (the war in heaven) and God's creation of a perfect world, then the fall from innocence to evil. After that we contemplate fallen human history in its horror and redemptive potential. There are images of salvation as the epic vision of the future comes to focus on the atonement of Christ. The magnificent final scene—the expulsion from the garden—is a Puritan paradigm of how people can live redeemed lives in a fallen world sustained by the consolations of human love and divine providence.

"FIT AUDIENCE, THOUGH FEW": HOW TO MEET THE CHALLENGE OF READING *PARADISE LOST*

For the uninitiated, *Paradise Lost* is a difficult poem (Milton himself spoke of writing it for a "fit audience . . . though few" [7:31]). The first difficulty is posed by the genre in which Milton wrote, namely, epic. C. S. Lewis, in what is still the best book on *Paradise Lost* (*A Preface to Paradise Lost*), was so convinced that recovery of the epic genre is the key to understanding the poem that he devoted the first third of the book to discussing epic as a genre.

An epic poem is a long, encyclopedic work that is so expansive that it sums up what a whole age wanted to say. Literary critic Northrop Frye calls epic "the story of all things."[5] The epic action is always built around a central epic feat, which in traditional epic is a variation of the martial theme of winning a battle and establishing an empire.

The epic story is never original but instead draws upon the ancient and authoritative myths of a culture. For a Christian epic writer, the Bible is the most plausible source. Epics are also built around a central hero who is regarded as representative of the culture from which the epic rises. As a didactic genre, epic incorporates the worldview and leading ideas of the culture that produced it. Milton wrote the last major literary epic.

It is not only the remoteness of subject matter that taxes a modern reader of epic. The epic style is an even more formidable obstacle. Epic is written in a high style, replete with allusions and stylistic traits like epithets (titles for persons and

---

[4]Milton repeatedly references the hermeneutical principle of accommodation, according to which the transcendent God accommodates his revelation of spiritual realities by picturing them in earthly and human terms. For a full discussion, see Leland Ryken, *The Apocalyptic Vision in "Paradise Lost"* (Ithaca, N.Y.: Cornell University Press, 1970), pp. 7-24.

[5]Northrop Frye, *The Return of Eden* (Toronto: University of Toronto Press, 1965), p. 3.

things) and extended epic similes. A modern reader is not accustomed to having long narrative presented in poetic form, but until relatively recently that was the preference. To enjoy an epic, we need to be ready to relish the poetry and not read simply to satisfy the narrative question of what happens next. Instead of expecting a "fast read," we need to settle down to the proverbial "slow read" extending over several weeks (epic lends itself to intermittent reading in a way that a novel does not).

The allusiveness of *Paradise Lost* is another potential obstacle for a modern reader. Milton is the most learned of English poets. He loads his epic with allusions to the Bible, to classical mythology, to events from history. Having acknowledged the difficulty, I need to assert that for all his allusiveness, Milton is a more accessible poet than many modern poets, such as T. S. Eliot and William Butler Yeats. One does not need to understand every allusion to read *Paradise Lost* with enjoyment. Usually the general meaning is clear, and I sometimes prefer simply to sit down with *Paradise Lost* in an edition without footnotes. The other option is to read the poem in a modern edition with good explanatory footnotes.[6] The reader will note that the first two books are the most laden with classical allusions, and this is part of Milton's design to render the whole satanic enterprise unsympathetic by linking it to the military values of classical epic, embodied in a classical idiom filled with mythological references. It is as though Milton was writing a commentary on Lady Macbeth's memorable one-liner in the sleepwalking scene in Shakespeare's *Macbeth*: "Hell is murky."

A DEVOTIONAL CLASSIC

I am what in my profession is known as a Miltonist, meaning that I wrote my dissertation on *Paradise Lost*, I teach Milton and I write and speak on Milton. Out of all the commentary that I have read on the poem, however, my favorite statement is the opening sentence of a testimony that someone penned upon becoming a member of Tenth Presbyterian Church in Philadelphia: "I was led to the Lord by John Milton." The accompanying narrative told of this person's taking stock of his own responses while reading *Paradise Lost*. At the same time that I first encountered that anecdote, I also read the story of a Chinese student in the United States who was converted when he "read afresh John Milton's *Paradise Lost* and connected it to the gospel story." Simultaneously, I received a long, effusive letter from a student who narrated her experience of understanding God's forgiveness at an unprece-

---

[6]See select bibliography at the end of the chapter.

dented depth for the first time after studying *Paradise Lost* in my course.

I relish these anecdotes because they confirm the truth of what I have told my classes for a long time, namely, that virtually everything Milton wrote can be read devotionally. This may not have been Milton's conscious intention, but it is the potential effect for any Christian reader. To read *Paradise Lost* as a devotional classic, all one needs to do is assimilate the poem by consciously contemplating the religious ideas and realities that the poem embodies, building bridges to one's own spiritual and moral experiences and allowing the poem to awaken godly affections.

The most influential book on *Paradise Lost* in modern times—Stanley Fish's *Surprised by Sin: The Reader in Paradise Lost*—draws a parallel between Milton's intention in the poem and the purpose of Puritan devotional writers of the day: "I believe Milton's intention to differ little from that of so many devotional writers, 'to discover to us our miserable and wretched estate through corruption of nature' and to 'shew how a man may come to a holy reformation and so happily recover himself' (Richard Bernard, *The Isle of Man*)."[7]

MERE CHRISTIANITY IN *PARADISE LOST*

I have divided my survey of the theological content of *Paradise Lost* into two sections. In this preliminary section, I will discuss that part of Milton's masterpiece that belongs to the realm of "mere Christianity"—those core ideas and values that all Christians embrace. It is a fact that for all its Puritan partisanship, *Paradise Lost* has spoken powerfully to Catholics and Anglo-Catholics as well as to evangelical Protestants. In a later section I will outline specifically Puritan emphases. In discussing the big ideas of *Paradise Lost*, I have chosen to arrange the material in the approximate order in which we encounter the ideas as we read the poem from beginning to end.

We begin Milton's poem with a prolonged meditation on *the sinfulness of sin* (as at least three Puritan writers termed it in titles of treatises on sin).[8] The vehicle by which this is embodied is the spectacle of Satan and his cohorts as they rouse themselves from the burning lake, get their act together, and hold a demonic council to decide how to get back at God for their expulsion from heaven. As we allow the emotions and attitudes that are displayed by this ungodly crew to serve as an anatomy of sinfulness, we need to read the story on two levels. On the most immediate level, Milton does, indeed, give us his understanding of Satan and spiritual evil as

---

[7]Stanley E. Fish, *Surprised by Sin: The Reader in Paradise Lost* (New York: St. Martin's, 1967), p. ix.

[8]William Bridge, *The Sinfulness of Sin*; Edward Reynolds, *The Sinfulness of Sin*; Jeremiah Burroughs, *The Evil of Evils, or the Exceeding Sinfulness of Sin.* A 1993 reprint of Ralph Venning's *The Plague of Plagues* retitled it *The Sinfulness of Sin.*

it exists among principalities and powers. But we must also read Milton's story on the premise that we are intended to look not only at the details of the story (in this case Satan and the fallen angels in hell) but also *through* it to life as we know it ourselves. Milton's pictures of Satan and hell are *metaphors of the human condition* as we know it in our own lives and society.

Of course Milton does more than give us such indirect and metaphoric pictures of human waywardness. He also portrays it directly, and here the emphasis is on sin as disobedience to God. In fact, the very first phrase of the poem, in which Milton names his epic subject, is, "Of man's first disobedience." Milton's portrayal runs true to the *Westminster Children's Catechism* assertion that sin consists of "doing what God forbids." Milton gives us a full-scale epic elaboration of the temptation and fall of Eve and Adam, buttressed by a modification of the conventional epic vision of the future, which in Milton's own words is a story of "supernal grace contending / With sinfulness of men" (2:359-360), not a patriotic celebration of the poet's own nation.

Also important to the ideational design of *Paradise Lost* is the character of God. Milton's portrayal of that character is approximately identical with what we find in the Bible. Overriding everything else is God's sovereignty. In Milton's poem, God the Father is emphatically in charge of the universe, including heaven, earth, and hell. This comes out in virtually every scene in which God is an actor in the drama but is perhaps best illustrated in the scene set in heaven in the first half of book three. Other attributes take their place under God's sovereignty. In a story of sin and its punishment, God's justice naturally looms large. But God's mercy and redemptive love come to overshadow his justice by the end of the story. As the Son states it in the dialogue in heaven (the first half of book three), "mercy first and last shall brightest shine" (3:134).

The active agent of God's love is the Son, and it is in connection with the Son that we can best see the outworking of Milton's theme of the redemption of the human race. This emphasis is asserted in the opening lines of the poem, where after announcing the subject of his story as being the loss of Eden, Milton immediately adds, "till one greater Man / Restore us, and regain the blissful seat" (1:4-5). In a dramatic moment in the dialogue in heaven, the Son volunteers to undertake the redemption of the human race:

> And now without redemption all mankind
> Must have been lost, adjudged to death and hell
> By doom severe, had not the Son of God,
> In whom the fullness dwells of love divine,
> His dearest mediation thus renewed. . . . (3:222-26)

After the Fall, too, it is the Son who intervenes in Adam and Eve's pitiable plight as "their great Intercessor" (11:19). Additionally, in the war in heaven, it is specifically Christ who defeats Satan, as Milton draws upon the *Christus Victor* tradition and lends a Christocentric emphasis to his epic.[9]

If the character of God is thus one of the big ideas in the poem, so are the acts of God, and once again those acts are familiar to anyone who knows the Bible and the outline of Christian doctrine. I have already implied that two divine acts that get major attention are judgment and redemption. Two further divine acts loom larger than we might predict, apparently because Milton regarded them as essential to his overall design. Milton devotes two whole books to narrating God's creation of the world and the first two humans. Secondly, Milton highlights the doctrine of providence, which was a lasting consolation for Milton throughout his life and writings. In his opening statement of epic theme, Milton announces that his purpose is to "assert Eternal Providence, / And justify the ways of God to men" (1:25-26). The Fall being Milton's story material, this is the interpretive slant that he proposes to take toward that material, thereby turning his story into a theodicy (a reconciliation of God's goodness and power with the fact of evil and suffering in the world). In the magnificent closing lines, too, as Milton narrates Adam and Eve's leaving the garden, he adds the information, "and Providence their guide" (12:647).

Complementing Milton's portrayal of God is his portrayal of Adam and Eve as representative humans, thereby making the Christian view of the person another of the big ideas in *Paradise Lost*. According to the poem, people have a dual capability—toward good and toward evil. They were created perfect by God, fell through their own disobedience, are capable of redemption through the atonement of Christ, and as part of that redemption live in hope of being glorified in eternity. This is what Thomas Boston eventually labeled "human nature in its fourfold state," an idea that William Perkins had already expressed in this form: "Man must be considered in a foure-fold estate, as he was created, as he was corrupted, as he is renewed, as he shall be glorified."[10] In Milton's portrayal, moreover, people are endowed with the power of moral choice, and they are held responsible by God for the choices they make.

Another of the main ideas that undergird *Paradise Lost* is the biblical/Christian view of history—the view that earthly history is bracketed by eternity.[11] It begins

---

[9] As a corrective to a lot of misinformation about Milton's portrayal of Christ, I commend Hideyuki Shitaka, *Milton's Idea of the Son in the Shaping of Paradise Lost as a Christocentric Epic* (Tokyo: Eihosha, 1996).

[10] William Perkins, *A Reformed Catholike*, in *The Workes of the Famous and Worthie Divine William Perkins* (Cambridge: John Legate, 1616-1618), 1:551.

in a state of perfection, which is lost by the fall of Adam and Eve into sin. It is succeeded by the long and painful history of the human race in its sinful state and is, in fact, a story in which "works of faith" are "rarely . . . found" (12:535-36). But time will eventually "stand fixed" (12:555), and there will be "new heav'ns, new earth, ages of endless date / Founded in righteousness and peace and love" (12:549-550).

Finally, Milton's story is the most powerful example we have in English litera- ture of the great spiritual/moral conflict between good and evil. This conflict, in fact, structures the entire story. On one side are God and his faithful followers (both angelic and human). On the other side are Satan, the demons and evil people. Heaven is pitted against hell, light against darkness. Deeds of good, whether done by angels or humans, are set over against deeds of evil. There is hardly a detail in Milton's story that does not contribute in big or small ways to this overriding spir- itual battle. Milton's poem is a literary elaboration of the mindset that Richard Sibbes expressed thus:

> There are two grand sides in the world, to which all belong: there is God's side and
> those that are his, and there is another side that is Satan's, and those that are his; two
> kingdoms, two sides, two contrary dispositions, that pursue one another.[12]

As I conclude this overview of leading ideas in Milton's poem, I need to under- score that while the Puritans certainly endorsed them, they are not distinctive to the Puritans. Although critics have related these ideas to marginal glosses in the *Geneva Bible*,[13] and the writings of Luther and Calvin,[14] one could also resort to Au- gustine and Aquinas and the Anglican *Book of Common Prayer* to find parallels.

PURITAN EMPHASES

Despite the way in which much of *Paradise Lost* belongs to the realm of shared Chris- tian faith, there is also much about the poem that is distinctly Puritan in its view- point.[15] We can profitably begin with the centrality of the Bible, as seen in the way in which Milton chose the Bible for his story material and for a large percentage of

---

[11]C. A. Patrides wrote a readable little book on the topic titled *The Grand Design of God: The Literary Form of the Christian View of History* (Toronto: University of Toronto Press, 1972).

[12]Richard Sibbes, *Works*, as quoted by Charles H. George and Katherine George, *The Protestant Mind of the English Ref- ormation, 1570-1640* (Princeton, N.J.: Princeton University Press, 1961), p. 109.

[13]George Wesley Whiting, *Milton and This Pendant World* (1958; reprint, New York: Octagon, 1969), pp. 129-68.

[14]Georgia B. Christopher, *Milton and the Science of the Saints* (Princeton, N.J.: Princeton University Press, 1982).

[15]In my discussion here I have provided only minimal quotation from Puritan sources; anyone wanting a copious Puritan context for my claims can find it in my book *Worldly Saints: The Puritans as They Really Were* (Grand Rapids: Zondervan, 1986).

his allusions. The Bible, as we know, was the ultimate authority for the Puritans, "the touchstone that trieth all doctrines" and "the Rule according to which we must believe."[16] Earlier in his life Milton had reached tentative decisions to write his epic on conventional epic subjects—first classical mythology and then the Arthurian material. His final choice of early Genesis was entirely in keeping with the Puritan impulse to root everything in the Bible. When in the opening lines of the poem Milton claims that he is pursuing "things unattempted yet in prose or rhyme" (1:16), he means that he is the first poet to take the story material of the Bible and cast it into the strict form of classical epic.

Equally Puritan is Milton's picture of the good life, which is in every way a Puritan vision. The chief repository is book four, with its picture of Adam and Eve's life of innocence in paradise. This narrative is Milton's picture of how God intends human life to be lived, anytime, anywhere. The chief ingredients in this Puritan vision are as follows.

First, the view of work fits exactly with the Puritan work ethic. There are few topics on which the Puritans said more than the topic of work. In just a few lines, Milton sums up what countless Puritan sermons and treatises had also said on the subject of work:

Man hath his daily work of body or mind
Appointed, which declares his dignity,
And the regard of Heav'n on all his ways. (4:618-620)

But that is only the core idea. We catch numerous glimpses of Adam and Eve at work pruning the garden. Someone who made a detailed comparison between Milton's paradisal vision and its long lineage of predecessors concluded that the most original feature of Milton's vision was not that he made work before the fall pleasurable (which was a conventional view) but that he made it *necessary*.[17]

A second Puritan bias in Milton's picture of the good life is his idealization of the companionate marriage and, as part of that ideal, the beauty of unfallen sexuality between husband and wife. Centuries of Catholic doctrine had claimed that sexual union was a result of the Fall but the Puritan tradition went out of its way to claim that it existed before the Fall. Marriage was ordained by God, said Thomas Becon, "and that not in this sinful world, but in paradise, that most

---

[16]William Tyndale, Prologue to "Genesis," in *Tyndale's Old Testament*, ed. David Daniell (New Haven, Conn.: Yale University Press, 1992), p. 7; Increase Mather, *David Serving His Generation* (Boston: B. Green and J. Allen, 1698), p. 10.
[17]J. M. Evans, *Paradise Lost and the Genesis Tradition* (Oxford: Oxford University Press, 1968), pp. 248-49.

joyful garden of pleasure."[18] Milton makes exactly the same claim, partly in his pictures of wedded romantic love, and partly in a famous passage in which he highlights the matter:

> nor turned, I ween,
> Adam from his fair spouse, nor Eve the rites
> Mysterious of connubial love refused;
> Whatever hypocrites austerely talk[19]
>
> Of purity and place and innocence,
> Defaming as impure what God declares
> Pure, and commands to some, leaves free to all. (4:741-47)

Milton's portrayal of life in paradise also illustrates to perfection Puritan sacramentalism. It is well known that the Puritans eschewed the multiplication of images and rituals in the church. What is not adequately acknowledged is that they had their own sacramental vision—one that consisted of seeing God in all of life, including the commonplace. The most attractive feature of Adam and Eve's prelapsarian ("before the Fall") life in Milton's story is the way in which nothing in the daily routine is self-contained but opens upward to God. If we simply listen to Adam and Eve's conversation, every topic they take up is related to God—work, nature, their mutual love, even sleep. For a good summary of the sacramental vision of *Paradise Lost*, read Adam and Eve's evening hymn, found in book four, lines 720-35.

A final Puritan trait of *Paradise Lost* is the primacy of the spiritual as we find it everywhere in the Puritans. Thomas Watson, for example, wrote that "blessedness does consist in externals," and that "happiness cannot by art of chemistry be extracted here. . . . The soul is a spiritual thing. . . . True blessedness must have *eternity* stamped on it."[20] Samuel Willard wrote in a similar vein that "the more of Christ that a people enjoy, the happier are they, and the less he is known and acknowledged in his great design of mediatorship, the greater is the infelicity of such a people."[21] Milton's poem espouses the same viewpoint. Milton even takes on the whole epic tradition, which had elevated military power and human success to the highest value. Milton makes Satan and his followers the exemplars of the old epic values to

---

[18]Thomas Becon, *The Christian State of Matrimony*, as quoted by Laurence Lerner, *Love and Marriage: Literature and Its Social Context* (New York: St. Martin's, 1979), p. 111.

[19]The hypocrites whom Milton here denounces are Catholics.

[20]Thomas Watson, *The Beatitudes* (1660; reprint, Edinburgh: Banner of Truth Trust, 1971), pp. 25-26, 31.

[21]Samuel Willard, *The Fountain Opened*, as quoted by Ernest B. Lowrie, *The Shape of the Puritan Mind: The Thought of Samuel Willard* (New Haven, Conn.: Yale University Press, 1974), p. 227.

show that he disapproved of those values. At this point Milton's choice of a pastoral (rural) subject becomes important. Milton replaces heroic values (military prowess and conquest) with the pastoral values of contentment, the humble estate, harmony with nature, and love. He also replaces heroic values with domestic values: instead of writing about kings and warriors, he writes about a husband and wife in their daily domestic routine. Furthermore, Milton replaces the warrior as hero with the Christian saint as hero, as seen in Adam and Eve's life of spiritual perfection before the Fall and their acts of repentance and coming to trust in Christ as savior after the Fall.

Milton makes all of this explicit in the moment of epiphany toward which the whole poem moves. The context is the conclusion of the vision of future history, which has come to focus on the atonement of Christ. Adam's final state of mind and soul in the poem is this:

> Henceforth I learn that to obey is best,
> And love with fear the only God, to walk
> As in his presence, ever to observe
> His providence, and on him sole depend,
> Merciful over all his works, with good
> Still overcoming evil, and by small
> Accomplishing great things, by things deemed weak
> Subverting worldly strong, and worldly wise
> By simply meek; that suffering for truth's sake
> Is fortitude to highest victory,
> And to the faithful death the gate of life;
> Taught this by his example whom I now
> Acknowledge my Redeemer ever blest. (12:561-573)

This is Milton's new epic norm—not winning a kingdom but coming to trust in Christ as Savior.

HOW TO READ *PARADISE LOST*

The best way by far to read Milton's masterpiece is to read it as a story, starting at the beginning, settling down for the archetypal "long read," and moving forward as fast or slowly as one's time and attention span allow. As C. S. Lewis once said of long poems, a reader needs to be prepared for flats and shallows as well as mountaintops. For people who find the prospect of reading the entire poem daunting, my advice is to read more topically and meditatively, foregoing the narrative as a whole. Here are the key passages that can comprise such a reading:

Book 1:

Satan and the demons in hell, a spectacle of evil and its punishment.

Book 3, lines 1-415:

God and the Son in heaven, determining what to do about the impending fall of Adam and Eve.

Book 4:

the best of the best! Milton's portrayal of life in paradise, offered as a picture of how God intends human life to be lived.

Book 9:

the temptation and fall of Adam and Eve.

Book 12, lines 552 to the end:

Adam's response to the vision of future history, followed by Milton's magnificent description of Adam and Eve's departure from the garden; everything is a balance between sadness and consolation here at the end.

SELECT BIBLIOGRAPHY

Currently Available Paperback Editions of Paradise Lost:

Bush, Douglas, ed. *The Portable Milton.* New York: Viking, 1977.

Campbell, Gordon, ed. *John Milton: The Complete English Poems*, Everyman ed. London: J. M. Dent, 1993.

Elledge, Scott, ed. *Paradise Lost.* New York: Norton, 1993.

Leonard, John, ed. *John Milton: The Complete Poems.* New York: Penguin, 1998.

Raffel, Burton, ed. *The Annotated Milton.* New York: Bantam, 1999.

Secondary Sources

Fish, Stanley. *Surprised by Sin: The Reader in Paradise Lost.* New York: St. Martin's, 1967.

Lewis, C. S. *A Preface to Paradise Lost.* New York: Oxford University Press, 1942.

Patrides, C. A. *Milton and the Christian Tradition.* Oxford: Oxford University Press, 1966.

Sims, James H. *The Bible in Milton's Epics.* Gainesville: University of Florida Press, 1962.

Sims, James H., and Leland Ryken, eds. *Milton and Scriptural Tradition.* Columbia: University of Missouri Press, 1984.

❧ 10 ❧

THE REFORMED PASTOR

BY RICHARD BAXTER (1615-1691)

Paul Chang-Ha Lim

IF A BOOK, WITH ITS PRIMARY INTENDED AUDIENCE BEING PASTORS, began its first chapter as follows, would it not be surprising to hear that it is, nearly 350 years after its publication, still in print and very much in demand as a textbook in pastoral theology?

> Many a preacher is now in hell, who hath a hundred times called upon his hearers to use the utmost care and diligence to escape it. Can any reasonable man imagine that God should save men for offering salvation to others, while they refuse it themselves; and for telling others those truths which they neglect and abuse? Many a tailor goes in rags, that maketh costly clothes for others; and many a cook scarcely licks his fingers, when he hath dressed for others the most costly dishes. . . . Take heed, therefore, to yourselves first, that you be that which you persuade your hearers to be, and believe that which you persuade them to believe, and heartily entertain that Saviour whom you offer to them.[1]

The full title of this treatise was *Gildas Salvianus: The Reformed Pastor*. Following its first printing in 1656, the second edition quickly came out in 1657, indicating the considerable interest generated from this book. Johann Zollikofer (1633-1692), a pastor at St. Gall in Switzerland, wrote on April 16, 1663, reporting the "high esteem we make of these two Chief Pieces, the [*Saints*] *Everlasting Rest* and *Reformed Pas-*

---

[1]Richard Baxter, *The Reformed Pastor*, ed. William Brown (Edinburgh: Banner of Truth Trust, 1989), pp. 53-55. Cited henceforth as *Reformed Pastor* unless otherwise cited from the original 1656 edition, *Gildas Salvianus: The Reformed Pastor*, which will be cited as *Gildas*. I would like to thank J. William Black for allowing me to read chapter four of his then unpublished monograph, *Reformation Pastors: Richard Baxter and the Ideal of the Reformed Pastor* (Carlisle, U.K.: Paternoster, 2004).

tor: in which latter you strike home to the very heart many Ministers." Thus we can see the international impact of Baxter's effort of pastoral reformation, now reverberating back to "Helvetia," one of the hallowed grounds for the reformed tradition.[2] Baxter's reformational strategy was formed in direct response to the immediate ecclesiastical context of the 1650s—the increased number of separatist churches—and in keeping with the best of the Calvinistic pastoral tradition, modifying it when he was called forth by his reading of Scripture and by his specific pastoral context. Baxter, therefore, focused especially on implementing pastoral discipline and seeking conversion through the means of catechizing the entire parish, in addition to preaching effective sermons on the same topic.

After the seventeenth century, *The Reformed Pastor* was substantially scaled down in length, edited and republished in a number of different languages and contexts. This resulted in presenting Baxter's pastoral practice without a well-contextualized picture of the historical events that gave rise to the treatise in the first place. In 1766, Samuel Palmer substantially abridged the treatise, which was originally 480 pages plus 78 pages of various letters, thus compromising both the immediacy of a hurriedly written treatise and the specific concerns and contexts which help the reader to understand its genesis. Palmer's first edition was followed by a second edition in 1808, both printed in London. Two separate American editions were published in Washington, Pennsylvania, in 1810 and in Cincinnati, Ohio, in 1811, respectively. Its German translation appeared before 1720, the Dutch translation before 1761, and by 1864 a Syriac translation of the same appeared as *Ktaba d-makrzana mhumna*, published in Urmia, Iran. However, the version which today's readers are most familiar with was abridged and edited by William Brown in 1829, and its popularity was substantial enough to require subsequent editions on both sides of the Atlantic in 1835, 1841, 1850, 1860 and 1862. The Banner of Truth edition of 1974 was a reprint of the Brown edition of 1862, and since then it was reprinted in 1979, 1983 and 1989.[3] This chapter seeks to provide both a brief context within which *The Reformed Pastor* needs to be understood and also a thematic and textual analysis.

Throughout its publication history, Baxter's *Reformed Pastor* has impacted a number of well-known Christians, including Philip Doddridge, Charles and John Wes-

---

[2] Baxter, *Reliquiæ Baxterianæ*, ed. Matthew Sylvester (1696), 2:443-4, § 442. Henceforth as *Reliquiæ*. See also *Calendar of the Correspondence of Richard Baxter*, 2 vols., ed. N. H. Keeble and Geoffrey F. Nuttall (Oxford: Oxford University Press, 1991), 2:38, no. 712.

[3] In addition, see editions by J. T. Wilkinson (London: Epworth, 1939); Hugh Martin (London: SCM Press, 1956); Jay Green (Grand Rapids: Sovereign Grace, 1971); and James Huston (Portland, Ore.: Multnomah, 1982).

ley, and Charles Haddon Spurgeon, the latter having his wife read it on Sunday eve-
nings to "quicken my sluggish heart." Before we delve into the book, it is necessary
to know the life of the man whose pastoral zeal and strategy were to become a
shaping influence upon his contemporary Puritan pastors and beyond.

BAXTER'S LIFE AND TIMES

Born as the only child of Richard Baxter and Beatrice Adeney on November 12,
1615, in Rowton, Shropshire, Richard Baxter the son was educated at Donnington
Free School, Wroxeter. On December 23, 1638, he was ordained as deacon by John
Thornborough, bishop of Worcester, then served as head of Sgt. Richard Foley's
school in Dudley for nine months. Between 1639 and 1640, Baxter was curate at
Bridgnorth, Shropshire. In April 1641, at the behest of eleven influential laymen
in the parish of St. Mary's, Kidderminster, Baxter accepted a call to be "lecturer"
at Kidderminster. Due to the utter negligence of the incumbent, George Dance,
who "preached but once a quarter," and "frequented Alehouses, and had sometimes been drunk," the selection of Baxter as preacher was a decisive step toward
fostering godliness at the initiative of the laity.[4]

In response to the English Civil War, Baxter left Kidderminster between 1642
and 1647, to serve as an army chaplain. Upon his return in 1647, he began to implement "laborious holiness," as a direct response to the Antinomian threat that he
witnessed while serving in Cromwell's New Model Army. Baxter was also seeking
ways to respond to the critique of radical separatists whose cry against the impurity
of the parochial system he acknowledged as legitimate, although he could not en-
dorse their practice of separatism. Between 1647 and 1661 Baxter endeavored to
implement a fundamental ecclesiological reconfiguration through his conversionistic preaching, private catechetical instruction with *all* households and implementation of pastoral discipline. He was also instrumental in the creation of the Worcestershire Association to foster an environment of godly unity and to facilitate the
overall aim of reformation. It was during his twenty-year tenure at Kidderminster
that Baxter became the "most outstanding pastor, evangelist and writer on practical
and devotional themes that Puritanism produced," and whose "sweet savour of
good . . . doctrine, works and discipline remained to this day," a day captured when
George Whitefield visited in December 1743.[5]

In addition to fulfilling his pastoral duty, Baxter penned forty-seven books
during his Kidderminster years. After the restoration of the monarchy in 1660,

---

[4]Geoffrey F. Nuttall, *Richard Baxter* (London: Thomas Nelson, 1965), p. 25.
[5]Cited in J. I. Packer, "Introduction," in *Reformed Pastor*, pp. 9, 12.

Baxter was made a royal chaplain ordinary, but declined the offer of bishopric so as to stand along with the soon-to-be marginalized group of nonconformist ministers. His appeal for an episcopacy—patterned after Archbishop James Ussher's "reduced episcopacy"—was comprehensive enough to embrace the ministers who were not episcopally ordained, but wanted to function within the restored Church of England. However, it failed to convince the restored Anglican party at the Savoy Conference in 1661; the breach that followed inexorably led to the expulsion of over 1,500 ministers on August 24, 1662. During the period after the Act of Uniformity of 1662, Baxter emerged as the leader for the conservative branch among the nonconformists. His constant self-designation as a "mere Catholic" (which influenced C. S. Lewis's own understanding of Christian orthodoxy as encapsulated in his *Mere Christianity*) clearly demonstrated Baxter's distaste for denominational labeling and a desire for ecclesiastical mutuality and unity. Baxter endured through two incarcerations, the results of stillborn endeavors for nonconformists' inclusion within the Church of England during the late 1660s until the mid-1680s. There was much misunderstanding regarding his occasional conformity—of attending weekly service at the local Anglican church but leaving when the Eucharist was celebrated—during the same period. During these years Baxter published another eighty-seven books, ranging from defense of nonconformity to pleas for church unity, from a highly complex systematic theology to guidebooks for the poor and their household instruction. Two years after the Act of Toleration of 1689, Baxter entered his "saints everlasting rest" on December 8, 1691, and was buried in London.

Among his 135 published books—and this does not include six posthumous publications—arguably the three best known would be *The Saints Everlasting Rest* (1650), which reached its twelfth edition by 1688, *A Call to the Unconverted* (1658), which reached its thirteenth edition by 1669, and the treatise we are considering, *The Reformed Pastor*.

THE REFORMED PASTOR: ITS CONTEXT AND CONTENT

In a contemporary pamphlet humorously titled *A Dialogue Between the Pope and the Devil, About Owen and Baxter*,[6] the Pope angrily protests, "Shall WE allow these Scribling Fellows, to write for ever? . . . They . . . extremely lessen our Number." The response of the putative devil illuminates the nature of Baxter's influence—even after he was ejected from his Kidderminster pastorate:

---

[6]Richard Baxter, *A Dialogue Between the Pope and the Devil, About Owen and Baxter* (London: n.p., 1681).

Yes, yes. Take away their Family Books, my Friend, in the first place, and call-in their CALLS in the next, and that will do the Business. . . . I have peep'd through the Glass-Windows and there have I seen such Swarms of the Ordinary sort of People . . . pooring [*sic*] upon *Baxter's* Family Book (as they call it) as wou'd have amazed thee. . . . I have heard them read on a Sunday night, till their very Eyestrings were ready to crack again.[7]

Such parody helps us situate the aim of Baxter's reformational endeavors of ecclesiological reconfiguration. Conversionistic emphasis on all his ministerial endeavors and a corresponding stress on the catechesis for all families were two overtly and repeatedly stated purposes of his pastoral work. His ultimate goal was to have each parish and family seek a disciplined life of piety of its own. Such were the literary origins and theological rationale for *The Reformed Pastor*.

The influence of Archbishop William Laud (1573-1645) on the religious milieu of early Stuart Puritanism was considerable, if only in negative terms. Laud was the ultimate "other" whose Arminianizing tendencies needed to be fought off. His emphasis on the Eucharist as the climax of worship (thus seemingly deviating from the centrality of the preached Word) was dangerously sacramentarian and his active harassment of zealous Puritans easily marked him to be the epitome of *the* religious problem facing England. He represented a stillborn reformation and the constant threat of Roman Catholicism, both real and perceived. Thus the word and the reality of reformation were of paramount concern for the Puritans as they sought to remove all vestigial elements of "popery" from their churches. As clearly indicated in "The Root and Branch Petition" (1640) in which the swift removal of all non-Protestant religious elements was called for, the signatories and other like-minded "hotter sort of Protestants" were hopeful such cleansing would usher in the elusive and long-awaited reformation to England.[8]

During the era of the Long Parliament, the Puritans could finally envisage a full implementation of a magisterial reformation, endorsed by pastors and enforced by the civil authority. However, due to the collapse of censorship and, more significantly, the rise of anticlericalism and the exponential growth of the sects, Baxter, as well as many Puritans, realized that the fight for reformation would have to confront a two-headed monster: one, the proscribed Laudian episcopacy, the other what the Presbyterian polemicist Thomas Edwards called the "gangrene" of radical separatism. Baxter encountered much of the latter during this period in the New Model Army, thus prompting him to abandon his previous high-Calvinistic con-

---

[7]Baxter, *Dialogue*, 1.
[8]See Nicholas Tyacke, ed., *England's Long Reformation 1500-1800* (London: UCL Press, 1998).

victions regarding justification, for he thought that such an espousal would inexorably lead to Antinomianism.

By the time Baxter came to Kidderminster and resumed his pastoral duties, his views on reformation began to shift:

> I can well remember the time when I was earnest for the reformation of matters of ceremony. . . . Alas! Can we think that the reformation is wrought, when we cast out a few ceremonies, and changed some vestures, and gestures, and forms! Oh no, sirs! It is the converting and saving of souls that is our business. That is the chiefest part of reformation, that doth most good, and tendeth most to the salvation of the people.[9]

Baxter certainly did have scruples with the infamous "Et Cetera Oath," delivered by the bishops in the Convocation of 1640, demanding from all Anglican clergy that they would never "consent to alter the government of this Church, by archbishops, bishops, deans, archdeacons, *et cetera,* as it stands now established."[10] However, as reflected in the quote above, Baxter came to realize that true reformation had more to do with conversion than structural changes, and to actualize this belief he was convinced that catechizing, discipline and unity among pastors were the three most significant factors. With the virtual disappearance of the national church and no substantially settled ecclesial structure in its place, Baxter's untiring effort toward reformation was given the most opportune time for its implementation.

Instead of looking at *The Reformed Pastor* as merely an occasional writing, we should view it as a culmination of Baxter's reformational priorities and perspectives in the 1650s.[11] In 1653, the associating ministers in Worcestershire published their first joint document, *Christian Concord,* in which they asserted, "Particularly, We are all convinced that it is the duty of each Minister to endeavour to know (if possible) *each person* of his charge, that so he may know where his special duty lieth, and how to perform it."[12] Three years after the first publication of *Christian Concord,* another similar treatise was written by the associating ministers, *The Agreement of divers Ministers of Christ in the County of Worcester . . . for Catechizing* (1656). Fifty-eight ministers shared Baxter's conviction that personal instruction was the best way to insure the salvation of the souls of parishioners and thus the reformation of the parish.

---

[9]Baxter, *Reformed Pastor,* p. 211.

[10]For the text of the *Et Cetera Oath,* see William Land, *The Works of William Land,* 7 vols. (Oxford: Parker Society, 1847-60), 5:623.

[11]Black, *Reformation Pastors,* pp. 82-83.

[12]*Christian Concord* (1653), Proposition III, sig. A3v. On the origin of the Worcestershire Association, see Paul Lim, "Richard Baxter's Puritan Ecclesiology in Context" (Ph.D dissertation, University of Cambridge, 2001), chap. 5.

Shortly after the subscription of the *Agreement*, they were to hold a day of prayer on December 4, 1655, an act deemed necessary considering the stupendous nature of the task. The associating ministers urged Baxter to preach for that occasion, but due to an illness, he was not able to attend. Thus, he published the enlarged version of the sermon in 1656 as *The Reformed Pastor*.

Baxter's text was Acts 20:28 wherein St. Paul urges the Ephesian elders to "Keep watch over yourselves and over all the flock, of which the Holy Spirit has made you overseers," and Baxter, in painstaking detail and exegetical rigor, showed the nature of biblical eldership, its scope, origin and blueprint of pastoring; the nature, motive, subject, object and scope of the oversight of the elder's own self; the nature, manner and motives of the oversight of the flock; and the special significance of catechizing and pastoral discipline, the proper administration of which would ensure the elder to be a truly "reformed pastor." Inevitably this book reads like a specific directive for pastors, with seemingly relatively little relevance and value for nonclerical readers. However, by way of discussing the nature of the pastorate and its corresponding task, Baxter opens the windows to Puritan spirituality, its contours and priorities. Consequently, *The Reformed Pastor* provides helpful correctives to our individualistic tendencies and challenges us to think about the purity of the embodiment of the gospel, the church. Finally, the emphasis on catechizing shows the reality not only of our being-in-communion but also our learning-and-growing-in-communion. To be sure, Baxter's communal conception is neither a radical egalitarian position nor was it obtained without its due emphasis on the cognitive dimensions, two notable current tendencies in the way the ideas of community and relationality are often understood.

Baxter was unalterably convinced that before the hoped-for implementation of catechizing, establishment of discipline and the procurement of ecclesial unity, pastors themselves had to be "reformed." Thus there is an overriding concern to insure that those catechizing pastors themselves would not be disqualified after having preached to others. This partly explains the ostensibly "harsh" tone of Baxter's rhetoric. As a corollary, it must be noted that *The Reformed Pastor* depicts in bold strokes a reformational vision of the Christian community and the crucial role to be played by pastors. For Baxter a church comprised of a largely absentee diocesan bishop and thousands of parishioners who preferred to pursue hedonistic trivialities and pleasures rather than wayfaring and warfaring on the "plain man's pathway to heaven" was no true church. Nor was the true church made up of a "society of friends," as Quakers referred to themselves, whose radical anticlerical tendencies eliminated the office of pastor. Rather it was to be a covenanted community, whose catchment area was the entire parish, and whose pastor was *de facto* the congregational bishop, the *episkopos*, whose primary role was shepherding the flock. The pastor was to be an indispensable human instrument in mediating *"de regno Christi"*[13] and communicating the twofold benefits of Christ's redemptive work. As such, it is hardly surprising to find that for a true reformation to be obtained, there must first be an awakened and "reformed" ministry.

Catechizing. The first aspect to highlight about *The Reformed Pastor* is its heavy emphasis on catechizing. Ian Green, in his *The Christian's ABC*, has conclusively shown the widespread use of catechizing in England after the Reformation, and has highlighted Baxter's own contribution in the matter.[14] One unique aspect of Baxter's emphasis on catechizing has to do with the scope and the age of those catechized. Baxter was convinced that conversion needs to—and can—happen irrespective of age, and the most effective means of finding out whether one needs to be converted was *not* by public preaching, but by private discourse in the form of the catechesis. In his autobiography, Baxter spoke of his ministry at Kidderminster this way:

> The congregation was usually full, so that we were fain to build five galleries after my coming thither.... On the Lord's days ... you might hear an hundred families singing psalms and repeating sermons as you passed through the streets.... When I came thither first there was about one family in a street that worshipped God ... and when I came away there were some streets where there was not past one Family in the side that did not so.[15]

Baxter credits his catechizing as one of the main ingredients for such phenomenal pastoral effectiveness, and that "Of all the Works that I ever attempted, this yielded me most Comfort in the Practice of it."[16] He confessed that before the implementation of parish catechizing, he "only catechized them in the Church; and conferred with, now and then, only occasionally." Thus, before Baxter came to the recognition that catechizing was clearly indispensable for procuring genuine reformation, it seems that he catechized his flock more occasionally. However, as the Worcestershire Association pastors declared their resolution to catechize all ages and by families, Baxter purchased catechisms for each household within his parish. Thus, before any catechizing effort could be fruitful, Baxter and his associating

---

[13] Literally "the rule of Christ." It was also the title of Martin Bucer's treatise on the way a truly reformed church should look, which, as William Black argues persuasively, was a shaping influence in Baxter's own vision of the ministry. See Black, *Reformation Pastors*, chap. 4.

[14] Ian Green, *The Christian's ABC: Catechisms and Catechizing in England c. 1530-1740* (Oxford: Oxford University Press, 1996), pp. 131, 139, 222-27.

[15] Baxter, *Reliquiæ*, I:84.

[16] Ibid., II, §41, p. 179; *Gildas*, sig. B2r.

ministers in Worcestershire decided to "instruct our people in divers Sermons about the Nature of a Church." Baxter clearly understood that much of his pastoral effort would be nothing without a fundamental reconfiguration in regard to both the understanding and practice of the church, its membership, unity, purity and the crucial role of the pastor and parishioners.[17]

Richard Sargent, his curate for a number of years, delivered copies of the *Agreement of the Pastors in Worcester . . . for Catechizing* to the parishioners' homes.[18] In the *Agreement*, there was an appendix containing the Apostles' Creed, the Ten Commandments, and the Lord's Prayer, the triumvirate badge of orthodoxy, as espoused so passionately by Baxter himself, along with a much simpler (than the *Westminster Shorter Catechism*) version of a catechism with twelve questions and answers. Then after six weeks of study, Baxter and Richard Sargeant would embark on the work of private familial catechizing. Baxter had families come to him on Mondays and Tuesdays, an hour per family, and Sargeant went to the parishioners' homes himself on the same days. Thus between the two of them, they managed to catechize "about 15 or 16 families in a week, (that we may go through the parish [which hath above 800 families] in a year)."[19] For Baxter, catechizing became an integral pastoral component, for he was convinced that it was "a most helpful means of the conversion of souls," which would (1) "promote the orderly building up of those who are converted," (2) "make our public preaching better understood" and (3) "be much assisted in the admission of them to the sacraments."[20]

Baxter called upon the authority of the Westminster Directory of Worship as the semi-official enjoining authority for the work of catechizing: "It is the duty of the minister not only to teach the people committed to his charge in public, but privately, and particularly to admonish, exhort, reprove, and comfort them. . . . He is to admonish them in time of health to prepare for death." What is noteworthy is that Baxter took this injunction in the Westminster Directory pertaining to the visitation of the sick and widened its application to *all* parishioners.[21] In other words, the best way to prepare the saints for their everlasting rest was conversion, which was the ultimate aim of reformation. Perhaps no other writer or pastor before or since Baxter showed such an unswerving commitment to the centrality of conversion and its crucial linkage with parochial reformation. Baxter thought it en-

---

[17]Ibid.

[18]Baxter's letter to Thomas Wadsworth in late January 1656. See *Calendar*, nos. 290, 202.

[19]Baxter, *Gildas*, sigs A6v-A7r. Cf. *Reliquiæ*, II. §51, p. 179, where the figure seems to be "fourteen Families every Week" (2, §41, p. 179).

[20]Baxter, *Reformed Pastor*, pp. 174, 176-78.

[21]Ibid., 44.

tirely inappropriate to "come once into the Pulpit with any lower ultimate Ends then these. . . . And he that preacheth one Sermon for lower ultimate Ends then these, will . . . be unfaithful in that Sermon."[22] As Baxter was well acquainted with the early church fathers, he was convinced that the renewal of the catechesis was no pastoral innovation, but rather "simply the restoration of the ancient ministerial work."[23] He was convinced that preaching alone could not adequately bring in a reformation by conversion, for he was acutely aware that "that which is spoken to *all* or to *many*, doth seem to most of them as spoken to *none*."[24] Thus a more hands-on pastoral strategy was needed to awaken many sleeping souls. Regarding this issue, William Perkins, the famed Elizabethan Puritan, surprisingly identified the absence of an appropriate substitute for the Roman Catholic confessional as the Achilles' heel of the religion of Protestants:

> Again, if the Minister be to confess his peoples sins . . . then it follows also that they must discover & confess them unto him. . . . The want of this is a great fault in our Churches: for however we condemn Auricular confession . . . yet we not only allow, but call and cry for that confession, whereby a Christian voluntarily at all times may refer to his Pastor, and open his estate . . . and crave his godly assistance, and holy prayers.[25]

Patrick Collinson has argued that the collapse of the confessional and the continued existence of a diocesan system left a black hole of disciplinary problems in English Protestantism.[26] Baxter's solution was catechizing, which was arguably Baxter's Protestantization of the Catholic confessional. Thus he urged the intended readers to recognize that

> we have been led to wrong the Church . . . by the contrary extreme of the Papists'. . . . auricular confession; for, in overthrowing this error . . . we have run into the opposite extreme, and have led our people much further into it. . . . I have no doubt that the Popish auricular confession is a sinful novelty. . . . But . . . our common neglect of personal instruction is much worse.[27]

Consequently, catechizing was to facilitate a greater sense of accountability and

---

[22]Baxter, *True Christianity* (1655), p. 2.

[23]Baxter, *Reformed Pastor*, p. 174.

[24]Baxter, *A Sermon of Repentance* (1660), p.10.

[25]William Perkins, *Of the Calling of the Ministerie, Two Treatises* (1606), p. 21. I have modernized the Elizabethan spelling of the original text, e.g., "confesse" is rendered as "confess," "onely" as "only," "vnto" as "unto," and "discouer" as "discover," among others.

[26]Patrick Collinson, "Shepherds, Sheepdogs and Hirelings," in *The Ministry: Clerical and Lay*, ed. W. J. Sheils (Oxford: Blackwell, 1989), 216-20.

[27]Baxter, *Reformed Pastor*, pp. 179-80.

mutuality. It was only through catechizing that he could find out those who

> have been my hearers eight or ten years, who know not whether Christ be God or
> man, and wonder when I tell them the history of his birth and life and death, as if
> they had never heard it before. . . . I have found by experience, that some ignorant
> persons . . . have got more knowledge . . . in half an hour's close discourse, than they
> did from ten years' public preaching.[28]

Pastoral discipline. Another crucial factor in our properly contextualized understanding of *The Reformed Pastor* is Baxter's tireless emphasis on the necessity of pastoral discipline. Baxter was well aware of the impact of the separatist zeal upon the parochial church, especially in its greater laicizing tendencies within English religion of the 1640s and 1650s. As the separatists enjoyed pure ordinances in their gathered churches, Baxter chose a less trodden path: creation of a covenanted community within the parochial bounds. He acknowledged that disciplinary neglect among non-separating churches was directly responsible for the growth of separatism:

> *We* keep up separation, by permitting the worst to be uncensored in our churches, so
> that many honest Christians think they are obliged to withdraw from us. I have spo-
> ken with some members of the separated churches, who were moderate men, and
> have argued with them against separation; and they have assured me, that they were
> of the Presbyterian judgment . . . but joined . . . other churches from pure necessity,
> thinking that discipline, being an ordinance of Christ, must be used by all that can,
> and therefore, they durst no longer live without it when they might have it . . . and
> that they separated only *pro tempore*, till the Presbyterians will use discipline, and then
> they will willingly return to them again.[29]

To overcome what he saw as a disciplinary inertia among the majority of pastors in England, Baxter reiterated his conviction that "man should be ejected as a negligent pastor, that will not rule his people by discipline, as well as he is ejected as a negligent preacher that will not preach; for ruling I am sure is as *essential* a part of the pastor's office as preaching."[30] Previously, in *The Reformed Pastor,* Baxter offered a syllogistic reasoning for the necessity of discipline: "that to be against discipline, is near to being against the ministry," and to be against the ministry is tantamount to being implacably opposed to the church, and consequently, to be against the church was almost equivalent to "being absolutely against Christ."[31]

---

[28]Ibid., p. 196.
[29]Ibid., p. 168. See also, Baxter, *Christian Concord,* pp. 30-31.
[30]Baxter, *Reformed Pastor,* p. 171.
[31]Ibid., p.111.

In this regard, Baxter was, as he acknowledged in the original edition of *Gildas Salvianus*, greatly indebted to John Calvin and Jerome Zanchius whom he called *"the most godly, laborious, judicious Divines that most ever the Church of Christ had since the daies of the Apostle."* These two men wrote of the indispensable nature of discipline for the well-being (*bene esse*) of the church.[32] Elsewhere he cited Martin Bucer, who himself influenced both the Edwardian church and Calvin as well, as a proponent of disciplinary purity. During the Cromwellian era, due to its relatively *laissez faire* approach to religious affairs, many concerned pastors thought it impossible to implement discipline when the magistrate was not actively enjoining it. Although Baxter acknowledged the crucial role of the magistrate in encouraging godliness, he was equally convinced that the key to establishing godliness depended more on the pastors of local churches. Thus he spoke of the purity of the church before the Roman emperor Constantine made Christianity the official religion of his empire in A.D. 312:

> What had the Church of Christ done till the daies of *Constantine* the great, if it had no better Pastors then you that will not Govern it without the joint compulsion of the Magistrate? Discipline, and severe Discipline was exercised for three hundred years, where the Prince did not give them so much as a Protection, nor Toleration, but persecuted them to the death. Then was the Church at the best, and Discipline more pure and powerful.[33]

Unsurprisingly, then, Baxter was convinced that "too much interposition of the sword with our Discipline, would do more harm than good."[34]

In fact, when Baxter listed some crucial nonnegotiable elements of pastoral work, he emphasized discipline, along with laboring "for the conversion of the unconverted," giving advice on "cases of conscience," studying to "build up those who are already truly converted," keeping a "special eye upon families," and finally, "visiting the sick."[35] Closely related to this line of reasoning is Baxter's firmly held belief that "every flock should have its own pastor, and every pastor his own flock. . . . Though a minister is an officer in the church universal, yet is he in a special manner the overseer of that particular church which is committed to his charge."[36] For Baxter, then, the idea of a "congregational episcopate" was not oxymoronic; in fact, that was the best way to respond to the critique of the separatists.

---

[32]Baxter, *Gildas*, sig. B3r. Baxter quotes from Calvin's *Institutes* 4.12.1-2, 4-5, and from Zanchius's *De Ecclesia*. See *Gildas*, sigs. B3r-6v.

[33]Baxter, *Gildas*, p. 227.

[34]Ibid., p. 228.

[35]Baxter, *Reformed Pastor,* pp. 94-104.

[36]Ibid., p. 88.

Thus the consent of the parishioner was actively sought, as of one agreed to be under the pastoral care of the minister; this structure amounted to a creation—as numerous Presbyterians would criticize Baxter of doing—of an *ecclesiola in ecclesia* (chapel within church), in which covenanted members were recipients of more full-orbed pastoral care, including discipline. The idea of Christian community and mutuality could, in this setting, be more fully realized.[37] On the other hand, Baxter also emphasized the critically communal and congregational nature of pastoral discipline; it involved the whole community to pray for the repentance of the recalcitrant sinner:

> It will be meet that we beg the prayers of the congregation . . . entreating them to consider what a fearful condition the impenitent are in. . . . And, accordingly, let us be very earnest in prayer for him, that the congregation may be excited affectionately to join with us; and who knows but God may hear our prayers, and the sinner's heart may relent under them, more than under all our exhortations.[38]

Contrary to contemporary cultural misconception of discipline, Baxter clearly pointed out its restorative, rather than merely punitive, nature. Since discipline was always designed to "restore the penitent to the fellowship of the church," pastors were to avoid "too much severity," and assure those disciplined "of the riches of God's love, and the sufficiency of Christ's blood to pardon his sins," and finally to charge the church that "they imitate Christ, in forgiving and in retaining the penitent person; or, if he were cast out, in restoring him to their communion." This was to provide a concrete occasion for the whole congregation to imitate Christ (*imitatio Christi*), a practice of piety that Baxter regarded as of paramount significance.[39] Similarly, one of the last pieces of advice he had for the pastors who might attempt a similar program for reformation—through private instruction and catechizing—was equally tender and pastoral:

> Lastly, If all this will not serve to bring any particular persons to submit, do not cast them off; but go to them, . . . learn what their reasons are, and convince them . . . of the danger of their neglect of the help. A soul is so precious that we should not lose one for want of labour, but follow them while there is any hope. . . . Charity beareth and waiteth long.[40]

CONCLUSION

In 1656, Baxter wrote twice—once in *The Reformed Pastor*, and the other in a letter

---

[37]See Baxter, *Christian Concord*, Proposition XVIII, sig. B2r.
[38]Baxter, *Reformed Pastor*, p.108.
[39]Ibid., p. 109.
[40]Ibid., p. 237.

to Thomas Wadsworth, a pastor from Surrey—that "we never took the best course for demolishing the kingdom of darkness, till now."[41] He was convinced that the church was both a hospital and a school: healing and learning could only come through truth rightly taught and embodied.[42] In that regard, the role of the pastor, both as a role model for others and also as a shepherd and teacher, was absolutely crucial. Baxter often stressed in his writings that to teach the flock publicly and privately was more likely to bring the stillborn reformation to its desired end than abolishing episcopacy or implementing a specific form of church government.

The challenge for postmodern readers is this: do we value learning from others? In spiritual matters, how much need do we sense of transparent—and transforming—conversations in which our ignorance can be dispelled and the status of our soul gauged and guided? Secondly, we have seen that Baxter's vision of the Christian community certainly incorporated lovingly motivated measures that would protect the purity and beauty of the community. What of us? Despite the popularity of the word and concept of "community" in postmodern parlance, we find that the difficult measures of correcting the mistakes of those in egregious errors have never been easy, especially so when the ideal of truth has been eviscerated, leaving it awash in the sea of subjectivities and opinions. The general issue of the centrality of the catechesis in fostering true spirituality and the corresponding emphasis on purity through communal discipline would be helpful as we strive after the beauty of God's holiness and the alluring purity of the church of Jesus Christ. Baxter urged the pastors to "carry on all, even the most earnest passages, with clear demonstrations of love to their souls, and make them feel through the whole, that you aim at nothing but their salvation," so that "the increase of the purity and the unity of his churches" could be manifested.[43] That towering vision, although not realized in Baxter's time, provides a strange appeal for us all to take seriously the call to watch ourselves and to give ourselves in the service of others and ultimately of the Other, who has become incarnate as our shepherd, ultimately laying down his life for the sheep.

SELECT BIBLIOGRAPHY

Primary Sources

Baxter, Richard. *Gildas Salvianus: The Reformed Pastor.* London, 1656. Edited by William Brown. Reprint. Edinburgh: Banner of Truth Trust, 1989.

————. *Reliquiæ Baxterianæ.* Edited by Matthew Sylvester. London, 1696.

---

[41]Ibid., p. 43.
[42]Baxter, *Saints Everlasting Rest* (1650), p. 122.
[43]Baxter, *Reformed Pastor,* pp. 255, 256.

————. *The Autobiography of Richard Baxter.* Abridged by J. L. Lloyd-Thomas. London: Dent, 1974.

Keeble, N. H. and G. F. Nuttall, eds. *Calendar of the Correspondence of Richard Baxter,* 2 vols. Oxford: Oxford University Press, 1991.

Secondary Sources

Black, J. William. *Reformation Pastors: Richard Baxter and the Ideal of the Reformed Pastor.* Carlisle, U.K.: Paternoster, 2004.

Keeble. N. H. *Richard Baxter: Puritan Man of Letters.* Oxford: Oxford University Press, 1982.

Lim, Paul C. H. *In Pursuit of Purity, Unity, and Liberty: Richard Baxter's Puritan Ecclesiology in Its Seventeenth-Century Context.* Leiden: Brill, 2004.

Nuttall, G. F. *Richard Baxter.* London: Thomas Nelson, 1965.

❧ II ❧

COMMUNION WITH GOD

BY JOHN OWEN (1616-1683)

Kelly M. Kapic

DOES IT MAKE ANY DIFFERENCE THAT THE GOD CHRISTIANS CLAIM TO worship has revealed himself as triune—as Father, Son and Holy Spirit? Throughout the ages a strong affirmation of the Trinity has been regarded as a key indicator of faithfulness to biblical authority and authentic worship. Having said that, how often does the upholding of trinitarian doctrine make its way into the actual experience of the believer's fellowship with God? Does a believer's trinitarian affirmation actually inform that believer's communion with God?

WHY READ JOHN OWEN'S *COMMUNION WITH GOD*?

According to the Puritan John Owen (1616-1683), if we do not understand how our conception of the Trinity informs our conception of communion with God, the result will be that our worship will be impaired. We will devalue the divine persons—problematically pit them against one another—or we will end up creating an inappropriate internal hierarchy within the Godhead. I have become convinced that Owen can greatly assist the church in addressing these vital questions, questions too often neglected in the life of the church.

Called by some "the Calvin of England" and by others "the greatest of the Puritan scholastics," Owen is widely considered *the* theological giant among the Puritans.[1] Born in a home of Puritan persuasion, young John was educated at Queen's College, Oxford University, receiving first a B.A. and then an M.A. During his life Owen would minister in several churches, serve as a chaplain to Oliver Cromwell,

---

[1] Peter Toon, *God's Statesman: The Life and Work of John Owen: Pastor, Educator, Theologian* (Exeter: Paternoster, 1971), p. 173.

become dean of Christ Church, Oxford, and finally receive the high honor of becoming the vice chancellor of Oxford University from 1652-1657. The final decades of his life were spent ministering through his preaching and writings.

Although Owen is a fascinating historical and political figure in seventeenth-century English history, for our purposes his theological writings are most relevant; his books have consistently remained in print for more than three hundred and fifty years. Writing masterful doctrinal expositions on almost every key area of the Christian faith, Owen faithfully displays both theological depth and pastoral wisdom, even though his complex sentences and detailed outlining apparatus are taxing to the reader. Owen's massive corpus (containing twenty-four volumes in the standard nineteenth-century edition) continues to provide fresh insight and intellectual rigor.

Versed in both historic trinitarian debates and current controversies of his day, in his classic book *Communion with God* (1657) Owen will not allow a division of theological reflection and practical application. For him the two are inseparable.[2] Thus the affirmation that God is triune must necessarily have practical implications, and indeed, Owen argues this is the case, for we worship not an undifferentiated Godhead, but rather a God who is Father, Son and Holy Spirit.

Defining communion. In order to understand fully Owen's *Communion with God*, we begin with some attention to vocabulary. The word *communion*, as employed by Owen, has a particular flavor to it, constantly requiring the reader to be mindful of the relational matrix that Owen adopts. From the beginning, Owen argues that communion assumes the idea of *mutual relations*, and that there can be no communion where there is no participation. An example of such communion appears in the biblical portrait of the rich friendship between David and Jonathan (1 Sam 20:17).[3] Furthermore, Owen disagrees with Aristotle, who saw friendship with God as impossible. Those who have communion with God partake of "mutual communication in giving and receiving" in their relationship with God.[4] By introducing the idea of mutuality, one might be tempted to think that Owen places too much weight on human response and consequently devalues God's sovereign grace, but this would be a grave misreading of Owen's more nuanced position. Instead, Owen avoids the danger of both Arminianism (which can put the burden of a person's salvation on that individual's

---

[2]See Kelly M. Kapic, "Communion with God: Relations Between the Divine and the Human in the theology of John Owen" (Ph.D., diss., King's College London, 2001).

[3]John Owen, *The Works of John Owen*, ed. William H. Goold, 24 vols. (1850-1855; republished, Edinburgh: Banner of Truth Trust, 1965-1991), 2:8. For extensive historical and theological reflection on Owen's trinitarian theology as represented in his volume *Communion with God*, see Kapic, "Communion with God," esp. pp. 152-212.

[4]Owen, *Works*, 2:9.

own shoulders) and of an apathetic Calvinism (which can cause people to think their actions are irrelevant). After much detailed and somewhat technical elaboration regarding the term communion, Owen concludes that communion with God presupposes a person's union with God in Christ, and this leads us to a subtle but key insight that helps him avoid both extremes.

To appreciate Owen's nuanced position, a careful distinction between *union* and *communion* with God is required. Within the Calvinist Puritan tradition, union with God is unilateral in that it designates divine movement and action that prompts, secures and preserves a person in the life of faith. Once united to Christ, there can be no final falling away; nothing is able to tear apart what God has brought together—clearly the underlying theology for the doctrine of perseverance. However, communion with God can be deeply affected by a believer's sin, unresponsiveness to God and neglect of God's ordinary means of grace. Struggling believers are never at risk of losing their union with Christ, but they surely experience times when intimate communion with God feels blocked.[5] One must remember that during the seventeenth century "to commune" became associated with spiritual communication; or to use the common language, it describes "intercourse" with God.[6] Obviously this imagery is not new. It has a long theological history that many Puritans drew from, especially in their use of allegorical readings of Song of Songs.[7]

Union with Christ, allowing renewed communion with God, and expressing itself through obedience, is fundamental to Owen's understanding of the gospel. To experience the delight of communion between persons, it must be "bottomed upon some union between them," since union is the "foundation" of communion.[8] This distinction between union and communion helps prevent many Puritan theologians from formulating a justification by works doctrine, while at the same time allowing them to place a high value upon human responsiveness for those inside the house of faith. Placed within this historical background and theological framework, Owen's definition may now be properly understood. "Our Communion . . . with God consisteth in his communication of himself unto us, with our returnal unto him of that which he requireth and accepteth, flowing from that union which

---

[5] Cf. Calvin's vision of "two communions": the first (justification) is "total" while the second (sanctification) "grows." See Dennis E. Tamburello, "Union with Christ: John Calvin and the Mysticism of St. Bernard," *Columbia Series in Reformed Theology* (Louisville: Westminster John Knox, 1994), pp. 86-87.

[6] See C. T. Onions, ed., *The Oxford Dictionary of English Etymology* (Oxford: Clarendon, 1966), p. 196. Cf. J. A. Simpson and E. S. C. Weiner, eds., *The Oxford English Dictionary*, 2nd ed. (Oxford: Clarendon, 1989), 3:577, 580.

[7] Examples of Puritan reflections on the Song of Songs are plentiful. See Jean Dorothy Williams, "The Puritan quest for Enjoyment of God: An Analysis of the Theological and Devotional Writings of Puritans in Seventeenth Century England" (Ph.D. diss., University of Melbourne, 1997), pp. 177-203.

[8] Owen, *Works*, 2:8.

in Jesus Christ we have with him."[9] Divine action is first, union with Christ is the result, and human response is the desired consequence. Here Owen moves between the priority of God's self-revelation to the necessity of human response, the latter assumed possible based on a christological observation—only when united to Christ can a person enjoy communion with God.

Approaching the triune God. Yet how does a person enjoy communion with God as Father, Son, and Holy Spirit, without ending up with three different gods? Guiding Owen's perspective is the idea that our communion with God is always experienced in terms of our communion with the divine persons. In Owen's words, "there is no grace whereby our souls go forth unto God, no act of divine worship yielded unto him, no duty or obedience performed, but they are distinctly directed unto Father, Son and Spirit."[10] Although God is one, it is appropriate to recognize distinctions (although not separations) between the divine persons, thus allowing for distinct communion with each. When a believer has "distinctive" communion with one of the divine persons, the other divine "persons" are not excluded, "for the person, as the person, of any one of [the three], is not the prime object of divine worship, but as it is identified with the nature or essence of God."[11] The idea behind much of Owen's argument comes from a dictum commonly found in the early church, that the external acts of the triune God are undivided (*opera Trinitatis ad extra sunt indivisa*). To put it simply, God is the One who wills and acts, and this means that no divine Person functions as a maverick—the Son does not go off to do his own thing, or the Spirit will what is contrary to the Father and the Son. An example Owen gives is that of faith: it is *bestowed* on us by the Father, *purchased* for us by the Son and *worked* in us by the Holy Spirit.[12] As triune, God is and reveals himself to be Father, Son and Holy Spirit, and therefore we must approach him as such.

Throughout his writings, Owen uncompromisingly maintains that "God is one," the Father is Father of the Son, the Son is Son of the Father, and the Spirit is the Spirit of the Father and Son, which thus testifies to their "mutual relation" in which "they are distinct from each other."[13] What is most fascinating is that, in light of his monotheism, Owen never devalues communion with the persons, since that is communion with God. Owen's commitment holds together God's unity and distinction of divine persons.

---

[9]Ibid., 2:8-9.
[10]Ibid., 2:15.
[11]Ibid., 2:18.
[12]Ibid.
[13]E.g., Owen, *Works*, 2:377, 407. These references are both found in Owen's later work, *A Brief Declaration and Vindication of the Doctrine of the Holy Trinity* (1669).

Our access in our worship is said to be "to the Father;" and this "through Christ," or his mediation; "by the Spirit," or his assistance. *Here is a distinction of the persons, as to their operations, but not at all as to their being the object of our worship.* For the Son and the Holy Ghost are no less worshipped in our access to God than the Father himself. . . . *When, by the distinct dispensation of the Trinity, and every person, we are led to worship . . . any person, we do herein worship the whole Trinity;* and *every person,* by what name soever, of Father, Son, or Holy Ghost, *we invocate him.*[14]

Here, Owen maintains a trinitarian monotheism that provides the basis and parameters for the worshiping church, and in this way his message remains vitally relevant.[15]

Following the structure of Owen's book we will now take in turn an exploration of communion with each person of the Trinity.

COMMUNION WITH THE FATHER

How should a person conceive of and approach God the Father? The pastorally attuned Owen clearly recognizes a common experience among believers: Christians often believe Jesus loves them, but they fear the Father and therefore avoid him. The Father seems judgmental, harsh, distant and unapproachable.

Owen enters this discussion through a fascinating exegetical observation from the farewell discourse in John's gospel, where Jesus is speaking with the disciples and preparing them for his death and departure. Jesus anticipates that the disciples will ask him to pray to the Father for them, a request to which Jesus gives a most intriguing response: "I do not say to you that I will ask the Father on your behalf; *for the Father himself loves you*" (Jn 16:26-27).[16] What is going on here? According to Owen, the disciples are convinced of Jesus' love for them, but with his imminent departure their thoughts turn to the Father, and they find themselves uneasy—they have exceedingly "troubled hearts, concerning the Father towards them. . . . What is his heart towards them?"[17] In this particular passage, Jesus promises to pray for the Father to send the Comforter, who will bring the fruit of the triune God's love into the life of the believer. Owen makes it abundantly clear, however, that there is no need for Jesus to pray for the Father to love the disciples, since Jesus' very pres-

---

[14]Owen, *Works*, 2:269. Emphases mine. Cf. *Works*, 1:20-21. Owen sees this rule in many of the fathers, including Augustine in *Enchrid.* xxxviii: "Quando unus trium in aliquo opere nominatur, universa operari trinitas intelliguitur." English translation: "When one person of the three is named in any work, the whole Trinity is to be understood to effect it."

[15]Owen, *Works*, 1:20-21.

[16]Ibid., 2:20. Emphasis mine.

[17]Ibid., 2:21-22.

ence among them is testimony of the Father's already existent love.

In Owen's trinitarian theology of communion he will not fall into the trap of viewing the Father as full of wrath and Jesus as full of love. Instead, he consistently argues that the Father is the very "fountain" and "source" of love.[18] Out of this love the Father is prompted to send the Son and the Spirit, but their coming is the fruit of his love, rather than the source of it.

> Though there be no light for us but in the beams, yet we may by beams see the sun, which is the fountain of it. Though all our refreshment actually lie in the *streams*, yet by them we are led up unto the *fountain*. Jesus Christ, in respect of the love of the Father, is but the beam, the stream; wherein though actually all our light, our refreshment lies, yet by him we are led to the fountain, the sun of eternal love itself.[19]

Christians can rest and delight in God, because the Father has expressed his love in terms of rest and delight in them. But what does he mean by speaking of God resting in this sense? According to Owen, "to rest with contentment is expressed by being silent." Strangely, such silence is exactly what we find with the Father concerning his children. His love is "so full, so every way complete and absolute, that it will not allow him to complain of any thing in [believers] whom he loves, but he is silent on the account thereof . . . he will not seek farther for another object."[20] God delights in his children with an uncompromising and satisfied love.

With passionate language Owen captures the main characteristics of the Father's love.[21] He is convinced that it is eternal, thus not open to beginning and ending. Lest the eternal nature of God's love be misunderstood, Owen makes clear that the Father's love is also free: he loves not out of compulsion or necessity, not because there is something intrinsic in us which obligates him. God is not indebted to love, but rather it is an expression of his freedom, a freedom that is necessary for it to be conceived of as a gracious love. Furthermore, the Father's love remains unchangeable since it does not grow and wane.[22]

It must be clear that while there are similarities between human love for God and the reality of the Father's love, there are some striking differences that must be maintained.[23] First, drawing again from the image of an overflowing fountain, Owen sees the Father's love as one of *bounty*, while a believer's love is one of *duty*.

---

[18]Here he employs such texts as Rom 5:5, Jn 3:16, 2 Cor 13:11, etc.
[19]Owen, *Works*, 2:23. Emphasis in the original.
[20]Ibid., 2:25.
[21]Ibid., 2:33-34.
[22]Ibid., 2:29.
[23]Ibid., 2:28-31.

Behind all divine action Owen sees this key idea—God is motivated out of the depths and overflow of his love. Second, the Father's love is *antecedent* love, whereas a Christian's love is *consequential*. While God is by nature a lover of humanity (*philan-thropos*), fallen humans are by nature "haters of God" (*theostugeis*), a condition that can only be remedied by divine love. Here Owen is making a case found throughout his writings and common to the Reformed tradition: divine movement and grace always precede and provide the basis for human response. Slightly modifying Psalm 116:1, he proclaims, "we love the Lord, BECAUSE!" Third, love is always like one's character, and here we see a major difference between the Father and human-ity. "The love of God is like himself—equal, constant, not capable of augmenta-tion or diminution; our love is like ourselves—unequal, increasing, waning, grow-ing, declining." Owen uses this truth to bring pastoral comfort, for he knows that rarely does "a day stand" in which our love for God is not lost and then found growing again. Coming to an understanding of the depth of the Father's love, be-lievers are to respond in turn: "God loves, that he may be beloved." Communion with the Father "begins in the love of God, and ends in our love to him."[24]

Owen argues that the Father's love is made secure and known in the incarnate Son. "The Father communicates no issue of his love unto us but through Christ; and we make no return of love unto him but through Christ." The Father's love is clearly communicated to believers in Christ, and "our love is fixed on the Father; but it is conveyed to him through the Son of his love." If believers do not frame communion in this way, then they risk subverting the biblical truth that the only way to the Father is through the Son. "This is that which Christ came to reveal, God as a Father."[25]

COMMUNION WITH THE SON

When describing communion with the Father, Owen stresses the idea of love. Yet by doing this he is not denying the Son or the Spirit's love, since he freely ascribes this attribute to the other persons of the Trinity elsewhere.[26] His point is to stress what believers ought to think specifically of the Father, without taking away from the Son or the Spirit. In his discussion of the Son, Owen highlights the idea of grace (although this consistently moves him back to observations about Christ's love). It is not that the Father and Spirit are without grace—we are speaking of one God—but rather, "peculiar communion" with the Son is through grace. Owen in-

---

[24]Ibid., 2:29; 29-30; 31; 24.
[25]Ibid., 2:26-27; 23.
[26]E.g., Owen, *Works*, 2:35, 62, 63, 118, 342; 6:466; 9:522.

terprets John 1:14-17 as fully attesting to this reality: Jesus came in "grace and truth" and believers receive "grace upon grace," which means their fellowship is secured by his grace toward them. Likewise, the apostolic benediction, which refers to the *love* of God and the *fellowship* of the Holy Spirit, emphasizes this truth by speaking of the *"grace* of the Lord Jesus Christ."[27] Key to the grace of Christ is his revelatory function.

While creation itself reveals and testifies to many of God's "properties," only through Christ does one learn of God's pardon and mercy. God's particular "love unto sinners" is discovered in the gospel alone.[28] Beyond simply the property of God's love, one sees more clearly and "savingly" God's vindictive justice in the punishment of sin, his patience, wisdom and all-sufficiency.[29] In sum, to have a true knowledge of God one must look specifically to Jesus.

Additionally, only through Christ does a person gain a true knowledge of self, which includes a deeper knowledge of sin, righteousness and judgment. The Christ who sends his Spirit convinces the world of sin in a way that surpasses the conviction caused by the law and conscience.[30] Human sin and rebellion against God are so serious that the death of Jesus became necessary for fellowship between the divine and human to be reestablished. Apart from Christ there can be no "true saving knowledge of sin," for "in him and his cross is discovered our universal impotency, either of atoning God's justice or living up to his will."[31] Through Christ's life, death and resurrection sinners learn not only of their need to be freed from guilt, but also of their need to be "actually righteous." Just as clearly as Jesus on the cross demonstrates the reality of human sin, so through his life of obedience does he demonstrate true human righteousness.

Reflecting on the knowledge of God and of oneself gained through Christ naturally leads Owen to apply these ideas to a consideration of how, in Christ, one gains a knowledge of "walking with God." Just as in any relationship, fellowship with God necessitates an agreement between the two parties to walk together. Such an agreement, however, would be impossible had not Christ first taken away the cause and continuation of enmity, bringing reconciliation and establishing lasting peace with God. Since God remains wholly loving and just, one cannot approach the Father outside of the blood of Christ—to attempt such a thing would be to

---

[27]Owen, *Works*, 2:47. The Scriptures he uses are John 1:14, 16,17; 2 Cor 13:14.
[28]Owen, *Works*, 2:79, 81.
[29]Ibid., 2:83-91.
[30]Ibid., 2:95.
[31]Ibid., 2:101, 105.

undervalue the incarnation and death of Jesus.[32]

The Son's affection for believers. A common misconception of the Puritans suggests that they focused on their own subjective internal disorders to the neglect of an assurance gained through the objective person and work of Christ. Usually Calvin is contrasted at this point with later Calvinism, claiming the former was Christocentric while the latter was dangerously anthropocentric.[33] Challenging this stereotype, Owen's emphasis is on the objective reality of the Son's affection for believers, a truth he believes brings liberation.

There are four particular expressions of the Son's love and affection for believers: delight, valuation, compassion, and bounty.[34] Demonstrating an abundance of delight in believers, Christ values even the "meanest, the weakest, the poorest believer on the earth . . . more than all the world besides."[35] Willing to endure temptations and afflictions in the incarnation, the Son gains a "fellow feeling" with humanity, able to comfort believers "in his tenderness."[36] Furthermore, believers' responsive obedience is understood with the backdrop of Christ's bountiful love, which supplies all needed resources for those who seek to follow the Son.[37]

From his pastoral experience Owen is aware that unhindered communion with God is the exception rather than the rule. Consequently, Owen acknowledges that sin will always disturb the rest that believers have when they commune with the Son. Here he makes an important distinction: the problem is not that Christ's love fades or lessens with the believer's struggle against sin, but rather the soul becomes distracted by or entangled in sin and thus avoids communion. While communion is not purely a human act, it nevertheless takes seriously the human response to God's love—otherwise it ceases to meet the definition of *mutual* relations, which Owen established from the beginning. Once the restless soul again allows itself to ponder and accept Christ's goodness toward it, a new level of rest and alertness materializes, with a renewed obedience as the natural outflow. Christians tasting such communion seek to avoid temptations that can cause "disturbance of that rest and complacency" found in Christ, avoiding sin not out of fear, but out of a growing desire to have nothing between themselves and their Lord. "A believer that hath gotten Christ in his arms, is like one that hath found great spoils, or a pearl of price.

---

[32] Ibid., 2:107-8.

[33] The classic statement expressing this line of argument is found in R. T. Kendall, *Calvin and English Calvinism to 1649*, Oxford Theological Monographs (Oxford: Oxford University Press, 1979).

[34] Owen, *Works*, 2:118-54.

[35] Ibid., 2:136.

[36] Ibid., 2:141, 145.

[37] Ibid., 2:152-54.

He looks about him every way, and fears every thing that may deprive him of it."[38] The fear of the believer in this quotation is not that Christ is desperately trying to escape their grasp, for this is the Son who delights in his people. Rather, believers fear their own waywardness, knowing how often they have been lured by the world and distracted from Christ, only to realize much later how far they have gone from the one they once held so dear.

As noted above, one must not confuse a discussion of disrupted communion with that of undisturbed union. At no time is the believer's union with Christ at risk. Readers are encouraged to be careful in their communion with the Son not because the Son will arbitrarily depart, but because the human heart so easily strays. During times of darkness, the believer must willingly engage in self-examination, seeking to discover where he has gone wrong. Owen bases his reflections on the common allegorical reading of the Song of Songs. The woman of the story seeks the source of her spouse's absence: "Have I demeaned myself, that I have lost my Beloved? Where have I been wandering after other lovers?"[39] Beyond private introspection, use of the public means of grace (prayer, preaching and the sacraments) is encouraged. Furthermore, since this is not a question of objective reality (God remains lovingly disposed toward and delighted in the believer who is united to Christ) but of subjective experience, the despairing soul may also turn to a "faithful watchman" who may advise the struggling believer.[40] Here we find classic Puritan pastoral counseling: the troubled believer gains assurance of Christ's deep affection toward his followers from those further along in their pilgrimage.

Communion with Christ through purchased grace. Throughout Owen's writings one often comes across the terms *purchased* and *grace*, but only in this book does he put them together as a unit. This phrase serves as a basic summation of the work of Christ, particularly his obedience, his suffering of death and his continued heavenly intercession.[41] As the second Adam, Jesus needed to live a life of active obedience in order that he might take away believers' unclean robes and replace them with garments of righteousness.

Purchased grace is subdivided into three graces. First, Owen believes that purchased grace removes the alienation caused by sin and provides the grace of acceptance with God. Second, through the grace of sanctification the Son "makes us not

---

[38]Ibid., 2:126. Cf. Song of Songs 3:4.

[39]Owen, *Works*, 2:129.

[40]Ibid., 2:131. See Timothy J. Keller, "Puritan Resources for Biblical Counseling," *Journal of Pastoral Practice* 9, no. 3 (1988): 11-43.

[41]Owen, *Works*, 2:154-68.

only accepted but acceptable."[42] Third, the grace of privilege—another way of speaking of *adoption*—is discovered by communion with the Son through purchased grace.

Owen concludes his reflections on communion with the Son by outlining the fullness of fellowship with the Son made possible through adoption. Table 11.1, which captures the consequences of adoption, quickly illustrates the centrality of Christology as it informs Owen's overall approach to human communion with the triune God. [43]

Table 11.1. Owen's theology of fellowship with the Son

Fellowship in name	We are (as he is) sons of God
in title and right	We are heirs, coheirs with Christ
in likeness and conformity	We are predestined to be like the firstborn of the family
in honor	He is not ashamed to call us brethren
in sufferings	He learned obedience by what he suffered, and every son is to be scourged that is received
in his kingdom	We shall reign with him

Apart from Christ no union or communion can take place. In Christ the believer has the privilege to commune with God and to be transformed into his image, preparing to reign with him.

COMMUNION WITH THE HOLY SPIRIT

In the third and final section of the book, Owen turns his attention to the person and ministry of the Holy Spirit, and in doing so he follows his set pattern of drawing attention to what this means for the believer's communion with God. *Paracletos*, a Greek term used throughout the New Testament in reference to the Holy Spirit, can be rendered either *advocate* or *comforter*. Focusing on the latter title, Owen explores how it is that the Spirit brings comfort to Christians by first understanding who the Comforter is.

Scripture often refers to the Spirit as someone who is sent, a point Owen is quick to affirm. Owen affirms that the Father and the Son send the Spirit, but he fears that this truth might cause a neglect of the reality that the Spirit comes not

---

[42] Ibid., 2:170.
[43] Ibid., 2:222.

from necessity, nor compulsion, but freely. Just as the freedom of the Father is important to Owen, so also the freedom of the Spirit. Jesus declares that "If I go, I
will send him [the Spirit]," a promise that Owen understands to mean that the
Spirit's coming is of "his own will."[44] Thus he proclaims about the Spirit: "He, of
himself and of his own accord, proceedeth."[45] So although the Spirit has the authority of one sent by the Father and the Son, he comes voluntarily as an advocate
and comforter of believers. Although one might confuse this language of the Father
willing, the Son willing, and the Holy Spirit willing with trithesim, in fact it was
common to speak this way while also holding to the one will of God. God is free,
and he is free as Father, Son and Spirit:

> so the love of the Father in sending the Son is free, and his sending doth no ways
> prejudice the liberty and love of the Son, but that he lays down his life freely also; so
> the satisfaction and purchase made by the Son doth no way prejudice the freedom
> of the Father's grace in pardoning and accepting us thereupon; so the Father's and
> Son's sending of the Spirit doth not derogate from his freedom in his workings, but
> he gives freely what he gives. And the reason of this is, because the will of the Father,
> Son, and Holy Ghost, is essentially the same; so that in the acting of one there is the
> counsel of all and each freely therein.[46]

In other words, trinitarian speech requires one to uphold both truths: God wills,
and he wills as Father, Son and Holy Spirit, always in harmony and unity. Thus the
Spirit of God himself comes "freely," "voluntarily," and as God, he comes "powerfully."

With the above discussion in mind we will now be able to appreciate how Owen
handles the question of God's severity associated with sinning against the Holy
Spirit (cf. Mt 12:31-32; Mk 3:29; Lk 12:10). In this treatise, Owen is less concerned with what this sin is, than on why it is unpardonable. His answer is simple:
when you sin against the Spirit you uniquely sin against the triune God. Let us follow his logic. The Spirit does not come only by his own will or in his own name
(though this is not to deny his will and name), but rather "in the name and authority of the Father and Son, from whom and by whom he is sent." Owen adds:

> to sin against him is to sin against all the authority of God, all the love of the Trinity,
> and the utmost condescension of each person to the work of salvation. It is, I say,
> from the authoritative mission of the Spirit that the sin against him is peculiarly un-

---

[44]Ibid., 2:226.
[45]Ibid., 2:227.
[46]Ibid., 2:235.

pardonable;—it is a sin against the recapitulation of the love of the Father, Son, and Spirit.[47]

To sin against the Holy Spirit is to deny the fullness of God's loving movement toward fallen humanity. It is to accuse the triune God of not caring enough for his creation, to reject the outward operations of the "whole Trinity," in the end demonstrating "contempt" toward "their [i.e., Father, Son and Holy Spirit] ineffable condescension to the work of grace."[48] Such a rejection of God seems to Owen not only unthinkable, but unpardonable as well.

While the Holy Spirit is distinct from the Son, this distinction does not cause a chasm between the two. When the Spirit came after the incarnate Son's departure, he came to enable the remembrance of the things of Christ, overcoming frail minds and disjointed memories. Only when this testimony to the Son is recognized can the Spirit's role as Comforter be accomplished, for there is no true rest and consolation outside of Christ. Moving powerfully in believers' lives, the Spirit overcomes their despair when the "heavens are black over them, and the earth trembles under them," reminding them of the promises of Christ.[49]

Since the Spirit's work is always to glorify Christ, this provides a clear way to "test the spirits." Does a spirit bring the person and work of Christ, as attested to in Scripture, to one's mind? Does he glorify Christ? If a spirit gives "new revelations" which point away from Christ and the written word, then he is a false spirit.[50] The Spirit of God will never draw worship away from Christ, and if a spirit does, one may confidently assert that he is not the Holy Spirit: "we may see how far that spirit is from being the Comforter *who sets up himself in the room of Christ.*"[51]

By persuading believers of God's love expressed in the promises of Christ, the Spirit convinces them of God's particular kindness toward them. Capturing all of one's "faculties and affections" with this revelation, the Spirit brings delight to the weary soul.[52] Again, the Christian is equipped to test the spirits. The result of the Spirit's movement of "shedding God's love abroad" in one's heart is freedom in Christ, whereas a false spirit only brings bondage. Here Owen is taking a sideswipe at the "Enthusiasts" of his day, who "make men quake and tremble; casting them into an un-son-like frame of spirit, driving them up and down with horror and

---

[47]Ibid., 2:229.
[48]Ibid.
[49]Ibid., 2:236, 238.
[50]Ibid., 2:257.
[51]Ibid., 3:239. Emphasis added.
[52]Ibid., 2:240.

bondage, and drinking up their very natural spirits, and making their whole man wither away."[53] One must remember that William Sherlock, the later dean of St. Paul's and certainly not of Calvinistic leanings, includes Owen in the Enthusiasts' camp because of the somewhat mystical language he uses to describe intimacy with God.[54] But here is the fundamental difference: contrary to the tendency among Enthusiasts, Owen's "mysticism" affirms human faculties and sees communion only occurring through their proper operation. For Owen, the Holy Spirit engages all of a believer's natural faculties (mind, will, affections) as created in the image of God, whereas false spirits move against them. This helps explain why Owen reacted so harshly against two Quaker women, Elizabeth Fletcher and Elizabeth Homes, who caused a major stir at Oxford while Owen was vice chancellor. Both women seemed to act completely irrationally, according to Owen; Fletcher even removed her clothing and "walked semi-naked through the streets proclaiming the terrible day of the Lord."[55] Such behavior indicated, not a person acting like an Old Testament prophet, but someone following a false spirit.

Those who follow after false spirits are forced to deny their true humanity by suppressing their mind, will and affections, showing little physical control, and therefore attempting to commune with God in a manner outside of the original created order. Part of the Spirit's sanctifying work in believers is to renew—rather than suppress—their damaged faculties so that they are restored in a Godward direction. In Owen's mind, these false spirits inevitably bring cruelty and bondage rather than the freedom experienced when a believer is fully engaged—via his natural faculties—in communion with God. Instead of responding with fear and mistrust toward the spiritual, Owen boldly proclaims: "Let us be zealous of the gifts of the Spirit, not envious at them."[56]

CONCLUSION

In contemporary theology there has been what some have called a "renaissance" in trinitarian studies. Theologians from various traditions, such as T. F. Torrance, Wolfhart Pannenberg, Robert W. Jenson, Catherine Mowry LaCugna and Colin E. Gunton have all contributed to this exciting discourse by highlighting and building on the insights of past theological giants, including Gregory of Nazianzus, Augus-

---

[53]Ibid., 2:258. For an excellent sampling of seventeenth-century Enthusiasm, see Geoffrey F. Nuttall, *Studies in Christian Enthusiasm* (Wallingford, Penn.: Pendle Hill, 1948).

[54]William Sherlock, *Union and Communion with Him* (1678, 3rd ed.), pp. 88-119. See Kapic, *Communion with God: Relations Between the Divine and the Human*, pp. 158-61.

[55]Toon, *God's Statesman*, p. 76.

[56]Owen, *Works*, 2:256.

tine, Calvin and Barth.[57] Within the context of religious pluralism, creative attempts to explore the distinctiveness of the biblical God make sense. In the midst of renewed efforts to mine the history of trinitarian reflection, I suggest that Owen's *Communion with God* provides a rich, though much neglected, resource that will constructively add to this conversation, both in the academy and in the life of the Church. In creative form, Owen consistently encourages his readers to fellowship with God, and he accomplishes this by leading them to "peculiar" communion with Father, Son, and Holy Spirit. After all, he maintains, it is the Christian experience of God's love, grace and fellowship that points us to the triune reality of God. This Puritan's work challenges us to consider how impoverished our view of God becomes when we do not maintain a robust trinitarian consciousness. Throughout *Communion with God* Owen calls his readers to be unapologetically trinitarian, not in order to speculate about abstract metaphysics, but rather with the goal of finding a new understanding of and a delight in the living God.

SELECT BIBLIOGRAPHY

Primary Sources

Owen, John. *Communion with God* (Abridged). Carlisle, U.K.: Banner of Truth Trust, 1991. Part of The Treasures of John Owen for Today's Readers, a multivolume series printed by Banner of Truth and heavily abridged and edited by R. J. K. Law.

———. *The Works of John Owen.* Edited by William H. Goold. 24 vols. 1850-1855; republished, Edinburge: Banner of Truth, 1965, 1991. The standard collection of Owen's works, although the Banner edition omitted all of Owen's Latin writings and orations, thus rearranging and combining volumes sixteen and seventeen.

Secondary Sources

Ferguson, Sinclair. *John Owen on the Christian Life.* Edinburgh: Banner of Truth Trust, 1987.

Gleason, Randall C. *John Calvin and John Owen on Mortification: A Comparative Study in Reformed Spirituality.* Studies in Church History 3. New York: Peter Lang, 1995.

Kapic, Kelly M. "Communion with God: Relations Between the Divine and the Human in the Theology of John Owen." Ph.D. diss., King's College, University of Lon-

---

[57]E.g., Colin E. Gunton, *The Promise of Trinitarian Theology,* 2nd ed. (Edinburgh: T&T Clark, 1997); Robert W. Jenson, *Systematic Theology, Vol. 1: The Triune God* (New York: Oxford University Press, 1997); Catherine Mowry LaCugna, *God for Us: The Trinity and Christian Life,* 1st ed. (San Francisco: HarperSanFrancisco, 1991); Wolfhart Pannenberg, *Systematic Theology: Volume 1-3,* trans. Geoffrey W. Bromiley (Grand Rapids: Eerdmans, 1991-1998); T. F. Torrance, *The Trinitarian Faith: The Evangelical Theology of the Ancient Catholic Church* (Edinburgh: T & T Clark, 1988).

don, 2001.

Oliver, Robert W., ed. *John Owen: The Man and His Theology* (Phillipsburg, N.J.: P & R, 2002).

Rehnman, Sebastian. *Divine Discourse: The Theological Methodology of John Owen*. Texts and Studies in Reformation and Post-Reformation Thought. Grand Rapids: Baker, 2002.

Toon, Peter. *God's Statesman: The Life and Work of John Owen: Pastor, Educator, Theologian*. Exeter: Paternoster, 1971.

Trueman, Carl. *The Claims of Truth: John Owen's Trinitarian Theology*. Carlisle, U.K.: Paternoster, 1998.

❧ 12 ❧

PILGRIM'S PROGRESS

BY JOHN BUNYAN (1628-1688)

J. I. Packer

NEXT TO THE BIBLE, JOHN BUNYAN'S *PILGRIM'S PROGRESS* IS THE BEST-selling Christian book of all time.[1] At its first appearance (part one, 1678; part two, 1684), it was an instant hit, and it has never been out of print; there have been literally hundreds of editions and dozens of translations. By common consent it is Bunyan's masterpiece and a milestone in English literature, both sacred and secular. Yet, ironically, this book began as a distracting byproduct of something else. In the versified "Apology" prefacing part one, Bunyan explains:

> And thus it was: I writing of the Way
> And Race of Saints, in this our Gospel-Day,
> Fell suddenly into an Allegory
> About their journey, and the way to Glory,
> In more than twenty things, which I set down;
> That done, I twenty more had in my Crown,
> And they again began to multiply,
> Like sparks that from the coals of fire do fly.

Bunyan made notes and put them aside till he had completed what he was in the middle of, and then he turned to writing up this allegory, as we would say, for fun, to amuse himself through the long days in prison. Soon, though, he was set free, and the work was only completed after his release.

> But yet I did not think
> To show to all the world my Pen and Ink

---

[1] See S. H. Steinberg, *Five Hundred Years of Printing* (Baltimore: Penguin Books, 1966), p. 337.

In such a mode; I only thought to make
I knew not what; nor did I undertake
Thereby to please my Neighbor; no not I;
And did it mine own self to gratify.

He wrote it as an experiment (for he had written nothing like this before), as a novelty (for nobody else had either), and as a pastor's *jeu d'esprit*, almost a one-man game.

Neither did I but vacant seasons spend
In this my scribble . . .
Thus I set Pen to Paper with delight,
And quickly had my thoughts in black and white,
For having now my Method by the end,
Still as I pull'd, it came; and so I penn'd
It down; until at last it came to be,
For length and breadth, the bigness which you see.

The fantasy that had, as it were, whispered in his ear, "Write me," was now done: *Pilgrim's Progress* (part one) had come to birth.

Bunyan himself liked it; but because a parabolic presentation of holy things in the form of a racy adventure story was such a novelty in the world of Puritan culture, he saw need to ask around as to whether it would be wise to publish it. He got conflicting answers:

Some said, John, print it; others said, Not so:
Some said, It might do good; others said, No.

But finally the great John Owen, who had once told King Charles II that he would gladly trade all his learning for Bunyan's power to preach, arranged for his own regular publisher to put on the market the first edition, and thus Bunyan's success story began.

What sort of book is *Pilgrim's Progress*? Bunyan called it an allegory, and so from one standpoint it is. In the mind of Bunyan the pastor/preacher it grew as a series of connected cameos illustrating the application of all that he was concerned to teach about the Christian life. It stands, indeed, as a full-scale index in picture form to the entire range of the Puritan understanding of Christian existence. The themes and images in both parts are biblical, and all the ups and downs of real and phony Christianity are presented for the reader's instruction and self-assessment.

This Book is writ in such a Dialect,

As may the minds of listless men affect;
It seems a Novelty, and yet contains
Nothing but sound, and honest Gospel-strains.

Literary critics hail *Pilgrim's Progress* as a pioneer English novel, meaning by that a biographical fiction in which realistic characters and a dramatic plot combine to suck readers in and pull them along. They note that Bunyan's vividness in drawing characters, in composing for them what sounds like real-life dialogue, and in using man-in-the-street Anglo-Saxon—which has hardly dated at all—to tell his tale, is simply stunning, the more so for being instinctive, wholly unschooled and self-taught. Critics admire the way in which his Bible-echoing rhetoric reaches heights of poignancy and power, and how when the Bible's imagery fires his imagination the incantatory impact of his prose becomes spellbinding. Yet the supreme excellence of *Pilgrim's Progress* is as a didactic allegory setting forth Puritan profundities on spiritual life and death—as, in other words, the evangelistic and pastoral teaching tool that Bunyan meant it to be—and this is the wavelength on which we tune in to it now.

How does the allegory work? Allegory, the illustrative representation of one thing by another (word, sign, emblem or narrative, as the case may be) is for Bunyan a generic term covering parables, metaphors, "fancies" (fantasies) and "similitudes" of every sort. The "method" that Bunyan employed as he wrote was: First, to picture personal spiritual life as a pilgrimage—a trek to a religiously significant destination, in this case heaven, the Celestial City. Second, to develop Jesus' image of the pilgrim path as straight, narrow and taxing, by dotting it with dangers and false trails alongside its helps and helpers. Third, to follow real-life individuals bearing character-label names through the ups and downs of their travels along it, seeing sights, visiting places, overcoming obstacles, resolving problems and relating to friends, foes, fools and failures whom they meet en route. Bunyan's blend of allegorical with realistic scenes and characters, the latter either sharing real spiritual experiences with Christian (part one) and Christiana (part two) or modeling for our instruction the world's manifold mistakes about Christianity, yields a story that jolts the mind, haunts the imagination and searches the heart. The mixture of allegorical externals with spiritual authenticities, drawn from Bunyan's own experience both as seeker and as pastor, and spelled out in the characters' conversations, is what gives *Pilgrim's Progress* its unique flavor. Bunyan himself never equaled his achievement here: his other great allegory, *The Holy War*, packs far less of a punch than *Pilgrim's Progress* just because this distinctive ingredient is absent. What was first said of Tabasco sauce—"often imitated, never duplicated"—can be said of *Pilgrim's*

Progress too. Never was the Puritan understanding of the Christian life presented in a way so transparent, forthright, childlike, profound and in experiential terms so realistic and lifelike, as it is here.

ABOUT JOHN BUNYAN

Who was the man who gave us this jewel? Born in the village of Elstow in 1628, he joined a Baptist church in Bedford, moved there, and became one of its preachers in the 1650s, was its pastor from 1672, and died in London in 1688. Three particular things need to be said about him.

First, he was a Puritan to his fingertips. Sociologically, to be sure, he was a Puritan outsider. He was an artisan, a tinker, what in my youth was called a "blue-collar" worker to mark him off from "white-collar" people in the professions, and in Bunyan's day was called a "mechanick" for the same purpose. The core of the Puritan constituency was a brotherhood of university-educated preachers who favored some form of paedobaptist national church, and who themselves had status in the landowning segment of society. Bunyan, the self-educated preacher from the little Baptist church in Bedford, was something else, and apart from John Owen, the great exponent of the gathered-church polity that Baptists held to, Puritan leaders took no notice of him. Theologically, however, Puritanism was in essence a commitment to a Reformed piety that sought to make all life "holy to the Lord" by living it within a frame of personal conviction, Bible-based, Christ-centered and God-fearing devotion, and thorough sanctification of family, church and community life; and in this sense Bunyan was as much a Puritan insider as any. It is true, as historians like Christopher Hill underline, that Bunyan's mindset had in it something of the poor man's perkiness in deliberately deflating the privileged and well-heeled,[2] as well as of the pastor's sense that pride of place and possessions will in every case keep sinners from self-knowledge and so from true faith in Christ. Yet his mature view of godliness, as set forth in the sixty books he wrote during his thirty years of ministry (twelve of them in prison for nonconformity), is Puritan in every way.[3]

---

[2]Christopher Hill, *A Tinker and a Poor Man* (New York: Norton, 1990), pp. 16-25 and *passim*.

[3]Bunyan's whole works, doctrinal, devotional, allegorical, poetical and controversial, can be found in the three-volume, large-page, small-print edition of George Offor (Glasgow: Blackie, 1854; Edinburgh: Banner of Truth Trust, 1991), and in seventeen volumes of which Roger Sharrock was the general—and in four instances the specific—editor (Oxford: Clarendon, 1960-1994). Pagination of *Pilgrim's Progress* in these notes is from the Penguin English Library edition, ed. Roger Sharrock (Harmondsworth U.K.: Penguin, 1965), though in the extracts Bunyan's capitalization has been restored, in the belief that it often affords a clue to his intended emphasis. His overall emphasis and interest is made clear by his original title page, which reads: *The Pilgrim's Progress from This World, to that*

Second, Bunyan was a very able Puritan. The reason he was a tinker by trade was that he was his father's son; after a brief time at school learning to read and write, he was apprenticed to his brazier sire, evidently with the thought that he would in due course take over the family business. Plying his trade as an itinerant, however, going the rounds with portable anvil, tinderbox and tools on his back (doubtless the source of his later image of Christian burdened with unforgiven sin), he met the Bedford believers who set his feet on the path of life, and who some years later, when he had won through to firm faith, appointed him a preacher. In Bedford his preaching regularly drew hundreds, and in London up to three thousand at a time. From the sustained imaginative power that produced *Pilgrim's Progress*, and from the effortless flow throughout his work of the most forceful, down-to-earth, dignified colloquial English since William Tyndale, plus his power to produce edifying rhymes at the drop of a hat (granted, most were doggerel, but some of his verse is true poetry), it becomes obvious that Bunyan's natural ability—needing to be sanctified, certainly, but there from the start—was simply enormous.

Third, Bunyan was a Puritan who suffered. That in itself was hardly remarkable; all Puritans in the turbulent seventeenth century expected to suffer, and most did. Suffering, which the world would inflict out of malice and God would send and sanctify as a nurturing discipline, was par for the Puritan course. In *The Character of an Old English Puritane, or Nonconformist* (1646) John Geree writes that the Puritan saw all life as warfare—meaning what we would call spiritual warfare—and his motto as he squared up to it was *Vincit qui patitur* (he who suffers wins).[4] Inwardly, Bunyan suffered five years of intense agony as he sought an assured faith in Christ, and outwardly he suffered twelve years in jail between 1660 and 1672, with six months more in 1676-1677, for his nonconformity.

He was sent to jail because he would not stop preaching at the unauthorized, un-Anglican gatherings that in those days were called *conventicles*. Though in the ecclesiastical sense a layman, Bunyan had become Bedford's best-known and best-attended preacher; in 1660 the local magistrates decided to make an example of him, as a sign of their commitment to the restored Church of England. In prison Bunyan had no heating and slept on straw, but he enjoyed fair health, made himself a flute, wrote books, pastored the inmates and impressed everyone by his cheerful-

---

which is to come: *Delivered under the Similitude of a DREAM Wherein is Discovered, The manner of his setting out, His Dangerous Journey: and safe Arrival at the Desired Country.* (Facsimile in Sharrock, p. 29, and with minimal alteration for part two, p. 209.)

[4]Cited from Gordon Wakefield, *Puritan Devotion* (London: Epworth, 1957), p. x.

ness. The account he later wrote of his imprisonment is remarkably free from bitterness. He saw it as part of God's plan for him, and was content.[5]

GOOD THINGS

Puritan pastors, as physicians of the soul, responded to their particular situation—their listeners faced cultural instability and personal depression, and large numbers of them were yet unconverted—by preaching in a way designed to lead people along the path of assurance, joy, and peace in Christ. *Pilgrim's Progress* is a narrational, novelistic template of this ministry. The spiritual lives of such as Christian and Christiana and their companions as they progress through this world to glory embody the realities that were covered in this preaching and teaching, and their constant conversations monitor most aspects of the impact that the teaching made. The key themes of Bunyan's two-part story, and of the pastoral instruction that it reflects and represents, may be set out as follows.

The good word. It has been truly said that through Puritanism the English became the people of a book, namely the Bible, first in the Geneva version, then in the King James. The Bible was read as the Reformers had read it—as the inspired, infallible and authoritative Word of God, God's utterance to every reader, the true and trustworthy declaration of all that one needs to know for sound belief and the fullness of new life in and through Christ. That life was seen and lived as one of faith, hope, love, holiness, service and praise; and wisdom from the Bible, mediated through human teachers and personal reading, and inwardly grasped through the Holy Spirit's illumination, was the means of entering into it and adhering to it, despite opposition and distraction coming in many forms from the world, the flesh and the devil. The book in which Christian read of heaven and hell, and which he rated true "for it was made by him that cannot lie,"[6] also told him vis-à-vis the life of heaven that "if we be truly willing to have it, he (God) will bestow it on us freely,"[7] and extended to him divine promises to sustain him on his journey to it. These promises are pictured as the steppingstones through the Slough of Despond, the key that opens the exit doors from Giant Despair's Doubting Castle, and the crutches that

---

[5]The background to *Pilgrim's Progress* in Bunyan's own mind is found in *Grace Abounding to the Chief of Sinners* (1666), *The Life and Death of Mr. Badman* (1680), and *The Holy War* (1682). *Grace Abounding* and *Mr. Badman* were put together in an Everyman's Library volume (London: J. M. Dent, 1928); Roger Sharrock edited *Grace Abounding* (Oxford: Clarendon, 1962); *Mr. Badman*, with J. F. Forrest (Oxford: Clarendon, 1988); *The Holy War*, with J. F. Forrest (Oxford: Clarendon, 1980).

[6]Ibid., p. 44. Similarly, Faithful tells Hopeful "concerning that Book, that every jot and tittle thereof stood firmer than Heaven or earth," p. 181.

[7]Ibid., p. 45.

enabled crippled Mr. Ready-to-Halt to keep hobbling forward. We are to see these promises, then, as of prime importance for living a faithful—read that as faith-full—Christian life.

In part two the Puritan approach to the Bible is formulated explicitly in Prudence's catechizing of Matthew:

P.   What do you think of the Bible?

M.   It is the Holy Word of God.

P.   Is there nothing written there but what you understand?

M.   Yes, a great deal.

P.   What do you do when you meet with such places therein that you do not understand?

M.   I think God is wiser than I. I pray also that he will please to let me know all therein that he knows will be for my good.[8]

And three vivid images indicating the right use of the Bible also appear. First, Scripture is the *mirror* that Mercy asked for in the Shepherd's palace.

The Glass was one of a thousand. It would present a man one way, with his own Features exactly, and turn it but another way, and it would show one the very Face and Similitude of the Prince of Pilgrims himself. Yea I have talked with them that can tell, and they have said that they have seen the very Crown of Thorns upon his Head, by looking in that glass they have therein also seen the holes in his Hands, in his Feet, and his Side. . . . It will show him to one where they have a mind to see him; whether living or dead, whether in Earth or Heaven, whether in a State of Humiliation or in his Exaltation, whether coming to suffer, or coming to Reign.[9]

Second, Scripture is the *map* that Mr. Great-heart consulted, to avoid pitfalls on the Enchanted Ground.

He had in his pocket a Map of all ways leading to or from the Celestial City; wherefore he . . . takes a view of his Book or Map, which bids him be careful in that place to turn to the right-hand-way. And had he not been careful to look in his Map, they had all, in probability, been smothered in the Mud. . . .

Then thought I with myself, who that goeth on Pilgrimage, but would have one of these Maps about him, that he may look when he is at a stand, which is the way he must take.[10]

Third, Scripture is the *sword* with which Mr. Valiant-for-Truth fought off the

---

[8]Ibid., p. 276.

[9]Ibid., p. 345ff. Jas 1:23 is echoed.

[10]Ibid., p. 357.

three thieves, Wildhead, Inconsiderate, and Pragmatick. Great-heart recognized it as "a right Jerusalem blade," and the dialogue proceeds as follows:

> V. It is so. Let a man have one of these Blades, with a hand to wield it, and skill to use it, and he may venture upon an Angel with it. . . . Its Edges will never blunt. It will cut Flesh, and Bones, and Soul, and Spirit, and all.

> G. But you fought a great while, I wonder you was not weary?

> V. I fought till my sword did cleave to my Hand; and when they were joined together, as if a Sword grew out of my Arm, and when the Blood ran through my Fingers, then I fought with most Courage.

> G. Thou hast done well. Thou hast resisted unto Blood, striving against Sin.[11]

Central to Puritanism was prayerful reliance on the Bible as a God-given touchstone of spiritual truth, setting forth the person, place and grace of Jesus Christ as a source of vision, direction and strength for faithful discipleship to him; as a safe guide for Christians making decisions and ordering their lives; and as a powerful resource for resisting theological and moral error. *Pilgrim's Progress* shows all this clearly.

The good news. Puritanism was an evangelical movement shaped by the gospel as the Reformers had proclaimed it. That gospel, Bible based as it was, is best understood as Augustinianism adjusted. With great energy Augustine had echoed the biblical insistence on our natural inability in our fallenness to love God, or turn to him in repentance, or do anything meritorious in his sight, and had insisted that the faith, love and obedience he commands only ever appear when he himself works them in us. It follows that we who believe should praise God for the gift of our conversion no less than for the gift of the Savior himself. The Puritans agreed.

Bunyan's version of the good news highlights three things. The first two are the stages of what Luther called the wonderful exchange, namely first, the atoning death of Christ, in which our punishment was diverted on to his shoulders, and second, our justification through faith, in which we are clothed in his righteousness set as it were on our shoulders (the "broidered coat" given to Christian as he stood before the cross). The third aspect of the good news Bunyan highlights is the heart-changing effect of God's gift of faith in Christ. Bunyan works statements of these things into his story in several places, but they come together most directly in Hopeful's account of how Faithful pointed him to Christ and in what followed.

---

[11]Ibid., p. 349. Eph 6:17 and Heb 4:12 are echoed.

Faithful first explained atonement and justification:

H. He told me, That unless I could obtain the righteousness of a man that never had sinned, neither mine own, nor all the Righteousness of the World could save me.

C. And did you ask him what man this was, and how you must be justified by him?

H. Yes, and he told me it was the Lord Jesus. . . . Thus, said he, you must be justified by him, even by trusting to what he hath done by himself in the days of his flesh, and suffered when he did hang on the Tree. . . . He bid me go to him . . . for I was invited to come. . . . Then I asked him, What must I do when I came? And he told me, I must entreat upon my knees, with all my heart and soul, the Father to reveal him to me.

Faithful then taught Hopeful the Puritan equivalent of what nowadays is often called the sinner's prayer.

H. Then I asked him further, How I must make my supplication to him? . . . and he bid me say to this effect, God be merciful to me a sinner, and make me to know and believe in Jesus Christ. . . . Lord, I have heard that thou art a merciful God, and hast ordained that thy Son Jesus Christ should be the Savior of the World; and moreover, that thou art willing to bestow him upon such a poor sinner as I am. . . . Magnify thy grace in the Salvation of my soul, through thy Son Jesus Christ, Amen.

Hopeful prayed this way till he was given a strong sense that Christ was declaring to him his saviorhood and making clear that believing on him and coming to him were the same thing, so that "he that came, that is, ran out in his heart and affections after salvation by Christ, he indeed believed in Christ," and he realized that wholehearted trust in Christ as his own Savior had become a reality for him.

H. And now was my heart full of joy, mine eyes full of tears, and mine affections running over with love to the Name, People, and Ways of Jesus Christ.

C. This was a Revelation of Christ to your soul indeed. But tell me particularly what effect this had upon your spirit.

H. It made me see that God the Father, though he be just, can justly justify the coming sinner. It made me greatly ashamed of the vileness of my former life, and confounded me with the sense of mine own Ignorance; for there never came thought into my heart before now that showed me so the beauty of Jesus Christ.

It made me love a holy life, and long to do something for the Honour and Glory of the name of the Lord Jesus.[12]

---

[12] Ibid., pp. 180-83.

Bunyan underlines the cruciality of all this by at once bringing in Ignorance, the conventional self-deceived religionist, to whom Christian eventually has to say:

> Ignorant thou art of what Justifying righteousness is, and as ignorant how to secure thy Soul through the faith of it, from the heavy wrath of God. Yea, thou also art ignorant of the true effects of saving faith in this righteousness of Christ, which is [sic], to bow and win over the heart to God in Christ, to love his Name, his Word, Ways, and People: and not as thou ignorantly imaginest.[13]

That the good news continues with promises of ongoing help and final preservation to glory is also on occasion made plain. But the call for a deliberate turning to God, so as to seek and find the wicket-gate (the small doorway, narrow and often overlooked) through such a conversion as Hopeful describes, is the part of the message that Bunyan highlights. Since he wrote at a time when the need and nature of such a conversion was widely ridiculed and rubbished (Ignorance, to whom it was nonsense, Talkative, "a man whose Religion lies in talk," Formalist and Hypocrisy, who ignored the gate, and Worldly-Wiseman, who led Christian away from it, illustrate this), and since he wrote against the background of his own agonized five years of ups and downs in the conversion process, this emphasis is entirely understandable. Indeed, it is doubly so in light of its demonstrable centrality in the New Testament itself.

The good way. Both parts of Bunyan's narrative are about pilgrims following, or failing to follow, the path to the Celestial City that the New Testament itself calls the Way (Acts 9:2; 22:4; 24:14). *Pilgrim's Progress* is a road story, and like a road movie its episodes take place on, and are linked through, a journey to a destination. The Way begins with passage through the wicket-gate, where, having left the world behind, one knocks and is received and first becomes a Christian. At this entrypoint one's feet are set on the path of discipleship where soon one finds assurance of salvation (pictured as the sealed scroll that Christian received when, facing the cross, he was relieved of the burden of his sins). Then, still following the path, the believer makes strides toward holiness, observing these principles:

One must constantly labor to learn the spiritual truths by which one must live (as Christian did from Evangelist, an emblem of a gospel minister, and in the House of the Interpreter, a figure for the Holy Spirit as teacher, and in the Palace Beautiful, a picture of the local church, and from the Shepherds, a corporate embodiment of pastoral insight,

---

[13]Ibid., p. 188ff.

and also as Christiana did from Gaius, the hospitable veteran and wiseacre).

One must constantly counter one's spontaneous "inward carnal cogitations," which, says Christian, "are my grief: and might I but chuse mine own things, I would chuse never to think of these things more; but when I would be doing of that which is best, that which is worst is with me."

Prudence asks Christian how he fares in this continual conflict of thoughts.

P.   Do you not find sometimes, as if those things were vanquished, which at other times are your perplexity?

C.   Yes, but that is seldom; but they are to me golden hours, in which such things happen to me.

P.   Can you remember by what means you find your annoyances at times, as if they were vanquished?

C.   Yes, when I think what I saw at the Cross, that will do it; and when I look upon my broidered Coat, that will do it; also when I look into the Roll that I carry in my bosom, that will do it; and when my thoughts wax warm about whither I am going, that will do it.[14]

One must constantly resist all persuasions to leave the road (Demas, the Flatterer, etc.), all seductions by the world (Madam Wanton, Madam Bubble, etc.), all allurements into the self-serving ease and comfort of By-path Meadow (pictured as leading to incarceration by Giant Despair in Doubting Castle), and all temptations to become thoughtless and careless about eternal issues (pictured as going to sleep by the roadside). Christian tells By-ends the time-server:

You must go against Wind and Tide. . . . You must also own Religion in his Rags, as well as when in his Silver Slippers, and stand by him too, when bound in Irons, as well as when he walketh the Streets with applause.[15]

One must be prepared for constant buffetings from tears and threats of all kinds (Satanic attacks, pictured by Apollyon and the lions; Vanity-Fair, an emblem of unfriendly society; hostile energies here imaged as malevolent giants; and so forth). These cannot be avoided; they have to be faced and overcome. God provides pilgrims with armor "of proof" (that is, of tested quality), but they themselves must come to terms with their own fears and actually fight, and that is something that proves to be necessary over and over again. As Bunyan versifies:

---

[14]Ibid., p. 83.
[15]Ibid., p. 137.

> A Christian man is never long at ease,
> When one fright's gone, another doth him seize.[16]

And as Christian, fighting his way up the hill called Difficulty, declares:

> This hill, though high, I covet to ascend;
> The difficulty will not me offend;
> For I perceive the way to life lies here;
> Come, pluck up, Heart; let's neither faint nor fear;
> Better, tho' difficult, th'right way to go,
> Than wrong, though easy, where the end is woe.[17]

One must practice repentance regularly. When Mr. Skill's pills, made up from the flesh and blood of Christ "with a Promise or two" and some salt (a purge and emetic for the poison of sin), had cured Matthew of the life-threatening "Gripes" brought on by eating fruit from the devil's garden, the physician told Christiana:

> These Pills are good to prevent Diseases, as well as to Cure when one is sick. . . . If
> a man will but use this Physick as he should, it will make him live for ever. But . . .
> thou must give these Pills no other way but as I have prescribed; for if you do, they
> will do no good.

"Fasting, in half a quarter of a Pint of the Tears of Repentance," was how Skill said Matthew must take them, and Bunyan repeats this in his margin to make sure we shall not miss the point.[18] Christ's death can benefit us no further than we repent of our sin as we invoke it, and clearly Bunyan believes we should be doing this over and over again.

One must value and practice fellowship constantly. Every Christian needs peer friendship and companionship; it is not good for any of us to be alone. Bunyan shows this by giving Christian first Faithful and then Hopeful as a fellow traveler and conversation partner, and by giving Christiana Mercy as a companion along with Greatheart as a guide and friend. They share their testimonies, and tell tales of others on the pilgrim path, and much spiritual wisdom emerges as they do so. That this is more than Bunyan's narrative device for getting edifying exchanges into the text appears from the verse he inserts when Christian and Hopeful resolve on "good discourse" to keep them from going to sleep in the enchanted grounds, the land of drowsy and soporific air:

---

[16]This couplet is not printed in Sharrock's edition. I cite it from the older Oxford Standard Authors text (Oxford: Oxford University Press, 1904), p. 58.

[17]Sharrock, *Grace Abounding*, p. 74.

[18]Ibid., pp. 280-82. Bunyan's margin reads: "In a Glass of Tears of Repentance."

When Saints do sleepy grow, let them come hither,
And hear how these two Pilgrims talk together:
Yea, let them learn of them, in any wise.
Thus to keep ope their drowsy slumb'ring eyes.
Saints' fellowship, if it be manag'd well,
Keeps them awake, and that in spite of hell.[19]

Thus Bunyan enforces our need for fellowship as we travel the Christian path, which is the way of life.

The good guide. Bunyan, a working pastor himself, was largely a product of the pastoral ministry of John Gifford, who discipled and baptized him and under God shaped his mind on all the main matters of faith and life. Gifford died in 1655; in 1672 Bunyan became his successor as minister of Bedford Baptist Church. "Holy Mr. Gifford," as Bunyan called him,[20] was evidently the model for at least three of the characters in *Pilgrim's Progress.* The first is Evangelist, who directed Christian to the wicket-gate and twice reappeared to redirect him when he needed it. The second is the "very grave Person" with "the best of Books in his hand" and the World "behind his back," whose portrait Christian saw in the house of the Interpreter, "one of a thousand" who "can beget Children, travail in birth with Children, and nurse them himself when they are born."[21] The third is Mr. Great-heart, the Interpreter's heroic servant, who is appointed as guide to Christiana and her family and couriers them with others all the way to the river of death, explaining dangers, teaching faith and killing giants (figures of menace and fear) as they travel; finally seeing the pilgrims one by one safely through the river, to be welcomed into the Celestial City.

Those who joined Great-heart's party on the road were a mixed bag. Traveling with old Mr. Honest, Mr. Valiant-for-Truth and Mr. Stand-fast, all of whom could stand spiritually on their own feet and fight off any who attacked them, was also sickly Mr. Feeble-mind, rescued in the nick of time from Giant Slay-good, lame Mr. Ready-to-halt, who could only move slowly, and on crutches, and fear-ridden Mr. Despondency, the starving prisoner in Doubting Castle, with his daughter, Much-afraid. But Great-heart took care of them all. Bunyan means us to see him as the model pastor, showing at this point the patience and kindness that every pastor should maintain toward needier souls in the congregation who require of them special attention and more than a fair share of their ministry time. Most congrega-

---

[19]Ibid., p. 176. This is where Hopeful tells his conversion story.
[20]*Grace Abounding*, secs. 77, 117.
[21]Bunyan, *Pilgrim's Progress*, p. 60.

tions have such members (it has always been so), and all pastors must be ready to serve them as necessary.

Great-heart's protective leadership of Christiana's party, a natural enough feature in a story that comes from a time when women did not take long journeys on their own, is actually making the spiritual and theological point that over and above at least one "bosom friend," to use the standard Puritan phrase, all Christians need and should humbly accept a pastor's oversight and care. This becomes explicit when the Interpreter explains to Christian the significance of the portrait of the "very grave Person":

> His work is to know and unfold dark things to sinners. . . . The Man whose Picture this is, is the only Man, whom the Lord of the Place whither thou art going, has authorized to be thy Guide in all difficult places thou mayest meet with in the way: wherefore take good heed to what I have shewed thee, and bear well in thy mind what thou hast seen; lest in thy Journey thou meet with some that pretend to lead thee right, but their way goes down to death.[22]

Only in part two do we see this principle in action, but it is clearly a major part of Bunyan's message.

The good end. Death was everyone's near neighbor in Puritan England. Many adults died young, more than half the children born died before they reached their teens, and ordinarily everyone died at home, conscious to the last and in the presence of family and friends, who hung on their dying words as likely to be specially solemn and revealing. The Puritans taught that a life lived well, to the glory of God, should be rounded off by dying well, to the glory of God, and they sought to explain how. The agenda was not new: medieval scripts on the art of dying had abounded and the theme had been pursued in Protestant England in such works as William Perkins's *Salve for a Sick Man* and Jeremy Taylor's *Holy Dying.* The title page of both parts of *Pilgrim's Progress* promises an unfolding of the pilgrims' "safe arrival at the desired country," and that required deathbed and heavenly welcome scenes to conclude the story. Bunyan's inbuilt literary and ripened didactic instincts combined to show him the way to do this in each case.

Throughout part one, the emphasis is on difficulties and dangers, so it is no surprise that Christian, crossing the river together with Hopeful, should be depicted as having a difficult death. Memories of past sins, and "apparitions of Hobgoblins

---

[22]Ibid., p. 61, cf. Bunyan's comment as he narrates Christiana's journey through the Valley of the Shadow of Death: "You cannot imagine, how many are killed here about, and yet men are so foolishly venturous, as to set out lightly on Pilgrimage, and to come without a Guide," p. 296.

and Evil Spirits" pressed him down. Hopeful encouraged him:

> These troubles and distresses, that you go through in these waters, are no sign that God hath forsaken you, but are sent to try you, whether you will call to mind that which heretofore you have received of his goodness, and live upon him in your distresses. . . . Be of good cheer, Jesus Christ maketh thee whole.
>
> And with that, Christian brake out with a loud voice, Oh I see him again! And he tells me, When thou passest through the waters, I will be with thee, and through the Rivers, they shall not overflow thee. Then they both took courage, and the enemy was after that as still as a stone, until they were gone over.[23]

Then Bunyan concludes part one celebrating the glory of celestial Jerusalem, to which they had now come, and so Christian's story comes to an end.

Throughout part two, however, the emphasis is on pastoral care rather than personal adventures, and its set piece climax is a series of deathbed close-ups of different pilgrims, one after another, dying out of their present life, into the glory beyond. He pulls out all the stops, and the poignancy of his blend of allegory and realism becomes almost unbearable. The vivid imagery of terminal old age in Ecclesiastes 12 is woven into the narrative as (so to speak) we stand by each bedside in turn. Last words are recorded. Says Christiana: "I come Lord, to be with thee and bless thee." Says Mr. Ready-to-Halt: "Welcome life." Says Mr. Feeble-mind: "Hold out Faith and Patience." Says Mr. Despondency, the archetypal depressive, having abjured his "Desponds and slavish Fears" as "Ghosts," and now entering the river with his daughter Much-afraid: "Farewell Night, Welcome Day." ("His Daughter went through the River singing, but none could understand what she said.") Says Mr. Honest, "Grace Reigns." Says Mr. Valiant-for-truth: "Death, where is thy Sting? Grave, where is thy Victory?" ("And all the Trumpets sounded for him on the other side.") Last in line, and "about half way in," Mr. Stand-fast declares:

> The Waters indeed are to the Palate bitter, and to the Stomach cold, yet the thoughts of what I am going to, and of the Conduct that waits for me on the other side, doth lie as a glowing Coal at my Heart. . . . I am going now to see that Head that was Crowned with Thorns, and that Face that was spit upon, for me. . . . I have formerly lived by Hear-say and Faith, but now I go where I shall live by sight, and shall be with him in whose company I delight myself.

Then come his last words: "Take me, for I come unto thee."[24]

---

[23]Ibid., p. 198ff.
[24]Ibid., pp. 365-73.

Bunyan wants us to realize that, from one standpoint, death-day is the most momentous occasion of any Christian's life, and so writes as to convince us that this is so. The result is the most powerful few pages he ever put on paper.

CONCLUSION: FANTASY AND FACT

"I only thought to make / I knew not what." Thus Bunyan, of his composing of part one. Our age, the era of C. S. Lewis's *Narnia*, J. R. R. Tolkien's *Lord of the Rings*, Charles Williams's power myths, Madeleine L'Engle, Ursula Le Guin, *Star Wars* and *Harry Potter*, has accustomed us to the kind of story that Bunyan tells, in which real people are set in relationships in more or less imaginary, unreal worlds, and has given us a name for it: we call it *fantasy*. But unlike other fantasies, Bunyan's tale is allegorical to a degree: it is, in fact, a narrative presentation of the rock-bottom realities of spiritual life and death, as they always were and still are. Basically, it is a pastor's didactic device for anchoring God's truth in human hearts.

> Art thou forgetful? Wouldest thou remember
> From New-year's-day to the last of December?
> Then read my fancies, they will stick like Burrs,
> And may be to the Helpless, Comforters.[25]

As now we know in scientific terms, good communication involves both lobes of the brain together, the left for logic and the right for every form of imagination. By this standard our Lord Jesus Christ, whose word-pictures were all arguments and whose arguments were all parabolic and pictorial, was a supreme communicator. And on a lower level, Bunyan already saw the benefit of presenting theology imaginatively and dramatically and in personal relational terms, as well as logically.

> I also know, a dark Similitude
> Will on the Fancie more itself intrude,
> And will stick faster in the Heart and Head
> Than things from similes not borrowed.[26]

For two centuries *Pilgrim's Progress* was the best-read book, after the Bible, in all Christendom, but sadly it is not so today. When I ask my classes of young and youngish evangelicals, as I often do, who has read *Pilgrim's Progress*, not a quarter of the hands go up. Yet our rapport with fantasy writing, plus our lack of grip on the searching, humbling, edifying truths about spiritual life that the Puritans under-

---

[25]Ibid., p. 37.
[26]Ibid., p. 215.

stood so well, surely mean that the time is ripe for us to dust off *Pilgrim's Progress* and start reading it again. Certainly, it would be great gain for modern Christians if Bunyan's masterpiece came back into its own in our day. Have you yourself, I wonder, read it yet?

SELECT BIBLIOGRAPHY

Primary Sources

Keeble, N. H., ed. *Pilgrim's Progress.* World's Classics. Oxford: Oxford University Press, 1984.

Sharrock, Roger, ed. *Pilgrim's Progress.* Penguin English Library. Harmondsworth: Penguin, 1965. Although there are many editions of *Pilgrim's Progress*, this and the following edition are perhaps the best.

Wharey, J. B., ed. *Pilgrim's Progress.* 2nd ed. revised by Roger Sharrock. Oxford: Clarendon, 1960.

Secondary Sources

Brown, John, rev. F. M. Harrison. *John Bunyan 1628-1688: His Life, Times and Work.* London: Hurlburt, 1928. The standard large life.

Cheever, G. B. *Lectures on The Pilgrim's Progress and on the Life and Times of John Bunyan.* Edinburgh: Blackie, 1872. An elderly classic.

Davies, Gaius. *Genius, Grief and Grace.* Fearn, U.K.: Christian Focus, 2003. See chapter 2, pp. 53-90.

Greaves, R. *John Bunyan.* Grand Rapids: Eerdmans, 1969.

Hancock, Maxine. *The Key in the Window: Marginal Notes in Bunyan's Narratives.* Vancouver: Regent College Publishing, 2000.

Hill, Christopher. *A Tinker and a Poor Man.* New York: Norton, 1990.

———. *A Turbulent, Seditious and Factious People: John Bunyan and his Church, 1628-1688.* Oxford: Clarendon, 1988. The British edition of the preceding item.

Kaufman, U. M. *The Pilgrim's Progress and Traditions in Puritan Meditation.* New Haven, Conn.: Yale University Press, 1966.

Keeble, N. H., ed. *John Bunyan—Conventicle and Parnassus: Tercentenary Essays.* Oxford: Clarendon, 1988.

Mullett, Michael. *John Bunyan in Context.* Pittsburgh: Duquesne University Press, 1997.

Sharrock, Roger, ed. *The Pilgrim's Progress: A Casebook.* London: Macmillan, 1976.

Talon, Henri. *John Bunyan.* London: Rockliff, 1951. The best all-round introduction.

Wakefield, Gordon. *Bunyan the Christian.* London: HarperCollins, 1992.

❧ 13 ❧

A BODY OF DIVINITY

BY THOMAS WATSON (D. 1686)

William S. Barker

THE AUTHOR OF *A BODY OF DIVINITY*, THOMAS WATSON, WAS A PURITAN pastor in London from 1646 until near the time of his death in July 1686. Active in the tumultuous times of the English Civil War and the Westminster Assembly of the 1640s, the Commonwealth of Oliver Cromwell in the 1650s, the Restoration of the Monarchy in 1660, the Great Ejection of many nonconforming ministers in 1662 and the subsequent persecutions of Puritan nonconformists into the 1680s, he was recognized as a popular preacher who was called upon to speak on some significant public occasions.

The exact date and place of his birth are unknown, but he was educated at Emmanuel College, Cambridge, receiving his B.A. in 1639 and his M.A. in 1642.[1] After preaching at Hereford in 1641, he resided for some time with the family of Mary Vere, the widow of Sir Horace Vere, Baron Tilbury, who had been military leader of the English Protestant forces in the Netherlands. Lady Vere, whose religious views were "of Dutch complexion," and thus favored Parliament in the Civil War, nevertheless had the care of King Charles I's children (Elizabeth and Henry) for a short time in the spring of 1645.[2]

In 1646 Watson married Abigail, daughter of John Beadle, rector of Barnston, Essex.[3] In the same year he was appointed rector of the parish of St. Stephen's, Wal-

---

[1] Iain Murray, ed., *Sermons of the Great Ejection* (London: Banner of Truth Trust, 1962), p. 113.

[2] *Dictionary of National Biography*, ed. Leslie Stephen and Sidney Lee, 22 volumes (London: Oxford University Press, 1908-1909), 20:238, under "Vere, Sir Horace."

[3] Hamilton Smith, ed., "Biographical Introduction," in *Gleanings from the Past: Extracts from the Writings of Thomas Watson* (London: Central Bible Truth Depot, 1915), reprinted as *Gleanings from Thomas Watson* (Morgan, Penn.: Soli Deo Gloria, 1995), p. xi.

brook, in the heart of London. For nearly sixteen years he served there as a faithful pastor, known for his effective preaching and also for his public prayer. Dr. Edmund Calamy told of the time "when the learned Bishop Richardson came to hear Watson at St. Stephen's and was much pleased with his sermon, but especially with his prayer after it, so that he followed [Watson] home to give him thanks, and earnestly desired a copy of his prayer. 'Alas!' (said Mr. Watson) 'that is what I cannot give, for I do not use to pen my prayers; it was no studied thing, but uttered, *pro re nata*, as God enabled me, from the abundance of my heart and affections.' Upon which the good bishop went away wondering that any man could pray in that manner extempore."[4]

Watson was of Presbyterian convictions. After Cromwell's Colonel Pride had purged Parliament of its Presbyterian members, because of their willingness to negotiate with the king, on December 6, 1648, Watson was nevertheless selected, along with the Independent Thomas Brooks, to preach before the "Rump Parliament" on December 27. Whereas Brooks urged that justice be done to malefactors (meaning the king), Watson warned Parliament that all things were naked to the eye of God. Significantly, Parliament authorized the printing of Brooks's sermon, but not that of Watson.[5] He joined some sixty Presbyterian ministers in a remonstrance to Cromwell and the council of war against the death of Charles I, who was, however, executed on January 30, 1649. In 1651 Watson was implicated in the plot of fellow Presbyterian minister Christopher Love to negotiate with Charles II, then in Holland, against the Commonwealth. Love was executed by Cromwell, but Watson and some other ministers were released after several months' imprisonment in the Tower, and on June 30, 1652 he was formally reinstated as vicar of St. Stephen's, Walbrook.[6]

Upon the restoration of the monarchy in the person of Charles II in 1660, Watson continued at St. Stephen's until the Great Ejection of some 2000 Puritan ministers on St. Bartholomew's Day, August 24, 1662, when he was among those who could not agree to the Act of Uniformity. Sunday, August 17 he delivered two farewell sermons to his congregation (from Jn 13:34 and 2 Cor 7:1), and a third on

---

[4]Quoted in C. H. Spurgeon, "Brief Memoir of Thomas Watson," in Thomas Watson, *A Body of Divinity* (London: Banner of Truth Trust, rev. ed. 1965, reprinted from the 1890 edition), p. viii.

[5]William Haller, *Liberty and Reformation in the Puritan Revolution* (New York and London: Columbia University Press, 1955), pp. 336, 383 n. 23. Hugh Trevor-Roper calls this "one of the boldest sermons that was ever uttered to the Long Parliament" (*The Crisis of the Seventeenth Century* [New York and Evanston, Ill.: Harper & Row, 1968], pp. 334-35); cf. John F. Wilson, *Pulpit in Parliament* (Princeton, N.J.: Princeton University Press, 1969), pp. 95, 155-57.

[6]*Dictionary of National Biography*, ed. Leslie Stephen and Sidney Lee, 22 volumes (London: Oxford University Press, 1908-1909), 20:949, under "Watson, Thomas."

the following Tuesday from Isaiah 3:10-11. In the second of these he said:

> I have now exercised my ministry among you for almost sixteen years; . . . I have received
> many signal demonstrations of love from you. Though other parishes have exceeded
> you in number of houses, yet I think, none for the strength of affection. I have with
> much comfort observed your reverent attention to the word preached; you rejoice in
> this light, not for a season, but to this day. I have observed your zeal against error in a
> critical time, your unity and amity. This is your honour. If there should be any inter-
> ruption in my ministry among you, though I should not be permitted to preach to you
> again, yet I shall not cease to love you, and to pray for you. But why should there be any
> interruption made? Where is the crime? Some, indeed, say that we are disloyal and se-
> ditious. Beloved, what my actions and sufferings for his Majesty has been is known to
> not a few of you. However, we must go to heaven through good report and bad report;
> and it is well if we can get to glory though we press through the pikes.[7]

In spite of legal penalties Watson and other nonconformists managed to
preach from time to time in a variety of secret places. As the English Presbyterians divided between the "Dons" and the "Ducklings" after the Five Mile Act of
October 1665, Watson belonged to the latter group, those who "did not fear the
water," or who were willing to take the plunge in breaking the law and setting up
conventicles.[8] After the great fire of London in 1666, when many of the churches
were burned, he fitted up a large room for public worship for any who wished to
attend. Upon the Declaration of Indulgence in 1672, he obtained license for use
of the great hall in Crosby House, on the east side of Bishopsgate Street in London. He preached there for several years, Stephen Charnock becoming copastor
with him of the Presbyterian Church at Crosby Hall from 1675 until Charnock's
death in 1680.[9] Watson published several works in the 1650s and 1660s, but his
Body of Divinity, published posthumously in 1692, probably represents some
three-and-a-half years of his preaching on Sunday afternoons at the Crosby Hall
church before his own death.[10] His health failed in the mid-1680s, and he retired
to Barnston in Essex, where he died suddenly while at prayer and was buried in
the grave of his father-in-law, John Beadle, on July 28, 1686.

---

[7] Watson, *Sermons of the Great Ejection*, pp. 136-37; also quoted by Spurgeon, "Brief Memoir," pp. ix-x, in Watson, *Body of Divinity*.

[8] C. G. Bolam and Jeremy Goring, "The Cataclysm," in C. Gordon Bolam et al., *The English Presbyterians: From Eliz-abethan Puritanism to Modern Unitarianism* (Boston: Beacon, 1968), p. 87.

[9] *Dictionary of National Biography*, 2:134, under "Charnock, Stephen"; William Symington, "Life and Character of Charnock," in Stephen Charnock, *Discourses Upon the Existence and Attributes of God*, 2 vols. (1853; reprint, Grand Rapids: Baker, 1979), I:7-8.

[10] Watson, *Body of Divinity*, p. 5.

A BODY OF PRACTICAL DIVINITY

Thomas Watson's best-known work was originally published in 1692 as *A Body of Practical Divinity*. It consists of 176 sermons based on the *Shorter Catechism* produced by the Westminster Assembly of Divines in 1647. The modern edition available to-day was published in three separate volumes by the Banner of Truth Trust in Edin-burgh and Carlisle, Pennsylvania, as *A Body of Divinity* (1958), *The Ten Commandments* (1959) and *The Lord's Prayer* (1960), all reprinted from the 1890 edition which was superintended by Rev. George Rogers, principal of Charles Haddon Spurgeon's Pastors' College, who reported:

> The style has been modernized, so far as could be done without detracting from its own peculiar characteristics. Long sentences have been divided into two or three, when it could be done without injury to the clearness or force of the signification. Modern words have been substituted for such as had become obsolete; Latin quota-tions restored to their correct form, as far as their sources could be ascertained; and divisions of subjects more perspicuously arranged.[11]

Spurgeon stated in this 1890 edition concerning the original one-volume folio of 1692, "For many a year this volume continued to train the common people in theology, and it may still be found very commonly in the cottages of the Scottish peasantry."[12] There were numerous subsequent editions, including one in London (1838) and one in New York (1855).

The *Westminster Shorter Catechism* is the most concise statement of the theology of the Assembly which met from 1643 to 1648 to provide a clarified declaration of the Ref-ormation doctrines of the English Church and produced also the fuller Westminster Confession of Faith and Larger Catechism. These documents were adopted by the Parliament in England, where they had temporary official standing, and also by the Church and Parliament of Scotland, where they had more lasting influence among Presbyterians, but also among Congregationalists and Baptists in America and all the English-speaking world. Generations of believers in such circles have been brought up on the Shorter Catechism and thus have had their piety shaped by the doctrine that Thomas Watson expounded in the three volumes of *A Body of Divinity*.

Watson follows the general outline of the Shorter Catechism as indicated in its third question and answer, "The Scriptures principally teach what man is to believe concerning God, and what duty God requires of man." Volume one goes up through Q. & A. 38, covering "what man is to believe concerning God." Watson

---

[11]Quoted in Spurgeon, "Brief Memoir," in Watson, *Body of Divinity*, pp. xi-xii.
[12]Spurgeon, "Brief Memoir," p. xi.

treats the classic definition of the chief end of man ("to glorify God and to enjoy him forever") and then the doctrine of Scripture as the foundation. Then almost one-third of the volume is on "God and His Creation," with a detailed treatment of the attributes of God, then God's unity, the Trinity, and creation and providence. Under "The Fall" Watson deals with the covenant of works, sin, Adam's sin, original sin, and man's misery by the Fall. Under "The Covenant of Grace and the Mediator," Watson describes Christ's prophetic, priestly and kingly offices, giving twice the space to the priestly office as to each of the others, before covering Christ's humiliation and exaltation. Under "The Application of Redemption" Watson deals with faith, effectual calling, justification, adoption, sanctification and assurance, then breaks out from "the benefits of redemption" separate sections on peace, joy, growth in grace and perseverance, thus showing his special concern for the practical application of doctrine. Finally, he deals with the death of the righteous and the resurrection.

In volume two, "The Ten Commandments," covering Catechism questions 39-98, Watson moves into the latter half of what "the Scriptures principally teach" with the "duty that God requires of man." After introductory sections on obedience and love, he describes at length the preface to the Ten Commandments, and then deals with each one of the Commandments in turn. The second Commandment, on worship, and the fourth Commandment, on the sabbath, receive the longest treatments, in characteristic Puritan fashion. Then, under "The Law and Sin," he deals with humanity's inability to keep the moral law, degrees of sin, and the wrath of God. Finally, under "The Way of Salvation," he treats faith, repentance, and then in separate sections the means of grace: the Word, baptism, the Lord's Supper, and prayer.

In volume three, "The Lord's Prayer," covering Catechism questions 99-107, Watson takes up the preface to the Lord's Prayer and then each of the six petitions in turn. The fact that this third volume has more pages (332) than either volume one (316 pages) or volume two (245 pages), even though it covers far fewer catechism questions than the others, shows Watson's emphasis on the Christian's piety in terms of worship and private devotion.

Although Watson follows closely the outline and content of the Shorter Catechism, he typically begins a section with an exposition of Scripture. Then the Scripture quotations and allusions tend to tumble over each other in his development of a doctrinal topic. Other sources that frequently come into play are church fathers—including Irenaeus, Tertullian, Cyprian, Athanasius, Ambrose, Basil, Jerome, Chrysostom and Gregory the Great, but especially Augustine—and also Reformers such as Luther, Oecolampadius, Melanchthon, Calvin, Bullinger and Beza. He includes even medieval figures such as Anselm, Bernard, Aquinas, and other Scholastics, plus more recent theologians such as William Perkins, Joseph Scaliger and Hugo Grotius. Mingled with these are numerous references to classical sources, including Socrates, Plato, Aristotle, Plutarch, Caesar and others. The fruit of Watson's diligent study at Emmanuel College, Cambridge is clearly displayed.

As learned as Watson was, his style was that of a popular preacher. He is eminently readable, racy and rich with abundant illustrations from common life of the time or from biblical or classical literature. He is also repetitious in a way that can be as tedious as ringing the changes on church-tower bells or as beautiful and interesting as Brahms's *Variations on a Theme by Haydn*.

A taste of some of his aphorisms may whet the appetite of the potential reader. "In the Word we hear God's voice, in the sacrament we have his kiss."[13] "Let us pray that God will preserve pure ordinances and powerful preaching among us. Idolatry came in at first by the want of good preaching. The people began to have golden images when they had wooden priests."[14] Commenting on distractions during sabbath worship, he says: "Does it not please Satan to see men come to the word, and as good stay away? They are haunted with vain thoughts; they are taken off from the duty while they are in it; their body is in the assembly, their heart in their shop."[15] "Prayer is the gun we shoot with, fervency is the fire that discharges it, and faith is the bullet which pierces the throne of grace. Prayer is the key of heaven, faith is the hand that turns it."[16] Speaking of a person's particular besetting sin, he says: "Men can be content to have other sins declaimed against; but if a minister put his finger upon the sore, and touches upon one special sin, then *igne micant oculi* [their eyes flash with fire], they are enraged, and spit the venom of malice."[17] Comparing the glory of creation and the glory of redemption, he says:

> Great wisdom was seen in making us, but more miraculous wisdom in saving us. Great power was seen in bringing us out of nothing, but greater power in helping us when we were worse than nothing. It cost more to redeem than to create us. In creation it was but speaking a word (Psa cxlviii 5); in redeeming there was shedding of blood. I Pet i 19. Creation was the work of God's fingers, Psa viii 3, redemption was

---

[13] Watson, *Body of Divinity*, p. 21.

[14] Watson, *Ten Commandments* (Edinburgh: Banner of Truth Trust, rev. ed. 1965, reprinted from the 1890 edition), p. 64.

[15] Ibid., p. 111.

[16] Watson, *The Lord's Prayer* (Edinburgh: Banner of Truth Trust, rev. ed. 1965, reprinted from the 1890 edition), p. 32.

[17] Ibid., p. 117.

the work of his arm. Luke i 51. In creation, God gave us ourselves; in the redemption, he gave us himself. By creation, we have life in Adam; by redemption, we have life in Christ. Col iii 3. By creation, we had a right to an earthly paradise: by redemption, we have a title to a heavenly kingdom.[18]

These are but a few samples of his eloquence and of the vivid analogies that tend to come in almost every paragraph.

Always concerned with the practical application of doctrine, Watson is not without a polemical side. Frequently he contrasts the biblical teaching with that of Roman Catholicism or Islam ("the Pope" or "Papist," "the Turk"), that of the Arminians or the Antinomians, or that of the Anabaptists or the Socinians. There is an awareness of false teaching in the knowledge that right behavior or practice finds its foundation only in scriptural truth.

THEOLOGICAL ANALYSIS

The theology of Watson and *A Body of Divinity* is standard seventeenth-century Calvinism. This is to be expected since his work is an exposition of the Westminster Shorter Catechism. As such it furnishes a helpful elaboration on the Westminster standards for those desiring deeper interpretation of the Catechisms and Confession of Faith. For example, on the question of preparation for salvation, he says concerning effectual calling: "Before this effectual call, a humbling work passes upon the soul. . . . Conviction is the first step in conversion."[19] In regard to assurance, he says: "the heart must be ploughed up by humiliation and repentance, before God sows the seed of assurance."[20] On the other hand, in answer to the question "How may deserted souls be comforted who are cast down for want of assurance?" he answers "(1.) Want of assurance shall not hinder the success of the saint's prayers," and "(2.) Faith may be strongest when assurance is weakest" and "(3.) When God is out of sight, he is not out of covenant."[21] Here is his definition of assurance:

> It is not any vocal or audible voice, or brought to us by the help of an angel or revelation. Assurance consists of a practical syllogism, in which the word of God makes the major, conscience the minor, and the Spirit of God, the conclusion. The Word says, "He that fears and loves God is loved of God"; there is the major proposition; then conscience makes the minor, "But I fear and love God"; then the Spirit makes

---

[18]Watson, *Ten Commandments*, p. 96.
[19]Watson, *Body of Divinity*, p. 224.
[20]Ibid., p. 252.
[21]Ibid., pp. 256-57.

the conclusion, "Therefore thou art loved of God"; and this is what the apostle calls "The witnessing of the Spirit with our spirits, that we are his children" Rom viii 16.[22]

Like the Westminster Confession and Catechisms, *A Body of Divinity* reflects the structure of covenant theology, with sections on the "Covenant of Works" and the "Covenant of Grace." Its section on the doctrine of adoption reflects Westminster's unique inclusion of this element in a confessional statement along with justification and sanctification. In his exposition of the second Commandment, Watson expresses what would later become "the regulative principle of worship":

> Avoid superstition, which is a bridge that leads over to Rome. Superstition is bringing any ceremony, fancy, or innovation into God's worship which he never appointed. It is provoking God, because it reflects much upon his honour, as if he were not wise enough to appoint the manner of his own worship. He hates all strange fire to be offered in his temple. Lev x I.[23]

Watson's view of Communion is that in the Lord's Supper there is a real spiritual presence of the Lord, in contrast to the Roman Catholic view of transubstantiation: "We say, we receive Christ's body spiritually."[24] Faith is the instrument for the believer's reception of Christ: "Faith makes Christ present to the soul. The believer has a real presence in the sacrament."[25] On the role of the law in the believer's life, Watson provides eight rules for rightly interpreting the Ten Commandments that correspond fairly closely to the eight rules of interpretation that are given in the Larger Catechism question 99. In almost all respects Watson's work is perfectly consistent with the Westminster Assembly's position.

In some places he so expands on the Shorter Catechism's teaching that he signals some personal distinctive tendencies. His exposition of the second petition of the Lord's Prayer, "Your kingdom come," constitutes almost one-third of the volume on the Lord's Prayer and practically amounts to a theological treatise on its own. He rings the changes on the kingdom of grace and the kingdom of glory: "The kingdom of grace is glory in the seed, and the kingdom of glory is grace in the flower. The kingdom of grace is glory in the daybreak, and the kingdom of glory is grace in the full meridian. The kingdom of grace is glory militant, and the kingdom of glory is grace triumphant."[26] Toward the conclusion of this section he pro-

---

[22]Ibid., p. 251.
[23]Watson, *Ten Commandments*, p. 63.
[24]Ibid., pp. 225-26.
[25]Ibid., p. 237.
[26]Watson, *Lord's Prayer*, p. 59.

vides "twenty-three persuasives or arguments to exert and put forth your utmost diligence for obtaining the kingdom of heaven."[27] These are similar in spirit to the "twenty directions" he gave to his parishioners "as advice and counsel with you about your souls" in his second farewell sermon to the St. Stephen's, Walbrook congregation in the Great Ejection of 1662, and which can be given here more concisely:

1. I beseech you, keep your constant hours every day with God.
2. Get good books in your houses.
3. Have a care of your company.
4. Have a care whom you hear.
5. Follow after sincerity.
6. As you love your souls, be not strangers to yourselves.
7. Keep your spiritual watch.
8. You that are the people of God, often associate together.
9. Get your hearts screwed up above the world.
10. Trade much in the promises.
11. To all you that hear me, live in a calling.
12. Let me entreat you to join the first and second tables of the law together, piety to God, and equity to your neighbor.
13. Join the serpent and the dove together, innocence and prudence.
14. Be more afraid of sin than of suffering.
15. Take heed of idolatry.
16. Think not the worse of godliness because it is reproached and persecuted.
17. Think not the better of sin because it is in fashion.
18. In the business of religion serve God with all your might.
19. Do all the good you can to others as long as you live.
20. Every day think upon eternity.[28]

These counsels were given in a time of crisis, but they represent the advice of Watson for every day of a believer's life and also commend *A Body of Divinity* for every generation in which it is read.

CONCLUSION

Three traits of *A Body of Divinity* stand out for application to the church of this generation of the twenty-first century. One is the importance of doctrinal truth. Watson's primary concern is for application to the Christian's life, yet he constantly rec-

---

[27]Ibid., p. 145; cf. p. 136.
[28]Watson, *Sermons of the Great Ejection*, pp. 137-45.

ognizes that truth is the foundation for behavior; doctrine must come before life. Hence *A Body of Divinity* is a compact and readable version of systematic theology and Christian ethics.

A second distinctive trait of great usefulness to Christians today is Watson's recurring emphasis on meditation. This is a key to private devotion. It is not enough to hear sermons, engage in small-group Bible studies, or even to read the Word for oneself. One must also develop the ability to meditate on God's truth, to reflect on all that God has done, is doing and will do, on those things that transcend the natural and material, on eternity.

A third characteristic distinctive of Watson's *A Body of Divinity* is his emphasis on what he terms "the ordinances." These are the means of grace—the Word, the sacraments and prayer. And these are to be found preeminently in the fellowship of the church, in the regular services of worship on the sabbath. In all these respects, *A Body of Divinity* is indeed a Puritan classic that has ministered God's truth to generations and can continue to do so for those still to come.

SELECT BIBLIOGRAPHY

Primary Sources

Watson, Thomas. *A Body of Divinity: Contained in Sermons Upon the Westminster Assembly's Catechism*, first published as part of *A Body of Practical Divinity*, 1692. London: Banner of Truth Trust, 1958. Revised edition, 1965; reprinted from the 1890 edition.

———. *The Lord's Prayer*, first published as part of *A Body of Practical Divinity*, 1692. Edinburgh and Carlisle, Penn.: Banner of Truth Trust, 1960. Revised edition, 1965; reprinted from the 1890 edition.

———. *The Ten Commandments*, first published as part of *A Body of Practical Divinity*, 1692. Edinburgh and Carlisle, Penn.: Banner of Truth Trust, 1959. Revised edition, 1965; reprinted from the 1890 edition.

Secondary Sources

Bolam, C. Gordon, et al. *The English Presbyterians: From Elizabethan Puritanism to Modern Unitarianism*. Boston: Beacon, 1968.

Kevan, Ernest F. *The Grace of Law: A Study in Puritan Theology*. Grand Rapids: Guardian, 1976.

Lloyd-Jones, D. M. *The Puritans: Their Origins and Successors*. Edinburgh and Carlisle, Penn.: Banner of Truth Trust, 1987.

McGee, J. Sears. *The Godly Man in Stuart England: Anglicans, Puritans, and the Two Tables, 1620-1670*. New Haven, Conn., and London, 1976.

Trevor-Roper, Hugh. *The Crisis of the Seventeenth Century: Religion, Reformation and Social Change*. New York and Evanston, Ill.: Harper & Row, 1968.

Wilson, John F. *Pulpit in Parliament: Puritanism During the English Civil Wars, 1640-1648*. Princeton, N.J.: Princeton University Press, 1969.

❧ 14 ❧

THE MYSTERY OF PROVIDENCE
BY JOHN FLAVEL (1628-1691)

Sinclair B. Ferguson

I KNOW THE DATE EXACTLY, BECAUSE IT WAS MY TWENTY-FIRST BIRTH-day. The presents included a heavy parcel from two of my closest friends. Inside was the then recently republished six-volume set of *The Works of John Flavel.*[1] Thus I was introduced to a centuries-old, gold-rich mine of biblical and practical Christian wisdom.

Among several outstanding works from Flavel's pen, none speaks with more power than his *Divine Conduct: or, The Mystery of Providence.*[2] The doctrine of divine providence occupies a major place in classical Puritan practical theology and interpretation of the Christian life. It stands out for its insightful, biblical and pastorally sensitive realism. Here is truly a Puritan and spiritual classic.

JOHN FLAVEL: A SKETCH OF HIS LIFE

Born in 1627, the elder son of a Puritan minister, John Flavel went on to study at the University of Oxford. In April 1650 he was settled as an assistant minister in Diptford, Devon, and ordained to the ministry by the local presbytery some six months later. In 1656 he received and accepted (at some loss of income) a call to Dartmouth. Six years later (1662), along with two thousand other ministers who shared his Puritan convictions, he was ejected from his living. Prohibited by the Five Mile Act (1665) from residing in the area, he continued to minister in what-

---

[1] John Flavel, *The Works of John Flavel*, 6 vols. (1820; republished, Edinburgh: Banner of Truth Trust, 1968).
[2] First published in 1678 and reprinted in *Works*, 4:336-497. A paperback version, slightly edited, is also in print: *The Mystery of Providence* (Edinburgh: Banner of Truth Trust, 1963). References in the footnotes are to page references in *The Works*.

ever way he could. Meanwhile his parents, at that time settled in London, were arrested and confined in Newgate Prison. There they contracted the plague (rampant in 1665), and although bailed, both died of the disease.

Restrictions on Puritan ministers were eased following the Declaration of Indulgence (1672) and Flavel returned to Dartmouth until renewed persecution again took him away from his beloved people. In 1687 he was again reunited with them and continued to minister until his death on June 26, 1691. Married four times, he suffered the bereavement of three wives, the first of them in childbirth.

PURITAN MINISTRY

Flavel illustrated the Puritan vision of the godly minister and faithful preacher.[3] Sitting under his weekly preaching must have been a rich and nourishing spiritual privilege. He models the preaching method defined by the Westminster divines with its hallmarks:

1. An introduction to the text
2. An analysis of the main points it teaches
3. An exposition of these truths involving

    *   Clear explanation of how the truth arises *from this particular text*

    *   A straightforward explanation of the doctrine taught in the text, employing other carefully selected passages to confirm it, if necessary.

    *   Helpful illustrations of the principle

    *   A sensitive dealing with any difficulties that might arise in the minds of hearers

4. Application, which may involve

    *   Dealing with intellectual error

    *   Explaining how we should respond to the teaching

    *   Showing what sins the text reveals and how we are to be delivered from them

    *   Showing how the text helps Christians who are troubled, fearful or doubting

---

[3]Well illustrated in John Bunyan's famous description of the picture in Interpreter's House of "a very grave Person ... eyes lifted up to Heaven, the best of Books in his hand, the Law of Truth ... written upon his lips, the World was behind his back; it stood as if it pleased with men, and a Crown of gold did hang over its head." J. Bunyan, *The Pilgrim's Progress* (1678, 1974; reprinted, Edinburgh: Banner of Truth Trust, 1977), p. 25.

- Providing "notes of trial," i.e., answering the question: "How do I know what this text teaches is true for me and of me?"

- This is to be done in plain speech, with wisdom, seriousness of purpose, in love for the congregation.[4]

DIVINE CONDUCT, OR THE MYSTERY OF PROVIDENCE

All of this comes to fine expression in *The Mystery of Providence*. First published in 1678 it is ostensibly an exposition of Psalm 57:2 ("I cry to God Most High, to God who fulfills his purpose for me"). The work focuses entirely on the idea that God fulfills his purposes for his people.

Flavel begins with a brief explanation of the text, but his chief interest lies in ransacking the Scriptures to provide a practical, pastoral summary of the doctrine of providence for his readers (and presumably earlier his listeners—the book still bears some of the marks of originally being a series of spoken addresses). King David's words underline the universal influence of providence in the Christian's life; the efficacy of God's purposes; the beneficial nature of all God does for his people as he fulfils his decrees. With David, believers should reflect on the providences of God in every stage and condition of life.

Of course, our present perception is imperfect and partial. Like the apostle Peter, we do not understand what our Lord is doing, but afterwards we will (Jn 13:7). We see providence now like the "disjointed wheels and scattered pins of a watch"—only in glory will we see the complete timepiece. God, by contrast, sees providence as a unified working reality, like an "accurate Anatomist discerning the course of all the veins and arteries of the body."[5]

Three aspects of biblical teaching and Christian experience are stressed: (1) The way in which God's providence operates in every aspect of our lives. (2) The Christian's responsibility to meditate on God's providences, with practical counsel on how to do so and on the blessings this brings. (3) The value of keeping a record of God's providences as an aid to ongoing Christian living.

PROVIDENCE GOVERNS THE WHOLE OF LIFE

One of Flavel's aims is to press home the privileges that God's providence had showered—as he saw it—on seventeenth-century England. He surveys ten kinds

---

[4]See *The Directory for The Publique Worship of God* (London, 1645), printed in *The Confession of Faith* (Inverness: F. P. Publications, 1981), pp. 379-81.

[5]Flavel, *Mystery*, p. 348.

of "performance" or "fulfillment" of providence, tracing God's activity from our formation and protection in the womb, through birth, the point in history at which we live, the family in which we are reared, the dangers from which we are preserved, the temptations from which we are protected and finally the ways in which providence enables us to overcome sin and live for the Lord's glory. The chief concern here is to say: "Do you not realize how blessed you are?"

But the providence of God takes on special significance in our conversion to Christ. Apparently random events lead individuals to faith. A visitor from Ethiopia meets an evangelist in the desert (Acts 8:26-39); a Syrian general has a captured slave girl who knows a secret of which he is ignorant (2 Kings 5:1-4); a woman makes her lonely noon-time journey to the city well and finds a thirsty stranger (Jn 4:1-42). The same patterns, Flavel believed, could be seen in the contemporary world; for the providence of God is not limited to biblical times. Spanish soldiers going to war enter German cities to conquer them and are brought to faith in Christ; a random piece of paper "happens" to explain the way of salvation; a romantic attraction brings someone into contact with a truly Christian family; a minister wanders from the main point of his sermon—and through his "chance" remarks someone is converted; a Christian is imprisoned, and a fellow prisoner is converted through his testimony; Christians are "tragically" persecuted and scattered; but by this means the gospel spreads. In all this God is absolutely and gloriously sovereign.

Even evil deeds can be the occasion for God's working. Flavel records one particularly gripping personal example. In 1673, a ship returning from Virginia anchored at Dartmouth. A young ship's surgeon, deeply depressed, cut his throat in a suicide attempt. As he lay dying, Flavel went on board and spoke to him about the gospel. It is not difficult to imagine the congregation on the edge of their seats as the story unfolded (it takes fully two pages in the written version). The firmness with which Flavel spoke to the young man is itself remarkable. He revisited him and spent many hours with him. The young man was converted and recovered. An attempt at suicide becomes the occasion for conversion. God turns evil to good. Other experiences may not be so spectacular; but they are no less supernatural.[6]

God's providence can also be traced in his ordinary blessings, for example in our employment. Flavel has in view not our self-satisfaction but our eternal blessing: "If you had more of the world than you have, your heads and hearts might not be

---

[6]Indeed, Flavel presses home the importance of thinking about this: "And now suffer me to expostulate a little with thy soul. Reader . . . O therefore set a special mark upon that providence that set you in the way of this mercy." See *Mystery*, pp. 385-87.

able to manage it to your advantage."[7] This places corresponding obligations squarely on our shoulders: not to be lazy, not to give our calling in this world precedence over our calling to trust and serve the Lord; not to forget that God himself is our ultimate benefactor.

One of the greatest of all God's providences is the blessing of marriage and family life: "a prudent wife is from the LORD" (Prov 19:14). God works in his own wonderful and unexpected ways. There are lessons to be learned:

> Not what they [people] expect, but what his infinite wisdom judges best and most beneficial for them takes place. Improve relations, to the end Providence designed them: Walk together as co-heirs of the grace of life: Study to be mutual blessings to each other: So walk in your relations, that the parting day may be sweet. Death will shortly break up the family; and then nothing but the sense of duty discharged, or the neglects pardoned, will give comfort.[8]

Flavel spoke from experience. When *The Mystery of Providence* was first published (1678) he had already seen his first wife and their unborn child die while she was in labor. He now had the joy of a second marriage, but his second wife would also predecease him.

Meanwhile he makes some general applications. Never forget the kindnesses God's providence provides; learn not to distrust him in the future or to murmur at new difficulties; do not be discontent; do not neglect to pray; do not worry with sinful anxiety. To do so would be to mistrust the heavenly Father who is the author of all providences.

God also providentially preserves his people from evil, both spiritual and physical. He may do the former by the counsel of another; sometimes by his intervention in creating obstacles in the very things or people that would bring harm; sometimes by illness; sometimes by clearer understanding of the meaning of Scripture; sometimes by death. Flavel finds a striking illustration in the life of the great Puritan John Dod.[9]

> Being late at night in his study, he was strongly moved (though at an unseasonable hour) to visit a gentleman of his acquaintance; and not knowing what might be the design of providence therein, he obeyed and went. When he came to the house, after

---

[7]Flavel, *Mystery*, p. 390.

[8]Ibid., pp. 394-95.

[9]John Dod (1555-1645), son-in-law of Richard Greenham, was highly esteemed by many of the leading Puritans. William Haller well notes: "No one probably did more than he to fix by personal influence and example the way of life and style of preaching followed for generations by the rank and file of the Puritan ministry." W. Haller, *The Rise of Puritanism* (New York: Columbia University Press, 1938), p. 58.

a few knocks at the door, the gentleman himself came to him, and asked him whether he had any business with him? Mr Dod answered, No; but that he could not be quiet till he had seen him. O sir, (replied the gentleman) you are sent of God at this hour, for just now (and with that he takes the halter[10] out of his pocket) I was going to destroy myself. And thus was the mischief prevented.[11]

The Puritans placed great stress on the role of Scripture in finding the guidance of God. Like John Dod, Flavel believed in the ongoing supernatural operations of God in providence, even extending to the subjective "sense" an individual might have, prompting him to action (analogous to Calvin's "secret instinct of the Spirit"[12]). But he never dislocated it from the revealed will of God in Scripture.

In his providence God provides special protection for his children. Dartmouth was a busy port and Flavel wrote several works applying this principle to seafarers.[13] Thus he was able to appeal to his own people: "Many of you have seen wonders of salvation upon the deeps where the hand of God has been signally stretched forth for your rescue and deliverance."[14] How important, then, to "consider what is the aim of providence in all the tender care it hath manifested for you? Is it not that you should employ your bodies for God, and cheerfully apply yourselves to that service he hath called you to?"[15]

Finally, the providence of God cooperates with the internal ministry of the Holy Spirit to transform our lives, and particularly to enable us to "mortify" the sin that continues to plague regenerate believers. Here is one of the great themes of Puritan practical theology—"How can I overcome and mortify sin?"[16] While only the blood of Christ can purge us from sin, the application of its power may be effected within the context of the ministry of providential affliction: "Though a *cross* without a Christ, never did any man good, yet thousands have been beholden to the *cross*, as it hath wrought in the virtue of his death for their good."[17]

Thus external providences become the instruments by which God uncovers our

---

[10]I.e., the noose with which he intended to hang himself.

[11]Flavel, *Mystery*, p. 398.

[12]E.g., in *Institutes* 1.16.9; commentaries on Mt 21:8; Lk 19:5; Jn 19:20; I Cor 11:24 and many other places.

[13]These included his earlier work, *The Seaman's Companion wherein the Mysteries of Providence, relating to Seamen, are opened; their Sins and Dangers discovered; their Duties pressed, and their several Troubles and Burdens relieved. In six practicable and suitable Sermons* (1676).

[14]Flavel, *Mystery*, p. 403.

[15]Ibid., p. 405.

[16]John Owen's famous work on *The Mortification of Sin* grew out of sermons he preached in Oxford when many of his hearers must have been teenage boys. *The Works of John Owen*, ed. W. H. Goold (Edinburgh and London: Johnstone and Hunter, 1850-1853), 6:1-86.

[17]Flavel, *Mystery*, p. 408 (emphasis his).

indwelling sin, reveals its strength to us, shows us how attached we still are to sinful desires, and motivates us to greater holiness. Thus, Flavel says in a wonderfully quaint statement:

> These afflictions have the same use and end to our souls, that frosty weather hath upon those clothes, that are laid a bleaching: they alter the hue, and make them whiter, Dan. xi.35. "Some of the wise shall fall, so that they may be refined, purified, and cleansed."[18]

What, then, is our response to be? It is to meditate on God's providence. But how?

HOW TO MEDITATE ON THE PROVIDENCE OF GOD

Flavel himself was much given to meditation on two things: the Word of God and the providences of God. His facility with Scripture is outstanding. In many ways *The Mystery of Providence* is a tapestry woven from biblical principles and history, with additional illustrations and practical application. He seems to know every part, indeed every page, of Scripture well.

Failure to meditate on God's providence is sinful. It diminishes our praises of God. Moreover we deny ourselves benefit from the nourishment our faith would receive. We slight the God who acts. Meditation on God's providence is therefore essential if we are to come to him in prayer and know how to address him. But *how* are we to learn to meditate?

Answering "How to?" questions was a major element in Puritan preaching: "In exhorting to duties, he [the preacher] is, as he seeth cause, to teach also the means that help to the performance of them."[19] Flavel offers the following four principles.

Work hard at remembering and exploring the providence of God toward you. We should do this extensively, tracing his ways through our life, counting the blessings he has poured out on us. We must do it intensively also: "Let not your thoughts swim like *feathers* upon the surface of the waters, but sink like *lead* to the bottom."[20] Explore the timing of God's actions, and the care they express. Think about the means he has employed—sometimes a stranger or even an enemy rather than a friend, sometimes an evil act rather than a beneficent one. Consider the way in which "all things" work together for believers (Rom 8:28): "a thousand friendly hands are at work for them to promote and bring about their happiness." In particular we should try to trace the relationship between prayer and providence to

---

[18]Ibid., p. 407.
[19]*Directory for the Publique Worship of God*, p. 380.
[20]Flavel, *Mystery*, p. 417 (emphasis his).

see how "Providences have borne the very signatures of your prayers upon them."[21]

Trace the connection between the providences of God in your life and the promises of God in his Word. This confirms the reliability of Scripture and teaches us what course of action we should adopt in any given set of circumstances. The Christian life is lived on the basis of God's revealed will (in Scripture), not on the basis of his secret will (which comes to expression in providence). As the latter unfolds, we discover that God is always faithful to his promises.

Look beyond the events and circumstances of providence to God himself as author and provider. Think of the attributes and ways of God (his love, wisdom, grace, condescension, purposes, methods and goodness). Recognize how he reveals these things in his dealings with you. Remember too that God often works out his purposes through painful trials. He is sovereign in all things, gracious, wise, faithful, all sufficient and unchanging—this especially we need to know in the darkness of affliction: "God is what he was, and where he was."[22]

Respond to each providence in an appropriate way. Even if their response is sorrow, bib-lically instructed believers will always experience an element of comfort and even joy. For no element of God's providence should be read as a mark of his enmity against us. After all, "All your losses are but as the loss of a *farthing*[23] to a prince." God's "heart is full of love, whilst the face of providence is full of frowns."[24] The Christian who realizes that "the Lord is near" (Phil 4:5) will see all these things in their proper perspective.

But what are we to do when the providences of God do not seem to coalesce with his promises?

Learn how to resist discouragement. God is teaching us patience. It may not yet be God's time to act; we may be asking impatiently; he may be increasing our appetite for the blessing for which we long. What are we to do? We need to remember he is bringing about a yet greater blessing—our willingness to depend entirely on God and his good pleasure; he delights to come when we are at the end of our own re-sources. Furthermore, we may not be ready yet to receive the blessing. If all his mer-cies are of grace and we do not deserve them, then we need to learn to wait for them.

Learn not to assume you fully and clearly understand God's ways and purposes. "There are

---

[21]Ibid., pp. 418-19.
[22]Ibid., p. 428.
[23]The coin of least value in England until withdrawn from currency in the twentieth century.
[24]Flavel, *Mystery*, p. 429.

hard texts in the works, as well as in the word of God. It becomes us modestly and humbly to reverence, but not to dogmatize about them; a man may easily get a strain by over-reaching."[25] In Psalm 73, Asaph increased his depression by trying to understand all the intricacies of God's ways; the same can be true for us. This only breeds a sense of suspicion of God, a darkness of spirit, and tempts us to take matters into our own hands. But that would be to distrust providence, and to reject the wisdom and love of God.

Meditating in this way on God's providence leads to an ongoing communion with God, since he "manifests himself among his people by *providences*, as well as ordinances."[26] It is also a major pleasure of the Christian life to be able to trace the harmony of God's attributes as he expresses them in his providences.

Such meditation also serves to *"over-power and suppress the natural atheism that is in your hearts."* [27] Natural atheism? Flavel was a wise enough pastor to know that some true believers are afflicted with doubts about God's goodness and even his very existence. Here our meditations on the providence of God can serve like a bulwark as we trace the clear lines of his loving care and mighty power in our lives.

In this way faith is supported by what we have seen of God in the past (e.g., the young David drew strength for his conflict with Goliath from his memories of the providence of God in his past, I Sam 17:37). Thus a spirit of praise breathes a sweet melody into our lives and Christ becomes more important to us, since all of God's mercies come to us only in and through him. With melted hearts, inward poise in an unstable world, and an increased devotion to holiness, we are thus equipped to face death—in what Flavel realized was sometimes a time of considerable inner turmoil and special temptation from Satan.[28] Dying is one of the two most difficult acts of faith (the other is coming to Christ for the first time). But the dying believer who is able to rehearse the blessings of God's providence in his or her life will surely know God's peace.

QUESTIONS

Such a perspective on God's providence draws us to a fuller appreciation of his presence and power; it leads us to trust him when fresh difficulties face us; it calls

---

[25] Ibid., p. 435.

[26] Ibid., p. 436.

[27] Ibid., p. 442.

[28] A view he held in common with many other Puritan pastors. Cf. the remarks by Owen in the preface to his *Glory of Christ* (1684), *Works*, I: 280-84 and the vivid descriptions of Christian's experience in the closing sections to both parts one and two of Bunyan's *Pilgrim's Progress*.

us to renewed consecration to his will. Yet perhaps there are still unanswered questions. Flavel deals briefly with five:

I. *What are we to do when we find it difficult to discern God's will?* While God revealed his will in various ways in the past, he does so now through his Word: "All are tied up to the ordinary standing rule of the written word, and must not expect any such extraordinary revelations from God."[29] If Scripture does not speak directly to our situation, our task is prayerfully to apply its general principles. Admittedly "God doth give men secret hints and intimations of his will by his providence . . . but yet providences in themselves, are no stable rule of duty nor sufficient discovery of the will of God."[30]

Here is Flavel's counsel:

If therefore in doubtful cases, you would discover God's will, govern yourself in your search after it by these rules:

- Get the true fear of God upon your hearts; be really afraid of offending him. . . .

- Study the *word* more, and the concerns and interests of the world less. . . .

- Reduce what you know into practice, and you shall know what is your duty to practice. . . .

- Pray for illumination and direction in the way you should go; beg the Lord to guide you in straits, and that he would not suffer you to fall into sin. . . .

- And this being done, follow providence as far as it agrees with the word, and no further.[31]

Flavel's emphasis stands in stark contrast to the "inner light" movements of his time. It stands, too, in contrast with contemporary views of guidance that imply the Christian can bypass Scripture in order to have direct access to the (secret) will of God.

2. *How can we cope when God seems to be slow in working for our relief and blessing?* God has his own calendar. "The Lord doth not compute and reckon his seasons of working by our *arithmetic.*"[32] No doubt Satan will seek to make capital out of our uncertainty. So we need to be sure we are relying on the promise of God and not on wishful thinking, and that our motives are truly spiritual, and our wills truly

---

[29] Flavel, *Mystery*, p. 468.
[30] Ibid., p. 469.
[31] Ibid., pp. 470-71.
[32] Ibid., p. 472.

submissive to God's. "Enjoyment of your desires is the thing that will please you, but resignation of your wills is that which is pleasing to God."[33] The mercies of God are worth waiting for. After all, he has waited patiently for us! Indeed, our impatience with him is sufficient reason for the "delay" we experience in his fulfilling his promises to us!

3. *How can we tell whether a specific event in God's providence is an expression of his love—or not?* Events in themselves do not carry with them an infallible explanation of what God means to accomplish through them. We dare not insist that God explain himself in detail to us, as though he were accountable to us. And God's providences often work like medicine—bitter to taste, healthgiving in effect. Painful providences may be expressions of God's love designed to deal with specific sinful dispositions and to sanctify us.

On the other hand, pleasant providences are not necessarily evidences of God's love. If they do not come in the context of prayer, if we possess them through sin, if we abuse God's gifts and become proud and self-sufficient, neglect our duty to the Lord, become indifferent to the needs of others—then they are not evidences of his love for us. But if, on the other hand, these mercies humble us, safeguard us from sin, increase our love for God and never themselves become the objects of our satisfaction, but rather make us sensitive to the needs of others and more concerned to serve the Lord; if they lead us to praise him—then indeed such providences have been sanctified in our lives.

4. *How can we develop stability in our Christian lives when the providences of God are painful for us to bear?* Flavel insists that we need such providences. "The earth does not need more chastening frosts and mellowing snows than our hearts do nipping providences."[34] But nothing can separate us from the love of Christ, and anything that seems to be able to do so is of temporary duration. Anxiety is fruitless; we need to remember that all things are in our heavenly Father's power and purpose.

5. *How can we learn to be submissive to the will of God?* Remembering that we need tests and trials if we are to grow strong as Christians, five principles are fundamental:

- Recollect how infinitely wise God is, and how limited your own understanding is.

---

[33]Ibid., p. 476.
[34]Ibid., p. 487.

- Realize that anxious thoughts about God's ways are actually sinful as well as harmful.

- Reflect on the examples of submission you find in Scripture—"shame yourselves out of this quarreling temper with providence."[35]

- Recognize the advantages there are in a submissive will—it creates a perpetual sabbath in the Christian's heart.

- Remember that an insubordinate will is fatal to both our prayers and our profession of faith.

Thus Christians are called to "lie down meekly at your Father's feet, and say in all cases, and at all times, '*The will of the Lord be done*.'"[36]

It is typical of Flavel that he closes with very basic and very practical advice: learn to record in writing the providences of God in your life. In this way you will preserve the memory of them for future meditation and encouragement:

> Providence carries our lives, liberties and concernments in its hand every moment. Your bread is in its cup-board, your money in its purse, your safety in its enfolding arms: and sure it is the least part of what you owe, to record the favors you receive at its hands.[37]

Wise counsel indeed from a wise and good shepherd, John Flavel.

REFLECTIONS

John Flavel's grasp of the doctrine of providence and his pastoral wisdom in expounding and applying it are themselves adequate commendation of this wonderful book. It is easy to read yet deeply thought provoking; biblically focused yet throbbing with a sense of God's ongoing activity; rigorously Puritan yet wonderfully sensitive to human pain. Written for a generation living in times of social and political upheaval, for people who knew a great deal of the angst which we moderns often mistakenly view as peculiarly postmodern, it speaks to the twenty-first century with the same power as it did to the seventeenth. More than that, it spells out loudly and clearly a number of biblical principles which Christians today desperately need to hear:

- God is in control of his universe.

---

[35]Ibid., p. 494.
[36]Ibid., p. 495.
[37]Ibid., p. 496.

- God is working out his perfect purposes.

- God is not my servant.

- God's ways are far more mysterious and wonderful than I can understand.

- God is good—all of the time; I can trust him—all of the time.

- God's timetable is not the same as mine.

- God is far more interested in what I become than in what I do.

- Freedom from suffering is no part of the promise of the Christian gospel.

- Suffering is an integral part of the Christian life.

- God works through suffering to fulfill his purposes in me.

- God's purposes, not mine, are what bring him glory.

- God guides me by enabling me to read his providences through the lenses of his Word.

- I have few greater pleasures than tracing the wonders of God's ways.

Learning these lessons from John Flavel will transform your life and do you endless and eternal good!

SELECT BIBLIOGRAPHY

Primary Sources

Flavel, John. *The Mystery of Providence*, in *The Works of John Flavel*, 6 vols. (1820). Republished, Edinburgh: Banner of Truth Trust, 1968. [The following works by Flavel also deal with the themes expounded at length in *The Mystery of Providence* and are contained his collected works: *The Righteous Man's Refuge* (3:321-413); *A Narrative of Some Later and Wonderful Sea Deliverances* (4:497-515); *The Seaman's Companion* (5:342-416); *Preparation for Suffering* (6:3-83)].

An edition of Flavel's work, in slightly modernized English, is also available: *The Mystery of Providence*. Edinburgh: Banner of Truth Trust, 1963.

Secondary Sources

Cohen, Charles L. *God's Caress, The Psychology of Puritan Religious Experience.* New York: Oxford University Press, 1986.

Morgan, Edmund S. *The Puritan Family.* New York: Harper & Row, 1966.

————. *Visible Saints, The History of an Idea.* New York: New York University Press, 1963.
Stannard, David E. *The Puritan Way of Death.* New York: Oxford University Press, 1977.
Von Rohr, John. *The Covenant of Grace in Puritan Thought.* Atlanta: Scholars Press, 1986.

❧ 15 ❧

A TREATISE OF
DELIGHTING IN GOD
BY JOHN HOWE (1630-1705)

Martin Sutherland

JOHN HOWE (1630-1705) WAS ONE OF THE MOST SIGNIFICANT PURITAN leaders of the later Stuart period. A prolific writer, he counted among his friends the leading churchmen of the day as well as key thinkers such as John Locke and Robert Boyle. His irenic qualities and personal piety made him an almost iconic figure among nonconformists in the eighteenth and nineteenth centuries. More recently, however, his contribution has been almost ignored. In large part this relegation is due to the challenges of Howe's style. He is constantly reaching down to first principles, qualifying and defining terms and arguments so that the main thread of his case can seem obscured, even lost. In an age that values brevity and directness, Howe is not fashionable. Nevertheless, the reader will find great rewards in the effort of carefully reading Howe's writings. In his devotional works, a deep understanding of Christian piety is evident.

A Treatise of Delighting in God appeared in 1674. Taking its cue from Psalm 37:4 ("Take delight in the LORD, and he will give you the desires of your heart"), it is a long reflection on what its author asserted to be "the very substance of religion . . . both the basis and foundation, and the top and perfection of practical godliness."[1] Unfortunately for what purports to be such an important work, it suffers from all Howe's stylistic faults. Yet a picture emerges of Howe at his best, supporting his rep-

---

[1] J. Howe, *A Treatise of Delighting in God* (London, n.p. 1674) reprinted in J. P. Hewlett, ed., *The Works of the Reverend John Howe M.A.* (Ligonier, Penn.: Soli Deo Gloria, 1990), 1:474-664, 474.

utation for "unfeigned and exalted piety."[2] This in turn signals that *Delighting in God*, a work of Puritan "practical religion," cannot be understood apart from its author, a man who had a long and remarkable career. So, before moving to examine the written text, we will first consider the "living text" of John Howe's life.

SHORT BIOGRAPHY

John Howe had clerical nonconformity in his blood. His father was ejected from his curacy in Loughborough, Leicestershire, in 1634 and the family spent some time in Ireland before returning to England in 1641-1642 where they settled in Winwick, Lancashire. Here John Howe received his early education. In May 1647 he entered Christ's College, Cambridge where he was influenced by the Cambridge Platonists, in particular Henry More (1614-1687). In 1648, having gained a B.A., he moved to Oxford. He was admitted to Brasenose College, became chaplain at Magdalen from 1650 and a fellow there from 1652 until 1655. In these six years Howe's platonic influences and his religious views were cultivated and enriched.

Though ordained in 1652 as a Presbyterian, Howe was never a narrow sectarian. The apparent ease and range of his associations were an important feature of his university years. In 1654 he took up a perpetual curacy at Great Torrington, succeeding "the famous Independent," Lewis Stucley (1632?-1687). This ministry was for the most part a happy one. Howe's first biographer, Edmund Calamy, asserted that "the more he spent himself in his Master's service, the more was he belov'd by the Inhabitants of his Parish."[3] Evidence of mutual affection is certainly not lacking. Howe maintained cordial links with Torrington after he had left. He dedicated *Delighting in God* to "much valued friends" in his first charge. Nevertheless, Calamy's assertion that Howe "had thought of no other, than of living and dying [at Torrington]" must be questioned. In a letter to Richard Baxter in 1658, Howe noted that "when I settled there, I expressly reserved to myself a liberty of removing" if so led.[4] As it happened, a change came after only two and a half years of the Torrington ministry.

In 1656 Howe moved to London to be private chaplain to Oliver Cromwell. He was unhappy in this job and within a short time was looking for a way out of a role he increasingly disliked. The answer was found in a continuation of his link to Tor-

---

[2]D. Bogue and J. Bennett, *History of the Dissenters from the Revolution in 1688, to the Year 1808* (London: Williams and Smith, 1809), 2:220.

[3]E. Calamy, *Memoirs of the Life of the Late Revd Mr John Howe* (London: n.p., 1724), p. 15.

[4]Letter, John Howe to Richard Baxter, May 25 [1658] Baxter Correspondence xi, f. 232. See N. H. Keeble and G. R. Nuttall, eds., *Calendar of the Correspondence of Richard Baxter*, 2 vols. (Oxford: Oxford University Press, 1991), no. 453.

rington via a series of interim ministers, with Howe himself spending three months there each year. After the fall of the Protectorate, Howe returned to Torrington, but on Bartholomew's Day in 1662 he was ejected under the provisions of the Act of Uniformity. For nine years he remained in Devon. Although he preached occasionally in the houses of sympathetic gentry, he did not set up conventicles or provoke the authorities. He published two well-received works based on Torrington sermons. In 1671 he accepted a position with Lord Massarene in Antrim, Ireland. Howe was given remarkable latitude by the Irish Church authorities. A divinity school was established in Antrim, run by Howe and the local Presbyterian incumbent. It was in Antrim that Howe wrote *Delighting in God.* By 1675 he was being noticed in the wider world and he was invited to take up a vacancy in the Presbyterian chapel at Haberdashers' Hall, London.

In London Howe published further works on theology and toleration. But during the early 1680s the Dissenters came under increasing pressure. In August 1685 Howe abruptly left London to travel to Europe; he would not return until 1687. The context of his sudden departure in August 1685 is important: Monmouth's rebellion had been crushed only one month previously. One who would be executed for his part in the uprising was John Hickes, Howe's brother-in-law. Another friend, Matthew Mead, had been implicated in the 1683 Rye House plot and was a principal figure in the Monmouth conspiracy. In the early 1680s Howe had contact with the conspirator Robert Ferguson. Along with several who would be subsequently implicated, Howe had met with Monmouth in the autumn of 1682. There can be little doubt where Howe's sympathies lay in the mid-1680s. His surprise departure for the Netherlands may not have been as a fugitive, but it was almost certainly prompted by his connections with those who were.

Settling in Utrecht, Howe preached regularly in the English church there and again assisted in the training of young men for ministry. The interval on the continent marks a definite turning point in his career. The five years following his return in 1687 were the most politically active of his life. His congregation, perhaps aware of how precarious his situation had been in August 1685, appears to have welcomed him back. With older figures such as John Owen dead and Richard Baxter failing, Howe now assumed a major role in nonconformist leadership.

Howe was an active supporter of William of Orange and presented the Dissenters' welcome after the Glorious Revolution of 1688-1689. After a limited toleration was granted he was an architect of the short-lived "Happy Union" of Presbyterians, Independents and Baptists in 1692. Until his death in 1705 he would work for toleration and unity within an increasingly divided Dissent.

John Howe's influence on later Dissent was profound. His status as a major icon of nonconformist piety was primarily due to his irenic approach to church disputes. What is less recognized is that he based this stance on a sophisticated theology for which he deserves to be ranked among the premier thinkers of his day.

Howe was a thinker of considerable depth. He combined this with a strong commitment to Christian fellowship and personal piety. *Delighting in God* appeared early in Howe's publishing career, as many of his key positions were coming into place. The importance of the Antrim years should not be missed. Here Howe took the opportunity to rebuild his theology after the shock and disappointment of the Interregnum and Restoration. *Delighting in God* was one of the fruits of that period. Although it was dedicated to his former parishioners in Torrington it was not merely the reissue of old material. Two earlier publications—*The Blessedness of the Righteous* (1668) and *The Vanity of Man as Mortal* (1671) were essentially revised versions of sermon series. Howe initially planned this for *Delighting in God*. Yet when he came to the task he found a new start altogether was required. The resultant work bears little relation to former sermons. "The first part is even altogether new. . . . The other part contains many things formerly delivered to you, though perhaps not in the same order, much less in the same words."[5] The shift in focus between the first and second parts of the treatise is important and has implications for the way we will approach the text. Crucially, *Delighting in God* belongs less to the Torrington years than to the Antrim period. This relatively peaceful interlude also produced Howe's key philosophical text, *The Living Temple*, and the provocative apologetics of *The Reconcilableness of God's Prescience*. In Antrim, Howe laid important new foundations. *Delighting in God* must be read in that context.

APPROACHING THE TREATISE

One of the characteristics of Howe's style, not at all uncommon in seventeenth-century theological writing, is a reliance on a complex structure of parts, divisions, subdivisions, sections and subsections. As an aid to the reader he numbers these consistently, employing words, capitalized words, Roman numerals, Arabic numerals, numerals in brackets, etc. Nevertheless the wave on wave of subdivision can be bewildering. I will not attempt to provide an exhaustive analysis of the structure of *Delighting in God*. The basic outline is important, however, as it will determine the way in which we attempt to understand the text.

As Howe signals in his *Dedication*, his treatise falls into two parts. The first is

---

[5]Howe, *Delighting in God*, p. 474.

more philosophical and addresses "the import and meaning of delighting in God." In other words, the question "*why* are Christians called upon to enjoy God in this way?" The second addresses the more practical issue of *how* this desired state is to be encouraged—that is, "the *practice* of delight in God." As noted above, this latter part had earlier origins than the first. It is not merely a rewriting of Torrington sermons but its general approach reflects the questions addressed there. The first part, on the other hand, is very clearly new and related more closely to Howe's growing theological confidence than to the pastoral concerns of part two. The effect of these different origins is evident in the content of the respective parts. Part one is a complex, technical treatment of subtle concepts. Part two consists largely of series of questions that might be put to people at various stages of belief or relation to God.

Given the chronological development of the ideas it might be thought possible to approach this divided text backwards—through its second part—then, with a clear understanding of Howe's practical suggestions, to turn to the theory of the first section. However, as will be seen, the theory developed in the 1670s was no afterthought, no mere justification of earlier proposals. The published form of part two depends completely on the theory outlined in part one. So to those ideas, as Howe intended, we will turn first.

"PART I: SHOWING THE IMPORT OF DELIGHTING IN GOD"

This first part of the treatise comes almost entirely from the most fruitful season in John Howe's theological development. The works of the Antrim period relate closely to one another. In *Delighting in God* the first concern is to establish the value of delighting in God. Once this is understood, motivation would not be a problem; indeed it would be almost automatic. In other words, the very idea contains its own purpose. Howe sets for himself the complex task of demonstrating this to be true. The aim of this first part is to bring his readers to a point where they are fervently seeking delight in God. He addresses the question from two sides. First he considers the object of the delight, then the nature of delight itself.

The *object* of the called-for delight is, of course, God. Significantly, Howe devotes only a few lines of text to the absolute nature of God. God "is in himself the best and most excellent being," and therefore is clearly a fitting object of delight. However to dwell on the inherent qualities of God would be, in Howe's view, sterile. This would be the God of the philosophers, not of the saints. Christianity is about relationship with God, who came to us in Jesus Christ. "And thus we are more principally to consider him . . . relatively than absolutely; and that relatedness . . . as now settled in Christ."[6]

This is a most crucial point, one that lies behind the whole of *Delighting in God*. The divine being in whom we are called to delight is not some remote figure, hardly in contact, distant from human experience. To work up a sense of "delight" in such a being would be heavy work indeed. No, the Christian God is the One come among us, who entered our experience, took on human nature. This is One who can genuinely be met, and in such a meeting, delight is as natural as "hello."

Howe, then, goes to considerable lengths to discuss the communication between God and humanity. This is a direct reflection of his Antrim thinking. As we have noted, the other major work from this period is the philosophical treatise *The Living Temple*, which has as its focus "God's existence, and his conversableness with man."[7] In that work Howe set out to counter philosophical trends that would distance God from humanity. It is thus a twin with part one of *Delighting in God*. Together these somewhat daunting treatises are an example of the Puritan insistence on fusing theory and practice, head and heart. In *The Living Temple* the issues are canvassed to establish foundations for good theology; in *Delighting in God* they are explored in order to sustain practical divinity.

But what is it about the communication of the nature of God in Christ that generates delight? Howe stresses that we do not by this encounter *possess* God in any sense. But then neither are we mere observers of some beautiful object. Rather, as with a human friend, we enjoy "intimate acquaintance." "And in such-like is God to be enjoyed also. But with this difference, that God's communications are more immediate, more constant, more powerful and efficacious, infinitely more delightful and satisfying, in respect to both the good communicated and the way of communication."[8]

When God is met there are consequences for the mind, the will and the heart. There is first "an inwardly enlightening revelation of himself." This is a work of the Holy Spirit which brings about a progressive apprehension of the beauty of God's truth and an assurance of its eternal significance. It is primarily an impact on the mind, but it goes beyond mere "rational certainty." Howe is aware that it is possible to know, and be intellectually convinced of the facts of the gospel. But intellectual assent is not enough. An understanding "which is only the product of the external

---

[6]Ibid., pp. 481-82.
[7]Howe wrote the first part of *The Living Temple* while in Antrim. The second part, though clearly planned in the 1670s, did not appear until 1702.
[8]Howe, *Delighting in God*, p. 486.

revelation . . . is too faint to command the soul."[9] Without reducing the importance of rational understanding, Howe insists that God communicates something more—an inward revelation, which "captivates the heart to an entire unitive closure with the great things contained in the outward one."[10] Theory and practice, heart and mind, these must remain inseparable.

But encounter with God does more than convince, it also brings "a transforming impression of his image." Here the impact is principally on the Christian's will. This communication of God changes people "as like an active quick flame, it passes through their souls, searches, melts them, burns up their dross, makes them a new lump or mass, forms them for God's own use and converse."[11] This effect, too, is cumulative, the greater the transformation, the greater the joy in the change and the greater the desire for more.

> In order whereto it must be considered, that wherein it is transforming it is also enlivening, and therefore furnishes the soul with the power of spiritual sensation; whereby it comes to apprehend its former temper as very grievous and detestable . . . and proportionably, the holy frame to be introduced as highly covetable and to be infinitely desired.[12]

As with the inward revelation, this "rectifying" effect of encounter with God is an essential element in Christian delight. Furthermore, Howe argues that knowledge of its importance provides a crucial safeguard. First, there are those who might imagine themselves moving toward "delight in God" when their lives bear no sign of Christlikeness at all. To these Howe's words are a wake-up call. Second, there are those who think they fail to enjoy God when they actually do, "supposing there was no enjoyment of him, but what consisted in the rapturous, transporting apprehension . . . of his particular love to them; and slightly overlooking all the work he hath wrought in their souls, as if it were nothing to be accounted of."[13] While calling always for heart religion, the Puritans refused to allow faith to be defined in terms of emotion alone.

This concern is again evident in the third of Howe's descriptions of the impact of an encounter with God: it is personal. "This divine communication is delectable, as it includes in it, *the manifestation of God's love to the soul in particular.*" The glory of the Gospel is that it is not a move of God to be celebrated only for its general application but also, essentially, because it comes to the individual. This is truly a de-

---

[9]Ibid., p. 495.
[10]Ibid., p. 494.
[11]Ibid., p. 500.
[12]Ibid., p. 503.
[13]Ibid., p. 527.

lightful thing. "How dignifying is the love of *God!* How honourable a thing to be his favourite!" Nevertheless, Howe is very cautious about this individualized ground for delight. Concerned lest it open the door to mere "enthusiastical assurance . . . as excludes reference to his external revelation," he expounds ten cautions, mainly designed to prevent any notion that this internal joy is an end in itself, or that on its own is "the sum of religion."[14]

Having described the natural, indeed essential, connection between God in communication with humans and delight in God, Howe now moves to consider the significance of the nature of delight itself. This order of treatment is no small matter. Howe is determined that Christian faith be determined by divine, rather than human categories. Only when the nature of relationship with God is understood properly will he move to discuss the experience and eventually the practice of delight.

As with all his discussions, Howe sets up a series of categories, divisions and subdivisions. He first considers delight as a concept in general, arguing that it is "most intimately essential to love" but needs to be carefully distinguished from "desire." This latter concept implies a seeking or imperfection, whereas "delight" is a settled concept, reveling in the perfection of its object. When delight is fulfilled there is nothing more to be desired. "Pure and simple delight is love suited to a state of things in every way perfect, and whereto there is nothing lacking. Wherefore delight appears to be the perfection of love, or desire satisfied."[15]

Delight so defined is thus an ideal concept to apply to Christian faith. It is able to bear notions of rest and trust, completion and satisfaction. But it is not simply delight in general that Christians are called to, but delight in God—the communicating God and Father of Jesus Christ. Howe thus concludes part one of his discourse with a description of the particular nature of Christian delight. By now he feels enough has been said to justify its use as a "summary of all practical religion." Used in this way, "delighting in God" supposes

1. *knowledge* of God
2. *actual thoughts* of him
3. a *pleasedness* with even the first view of him
4. *desire* directed to gaining more of him, followed ultimately by
5. *satisfaction* or *repose* of the soul . . . as it finds its desire answered.
6. Finally, returning to his text (Ps 37:4) he notes a call to *"stirring up ourselves . . . to heighten our own delight."*[16]

---

[14]Ibid., pp. 530, 539, 542-46.
[15]Ibid., p. 548.
[16]Ibid., pp. 557-58.

Howe has now reached the point where he can move to his discussion of the exercise of this approach to practical religion. He has established a definition of delight that may be seen to be inherent in God's communication of himself to his people and in the natural response to that encounter. His final six points are programmatic of part two. In this section he will describe how believers may "stir themselves" (point six) to this state, using exercises which will employ the framework set out in elements one to five.

"PART 2: CONCERNING THE PRACTICE OF DELIGHT IN GOD"

Howe begins this segment by acknowledging that in part one he has extended the concept of "delight in God" to include "the sum of all holy and religious converse with God . . . and upon the same account, of all our other converse, so far as it is influenced by religion." Here, *converse* refers to the way we conduct our lives. Delight in God is now a very big concept, truly "the very substance of religion." Dividing his treatment, he considers the practice of this religious concept: "1, as a thing adherent to the other duties of religion and 2, as it is a distinct duty in itself."[17]

Howe deals with these headings in a model of Puritan practical divinity. In each case he sets out a rational explanation, followed by exercises to promote the desired outcome, followed in turn by "excitations" or motivations to encourage persistence in the quest.

Under the first heading the concern is to show how true delight informs and encourages the entire religious life. Indeed the presence of delight is argued to be a test for true religion. Here Howe relies on the rational arguments of part one. Religion that does not lead to delight must be rated as false. How, though, is the Christian to practice a religion of delight? Howe proposes rules for "direction"— exercises that will create the environment for delightful religion. Paraphrased, they may be summarized as follows:

1. Endeavor to have a mind well instructed in the essentials of faith.
2. Be intent to have your soul good and holy.
3. Maintain a constant watch on your spiritual health.
4. Be frequent and impartial in the actual exercise of gracious principles.
5. Be convinced that religion is in itself a delightful thing, but
6. Don't make your own delight the principal motivation. Yet, on the other hand,
7. Don't deny to yourself the pleasure of well-doing.
8. During times of spiritual dryness, do not wallow or despair but take action

---

[17]Ibid., pp. 565-66.

to restore delight to your relationship with God.[18]

To the modern mind these exercises can seem formal, reducing religion to positive thinking. This is of course not Howe's meaning. Rather he is stressing the Puritan conviction that, by grace, the individual Christian has a role to play in his or her connection to God:

> You must expect to be dealt with as a sort of creature capable of understanding your own concernments; not to be hewed and hammered as senseless stones that are ignorant of the artist's intent, but as living ones, to be polished and fitted to the spiritual building by a hand that reasonably expects your own compliance and cooperation to its known design. . . . Therefore if ever you would know what a life of spiritual delight means, you must constantly strive against all your spiritual distempers that obstruct it, in the power of the Holy Ghost. And do not think that is enjoining you a course wholly out of your power; for though it be true that the power of the Holy Ghost is not naturally yours, or at your disposal; yet by gracious vouchsafement and ordination it is.[19]

If there are practices or rules that secure religious delight, there are also "excitations," or reasons to seek it. Howe again refers to the case set out in part one, briefly reiterating that true religion, properly conceived, has delight at its heart. Why, then, seek a second-class spirituality? "And why should you be of so mean and abject a spirit, as to content yourself to be held at the door and in the outer courts of religion, when others enter in and taste the rich provisions of God's house?"[20]

Delight is more than an aspect of other religious practices. It is a good in itself. Howe now turns to the second of his major headings: delight as a distinct duty of itself. Again he addresses two types of people. The first are those alienated from God; the second are those who are in right relationship with God, but have not considered the value of directly seeking religious delight.

In keeping with the pattern established under the first heading, each group is first "expostulated" (i.e., challenged with rational argument). To the first group, Howe addresses a set of questions which probe the reasons for their disaffection and which point to the value, indeed the necessity, of seeking delight in God. Certain presuppositions are made, which signal that Howe is not addressing those we would now call atheists, nor even those in modern societies who have never been Christian. Howe acknowledges he is writing for a time in which belief in the existence of God is assumed and the Bible is accepted to be the authoritative word of

---

[18]Ibid., pp. 578-93.
[19]Ibid., p. 590.
[20]Ibid., p. 595.

God.[21] The second group is called on to consider how their resistance to seeking delight is contrary to the testimony of God's law, conscience, experience and all accepted aspects of the Christian faith. Indeed, it is "evil," in the sense that it fails to cohere with each of the other elements of faith. More than that it signals dangerous faults in the Christian life, such as blindness to God ("Is it possible any should have beheld his glory and not have been delighted therewith"?[22]), failure to reflect on God, carnality and "downright aversion." These outcomes will ultimately damage faith itself.

Howe moves from "expostulation" to "invitation"—beyond rational challenge to spiritual exercises. Here the structure of the treatise takes on a more complex look. Howe outlines three sets of religious mediations. Together these may be pictured as a spiral of movement towards God, which passes through three levels. On the lowest level is the first, alienated group. These are to consider their state through a set of exercises that culminate in "accepting Jesus Christ as thy Saviour and thy Lord."[23] Once they have risen to this new plane the now new Christians are in the same state as those in the next group: Christians who have not actively sought delight in God. This is the second level of the spiral. Here another set of exercises are proposed, which will draw the reluctant believer into active desire for delight. Once completed, these in turn give entry to a further level. "And when you are thus returned into the way and course of your duty, then may what follows concern you in common with all others, that . . . desire direction how to proceed and improve in this holy exercise of delighting in God." A final set of exercises is then outlined, aimed to bring the seeker to a vision of "an eternal abode in that presence where is 'fulness [*sic*] of joy, and pleasures for evermore.'"[24]

Howe lastly adds the element of "excitation," or motivation. His closing remarks are aimed to demonstrate above all that delight in God is the greatest good to which humans can aspire. A number of reasons are advanced. It is first a privilege that God should invite us to this state. Next, it is the best preparation for eternal life. "How easily tolerable and pleasant it will be to think, then, of going to Him with whom you have lived in delightful communion before!"[25] Finally, as the most perfect fulfillment, it delivers "from the vexation and torment of unsatisfied desire." The alternative is chillingly hopeless.

---

[21]Ibid., p. 597.
[22]Ibid., p. 617.
[23]Ibid., p. 627.
[24]Ibid., pp. 633, 657.
[25]Ibid., p. 660.

If you take no delight in God, your own souls will be a present hell to you. And it may be, it is not enough considered, how much the future hell stands also in unsatisfied desire; which desire (all suitable objects being for ever cut off from it) turns wholly to despair, rage and torture. . . . And the beginnings of this hell you will now have within you while you refuse to delight in God.[26]

The fundamental significance of this warning should not be lost. Puritan piety took an eternal perspective of all matters of spirituality. As noted, the ultimate exercise in seeking delight in God is contemplation of heaven—the "eternal abode." Conversely, delight in mere "sapless earthly vanities" leads to "perpetual distress." "For in these false vanishing shadows of goodness, you cannot have satisfaction, and in the blessed God you will not."[27]

CONCLUSION

Delighting in God is not an easy work, yet once Howe's distinctive brand of argumentation is grasped it yields very rich fruit. It is a remarkable example of the Puritan melding of head, heart and will in a balance of theology, experience and discipline. To Howe, in these elements is found "the very substance of religion." He weaves all three together in the singular motif of "delight in God," while constructing a stunning portrayal of the life of faith. It is a Puritan pearl of great price.

SELECT BIBLIOGRAPHY

Primary Source

Howe, John. *Delighting in God*. In *The Works of the Reverend John Howe M.A.*, edited by E. Calamy. London: n.p., 1724; reprint, Ligonier, Penn.: Soli Deo Gloria, 1990. (This book has not been published separately since the early nineteenth century. It is therefore accessible only in editions of Howe's entire works.)

Secondary Sources

Calamy, Edmund. *Memoirs of the Life of the Late Revd Mr John Howe*. London: n.p., 1724. (On Howe's life, the best source remains this dated volume by his first biographer.)

Greaves, R. L. *God's Other Children: Protestant Nonconformists and the Emergence of Denominational Churches in Ireland, 1660-1700*. Stanford: Stanford University Press, 1997.

Keeble, N. H. *The Literary Culture of Nonconformity in Later Seventeenth-Century England*. Leicester, U.K.: Leicester University Press, 1987.

---

[26]Ibid., pp. 663-64.
[27]Ibid., p. 664.

Spurr, J. *The Restoration Church of England, 1646-1689.* New Haven, Conn.: Yale University Press, 1991.

Sutherland, Martin. *Peace, Toleration and Decay: The Ecclesiology of Later Stuart Dissent.* Carlisle, U.K.: Paternoster, 2003. (A new analysis of Howe's life and theology.)

❧ 16 ❧

A METHOD FOR PRAYER

BY MATTHEW HENRY (1662-1714)

J. Ligon Duncan III

I FIRST ENCOUNTERED MATTHEW HENRY'S *A METHOD FOR PRAYER* WHILE in seminary. A number of us theological tadpoles, arrested by the richness and devotional quality of one particular professor's pre- and postlecture prayers, approached him to ask how we could improve our own feeble attempts at leading in public prayer. He pointed us to "the Bible and the closet," as the Puritans would have put it. That is, he indicated to us that edifying public prayer is cultivated by the use of the language and ideas of Scripture (we pray God's own words back to him), and by our own practice of prayer in private (we learn to pray God's own words back to him, sincerely, earnestly and naturally by doing so daily and constantly when we are alone with him). But he singled out one book for us to read that addressed this matter better than any other—Matthew Henry's *A Method for Prayer*. I won the race to the library.

Many Christians know the name Matthew Henry even if they know little of the man. He is famous to us because of his marvelous and massive *Commentary on the Whole Bible*. This work can now be found in electronic media, and is widely used in numerous print versions and editions to this day.[1] It was the labor of the last decade of his life. He began it in November of 1704 and left it incomplete upon his death.

---

[1]For instance, it has regularly been republished by Revell (now owned by Baker) in a six-volume set, *Matthew Henry's Commentary on the Whole Bible* (Old Tappan, N.J.: Fleming H. Revell, n.d.). Hendrickson Publishers (Peabody, Mass.) also produces the unabridged edition, handsomely bound. Leslie F. Church edited a Regency Reference Library one-volume abridged edition, *Commentary on the Whole Bible by Matthew Henry* (Grand Rapids: Zondervan, 1961). The whole commentary is in public domain in many places on the internet (a simple title-author search will yield dozens of sites where it is available), including Calvin College's theological resource project: the Christian Classics Ethereal Library at <www.ccel.org/h/henry/mhc2/MHC00000.htm>.

Ministerial colleagues, because of their appreciation and esteem for Henry, and out of a sense of the significance of the project, completed the work after his death, with reference to his notes and writings (Henry had finished the commentary from Genesis through Acts).

One could make an effective argument for the inclusion of Henry's *Commentary* in a volume on Puritan classics: its influence has been immense (George Whitefield, for instance, read it through four times, on his knees!). It is probably among the top three bestsellers among all the Puritan writings reviewed in this volume (despite its size—over seven thousand pages of text in small print—and its initial cost, about a quarter of the average working man's yearly wage when it was first published). But it is not the subject of this chapter. Rather, our focus is to be on an equally significant work, Matthew Henry's *A Method for Prayer with Scripture Expressions Proper to Be Used Under Each Head* (1710).[2] Along with Isaac Watts's *Guide to Prayer* (1715) it stands as the classic treatise in the Protestant English-speaking world for the promotion of the practice of biblical prayer, that is, praying Scripture, or praying with the intelligent use of the language of Scripture.

THE LIFE OF MATTHEW HENRY

Matthew Henry[3] was the second son of a prominent nonconformist minister named Philip Henry who was born in London of Welsh parents. Matthew Henry was born near Whitchurch, England (about 18 miles south, southeast of Chester, not too far from the border with Wales, and located in the area today known as Shropshire), in the year of "the Great Ejection" (1662) in which faithful evangelical ministers who refused to accede to the Parliament's Act of Uniformity were expelled from the Church of England. This is usually regarded as the end of Puritanism, at least as a movement within the Church of England, and it is certainly the beginning of English nonconformity as a new spiritual movement comprising Pres-

---

[2]It can be found in Matthew Henry, *The Complete Works of Matthew Henry-Treatises, Sermons, and Tracts,* 2 volumes (Edinburgh: A. Fullarton, 1855; reprinted, Grand Rapids: Baker, 1979; second printing, 1997). As a separate volume (combined with Henry's other book on prayer called *Directions for Beginning, Spending, and Closing Each Day with God*), it has been recently reprinted. See Matthew Henry, *A Method for Prayer* (Greenville, S.C.: A Press, 1992, reprinted from the 1819 Berwick edition); and also newly edited and republished, see Matthew Henry, *A Method for Prayer,* edited, revised and introduced by J. Ligon Duncan III (Greenville, S.C.: Reformed Academic, 1994), as well as Matthew Henry, *A Method for Prayer,* edited, revised and introduced by J. Ligon Duncan III (Fearn, Rossshire, Scotland: Christian Focus, 1998).

[3]See J. B. Williams, *The Lives of Philip and Matthew Henry* (London: W. Ball, 1839); reprinted, Edinburgh: Banner of Truth Trust, 1974); Alexander Gordon's entry on "Matthew Henry" in *Dictionary of National Biography,* ed. Leslie Stephen and Sidney Lee (London: Smith, Elder, 1891), 26:123-24; and Jack Seaton "Philip and Matthew Henry" in *The Banner of Truth* 137 (1975): 1-8, esp. 5-8.

byterians, Independents and Baptists with a common spiritual heritage.

Matthew Henry was early marked by his studious habits and delicate health. He was reading the Bible for himself at age three, and developmentally far ahead of his age group in knowledge and insight. The experience of a life-threatening fever when he was ten years old made a deep impression upon him and his lifelong concern for and practice of prayer is said to have originated with his recovery from this illness. In any case those around him noted an uncommon seriousness about him for a boy of his age. The universities being closed to nonconformists, he studied at a private academy in Islington (under the tutelage of Thomas Doolittle) and later at Gray's Inn in London. He began preaching at the age of twenty-three and spent most of his ministry as pastor of a church in Chester, England (1687-1712). His final two years of life and ministry were spent in London, pastoring a congregation in Hackney (1712-1714).

Throughout his life as a minister, Henry was a diligent student of the Word, sometimes rising as early as four o'clock in the morning and often spending eight hours a day in his study in addition to his pastoral labors. He was also, however, a man of prayer. The whole of his labors was marked by the wisdom that only those who are habitually dependent upon the Almighty in prayer may hope to attain.

THE MAKING OF *A METHOD FOR PRAYER*

Henry completed *A Method for Prayer* in 1710 after serving almost a quarter-century in the same congregation. Hence, it reflects a lifetime of prayer, ministry and Christian experience. In this book, Henry lays down an outline of a plan for prayer and supplies the contents of prayer from the Scriptures themselves. His extraordinary command of Scripture is evident throughout the work. In a day long before computer Bible programs, topical indices and Scripture treasuries, Henry draws out of his own memory and study a trove of pertinent, well-selected Scripture passages and arranges them in a coherent order. Readers who know the products of the Westminster Assembly of Divines (1643-1649) will recognize that Henry is following the themes of prayer noted in the *Westminster Directory for Public Worship*. His outline for prayer is thus not the more familiar and simple A-C-T-S model (adoration, confession, thanksgiving and supplication) but rather a six-part A-C-P-T-I-C model (adoration, confession, petition for ourselves, thanksgiving, intercession for others and conclusion).[4]

---

[4]Henry himself says of his "model," "though I have here recommended a good method for prayer, and that which has been generally approved, yet I am far from thinking we should always tie ourselves to it; that may be varied as well as the expression: Thanksgiving may very aptly be put sometimes before confession or petition, or our

He published another work on prayer in September of 1712, called *Directions for Daily Communion with God, in three Discourses, Showing How to Begin, How to Spend, and How to Close Every Day with God*, based on sermons preached in August and September of that same year, just four months after leaving Chester to take up his final post in Hackney. The title is explanatory of the contents, which are rich indeed. Henry here gives earnest exhortation and practical instruction on how a Christian may suffuse the day with prayer. Since at least 1819, these sermons have been attached to some editions of *A Method for Prayer*. This is still the case in the most common edition available in print today, so modern readers will benefit from both these works, though they were initially distinct.

A Tour Through Matthew Henry's *A Method for Prayer*

Adoration. To hear many Christians pray today, you would gather that praise of God for who he is and what he has done for us in creation, providence and redemption is a brief preliminary to be dispensed with before coming to the real substance of prayer, which is asking God to do and give the things we want. Matthew Henry's very first chapter—"the first part of prayer, which is address to God, adoration of Him, with suitable acknowledgments, professions, and preparatory requests"—in stark contrast to common contemporary practice, begins a program of biblical correction to our anemic prayer lives.[5] In it, he supplies Scripture to aid us in solemnly addressing God in light of his greatness, glory and majesty, and in reverently adoring God as a transcendent, blessed, self-existent, self-sufficient, infinite and eternal Spirit. He ransacks the Scriptures for references to God's attributes and turns them into matters of adoration: that God is an eternal and immutable God; that he is present in all places; that he has a perfect knowledge of all persons and things; that his wisdom is unsearchable; that his sovereignty is incontestable; that he is the Lord and owner of all; that his power is irresistible; that he is pure and upright; that he is just and never does wrong; that he is truthful and faithful and good. We still fall infinitely short describing him in all his glory when we have said all we can of him.

Henry's counsel to us about how to prepare for prayers of adoration is interesting and helpful. He says:

> Our spirits being composed into a very reverent serious frame, our thoughts gathered in, and all that is within us, charged in the Name of the great God, carefully to attend the solemn and awful [awesome] service that lies before us, and to keep close to it,

intercessions for others before our petitions for ourselves, as in the Lord's Prayer." *A Method for Prayer* (Christian Focus, Christian Heritage series, 1998), p. 15.
[5]Ibid., pp. 19-34.

we must with a fixed attention and application of mind, and an active lively faith, set the Lord before us, see his eye upon us, and set ourselves in his special presence, presenting ourselves to him as living sacrifices, which we desire may be holy and acceptable, and a reasonable service; and then bind these sacrifices with cords to the horns of the altar.[6]

It is obvious here how the language and thought of Scripture permeate even Henry's practical instruction. This is a foretaste of what he does throughout *A Method for Prayer*. After having provided a logical sequence for prayer based on God's attributes, he furnishes scriptural content for prayers of adoration for God's revelation of himself in creation, both in the heavens and on earth, and as providential ruler of the world, and specifically for God as Trinity. Here is a sample of Henry's adoration of God "as the Creator of the world, and the great Protector, Benefactor, and Ruler of the whole creation":

Thou art worthy O Lord, to receive blessing, and honor, and glory, and power; for thou hast created all things, and for thy pleasure, and for thy praise, they are and were created.

We worship him that made the heavens and the earth, the sea and the fountains of waters; who spake, and it was done; who commanded, and it stood fast; who said, let there be light, and there was light, let there be a firmament, and he made the firmament; and he made all very good; and they continue this day according to his ordinance, for all are his servants.

The day is thine, the night also is thine; thou hast prepared the light and the sun: Thou hast set all the borders of the earth, thou hast made the summer and winter.

Thou upholdest all things by the word of thy power, and by thee all things consist.

The earth is full of thy riches, so is the great and wide sea also. The eyes of all wait upon thee, and thou givest them their meat in due season: Thou openest thy hand, and satisfiest the desires of every living thing. Thou preservest man and beast, and give food to all flesh.

Thou, even thou art Lord alone; thou hast made heaven, the heaven of heavens, with all their host, the earth and all things that are therein, the sea, and all that is therein, and thou preservest them all; And the hosts of heaven worshippeth thee, whose kingdom ruleth over all.

A sparrow falls not to the ground without thee.

Thou madest man at first of the dust of the ground, and breathest into him the breath of life, and so he became a living soul.

And thou hast made of that one blood all nations of men, to dwell on all the face

---

[6]Ibid., p. 19.

of the earth, and hast determined the times before appointed, and the bounds of their habitation.

Thou art the most High who ruleth in the kingdom of men, and givest it to whomsoever thou wilt; for from thee every man's judgment proceeds.

Hallelujah, the Lord God omnipotent reigns, and doth all according to the counsel of his own will, to the praise of his own glory (Rev 4:11, 14:7; Ps 33:9; Gen 1:3, 6-7; Ps 119:91, 74:16-17; Heb 1:3; Col 1:17; Ps 104:24-25, 145:15-16, 36:6; Neh 9:6, Ps 103:19; Mt 10:29; Gen 2:7; Acts 17:26; Dan 4:25; Prov 29:26; Rev 19:6; Eph 1:11-12).[7]

The richness of Henry's Scripture-derived prayer of adoration is self-evident, and all the more impressive in light of the fact that he tells us "I have only set down such as first occurred to my thoughts."[8] His prayers of praise to God for his self-revelation and triunity are followed by sections in which we make further acknowledgments of our dependence upon God, our obligations to God, his ownership of us, the inestimable privilege of being invited to draw near to God in prayer, the sense we have of our own unworthiness to draw near and speak to God. Yet at the same time, Henry supplies Scripture that reminds us of the desire of our hearts toward God, as well as our believing hope and confidence in God.

Henry's chapter on adoration of God closes with several subdivisions of entreaty. He bids us appeal to God for his acceptance of us despite ourselves, and for the powerful assistance and influence of the grace of the Holy Spirit. Finally, Henry leads us to ask God's help to make his glory our highest aim in all our prayers, and to entirely rely on the Lord Jesus Christ alone for our acceptance with God.

Confession. The confession of sin is one of the most underappreciated and overlooked, but potentially encouraging aspects in the corporate and personal prayer of the church. However, many evangelical Christians today are uncomfortable with being asked to confess their sins regularly (or even at all), in public or private. Their logic often goes something like this. "We've already been forgiven so why should we go on asking for forgiveness? Once we become Christians we are saints, so why keep acting like people under condemnation for sin? All this dour confession of sin is depressing. It is unbecoming of joyful, forgiven children of God. Away with this 'worm theology.'" Henry, however, does not mince words about this vital aspect of prayer:

Having given glory to God which is his due, we must next take shame to ourselves, which is our due, and humble ourselves before him in the sense of our own sinfulness

---

[7]Ibid., pp. 25-26.
[8]Ibid., p. 15.

and vileness; and herein also we must give glory to him, as our Judge by whom we deserve to be condemned, and yet hope, through Christ, to be acquitted and absolved.[9]

Henry understood that without the inclusion of sufficient confession of sin in our prayers, we will never attain a real and right sense of divine forgiveness and reconciliation. We know in our hearts that even as renewed Christians we sin, and unless that ongoing sin is confessed we will be burdened by unresolved guilt—or else cope with that nagging guilt through denial, delusion and self-deception. Indeed, Henry knew that there are at least four biblical reasons why Christians must continue to confess sin. First, believers, though united to Christ, still sin. Hence to be realistic we must acknowledge it (Rom 6:12; I Jn 1:8). Second, repentance is not a one-time past action in the Christian life; it is an ongoing project (I Jn 1:9; Rev 2:5). We will not be finished with repenting until this life is over and the age to come has arrived. Third, sin is essentially displeasing to God. True, he has dealt with the punishment we deserved for our sin at the cross, but this does not make sins committed by believers any less displeasing to God (indeed all the more). The Lord does not take pleasure in evil. So when believers sin the Lord is displeased. This displeasure with sin will not be eradicated until he eradicates sin in all the saints in the last day (I Jn 3:4). Thus we confess our sins as grieving to our loving and longsuffering heavenly Father. Fourth, the goal of our salvation is not rescue from hell, or even justification. It is holiness and the glory of God (2 Cor 5:21). Until that goal is achieved, there will always be baggage in our lives that will have to be left behind (and which needs to be repented of) before we enter glory. For all these reasons, it is important that believers confess their sins in prayer, privately and congregationally.

Henry's second chapter, which deals with the confession of sin, has eleven main subsections and provides ample material to correct this regular omission from contemporary Christian prayer.[10] He supplies Scripture whereby we confess the reasons "we have to lie very low before God." But then immediately, he reminds us of "the great encouragement God has given us, to humble ourselves before him with sorrow and shame, and to confess our sins." Following this, he indicates five things we need to confess: (I) "our original corruption," (2) "our present corrupt dispositions to that which is evil, and our indisposedness to, and impotency in, that which is good," including—"the blindness of our understandings, . . . the stub-

---

[9]Ibid., p. 35.
[10]Ibid., pp. 35-52.

bornness of our wills, . . . the vanity of our thoughts, . . . the carnality of our affections, . . . and the corruption of the whole man," (3) "our omissions of our duty,"
(4) "our many actual transgressions, in thought, word, and deed," including pride,
rash anger, covetousness and love of the world, sensuality and flesh-pleasing, carnal
security, fretfulness, impatience, grumbling under affliction, distrust of God's providence, lack of love towards our brethren, tongue sins and spiritual slothfulness,
and (5) the sinfulness of sin, which includes the foolishness, unprofitableness, deceitfulness, offence, and damage of sin.

Next, Henry calls on us to "aggravate our sins," that is, to look at our sins in
light of factors that make them even "more heinous in the sight of God, and more
dangerous to ourselves." Henry provides Scripture that shows and presses us to
confess: (1) "The more knowledge we have of good and evil, the greater is our sin."
(2) "The greater profession we have made of religion, the greater hath been our
sin." (3) "The more mercies we have received from God, the greater has been our
sin." (4) "The fairer warning we have had from the world of God, and our own
consciences, concerning our danger of sin, and danger by sin, the greater is the sin
if we go on in it." (5) "The greater afflictions we have been under for sin, the
greater is the sin if we go on in it." (6) "The more vows and promises we have made
of better obedience, the greater has our sin been."

The outcome of this kind of confession, Henry says, is that "we must judge and
condemn ourselves for our sins, and own ourselves liable to punishment," "we must
give to God the glory of his patience towards us," and "we must humbly profess
our sorrow and shame for sin." The irony of such a full confession of sin, as Henry
outlines for us here, is that it leaves the believer (in receiving God's pardon) stag-
gered at the sheer magnitude and comprehensiveness of grace, and far more secure
in God's love than if sin had not been confessed in such excruciating detail.

Petition. Christian prayer today typically focuses on petition. But one is struck by
the superficiality and worldliness of much that is offered in petition, when it is
compared with the substance of biblical examples of believers' requests to God.
Henry, again, provides the Bible's remedy to this in the chapter concerning petition
or supplication.[11] According to Henry, petition consists of forgiveness of sins, objective and subjective aspects of reconciliation, and asking for the grace of God.

First, Henry leads us to "earnestly pray for the pardoning and forgiveness of all
our sins," pleading (1) the infinite goodness of God and his readiness to forgive sin,
(2) the merit and righteousness of our Lord Jesus Christ, which is our main plea

---

[11]Ibid., pp. 53-81.

for the pardon of sin, (3) the promises of God to pardon the repentant, (4) our own misery and danger because of sin, and (5) the blessed condition of the forgiven.

Second, from forgiveness, Henry then directs us to the scriptural theme of reconciliation, in which he leads us to pray "that God will be reconciled to us, that we may obtain his favor and blessing, and gracious acceptance." Five subpoints guide us with Scripture to seek "that we may be at peace with God, and his anger may be turned away from us," "that we may be taken into covenant with God, and admitted into relation to him," "that we may have the favor of God, and an interest in his special love," "that we may have the blessing of God," and "that we may have the presence of God with us." These are the objective aspects of reconciliation.

Now Henry moves to the subjective aspects of reconciliation in the third main section of the chapter, where he begins, "We must pray for the comfortable sense of our reconciliation to God, and our acceptance with him," specifically "that we may have some evidence of the pardon of our sins, and of our adoption," and "that we may have a well grounded peace of conscience; a holy security and serenity of mind, arising from a sense of our justification before God, and a good work wrought in us." Fourth and lastly, Henry guides us to "pray for the grace of God," and for various "kind and powerful influences and operations of that grace."

Using Henry's biblical outline of the substance of petitionary prayer will significantly correct the shallowness of our requests to God, as well as restore a God-centeredness even to our solicitations for ourselves. This change alone would bring a marked improvement to the quality of our discipleship.

Thanksgiving. A sense of entitlement is the death of gratitude. In our comfortable and affluent world in the Christian West, we must be constantly on guard for this bane of ingratitude to God. The prime prayer-weapon that God has given to us to fight against it is thanksgiving. Without thanksgiving in our prayers we will lack assurance because when we fail to rehearse God's answers and blessings we become forgetful of them and hence are opened up to discouragement. Matthew Henry supplies us with biblical substance for thanksgiving, which he calls "the fourth part of prayer, which is thanksgivings for the mercies we have received from God, and the many favors of his we are interested in, and have hope for benefit by."[12] This portion of Henry's comprehensive prayer outline has five sections, with numerous subpoints under sections 3-5. Henry explains the place of thanksgiving in prayer this way:

---

[12]Ibid., pp. 82-107.

Our errand at the throne of grace is not only to seek the favour of God, but to give unto him the glory due unto his name, and that not only by a grateful acknowledgment of his goodness to us, which cannot indeed add any thing to his glory, but he is pleased to accept of it, and to reckon himself glorified by it, if it comes from a heart that is humbly sensible of its own unworthiness to receive any favour from God, that values the gifts, and loves the giver of them.[13]

Intercession. Not surprisingly, Henry's chapter on intercession is replete with ideas for our praying on behalf of others.[14] Traditional Protestant pastoral prayer has involved five main matters for regular intercession: prayer for the sanctification of the congregation, for civil authorities, for the Christian ministry, for the salvation of humanity, and for the afflicted.

Henry covers and elaborates on these in twelve main sections, leading us to (1) "pray for the whole world of mankind, the lost world," (2) for "the propagation of the gospel in foreign parts, and the enlargement of the church," (3) for "the conversion of the Jews," (4) for God to preserve the church under Islamic persecution and for God to check the growth of Islam, (5) for the mission churches in the colonies, (6) for "the universal church, wherever it is dispersed," (7) for "the conviction and conversion of atheists, deists, and infidels, and of all that are out of the way of truth, and of profane scoffers, and those that disgrace Christianity by their vicious and immoral lives," (8) for "the amending of every thing that is amiss in the church, the reviving of primitive Christianity, and the power of godliness, and in order thereunto the pouring out of the Spirit," (9) for "the breaking of the power of all the enemies of the church, and the defeating of all their designs against her," (10) for "the relief of suffering churches, and the support, comfort, and deliverance of all that are persecuted for righteousness," (11) for the nations and countries around us, (12) for our own land (seeking God for its welfare, being "thankful to God for his mercies to our land," "humble before God for our national sins and provocations," praying "earnestly for the favour of God to us," for "the continuance of the gospel among us, and the means of grace," for "the continuance of our outward peace and tranquility, liberty and plenty," for civic virtue, for domestic unity, for "victory and success against our enemies abroad," for the national leadership, and for the various branches of government).

Henry urges us, with this plea, to intercede for others:

Our Lord Jesus hath taught us to pray, not only with, but for others: And the apostle

---

[13]Ibid., p. 82.
[14]Ibid., pp. 108-25.

hath appointed us to make supplication for all the saints: and many of his prayers in his epistles are for his friends: And we must not think that when we are in this part of prayer, we may let fall our fervency, and be more indifferent, because we ourselves are not immediately concerned in it, but rather let a holy fire of love, both to God and man here, make our devotions yet more warm and lively.[15]

CONCLUSION

After pausing in the sixth chapter to consider some special occasions for prayer and to offer scriptural substance for them (including ideas for blessings before and after meals, and prayers on such occasions as droughts, floods, plagues, fires and storms),[16] Henry's seventh chapter ("Of the Conclusion of our prayers") helps us to "sum up our requests in some comprehensive petitions."[17] We are, Henry says, to ask God's "acceptance of our poor weak prayers, for Christ's sake" and his "forgiveness of what has been amiss in our prayers," commend ourselves to his grace, conclude with "doxologies or solemn praises of God, ascribing honor and glory to the Father, the Son, and the Holy Ghost, and sealing up all our praises and prayers with an affectionate Amen." Henry suggests that we may appropriately conclude our prayers with the Lord's Prayer, which is especially interesting in light of John Owen's and English nonconformity's reticence about its use.

The eighth chapter of the book offers biblical material with which to paraphrase and elaborate on the outline of the Lord's Prayer.[18] The ninth chapter provides sample "forms" of prayer, which are worth their weight in gold.[19] What Henry calls a "children's prayer" will stagger many a mature adult Christian.

THE BENEFITS OF READING AND USING *A METHOD FOR PRAYER*

Reading and rereading Henry's book will train us in the use of biblical truth and language in prayer, and thus assist and encourage modern Christians in both public and private prayer. Resorting to a more scriptural pattern of prayer may be a simple (but profound) answer to many problems in our practice of prayer. Praying scripturally will teach us what prayer is, even while we do it. Biblically shaped prayer will correct the "shopping list" approach to prayer which abounds in the Christian

---

[15]Ibid., p. 108.

[16]Ibid., pp. 126-47. There are poignant prayers here for sick children, for families where the father has been lost, for women in childbirth, or recovering from it, for those parents "whose children are a grief to them, or such as they are in fear about," for "those that are in prison," and for those who are condemned "that have but a little while to live."

[17]Ibid., pp. 148-51.

[18]Ibid., pp. 152-66.

[19]Ibid., pp. 167-97.

community, even as it begins to solve in our own minds the question of "unanswered prayer." Availing ourselves of the comprehensive categories of scriptural prayer enumerated by Henry reminds us of just how much there is to pray about day by day. Utilizing the prayer language of Scripture will teach us of the extreme urgency of prayer (indeed, Henry once said that "those who live without prayer, live without God in this world"). Aiming for a biblical pattern for prayer will return proportion to prayers long on petition but short on adoration, confession, and thanksgiving. Henry's book will help us pray more biblically, and thus more effectively for ministers, missionaries and one another. It will show us the proper way to approach God in prayer and will remind us of the good things that God does for us, which we, more often than not, take for granted. Pillaging the Bible for aid in prayer will remind us to always give thanks to God (which, paradoxically, is important for our own assurance of his faithfulness in answering prayer), and will begin to engrave in our minds biblical patterns of thought that can help immunize us from the enticing folly of the world's view of life. Biblically saturated prayer forces us to rehearse the solemn warnings and precious promises of God (which will do eternal good to our souls) and moves us from our inherent human-focused prayer to a biblical, God-centered way of praying. For those who are called upon to lead the church in public prayer, or who simply desire to be more faithful and competent in their own private petitions, a scriptural manner of praying provides the order, proportion and variety that should characterize all our prayers. Matthew Henry's *A Method for Prayer* helps us in all these areas, and so may God use his little book to help us all become men and women mighty in prayer.[20]

SELECT BIBLIOGRAPHY

Primary Sources

Henry, Matthew. *A Method for Prayer: With Scripture-Expressions Proper to Be Used Under Each Head.* In *The Complete Works of Matthew Henry—Treatises, Sermons, and Tracts,* 2 vols. Edinburgh, London and Dublin: A. Fullarton, 1855. Reprinted, Grand Rapids: Baker, 1979. (*A Method for Prayer* is found in 2:1-96; several other works deal with prayer, including *Directions for Daily Communion with God, in three discourses, Showing How to Begin, How to Spend, and How to Close Every Day with God,* 1:198-247; *A Church in the House: A Sermon Concerning Family Religion,* 1:248-67; and *Family Hymns, gathered mostly out of the*

---

[20]In addition to *A Method for Prayer*, three books stand out as aids to the cultivation of a robust, biblical practice of prayer: Don Carson's extraordinary *A Call to Spiritual Reformation: Priorities from Paul and His Prayers* (Grand Rapids: Baker, 1992); Arthur Bennett's *The Valley of Vision: A Collection of Puritan Prayers and Devotions* (Edinburgh: Banner of Truth Trust, 1975); and Isaac Watts's *Guide to Prayer* (Edinburgh: Banner of Truth Trust, 2002).

translations of David's Psalms, 1:413-43.)

————. *A Method for Prayer,* ed. J. Ligon Duncan III. Fearn, Ross-shire, Scotland: Christian Focus, 1994, 1998. (This edition includes Henry's other book on prayer called *Directions for Beginning, Spending, and Closing Each Day with God.*)

Secondary Sources

Gordon, Alexander. "Matthew Henry." In *Dictionary of National Biography,* edited by Leslie Stephen and Sidney Lee, 26:123-24. London: Smith, Elder, 1891.

Seaton, Jack. "Philip and Matthew Henry." *The Banner of Truth* 137 (1975): 1-8, esp. 5-8.

Williams, J. B. *The Lives of Philip and Matthew Henry.* 1839. Reprinted, Edinburgh: Banner of Truth Trust, 1974.

⸲ 17 ⸲

THE POETRY OF
ANNE BRADSTREET
(1612-1672)
AND EDWARD TAYLOR
(1642-1729)

Mark A. Noll

REFORMED PROTESTANTS, INCLUDING THE PURITANS, DID NOT, AS A
rule, excel at the arts. Early on a principle was established by Ulrich Zwingli of Zu-
rich and others that could have allowed room for artistic development: artistic
forms not allowed in formal church services—because they were not commanded
in Scripture—could nonetheless be cultivated at home and in other noneccslesias-
tical venues. Despite this opening, the way in which the Regulative Principle usually worked out in practice—with visual art, sculpture, and elaborate choral music
banned from the worship service as well as the worship space, and with the worship
service functioning as the norm for public expressions of all kinds—prejudiced
Reformed communities against many of the arts. Exceptions could be found in the
Calvinist lands of southwestern Germany, the Netherlands, Scotland, Puritan England, Hungary and the Reformed cantons of Switzerland, like the exquisite music
of Louis Bourgeois written for the Genevan *Psalter* or the realistic landscapes of seventeenth-century Dutch painting.[1] But they were notable in great part because they
were exceptions to the usual Reformed rule.

---

[1]On the theological basis for that painting, see E. John Walford, *Jacob van Ruisdael and the Perception of Landscape* (New
Haven, Conn.: Yale University Press, 1992).

With words on the page, however, it was another matter entirely. The central place of the sermon in worship, the painstaking efforts to plumb the depths of the written Word of God, and the cultivation of a "plain style" of sermonic rhetoric—all gave a strong impetus to Reformed writing of many kinds, including belles-lettres. "It was," in the words of historian John Morgan, "the ability to write that allowed the godly to produce their daily testaments of struggle, and for separated relatives to encourage each other to labour for (and in) the covenant."[2] This affinity for disciplined words helps explain why poetry and allegory came so comparatively easily to so many in Reformed communities. Efforts at paraphrasing psalms into meter were a constant Calvinist exercise in the sixteenth and seventeenth centuries. In the Reformed world generally, as with the Puritans in particular, it was a relatively small step from meditating on Scripture (especially the Psalms), from putting great care into the composition of "plain style" sermons, and from sponsoring the production of metrical paraphrases, to writing poetry structured by biblical narratives (John Milton) or imaginative prose exemplifying biblical realities (John Bunyan). What may be considered surprising for the Reformed worlds of the seventeenth century is that poetry, and poetry of a high order, was written not only at the center of Puritan civilization in England but also at the cultural margins in New England.

The history of poetry in Puritan New England is almost coterminous with the history of New England. In 1640, only ten years after the founding of the Massachusetts Bay Colony, the press at Cambridge, which with its type had been imported at great cost, published as its first title, *The Whole Booke of Psalmes Faithfully Translated into English Metre*. This volume repeated in the new world what Reformed Christians had often done in the old, but the results, despite somewhat precarious rhythms, were still noteworthy, as in its very first lines:

> O Blessed man, that in th'advice
> Of wicked doeth not walk:
> Nor stands in sinners way, or sit
> In chayre of scornfull folk.
> But in the law of Jehovah,
> Is his longing delight:
> And in his law doth meditate,
> By day and eke by night.[3]

---

[2]John Morgan, *Godly Learning: Puritan Attitudes Towards Reason, Learning and Education, 1560-1640* (Cambridge: Cambridge University Press, 1986), p. 165.

From that beginning point the uses of poetry multiplied. They included the *New England Primer* of 1683, with verses written specifically for young people:

> I in the Burying Place may see
>   Graves shorter there than I;
> From Death's Arrest no Age is free,
>   Young Children too may die;
> My God, may such an awful Sight,
>   Awakening be to me!
> Oh! that by early Grace I might
>   For Death prepared be.[4]

Many New Englanders of the first generations added their efforts, like the leading minister, John Cotton, who in 1658 published "A Thankful Acknowledgment of God's Providence":

> In mothers womb thy fingers did me make,
> And from the womb thou didst me safely take:
> From breast thou hast me nurst my life throughout,
> That I may say I never wanted ought.[5]

Or Benjamin Woodbridge who in 1699 memorialized John Cotton's life with verses for his tomb:

> Here lies magnanimous Humility,
> Majesty, Meekness; Christian Apathy
> On soft Affections: Liberty in thrall;
> A Noble Spirit, Servant unto all.
> Learnings great Master-piece; who yet would sit
> As a Disciple at his Schollars feet.
> A simple Serpent, or Serpentine Dove,
> Made of Wisdome, Innocence, and Love.[6]

Among the many Puritan versifiers of early New England, Anne Bradstreet was singled out in her own time for unusual respect, and Edward Taylor has come in recent decades to be considered by literary scholars an unusually effective practitioner of Puritan poetics. For Christians in the twenty-first century to learn some-

---

[3] *Early American Writings*, ed. Carla Mulford, Angela Vietto and Amy E. Winans (New York: Oxford University Press, 2001), p. 351.
[4] Ibid., p. 353.
[5] Ibid., p. 354.
[6] Ibid., p. 356.

thing about the lives of Bradstreet and Taylor and to sample a small portion of their literary output rectifies an unfortunate situation where students in the general academy have paid them more attention than have Christian communities where their work by rights should be most at home. In addition, to make the acquaintance of Anne Bradstreet and Edward Taylor can contribute to the general picture of early American Puritanism by putting poetic flesh on the bones of doctrines, churches, migrations, wars and other external achievements that so often dominate the landscape of Puritan studies.

ANNE BRADSTREET (1612-1672)

Anne Bradstreet was the first person in the British colonies to publish a book of poetry and likewise the first British colonial woman to publish a book of any kind. Because of these distinctions, she became an object of increasing scholarly attention throughout the twentieth century. Debates over whether Bradstreet desired to subvert the era's standard male-female relationships, or over the quality of her commentary on contemporary events, can prove worthwhile but only after understanding the main themes of what she wrote. Those main themes came out of a life privileged in its intellectual training, but even more from an orientation to the wisdom and goodness of God as experienced on two continents amid the striking vicissitudes of a rich domestic life.

Anne Bradstreet was born in Northampton, England, probably in 1612, where her mother, Dorothy Yorke, enjoyed a considerable income, and her father, Thomas Dudley, was steward to the Earl of Lincoln.[7] Sometime before she was born, the Earl and his retinue, including the Dudley family, had cast their lot with the Puritan forces of reform. In 1627 the Earl of Lincoln would be among a number of others sent to the Tower of London for resisting Charles I's efforts at collecting an enforced loan from England's elite. From age six to sixteen Anne Dudley enjoyed free access to the Earl's considerable library, where from Latin and Greek classics, Sir Walter Raleigh's *History of the World* (1614), and above all the *Geneva Bible*, she received a much better education than most girls—and also than many boys—of her day. During a tumultuous sixteenth year, Anne survived an attack of smallpox, experienced conversion and was married. Her husband, Simon Bradstreet, was the

---

[7]For biographical information, I have benefited especially from Elizabeth Wade Wright, *Anne Bradstreet: The Tenth Muse* (New York: Oxford University Press, 1971); Robert Daly, "Anne Bradstreet," *American National Biography*, ed. John A. Garraty and Mark C. Carnes (New York: Oxford University Press, 1999), 3:385-86; and the editorial material in the Jeannine Hensley and Charles Hambrick-Stowe editions mentioned under the "Select Bibliography."

son of a nonconforming minister and had graduated from the Puritan stronghold, Emmanuel College, Cambridge, before coming into service with the Earl of Lincoln as Thomas Dudley's assistant.

About the time of this marriage in 1628, heightened tensions with Charles I and William Laud, then the bishop of London and chancellor of the University of Oxford, caused a few leading Puritans to explore the possibility of migration to the New World. Among those who took the lead in this plan were several individuals associated with the Earl of Lincoln, including Thomas Dudley and Simon Bradstreet. When the first major contingent of Puritans ventured forth in April 1630, the Dudley family, including Simon and Anne Bradstreet, were aboard the *Arbella* with Governor John Winthrop.

Anne later wrote that she bridled at the privations of her early days in Massachusetts Bay. But when she, like so many of the early settlers, became seriously ill, it seems to have reconciled her to life in the wilderness as a calling from God. Her recovery, in fact, prompted the first of her extant poems, "Upon a Fit of Sickness, Anno. 1632 Aetatis Suae, 19," in which she offered a standard Puritan opinion about the transitory character of life and the need to devote oneself to divine things:

> For what's this life, but care and strife?
> 　　since first we came from womb,
> Our strength doth waste, our time doth haste,
> 　　and then we go to th' Tomb. . . .
> O whil'st I live, this grace me give,
> 　　I doing good may be,
> Then deaths arrest, I shall count best,
> 　　because it's thy decree (66).[8]

The Bradstreets became concerned about their ability to have a family, until in 1634 Samuel, the first of their eight children, was born. From that time, domestic duties multiplied even as Anne's broader family became more deeply involved in the affairs of Massachusetts Bay. Her father served a term as governor in 1634-1635, as he would again several times in later years, and in the mid-1630s he joined the inaugural board of overseers at Harvard College. In 1635 the entire Dudley clan moved north on the Charles River to Ipswich, where other children were born to

---

[8] References to the poems of Bradstreet and Taylor are to *Early New England Meditative Poetry: Anne Bradstreet and Edward Taylor*, ed. Charles E. Hambrick-Stowe (New York: Paulist, 1988). This volume reprints a full, carefully edited selection of poems with their original spelling and punctuation, but also includes an introduction of unusual historical scope and theological insight.

the Bradstreets and where Anne benefited greatly from the ministry of the Rev.
Nathaniel Ward, one of the most important preachers in Puritan New England. In
1645 Simon and Anne Bradstreet moved again, this time to North Andover, where
she lived out the rest of her days. By that time, Anne was regularly writing poems
in odd moments stolen from an increasingly busy life as mother and household
manager. One of these was "A Dialogue between old England and New; Concerning Their Present Troubles, Anno, 1642," in which she offered a decidedly Puritan,
though also moderate and thoughtful, account of the outbreak of civil war between
the English Parliament and Charles I. The poem features graphic accounts of what
Puritans perceived as England's besetting sins:

> Idolatry supplanter of a Nation,
> With foolish Superstitious Adoration,
> Are lik'd and countenac'd by men of might,
> The Gospel troden down and hath no right (118).

This lengthy poem also shares fully in the Puritan's standard anti-Catholicism:

> Lets bring *Baals* vestments forth to make a fire,
> Their Mystires, Surplices, and all their Tire [attire],
> Copes, Rotchets, Crossiers, and such empty trash;
> And let their Names consume, but let the flash
> Light Christendome, and all the world to see
> We hate *Romes* whore, with all her trumpery (121).

Yet unlike more radical Puritan voices, the poem envisions a purified monarchy as
opposed to the execution of the king and the establishment of a Puritan commonwealth, as actually happened a few years later.

Apparently without thought of ever publishing them, Anne continued to write poems as her children multiplied and grew up, and as Simon became more deeply involved
in the political and economic life of the colony. When Anne's mother died at age sixty-
one in 1643, she memorialized her with conventional but also affectionate lines:

> Religious in all her words and wayes,
> Preparing still for death, till end of dayes:
> Of all her Children, Children, liv'd to see,
> Then dying, left a blessed memory (128).

The larger significance of this memorial poem was that it provided an early instance of much of her best later verse, which would also be written about family
members, often again as memorials at death.

Anne's emergence as a phenomenon—a published female poet—came about without her knowledge or intent. The minister of the Bradstreet's new residence in North Andover was her sister Mercy's husband, John Woodbridge, who in 1647 returned to England to aid the Puritan side in the last phase of the English Civil War. He took with him to England a manuscript of Bradstreet's poems that had apparently been circulating privately among friends and the domestic circle. Anne herself had spent time revising some of the poems in this manuscript and also fitting it out with an apology for her poetic efforts. This "Prologue" acknowledged that she was not capable of writing poems "To sing of Wars, of Captains, and of Kings, / Of Cities founded, Common-wealths begun" (113). She also noted, with respect to her sex, that in composing verse, "I am obnoxious to each carping tongue / Who says my hand a needle better fits" (114). But the poem also boldly suggested that, although "Men can do best, and women know it well," it was still appropriate for women to do what they could in the sphere of literature—"Yet grant some small acknowledgment of ours." And it closed with the kind of elaborate conceit that drew attention to its author's skill even in the act of demeaning it. Bradstreet, that is, justified her own poems to "ye high flown quills that soar the Skies" by the consideration that they would only make the verse of such ones seem all the better: "This mean and unrefined ure [ore] of mine / Will make you glistering [glistening] gold, but more to shine" (114).

John Woodbridge arranged in 1650 for the manuscript to be published in London under a title that Bradstreet did not appreciate, *The Tenth Muse Lately sprung up in America. Or Severall Poems, compiled with great variety of Wit and Learning . . . By a Gentlewoman in those parts*. Later, Bradstreet revised many of the poems from this book and prepared eighteen more for the press, which were then published in Boston after her death in 1678 with a modest title closer to her liking, *Several Poems . . . By a Gentlewoman in New England*. After the publication of *The Tenth Muse* in 1650, Anne saw her children married and begin to make their own families. She suffered several bouts of debilitating illness, her husband Simon journeyed to England in 1662 as a Massachusetts emissary charged with repairing relations with the restored king Charles II (successfully accomplished), the Bradstreets witnessed their house and all of their worldly goods consumed by fire in July 1666, and Anne's health declined over several years before her death at Andover on September 16, 1672.

The poems she left behind remain an impressive testimony to the vitality of Puritan intellectual life. In fact, John Woodbridge may have engineered the London publication of her book to make the point that the flourishing civilization of Puritan New England extended even to women. She was fully capable of formal, discursive meditations on standard themes of Puritan piety, like the security of heaven in contrast to the insubstantial pleasures of earthly life. This theme she explored in the lengthy "Contemplations" that appeared in her 1678 *Several Poems*; it closed with reference to the strikingly personal image of Revelation 2:17, where God writes on a white stone a secret name for the believer:

> O Time the fatal wrack of mortal things,
> That draws oblivions curtains over kings,
> Their sumptuous monuments, men know them not,
> Their names without a Record are forgot,
> Their parts, their ports, their pomp's all laid in th' dust
> Nor wit nor gold, nor buildings scape times rust;
> But he whose name is grav'd in the white stone
> Shall last and shine when all of these are gone (109).

Much more commonly, Bradstreet turned a poetic eye toward the domestic relationships that structured her daily life. In so doing, she produced one of the most affecting sets of personal, yet God-honoring verses in English literature. The poetry does not soar nor does it strive for unusual affects, but it is rooted solidly in the most ancient school of character.

On several occasions she wrote particularly poignant verses about her father, including an early poem that employed banking metaphors in gratitude to the one who had given Anne her "principle":

> Such is my debt, I may not say forgive,
> But as I can, I'le pay it while I live:
> Such is my bond, none can discharge but I,
> Yet paying is not payd until I dye (71).

When Thomas Dudley passed away at age seventy-seven in 1653, Bradstreet composed a long memorial poem, but also a simple, yet frank, epitaph that in passing referred to Dudley's role in enforcing Massachusetts's laws against sectarians ("Sectaryes") like Quakers and Baptists.

> Within this Tomb a Patriot lyes
> That was both pious, just and wise,
> To Truth a shield, to right a Wall,
> To Sectaryes a whip and Maul,
> A Magazine of History,
> A Prizer of good Company
> In manners pleasant and severe

The Good him lov'd, the bad did fear,
And when his time with years was spent
If some rejoyc'd, more did lament (127).

Several of Bradstreet's most memorable poems concern her affection for her husband. In one, "Before the Birth of One of Her Children," Anne addresses Simon with the expectation that she, like so many of her peers, might not survive the birth:

How soon, my Dear, death may my steps attend,
How soon't may be thy Lot to lose thy friend. . . .
The many faults that well you know I have,
Let be interr'd in my oblivious grave;
If any worth or virtue were in me,
Let that live freshly in thy memory.
And when thou feel'st no grief, as I no harms,
Yet love thy dead, who long lay in thine arms:
And when thy loss shall be repaid with gains
Look to my little babes my dear remains.
And if thou love thy self, or loved'st me
These O protect from step Dames injury.
And if chance to thine eyes shall bring this verse,
With some sad sighs honour my absent Herse;
And kiss this paper for thy loves dear sake,
Who with salt tears this last Farewel did take (67).

Bradstreet and her child survived this birth, but she would live to experience many other occasions for grief. The following lines were written in 1669 after the death of a grandchild not quite four years old:

With troubled heart and trembling hand I write,
The Heavens have chang'd to sorrow my delight.
How oft with disappointment have I met,
When I on fading things my hopes have set? . . .
Farewel dear child, thou ne're shall come to me,
But yet a while, and I shall go to thee;
Mean time my throbbing heart's chear'd up with this
Thou with thy Saviour art in endless bliss.

One of Bradstreet's most effective poems was written after the harrowing night of July 10, 1666, when her house was destroyed by fire (92-94). "In silent night when rest I took," she was roused by "thundering nois / and Piteous shreiks of dreadfull voice." Immediately Bradstreet prayed for God "To strengthen me in my Distresse," but she was forced to see "The flame consume my dwelling place." Her immediate response was pious resignation:

> And, when I could no longer look,
> I blest his Name that gave and took,
> That layd my goods now in the dust:
> Yea so it was, and so 'twas just.
> It was his own; it was not mine;
> Far be it that I should repine.

Yet then something like repining immediately took place as Bradstreet walked through the ruins and lingered over "the places . . . where oft I sate, and long did lye," contemplated where "stood that Trunk, and there that chest; / There lay that store I counted best," and thought about place-connected experiences that would never again brighten her life ("Under thy roof no guest shall sitt, / Nor at thy Table eat a bitt"). And so the mournful meditation continued until, in a rush of doctrinal correctness, which in her hands becomes also a moving exhortation, she caught herself up short:

> Then straight I gin my heart to chide,
> And didst thy wealth on earth abide?
> Didst fix thy hope on mouldring dust,
> The arm of flesh didst make thy trust?
> Raise up thy thoughts above the skye
> That dunghill mists away may flie.
> Thou hast an house on high erect
> Fram'd by that mighty Architect,
> With glory richly furnished,
> Stands permanent tho' this bee fled.
> It's purchased, and paid for too
> By him who hath enough to do. . . .
> Ther's wealth enough, I need no more;
> Farewell my Pelf [possessions], farewell my Store.
> The world no longer let me Love,
> My hope and Treasure lyes Above.

The strength of Anne Bradstreet's domestic connections and the sturdy Puritan faith illustrated by those connections became the theme of one of her prose meditations that was written "when my soul hath been refreshed with the consolation which the world knowes not." With its references to many biblical passages, including Isaiah 54:5, it is a fitting summary in prose for the poetic themes that she explored so well:

> Lord, why should I doubt any more when thou hast given me such assured Pledges of thy Love? First, thou art my Creator, I thy creature; thou my master, I thy servant. But hence arises not my comfort: Thou art my Father, I thy child. Yee shall [be] my Sons and Daughters, saith the Lord Almighty. Christ is my Brother; I ascend unto my Father and your Father, unto my God and your God. But least this should not bee enough, thy maker is thy husband. Nay, more, I am a member of his Body; he, my head. Such Priviledges, had not the Word of Truth made them known, who or where is the man that durst in his heart have presumed to have thought it? (80)

EDWARD TAYLOR (1642–1729)

In the inventory of Edward Taylor's estate, only one book of poetry was found, and it was by Anne Bradstreet.[9] Yet despite the commonalities that both were serious Puritans and serious poets, Taylor's life was very different from Bradstreet's. Unlike his notable poetic predecessor, Taylor came from humble origins, he lived his life on the fringes of colonial society, and his poetry was almost unknown in his own lifetime. But the greatest difference between the two is that while Bradstreet wrote clear, direct poems about God's loving sovereignty over her domestic life, Taylor wrote complex, highly metaphorical poems describing how his own psyche internalized the great themes of biblical theology. Anne Bradstreet was an entirely admirable poet who won renown in her own lifetime for her solid, God-honoring talent. Edward Taylor was a genius whose intricate poems, when they were finally published long after his death, transformed the image of the Puritan imagination.

Taylor was born in Leicestershire, England, to a farming family, probably in 1642. His intellectual abilities were recognized early on, and he was employed as a schoolteacher until in 1662 he refused to conform to the Act of Uniformity by which Charles II sought to purify the Church of England of the Puritans. After continued difficulties in his native land, Taylor in 1668 immigrated to New England, where he first stayed for two nights with Reverend Increase Mather, who was then also serving as president of Harvard College. Taylor was admitted to the college (he was then about twenty-six years old) and after a splendid undergraduate career graduated in 1671. At the commencement, Taylor declaimed a full-scale de-

---

[9]For biographical information, I have relied on Robert Daly, *God's Altar: The World and the Flesh in Puritan Poetry* (Berkeley: University of California Press, 1978); Jeffrey A. Hammond, "Edward Taylor," in *American National Biography*, ed. John A. Garraty and Mark C. Carnes (New York: Oxford University Press, 1999), 21:365-67; and the editorial material in the Donald Stanford and Charles Hambrick-Stowe editions mentioned under the "Select Bibliography."

fense of the English language in verse. He had, in fact, been writing poems for some time, and it is evident that he had heeded closely the metaphorical style and the metrical patterns of England's metaphysical poets, including the incomparable George Herbert (1592-1633). Soon after his Harvard graduation, Taylor was approached by citizens from the new town of Westfield, in south-central Massachusetts near to the Connecticut border, to serve as their inaugural pastor. He accepted this call, although it was not until 1679 that a church was formally organized. The delay was caused in large part by desperate clashes with Indian warriors that marked this entire decade. In 1674 Taylor married Elizabeth Fitch, the daughter of a clergyman. They would have eight children (three surviving) before she died in 1689. Three years after her death, Taylor married Ruth Wyllis, with whom he had six children.

Taylor left a large cache of manuscripts after his own death, but the sermons and many kinds of poems it contained reveal only hints about external life in Westfield. He was respected as a faithful preacher of Puritan doctrine and known for his conservative views on church practices. In the era's heated debates over whether it was necessary to make a full profession of faith before taking part in the Lord's Supper, Taylor stood against the practice of Solomon Stoddard in nearby Northampton, who offered Communion to all respectable citizens as a "converting ordinance."[10] Otherwise, however, not much is known about Taylor's day in, day out activities.

It was far otherwise with his internal spiritual life, once Taylor's poems and sermons were published. Therein also lies a tale. Taylor's writing was known by his family and a few others, but it was not until 1937 that Thomas H. Johnson of Yale University began to publish significant portions of these manuscripts. Immediately they created a sensation, especially by putting a lie to the notion of the Puritans as cold, doctrinally constricted dogmatists. Whether Taylor had requested that his poems not be published is unclear. What is clear is that when they finally did appear in print, they were recognized immediately for the forcefulness of their language, for Taylor's incredibly broad knowledge of crafts, agriculture, the sciences, history and the Bible, and for the extraordinarily complex life of piety they revealed.

Taylor's poems include a large number of occasional efforts, a long doctrinal-biblical sequence of thirty-five poems titled "God's Determinations," and a staggering 217 "Preparatory Meditations" that he wrote as a way of preparing his own heart for the administration of the Lord's Supper. He wrote these at regular intervals from July 23, 1682, until he retired at age eighty-three in 1725. The most dif-

---

[10]See for detailed attention and relevant texts, Thomas M. Davis and Virginia L. Davis, eds., *Edward Taylor vs. Solomon Stoddard: The Nature of the Lord's Supper* (Boston: Twayne, 1981).

ficult task of anyone trying to introduce Taylor briefly is the decision about what to quote from this extraordinarily rich treasure. The prime difficulty for readers is the patience required to handle Taylor's archaic spelling, diction, and word choice. (On that score, it works best to read the poems slowly and out-loud, procedures that greatly reduce the apparent distance between Taylor's seventeenth-century prosody and English usage of our own day.)

The occasional poems include a number of typological exercises whereby natural situations are used to provide spiritual instruction. One of the most memorable is "Upon a Spider Catching a Fly" in which the fly is likened to the sinner ensnared by sin and Satan:

> This Frey [fray] seems thus to us.
>   Hells spider gets
> His intrails spun to whip Cords thus
>   And wove to nets
>   And sets.
>
> To tangle Adams race
>   In's stratagems
> To their Destructions, spoil'd, made base
>   By venom things
>   Damn'd Sins (131).

The occasional verses also include unusually effective poems of affection for Taylor's first wife Elizabeth and for their offspring who died as very young children. Here is Taylor in a poem titled "Upon Wedlock, and Death of Children," in which the first lines speak rapturously of "the True-Love Knot, more sweet than spice / And set with all the flowres of Graces dress" that God provided in Christian marriage. The poem continues with heightened joy about the birth of children, but then turns starkly realistic concerning the illness and then the demise of the children who as flowers had adorned the "True Love-Knot" of matrimony:

> But oh! the tortures, Vomit, screechings, groans,
> And six weeks Fever would pierce hearts like stones.
>
> Griefe o're doth flow: and nature fault would finde
>   Were not thy Will, my Spell Charm, Joy, and Gem:
> That as I said, I say, take, Lord, they're thine.
>   I piecemeale pass to Glory bright in them.
>   I joy, may I sweet Flowers for Glory breed,
>   Whether thou getst them green, or lets them seed (134).

Taylor was just as graphic and even more moving after the death of Elizabeth herself, when he wrote "A Funerall Poem upon the death of my ever endeared, and tender wife Mrs. Elizbeth Taylor, who fell asleep in Christ the 7th day of July at night about two hours after sun setting 1689 and in the 39 yeare of her life." In this effort, Taylor's use of metaphysical devices like the extended catalogue, revealed to good effect his literary sympathy with English poets like George Herbert and Francis Quarles. At one point in the poem Taylor addresses God directly:

> Five Babes thou tookst from me before this Stroake.
> Thine arrows then into my bowels broake,
> But now they pierce into my bosom smart,
> Do strike and stob [stab] me in the very heart (136).

But mostly his wife and her virtues are in view:

> Her husbands Joy, Her Childrens Chief Content.
> Her Servants Eyes, Her Houses Ornament.
> Her Shine as Child, as Neighbour, flies abroad
> As Mistress, Mother, Wife, her Walke With God (137).

A poem that, with good reason, has been often reprinted is Taylor's conceit on the spinning wheel, titled "Huswifery," where apparatus and operation both serve as powerful metaphors for the believer's life in Christ. In the poem's first line, "compleate" means "fully equipped," "winde quills" in line eight means to fill spools with yarn, "Fulling mills" in line ten refers to places where cloth is cleansed (and also echoes Malachi 3:2), and "pinkt" in line twelve means "adorned."

> Make me, O Lord, thy Spinning Wheele compleate.
>   Thy Holy Worde my Distaff make for mee.
> Make mine Affections thy Swift Flyers neate
>   And make my Soule thy holy Spoole to bee.
>   My Conversation make to be thy Reele
>   And reele the yarn theron spun of thy Wheele.
>
> Make me thy Loome then, knit therein this Twine:
>   And make thy Holy Spirit, Lord, winde quills:
> Then weave the Web thyselfe. The yarn is fine.
>   Thine Ordinances make my Fulling Mills.
>   Then dy the same in Heavenly Colours Choice,
>   All pinkt with Varnisht Flowers of Paradise.
>
> Then cloath therewith mine Understanding, Will,

Affections, Judgment, Conscience, Memory
My Words, and Actions, that their shine may fill
   My wayes with glory and thee glorify.
Then mine apparel shall display before yee
That I am Cloathed in Holy robes for glory (132-33).

The six-line stanza of iambic pentameter rhyming a-b-a-b-c-c that Taylor used for "Huswifery" was the same that George Herbert had employed for the long prefatory poem, "The Church Porch," that introduced his own magisterial sequence, *The Temple*. More pertinent for Taylor's own work, this was the form he perfected in the "Preparatory Meditations," ranging from three to twelve stanzas, that he composed along with sermons for the celebration of Communion. Usually these meditations were keyed to the same text upon which Taylor preached; usually they provided full scope for frank personal examination; usually they breathed ardent praise for God's saving work in Christ.

Included in these meditations are some of the most moving statements about the work of redemption ever attempted in the English language. Thus in one of a series of poems on John 6:51, "I am the Living Bread," Taylor considered the richest imaginable human fare as nugatory in comparison to what Christ offered: "Their Spiced Cups, sweet Meats, and Sugar Cakes / Are but dry Sawdust to this Living Bread." (171) The poem ends, as the meditations often do, with Taylor being swept away by the magnitude of God's grace:

What wonder's here, that Bread of Life should come
   To feed Dead Dust? Dry Dust eate Living Bread?
Yet Wonder more by far may all, and some
   That my Dull Heart's so dumpish when thus fed.
   Lord Pardon this, and feed mee all my dayes,
   With Living Bread to thy Eternall Prayse (172).

It was similar with one of several meditations on John 6:55, where Jesus proclaimed that "my blood is true drink." Taylor wrote that, although he was sinsick—"My Soule had Caught an Ague, and like Hell / Her thirst did burn"—God had provided the most powerful medication imaginable: in his "bright blazing Love did spring a Well / of Aqua-Vitae in the Deity." The result was a bold statement about the effects of that love upon Taylor, but also with reference to God himself:

But how it came, amazeth all Communion.
   Gods onely Son doth hug Humanity,

Into his very person. By which Union
   His Humane Veans its golden gutters ly.
   And rather than my Soule should dy by thirst,
   These golden Pipes, to give me drink, did burst (173).

Taylor's metaphoric creativity with biblical themes was endless. Eleven stanzas written April 22, 1683, on Song of Solomon 2:1 ("I am a rose of Sharon") allowed him to elaborate upon the immense contrast between his own unworthiness and the supernal worth of Christ, a theme that was common to many of the meditations. In these stanzas, "Palma Christi" means "castor oil," "Unguent Apostolrum" is the "apostolic remedy" referred to in James 5:14, "Supple" means "anoint," "sheed" is "shed," and "a Physick" is "a medicine."

The Rosy Oyle, from Sharons Rose extract
   Better than Palma Christi far is found.
Its Billiads Balm for Conscience when she's wrackt
   Unguent Apostolorum for each Wound.
   Let me they Patient, thou my Surgeon bee.
   Lord, with thy Oyle of Roses Supple mee.

But, oh! alas! that such should be my need
   That this Brave Flower must Pluckt, stampt, squeezed bee,
And boyld up in its Blood, its Spirits sheed,
   To make a Physick sweet, sure, safe for mee.
   But yet this mangled Rose rose up again
   And in its pristine glory, doth remain (165, 166).

In another meditation four years later, but from Song of Solomon 4:8 ("my bride"), Taylor used in his own way the same idea from Isaiah 54:5 ("your Maker is your husband") that had been so important to Anne Bradstreet, but then he added characteristically metaphysical exaggeration to drive home the meaning of that unbelievable reality:

I know not how to speak't, it is so good:
   Shall Mortall, and Immortall marry? nay,
Man marry God? God be a match for Mud?
   The King of Glory Wed a Worm? mere Clay?
   This is the Case. The Wonder too in Bliss.
   Thy Maker is thy Husband. Hearst thou this? . . .

I am to Christ more base, than to a King
   A Mite, Fly, Worm, Ant, Serpent, Divell is,

Or Can be, being tumbled all in Sin,
     And shall I be his Spouse? How good is this?
     It is too good to be declar'de to thee.
     But not too good to be believ'de by mee (190-91).

The first of Taylor's meditations, which was not specified as keyed to a particular text, was shorter than most that followed. But it set out themes of divine love, Taylor's response, and mystical hope that never flagged over the four decades that followed. It is appropriate to end this brief introduction to Taylor's Christ-centered genius where he began it:

What Love is this of thine, that Cannot bee
     In thine Infinity, O Lord, Confinde,
Unless it thy very Person see,
     Infinity, and Finity Conjoynd'd?
     What hath thy Godhead, as not satisfied
     Marri'de our Manhood, making it its Bride?

Oh, Matchless Love! filling Heaven to the brim!
     O're running it: all running o're beside
This world! Nay Overflowing Hell; wherein
     For thine Elect, there rose a mighty Tide!
     That there our Veans [veins] might through thy Person bleed,
     To quench those flames, that else would on us feed.

Oh! that thy Love might overflow my Heart!
     To fire the same with Love: for Love I would.
But oh! my streight'ned Breast! my Lifeless Sparke!
     My Fireless Flame! What Chilly Love, and Cold?
     In measure small! In manner Chilly! See.
     Lord blow the Coal: Thy Love Enflame in mee (158-59).

Anne Bradstreet and Edward Taylor were in many ways entirely ordinary Puritans. One was a busy housewife whose life was encompassed round with a staggering weight of domestic duties, the other a hard-working minister who without any concern for his own literary reputation faithfully served his congregation and town for almost half a century. The ordinariness of their lives stands in striking contrast to what was, on the one hand, a remarkable flourishing of "The Tenth Muse" in the barbarian wilderness of the new world and, on the other, an extraordinary outpouring of poetry at the highest imaginable plane. The care that both in different ways took to record the mercies of God in their daily round, and to meditate upon the eternal significance of those mercies, was their most significant contribution to later generations who ponder what it would mean to recover even a portion of what was best in the Puritan movement.[11]

SELECT BIBLIOGRAPHY

Primary Sources

Ellis, John Harvard. *The Works of Anne Bradstreet in Prose and Verse*. Charlestown, Mass.: A. E. Cutter, 1867. This remains the definitive edition.

Grabo, Norman S., ed. *Edward Taylor's Christographia*. New Haven, Conn.: Yale University Press, 1962. A helpful edition of some of Taylor's sermons.

Hambrick-Stowe, Charles E., ed. *Early New England Meditative Poetry: Anne Bradstreet and Edward Taylor*. New York: Paulist, 1988. An outstanding collection with a very helpful introduction.

Hensley, Jeannine, ed. *The Works of Anne Bradstreet*, with a foreword by Adrienne Rich. Cambridge, Mass.: Harvard University Press, 1967. This edition modernizes Bradstreet's poetry and verse.

Mulford, Carla, Angela Vietto and Amy E. Winans, eds. *Early American Writings*. New York: Oxford University Press, 2001. A useful, recent anthology.

Stanford, Donald E., ed. *The Poems of Edward Taylor*. New Haven, Conn.: Yale University Press, 1960. An excellent edition with a helpful introduction.

Bradstreet—Secondary Sources

Daly, Robert. "Anne Bradstreet." *American National Biography*, vol. 3. Edited by John A. Garraty and Mark C. Carnes, pp. 385-86. New York: Oxford University Press, 1999.

Rosenmeier, Rosamond. *Anne Bradstreet Revisited*. Boston: Twayne, 1991.

Wright, Elizabeth Wade. *Anne Bradstreet: The Tenth Muse*. New York: Oxford University Press, 1971.

Taylor—Secondary Sources

Hammond, Jeffrey A. "Edward Taylor." *American National Biography*, vol. 21. Edited by John A. Garraty and Mark C. Carnes, 365-67. New York: Oxford University Press, 1999.

Hammond, Jeffrey A. *Edward Taylor: Fifty Years of Scholarship and Criticism*. Columbia, S.C.: Camden, 1993.

---

[11]I am pleased to thank Luke Harlow for research assistance with this essay.

General—Secondary Sources

Daly, Robert. *God's Altar: The World and the Flesh in Puritan Poetry.* Berkeley: University of California Press, 1978.

Hambrick-Stowe, Charles E. *The Practice of Piety: Puritan Devotional Disciplines in Seventeenth-Century New England.* Chapel Hill: University of North Carolina Press, 1982.

Hammond, Jeffrey A. *Sinful Self, Saintly Self: The Puritan Experience of Poetry.* Athens: University of Georgia Press, 1993.

❧ 18 ❧

HUMAN NATURE
IN ITS FOURFOLD STATE

BY THOMAS BOSTON (1676-1732)

Philip G. Ryken

SOMETIME IN THE EIGHTEENTH CENTURY A GENTLEMAN IN HANOVER, Virginia, stumbled across a few loose pages from an old Puritan book on sin and salvation. His spiritual interest was kindled and soon he came under the conviction of the Holy Spirit, repented of his sin, and committed his life to Jesus Christ.[1]

What the man read came from *Human Nature in Its Fourfold State* by Thomas Boston. The book was an eighteenth-century bestseller, with more than one hundred editions published in Scotland, England and America. Famous preachers of the Great Awakening (1725-1760) frequently recommended *The Fourfold State*—as it was called—to new converts. Jonathan Edwards liked the book "exceeding well" and considered its author "a truly great divine."[2] George Whitefield found it "of much service" to his soul.[3] John Wesley went so far as to publish an abridgment of the book in his Puritan library.[4] Boston's influence lasted well into the nineteenth century, when *The Fourfold State* was on the reading list at Princeton Seminary.[5] Even as late as 1910 a section from the book was published in *The Fundamentals*, the an-

---

[1]William Henry Foote, *Sketches of Virginia: Historical and Biographical* (1850; reprint, Richmond, Va.: John Knox, 1966), p. 120.

[2]Jonathan Edwards, *The Works of Jonathan Edwards*, ed. John E. Smith (New Haven, Conn.: Yale University Press, 1957), 2:489.

[3]George Whitefield, quoted in Donald Fraser, *The Life and Diary of the Reverend Ralph Erskine* (Edinburgh: William Oliphant & Son, 1834), p. 317.

[4]Thomas Boston, *The Doctrine of Original Sin*, ed. John Wesley (London, n.p. 1774).

[5]David B. Calhoun, *Princeton Seminary, Volume 1: Faith and Learning, 1812-1868* (Edinburgh: Banner of Truth Trust, 1994), 1:48, 128.

thology that launched American fundamentalism.[6]

All of this would have come as a great surprise to Thomas Boston, who at the time of his death in 1732 had little reason to believe that his influence would extend very far beyond the little churches he served in the Scottish Borders. Yet Boston would have recognized his book's ultimate success as the answer to his prayer that God would bless *The Fourfold State* "for the conviction and conversion of sinners, and edification of saints, for the time I am in life, and after I shall be in the dust."[7]

As an eighteenth-century Scottish Presbyterian, Thomas Boston lived too late and too far north to be considered a Puritan in the technical sense of the term. However, his approach to life and ministry can hardly be described as anything but Puritan. One of his earliest memories was visiting his father in the prison where he was jailed for failing to conform to the episcopal form of worship and government then imposed on the Church of Scotland. During this same period Boston was converted through the open-air preaching of another nonconformist, the Scottish Covenanter Henry Erskine.

After graduating from Edinburgh University, Boston entered the gospel ministry. He approached his pastoral work with typical Puritan vigor, preaching in the plain biblical, doctrinal and practical style that made the Puritans famous. He was well versed in Puritan literature, including many of the authors whose work is introduced in the present volume: William Ames, Samuel Rutherford, Thomas Goodwin, Thomas Shepard, John Milton, Richard Baxter and John Owen. But Boston's favorite book was one he discovered in a parishioner's cottage, a little volume called *The Marrow of Modern Divinity*.[8] This book was written in the form of a theological dialogue and it contained many quotations from Puritan authors. Among its distinctive emphases were evangelical doctrines such as the free offer of the gospel, assurance in Christ as the essence of faith, and sanctification by grace. Although *The Marrow of Modern Divinity* came under theological attack—an incident known in Scottish church history as the Marrow Controversy (1717-1722)[9]—Boston correctly perceived that its gracious doctrines

---

[6]Thomas Boston, "The Nature of Regeneration," in *The Fundamentals*, 12 vols. (Chicago: Testimony, 1910), 10:26-30.

[7]Thomas Boston, *Memoirs*, in *The Complete Works of the Late Rev. Thomas Boston of Ettrick*, ed. Samuel M'Millan, 12 vols. (1853; reprint, Wheaton, Ill.: Richard Owen Roberts, 1980), 12:402. Hereafter this multivolume set will simply be titled *Works*, followed by volume and page numbers.

[8]Edward Fisher, *The Marrow of Modern Divinity* (London: n.p., 1645).

[9]See David C. Lachman, *The Marrow Controversy, 1718-1723: An Historical and Theological Analysis*, Rutherford Studies in Historical Theology (Edinburgh: Rutherford House, 1988); William J. U. Philip, "The Marrow and the Dry Bones: Ossified Orthodoxy and the Battle for the Gospel in Eighteenth-Century Scottish Calvinism," *Scottish Bulletin of Evangelical Theology* 15:1 (1997), pp. 27-36.

were needed to preserve Calvinism from degenerating into legalism.

Thomas Boston was a faithful pastor. Although he was prone to melancholy and suffered from a variety of physical ailments, he never missed a week in the pulpit during more than three decades of public ministry. In addition to preaching twice on the sabbath, he lectured in mid-week and carried out an ambitious plan of pastoral care, riding on horseback to visit his widely scattered parishioners for the purpose of providing spiritual counsel and catechetical instruction.

Boston's partner in ministry was his wife Katharine, a devoted woman who also struggled with chronic physical and perhaps psychological problems. In addition to the ordinary trials of parish ministry, the Bostons suffered the loss of six children in infancy, with only four surviving to adulthood. But Thomas learned to pray for each "loss to be made up by the presence of the Lord,"[10] and despite all his difficulties, at the end of his life he was able to praise God "that ever he made me a minister of the gospel."[11]

THE STORY OF *THE FOURFOLD STATE*

Thomas Boston wrote many fine books, including a lengthy commentary on the Westminster Shorter Catechism, two volumes on covenant theology, and an intimate spiritual autobiography. But his most influential work was *Human Nature in Its Fourfold State*, a major book on the doctrine of man that arose out of the context of his pastoral ministry.[12]

In 1699 Boston arrived in the tiny village of Simprin to pastor the smallest church in Scotland. There were fewer than one hundred adults in the entire parish, and only seven came to hear the new minister preach his first sermon. Expounding Hosea 4:6 ("My people are destroyed for lack of knowledge"), Boston argued that preachers must answer to God for the spiritual condition of their congregations. Indeed, "Ministers by carelessness become the murderers of the souls of their people."[13]

Needless to say, Boston had no intention of being a careless minister. Immediately he embarked on a yearlong series of sermons on humanity's "wretched state by nature" and "Christ the remedy for man's misery."[14] When he was called to the rural parish of Ettrick in 1707 he began with the basics once again, only this time

---

[10]Boston, *Works*, 12:207.

[11]Ibid., 12:447.

[12]The word *man* is used in this chapter as Boston used it, to refer to humanity in general, both male and female.

[13]Thomas Boston, "MSS of Thomas Boston of Ettrick," Aberdeen University Library (MS.3245/2), p. 157.

[14]Boston, *Works*, 12:153.

he organized his preaching on sin and salvation into four parts: innocence, nature, grace, and eternity. In these "sermons of the Fourfold State,"[15] Boston carefully traced the story of humanity through the four stages of created perfection, fall into sin, redemption in Christ, and eternity in heaven or hell.

At first Boston did not intend to publish his sermons. However, when his ministerial colleagues pressed him to "Let respect to duty, and the salvation of perishing souls sway you,"[16] he was forced to relent. Boston spent several years revising his sermons, and the manuscript was finally published as *Human Nature in Its Fourfold State* (1720). The entire work was revised again for its definitive edition (1729), published a few years before the author's death.[17] Thus, in one form or another, these sermons occupied Thomas Boston for nearly his entire ministry.

The organizing principle for Boston's book came from Augustine (354-430), who in his *Treatise on Rebuke and Grace* distinguished between the grace God gave Adam to be able not to sin (*posse non peccare*) and the grace he will give the saints in heaven not to be able to sin (*non posse peccare*).[18] Various medieval and Reformation theologians picked up this distinction and expanded it to encompass four stages of the human condition: *posse peccare* (able to sin), *non posse non peccare* (not able not to sin), *posse non peccare* (able not to sin), and *non posse peccare* (not able to sin).[19] The same four categories appear in the Westminster Confession of Faith, where they are defined as the "state of innocency," the "state of sin," the "state of grace," and the "state of glory."[20]

Boston used "the fourfold state" because it was simple. As a pastor he wanted to give his congregation a memorable framework for understanding their Christian experience and these four points provided the perfect structure. In Boston's own words,

There are four things very necessary to be known by all that would see heaven: 1. What man *was* in the state of innocence, as God made him. 2. What he *is* in the state of corrupt nature, as he hath unmade himself. 3. What he *must be* in the state of grace, as created in Christ Jesus unto good works, if ever he be made a partaker of the in-

[15]Ibid., 12:209.

[16]Ibid., 12:238.

[17]The best one-volume edition is Thomas Boston, *Human Nature in its Fourfold State* (Edinburgh: Banner of Truth Trust, 1989).

[18]Augustine, *De Correptione et Gratia*, ed. J. P. Migne, Patrologiae Cursus Completus, Series Latina, 44 (Paris, 1863), cols. 915-46 (X. 28).

[19]The history of the fourfold state is traced in Philip Graham Ryken, *Thomas Boston as Preacher of the Fourfold State*, Rutherford Studies in Church History (Carlisle, U.K.: Paternoster, 1999).

[20]*Westminster Confession of Faith*, 9.1.5.

heritance of the saints in light. 4. What he *will be* in his eternal state, as made by the Judge of all, either perfectly happy, or completely miserable, and that for ever.[21]

Boston's innovation was to use this venerable theological framework to organize his preaching. He wanted his largely illiterate parishioners to know their origins (Creation) and their destiny (Eternity). He also wanted them to recognize their sin (Fall) and come to Christ for salvation (Grace). To put all this another way, Boston was trying to help his people find their place in the story of God's salvation. He wanted them to know where they were, where they had been, and where they were going. To that end, he gave them a simple four-point theological system for all of life: "The State of Innocence," "The State of Nature," "The State of Grace" and "The Eternal State."

THE STATE OF INNOCENCE

The Fourfold State begins with the creation of Adam and Eve. Taking Ecclesiastes 7:29 for his text ("Lo, this only have I found, that God hath made man upright; but they have sought out many inventions" KJV), Boston shows that man was created innocent,

> without any imperfection, corruption, or principle of corruption, in his body or soul. He was made "upright," that is, straight with the will and law of God, without any irregularity in his soul. . . . God made him thus: he did not first make him, and then make him righteous; but in the very making of him, he made him righteous. Original righteousness was created with him; so that in the same moment he was a man, he was a righteous man.[22]

This "Original Righteousness," as Boston calls it, "was diffused through the whole man."[23] The Puritans typically described the soul as having three primary faculties: the mind, the will and the affections. Boston shows that each of these faculties was created righteous. Before sin entered the world, the mind understood God's law, the will followed God's pleasure and the affections desired God's glory. Adam was "upright" all the way through. However, his righteousness was also mutable. In other words, it could be lost, as events were later to prove. Although God gave the man "a sufficient power to stand," he was also free to fall.[24] This was an idea that went back to Augustine and the expanded medieval expression: Adam was able to sin (*posse peccare*).

---

[21]Boston, *Human Nature in Its Fourfold State*, in *Works*, 8:9.
[22]Ibid., 8:10.
[23]Ibid., 8:14.
[24]Ibid., 8:15.

The state of innocence was a state of happiness as well as righteousness. The first man was "the favourite of Heaven" and the "emperor of the whole earth." Together our first parents "lived in perfect amity," sharing "a life of pure delight, and unalloyed pleasure."[25] And part of their happiness was having a relationship with God based on covenant. In this covenant—the covenant of works—man was obligated to obey God, specifically by not eating from the tree of the knowledge of good and evil. This command made Adam's obedience "turn upon the precise point of the will of God,"[26] and thus provided the best possible test of his righteousness. According to the terms of the covenant, God promised Adam "life, the continuance of natural life, in the union of soul and body, and of spiritual life, in the favour of his Creator: he promised him also eternal life in heaven, to be entered into when he should have passed the time of his trial upon earth, and the Lord should see meet to transport him into the upper paradise."[27] However, if the man failed to obey God's law, the penalty was death.

Like any good Puritan, Boston invariably ended his sermons with practical application. Each section of *The Fourfold State* concludes with what Puritans called the "use" of the doctrine. One use of "The State of Innocence" was apologetic: Man's original innocence defended God from the charge of injustice. If he was made righteous, then obviously "man was, and is, the cause of his own ruin";[28] God is not to blame. Boston sees this point made directly in his sermon text: "God hath made man upright; but *they* have sought out many inventions" (emphasis added). As Boston explains it, "Their ruin was from their *own* proper motion; their depravity was not from God, but from themselves."[29] Another "use" Boston makes of his preaching on "The State of Innocence" is "lamentation." To contemplate man's original righteousness and happiness is to feel a sense of overwhelming sadness at its loss. As he surveys the ruins of fallen humanity, Boston takes up the lament:

> Here was a stately building; man carved like a fair palace, but now lying in ashes: let us stand and look on the ruins and drop a tear. . . . Where is our primitive glory now? once no darkness in the mind, no rebellion in the will, no disorder in the affections. . . . Happy wast thou, O man! who was like unto thee? No pain nor sickness could affect thee, no death could approach thee, no sigh was heard from thee, till these bitter fruits were plucked from the forbidden tree. Heaven shone upon thee, and earth

25 Ibid., 8:16-21.
26 Ibid., 8:17.
27 Ibid.
28 Ibid., 8:22.
29 Ibid., 8:11.

smiled. . . . But how low is he now laid, who was created for dominion, and made lord of the world!³⁰

THE STATE OF NATURE

"The State of Innocence" is the shortest section of *The Fourfold State*, and for an obvious reason: this stage of human history was short-lived. As Boston wrote elsewhere, "Adam broke fair off, but he tripped quickly."³¹ Whereas humanity's fall into sin happens in the first two or three pages of the Bible, it takes the whole rest of Scripture to deal with the consequences. Thus there is far more to say about the fallen nature than about original righteousness.

Boston believed that gaining a "sight and sense" of "man's natural state" was the "foundation of all real religion."³² With this in mind, he intended his sermons on "The State of Nature" to help sinners perceive their true spiritual condition. Whereas innocence was a state of righteousness and happiness, nature is a state of sin and misery, and it is only by seeing this that anyone ever enters the state of grace.

To show the sinfulness of the state of nature, Boston chooses a text from the biblical account of Noah and the great flood: "The LORD saw that the wickedness of humankind was great in the earth, and that every inclination of the thoughts of their hearts was only evil continually (Gen 6:5)." Boston's exposition underscores the sweeping vocabulary of this verse (*every* inclination; *only* evil; *continually*) to show that nature is a state of total depravity: "Innumerable sins compass thee about: mountains of guilt are lying upon thee; floods of impurities overwhelm thee, living lusts of all sorts roll up and down in the dead sea of thy soul, where no good can breathe, because of the corruption there."³³ In short, "Thou art loathsome in the sight of God; for thou art altogether corrupt; thou hast no good in thee."³⁴

It all started with Adam. What he did in eating the forbidden fruit is what we all do. We are guilty of the same sinful curiosity, blindness to temptation, susceptibility to physical desire, willful disobedience, aptitude for deception, unwillingness to confess our sin and lack of contentment that our first parents were guilty of when they committed the first sin. We do this because we have inherited a sinful nature from Adam—what theologians call "original sin." When God established

---

³⁰Ibid., 8:24.

³¹Boston, *A View of the Covenant of Grace from the Sacred Records*, in *Works*, 8:630.

³²Boston, *Memoirs*, in *Works*, 12:91.

³³Boston, *Fourfold State*, in *Works*, 8:88.

³⁴Ibid., 8:87.

the covenant of works he appointed Adam as our representative. His obedience would secure our reward; his disobedience would result in our death. According to the terms of God's covenant, what Adam did (or failed to do) would count for all his posterity; "we were in him representatively, being represented by him as our moral head in the covenant of works . . . ; hence we fell in him, and by his disobedience were made sinners."[35]

The sin we have inherited from Adam corrupts our whole nature. The faculties that God created righteous—the mind, the will and the affections—are now corrupted by sin. Boston writes: "Now, here is a threefold cord against heaven and holiness, not easily to be broken; a blind mind, a perverse will, and disorderly distempered affections. The mind, swelled with self conceit, says, the man should not stoop; the will, opposite to the will of God, says, he will not; and the corrupt affections, rising against the Lord, in defence of the corrupt will, say, he shall not."[36]

The state of nature is not only sinful, but also miserable. Here Boston takes Ephesians 2:3 for his text: "we were by nature children of wrath, like everyone else." He explains that God's wrath is not an angry passion, but "a most pure and undisturbed act of his will, producing dreadful effects against the sinner." Although many of these "dreadful effects" will be delayed until the final judgment, some of them are taking place right now. Thus the state of nature is a state of wrath. "All thy sufferings in this world," Boston says to unrepentant sinners, "are but an earnest of what thou must suffer in the world to come." Even now, sinners are "under the wrath of God; that they are wholly under wrath: wrath is, as it were, woven into their very nature, and mixes itself with the whole of the man, who is, if I may so speak, a very lump of wrath, a child of hell."[37]

This frightening portrait of fallen humanity serves a number of purposes. One is to explain why there is so much suffering in the world. Life was difficult in eighteenth-century Scotland, and then, as now, people needed a theology that addressed the problem of pain. Boston asks:

> Who sees not a flood of miseries overflowing the world? Whither can a man go where he shall not dip his foot, if he go not over head and ears, in it? Every one at home and abroad, in city and country, in palaces and cottages, is groaning under some one thing or other, ungrateful to him. Some are oppressed with poverty, some chastened with sickness and pain, some are lamenting their losses, every one has a cross of one sort or another. No man's condition is soft, but there is some thorn of

---

[35]Ibid., 8:73.
[36]Ibid., 8:81.
[37]Ibid., 8:101, 128, 98.

uneasiness in it. At length death, the wages of sin, comes after these its harbingers, and sweeps all away.—Now, what but sin has opened the sluice of sorrow?[38]

What brings suffering into the world is sin and its deadly consequence, the wrath of God. But Boston had another, more important purpose for showing people the misery of their depravity: he wanted them to see their need of salvation. "For I testify unto you all," he writes, "there is no peace with God, no pardon, no heaven, for you, in your natural state: there is but a step between you and eternal destruction from the presence of the Lord; if the brittle thread of your life, which may break with a touch ere you are aware, be broken while you are in this state, you are ruined for ever, without remedy." Only by knowing what state we are in by nature can we ever see our need for grace. As Boston goes on to say, "You cannot be in the way to heaven, who never saw yourselves by nature in the high road to hell."[39]

THE STATE OF GRACE

The depraved mind, will and heart are so entirely corrupt that sinners are unable to rescue themselves from the state of nature. This is the doctrine of total inability, or as Boston calls it, "Man's Utter Inability to Recover Himself." Only God can save us. Thus Boston's teaching on "The State of Nature" ends with a fervent appeal to abandon every last hope of saving ourselves and to turn instead to Christ: "O be convinced of your absolute need of Christ, and his overcoming grace; believe your utter inability to recover yourself; so that you may be humbled, shaken out of your self-confidence, and lie down in dust and ashes, groaning out your miserable case before the Lord."[40]

God answers the sinner's prayer by working a "supernatural real change" in his soul, and thereby "bringing him into the state of grace."[41] This "real, thorough change, whereby the man is made a new creature" is called regeneration, or the new birth. In regeneration, God transforms every faculty of the soul: "Man is, in respect of his spiritual state, altogether disjointed by the fall; every faculty of the soul is, as it were, dislocated: in regeneration, the Lord loosens every joint, and sets it right again." The sinner's mind is enlightened with spiritual knowledge, his affections are turned "upside down," so that now the "main stream of his desires is turned to run towards God."[42]

---

[38]Ibid., 8:33.
[39]Ibid., 8:97, 100.
[40]Ibid., 8:137.
[41]Ibid., 8:162.
[42]Ibid., 8:141, 149.

But the biggest transformation occurs in the will, which is released from its bondage to sin when "the Spirit of God comes and opens the prison door, goes to the prisoner, and, by the power of his grace, makes his chains fall off."[43] Boston uses the will to summarize his teaching on the first three states of human nature:

> When *God made man*, his will, in respect of its intention, was directed towards God, as his chief end; in respect of its choice, it pointed towards that which God willed. When *man unmade himself*, his will was framed to the very reverse hereof: he made himself his chief end, and his own will his law. But when *man is new made*, in regeneration, grace rectifies this disorder in some measure, though not perfectly: because we are but renewed in part, while in this world.[44]

Boston proves the necessity of regeneration by emphasizing Jesus' words to Nicodemus: "You *must* be born from above" (Jn 3:7). He also shows that the new birth is a matter of eternal significance; the state we are in now is directly connected to our state in eternity. "Be not deceived," he writes, "grace and glory are but two links of one chain, which God has joined, and no man shall put asunder. None are transplanted into the paradise above, but out of the nursery of grace below." There is an equally "infallible connexion between a finally unregenerate state and damnation." Boston concludes: "Thus you see what affinity there is between an unregenerate state, and the state of the damned, the state of absolute and irretrievable misery. Be convinced, then, that you must be born again; put a high value on the new birth, and eagerly desire it."[45] It is only by regeneration that anyone ever enters the state of grace and thus proceeds to the state of glory.

Once we are born again by the regenerating work of God's Spirit, we are joined to Jesus Christ. To use the proper theological term, we are united to Christ. In the state of nature we are joined to Adam by the covenant of works. But in the state of grace we are joined to Jesus Christ in the covenant of grace. Boston defines union with Christ as a real, spiritual union that establishes an intimate and unbreakable bond between Christ and the Christian. Union with Christ was a favorite Puritan doctrine. Boston's innovation was to use it as the organizing principle for his teaching on justification, adoption, sanctification, perseverance, and many other aspects of salvation. Once we are united to Christ, everything he has belongs to us. All the blessings of salvation are ours in him. Thus union with Christ is the doctrine that ties together all the great truths of salvation.

---

[43] Ibid., 8:146.
[44] Ibid., 8:147 (emphasis added).
[45] Ibid., 8:174-76.

THE ETERNAL STATE

The last section of *The Fourfold State* is the longest because Boston preached on the eternal destiny of both the righteous and the wicked. Traditionally the four states of man were innocence, nature, grace, and glory. However, Boston believed in hell as well as heaven and thus he ends his book with six long sermons titled "Death," "Difference between the Righteous and the Wicked in their Death," "Of the Resurrection," "Of the General Judgment," "The Kingdom of Heaven" and "Of Hell."

The doctrine for the sermon on death is very simple: "All must die." Boston defends this proposition from both reason and Scripture, proving that "we have no life in this world, but as runaways from death, which stretches out its cold arms, to receive us from the womb; but though we do then narrowly escape its clutches, we cannot escape long."[46] By now Boston's application of this doctrine is predictable: the present life is "but a short preface to long eternity." Therefore, we should reflect on our spiritual condition to determine whether we are still in the state of nature or whether we have come into the state of grace through faith in Jesus Christ. Boston warns: "Your eternal state will be according to the state in which you die: death will open the doors of heaven or hell to you. As the tree falls, so it shall lie through eternity. If . . . one die out of Christ, in an unregenerate state, there is no more hope of him for ever."[47]

For those who are in Christ, death marks the entrance into glory. This gives abiding hope to believers as they approach the time of death. In typical Puritan fashion, Boston considers ten different fears that people commonly have about death, showing in each case how faith in Christ brings peace and comfort. His purpose is pastoral: he wants to help people prepare to die and to die well.

After death comes the resurrection, which Boston again defends on the basis of both reason and Scripture. The glorious resurrection of the body is a further benefit of union with Christ. In the same way that God raised Jesus from the dead, so he will raise everyone who believes in Jesus. Yet, like many preachers, Boston had difficulty describing what the resurrection life would be like, admitting that he "found it no easy thing to believe the greatness of that glory which is to be revealed."[48] His strategy for dealing with this difficulty in *The Fourfold State* is to gather the biblical descriptions of heaven as a kingdom. This metaphor is effective because kingdoms contain the "greatest number of earthly good things" (cities, palaces,

---

[46]Ibid., 8:233.
[47]Ibid., 8:244.
[48]Boston, *Memoirs*, in *Works*, 12:249.

treasures, courtiers, kings, crowns, thrones, etc.), and thus this imagery points us to heaven.[49]

In his description of heaven Boston brings his teaching on the mind, the will and the affections to its completion. In glory the mind becomes "a globe of pure and unmixed light," the will is "brought to a perfect conformity to the will of God" and the affections are given a "fixed habit of purity." As a result of this glorious transformation, the saints will be "set beyond the possibility of sinning, for they shall be confirmed in goodness." To use Augustine's terminology, they will have the grace to be unable to sin (*non posse peccare*). But the brightest blessing is to enjoy "society with the Lord himself in heaven, glorious communion with God in Christ, which is the perfection of happiness."[50]

The blessings of God's heaven only belong to those who first enter the state of grace. Boston cannot leave his preaching on God's eternal kingdom without clarifying the terms of its citizenship:

> If you are yet in your natural state, you are children of wrath, and not children of this kingdom; for that state, to those who live and die in it, issues in eternal misery. If you be brought into the state of grace, you have a just claim to the state of glory; for grace will certainly issue in glory at length. This kingdom is an inheritance, which none but the children of God can justly claim. Now, we become the children of God by regeneration, and union with Christ his Son.[51]

The Fourfold State ends with a sobering account of the eternal state of those who never enter God's kingdom. The death of the wicked—unlike the death of the righteous—is utterly hopeless. After death they will not receive "one offer of Christ, one day, or but one hour more, to make up their peace with God"; they will have "no access to get their ruined state and condition retrieved, though they be ever so desirous of it."[52] Instead of enjoying "a joyful resurrection to life," they will suffer "a dreadful resurrection to damnation."[53] Boston describes the resurrection of the damned in terms reminiscent of a frightening encounter with a rotting corpse that he had when he was a child: "The greatest beauties, who now pride themselves in their comeliness of body, not regarding their deformed souls, will then appear with a ghastly countenance, a grim and deathlike visage. Their looks will be frightful, and they will be horrible spectacles, coming

---

[49]Boston, *Fourfold State*, in *Works*, 8:318.
[50]Ibid., 8:320-21, 330.
[51]Ibid., 8:343.
[52]Ibid., 8:252-53.
[53]Ibid., 8:271.

forth from their graves, like infernal furies out of the pit."[54]

After death comes the final judgment, when God determines where he will send every human being for all eternity. There are only two destinations, as Boston has insisted throughout *The Fourfold State:* a place for the redeemed and a place for the damned. "And remember," he writes, "thou shalt not be a mere spectator, to look at these two such different companies; but must thyself take thy place in one of the two."[55]

Boston's description of hell is remarkably vivid. In hell the damned will suffer both the pain of loss and the pain of sense, according to the justice of God. The pain of loss is separation from fellowship with God, a deprivation Boston considers to be "the very hell of hell." The pain of sense is the exposure of both body and soul to the "fiery torments" of hell. In Boston's words, "Their eyes shall be kept in blackness of darkness, without the least comfortable gleam of light; their ears filled with frightful yellings of the infernal crew. They shall taste nothing but the sharpness of God's wrath, the dregs of the cup of his fury. The stench of the burning lake of brimstone will be the smell there; and they shall feel extreme pains for evermore."[56]

READING *THE FOURFOLD STATE* TODAY

Why did Thomas Boston end *The Fourfold State* by preaching about hell? Not only would preaching on glory have made for a happier ending, but it also would have been fully consistent with the book's Augustinian heritage. However, Boston wanted to take sin seriously, and this is one of the many ways his Puritan theology can help the contemporary church.

We live at a time when most people have trifling views of sin and its consequences. But men like Thomas Boston knew what many ministers have forgotten, namely, that God uses the preaching of his wrath to bring sinners to Christ. As Boston put it, hell is an "awful subject! but necessary."[57] It is necessary because it helps us to see the state we are in, and thus compels us to look for a savior. Boston closes *The Fourfold State* with this invitation:

> And now, if you would be saved from the wrath to come, and never go into this place
> of torment, take no rest in your natural state; believe the sinfulness and misery of it,

---

[54]Ibid., 8:285.

[55]Ibid., 8:299.

[56]Ibid., 8:354, 357, 361.

[57]Boston, "The Believer's Hundredfold in this Life Considered; and a View of the Reality, Parts, Inhabitants, Passage into, and State of Men in the World to Come," in *Works,* 5:432.

and labour to get out of it quickly, fleeing unto Jesus Christ by faith. . . . And the terrors of hell, as well as the joys of heaven, are set before you, to stir you up to a cordial receiving of him, with all his salvation; and to incline you unto the way of faith and holiness, in which alone you can escape the everlasting fire. May the Lord himself make them effectual to that end![58]

There are many benefits to reading Boston's *Fourfold State*. The book's four-part structure provides a simple, memorable framework for understanding the world and our place in it. It has a strong, evangelical emphasis on the necessity of the new birth. By using the doctrine of union with Christ to organize the theology of salvation, it properly shows the centrality of Christ and the benefits of a personal saving relationship with him. But perhaps the book's greatest strength is the way it forces us to evaluate our spiritual condition. Have we been born again? Are we united to Christ in the state of grace? Or are we still in the sinful, miserable state of nature, in which case we have no legitimate hope of reaching the state of glory?

These are excellent questions, and Boston kept asking them to the very end of his life. In his final sermon—preached from his deathbed as people gathered outside the window of his manse—he reminded his parishioners how necessary it is to gain "certain knowledge of our estate, whether we be in the faith or not."[59] Personal knowledge of our place in the fourfold state will always be a matter of life and death.

SELECT BIBLIOGRAPHY

Primary Sources

Boston, Thomas. *The Complete Works of the Late Rev. Thomas Boston of Ettrick,* edited by Samuel M'Millan, 12 vols. London: William Tegg & Co., 1853. Reprint, Wheaton, Ill.: Richard Owen Roberts, 1980. Recently reprinted again: Lafayette, Ind.: Sovereign Grace Trust, 2002.

———. "Fourfold State of Man" (original manuscript). Philadelphia: Presbyterian Historical Society.

———. *Human Nature in Its Fourfold State.* 1729. Reprint, Edinburgh: Banner of Truth Trust, 1989.

———. *Memoirs.* Edinburgh: Banner of Truth Trust, 1988.

Secondary Sources

Addison, William. *The Life and Writings of Thomas Boston of Ettrick.* Edinburgh: Oliver and

---

[58] Boston, *Fourfold State,* in *Works,* 8:374-75.
[59] Boston, "The Necessity of Self-Examination Considered," in *Works,* 2:504.

Boyd, 1936.

Bruggink, Donald Jay. "The Theology of Thomas Boston, 1676-1732." Unpublished doctoral thesis, University of Edinburgh, 1956.

Lachman, David C. *The Marrow Controversy, 1718-1723: An Historical and Theological Analysis*, Rutherford Studies in Historical Theology. Edinburgh: Rutherford House, 1988.

McGowan, Andrew T. B. *The Federal Theology of Thomas Boston*, Rutherford Studies in Historical Theology. Carlisle, U.K.: Paternoster, 1997.

Ryken, Philip Graham. "Thomas Boston: The Evangelical Minister," in *The Compromised Church: The Present Evangelical Crisis*, edited by John H. Armstrong, pp. 303-20. Wheaton, Ill.: Crossway, 1998.

————. *Thomas Boston as Preacher of the Fourfold State*. Rutherford Studies in Historical Theology. Carlisle, U.K.: Paternoster, 1999.

Woodruff, Stephen Albert, III. "The Pastoral Ministry in the Church of Scotland in the Eighteenth Century, with Special Reference to Thomas Boston, John Willison and John Erskine." Unpublished doctoral thesis, University of Edinburgh, 1966.

19

RELIGIOUS AFFECTIONS

BY JONATHAN EDWARDS (1703-1758)

Stephen R. Holmes

HALFWAY THROUGH MY TIME IN TRAINING FOR MINISTRY AT SPUR-geon's College, London, something unusual happened in the community there. It started, I recall, during the summer vacation, and so disconnected rumors were the beginnings, but as the college reassembled in September, it was clear that some of our fellows believed they had met God in a new and special way during regular meetings for prayer ministry at one of the local churches. Some spoke of a new joy in the Lord, others of new power in preaching, still others of the healing of deep-seated hurts. There was clearly much that was good and positive going on. We soon learned that their experience was part of a much wider phenomenon, traceable to the Toronto Airport Vineyard Church, and so soon known as the "Toronto Bless-ing."[1] We also learned that alongside the very positive experiences our friends were claiming, there was much that was strange or even disturbing associated with the movement: apparently uncontrollable fits of laughter and falling during prayer; later animal noises, weeping and many other things were reported. Some saw these as dangerous and irrational emotional manifestations that demonstrated that what was happening had no relation to a true work of God's Spirit; others claimed that the Spirit might well do such things in a person's life, citing scriptural references to laughter (Ps 126:2 was much in evidence; a poor piece of exegesis, whether the point it supported was correct or not). There was sufficient controversy that the faculty judged it right to bring the college community together to discuss these things. At that time our doctrine tutor, Dr. John Colwell, spoke of similar events

---

[1]A very worthwhile theological examination of the Toronto phenomenon has recently appeared: David Hilborn, ed., *Toronto in Perspective* (Carlisle, U.K.: Paternoster, 2003).

resulting in similar controversy some 250 years ago, and pointed us to an acute theological analysis of that time, a work he then described as still unsurpassed on the subject. That was my first introduction to Jonathan Edwards's *Treatise Concerning Religious Affections, in Three Parts.*[2]

A SURPRISING WORK OF GOD

Edwards came to the analysis of human religious experience by accident; the book, undoubtedly a classic, is all but incidental to his main theological endeavor, as are the three smaller works that preceded it. Edwards was born in 1703 into Puritan New England, his father Timothy a minister, his maternal grandfather, Solomon Stoddard, one of the pillars of the church in the colonies. He trained for the ministry himself and soon went to assist his grandfather, who was then eighty-three, in the church at Northampton. Not long afterwards, when Stoddard died, Edwards succeeded to the pulpit. Five years into his solo ministry, in 1734, Edwards was concerned with the growth of Arminianism and began to preach against it. Those sermons were later published; they are careful doctrinal treatments (the two most lengthy are on "Justification by Faith Alone" and "The Justice of God in the Damnation of Sinners").[3] Indeed, even allowing for the inevitable editing for publication, Edwards was then, Sunday by Sunday, offering his congregation technical theological discussions of sufficient complexity to tax many seminary professors today. The response, however, was startling: a number of people were suddenly and spectacularly converted, beginning a revival which lasted for months and spread across the Connecticut River valley. Edwards described the events in his own town, suggesting that the common interest of the people was in the state of their souls, and that "Pressing into the Kingdom of Heaven" (the title of another of his anti-Arminian sermons) seemed the great concern of every person who lived there.[4]

Happenings like this had been known in New England before Edwards's day, but they tended to be brief in duration, confined to one congregation and truly effective only among the young. Stoddard had known five such "harvests" in his min-

---

[2]Many editions are available. There are two collected editions of Edwards's works currently published: for scholarly work, the Yale *Works of Jonathan Edwards* series is invaluable; *Religious Affections* is vol. 2 of the series, edited by John E. Smith (New Haven, Conn.: Yale University Press, 1959), and I have used this edition throughout. The older Dwight/Hickman *Works of Jonathan Edwards* is still available in two volumes (Edinburgh: Banner of Truth Trust, 1974) and still useful; *Religious Affections* is in vol. I, pp. 234-343.

[3]These were published in Edwards's lifetime as *Five Discourses on the Soul's Eternal Salvation*; they can most easily be found now in the Dwight/Hickman *Works*, I:620-89.

[4]Edwards's description is in *A Faithful Narrative*, 4:144-211, of the Yale edition (titled *The Great Awakening*), or I: 344-64 of Dwight/Hickman.

istry.[5] An event so geographically widespread, lasting for months and seemingly touching the whole community was unprecedented, however, and attracted great notice. Edwards described the events in a letter to a colleague, which found its way across the Atlantic and was published in England by John Guyse and Isaac Watts (the hymn writer). Edwards heard of the interest and undertook to expand the letter into a full account of what had gone on, published as *A Faithful Narrative of the Surprising Work of God . . .* (1736).[6] Amid description and rejoicing, this work contains only one paragraph noting that some were opposed to the revival, an attitude that Edwards seems to imply must come from ignorance and/or jealousy. It ends with a lament that the revival has come to an end, which was brought about through certain unfortunate excesses (a man who committed suicide; one or two other people pretending to special revelations from God), and a request for prayer that the flame might be re-ignited.

These prayers were answered in 1740, when George Whitefield landed at Rhode Island to begin a grueling preaching tour of the colonies. Revival began again, and in sensational fashion. Conversions were frequent, sudden and often spectacular, involving seekers with troubled consciences screaming and shaking, and then sobbing with relief as they grasped the promise of the gospel. Whitefield's diary records that "Good Mr. Edwards wept" with joy as the visitor preached in his pulpit and the scenes of six years before returned.[7] Following this, Edwards took his part in revival preaching, most famously addressing "Sinners in the Hands of an Angry God" at Enfield in 1741.[8] Alongside these labors, however, he devoted himself to the defense of the revival against its Christian opponents and detractors.

LEARNING TO ASK THE RIGHT QUESTIONS

These opponents had a number of complaints that they leveled against the apparent excesses. Some were theological, notably concerning the nature of conversion; others had to do with the biblical demand for good order in worship; others again focused on the apparent excesses connected to the revival, of which there were undeniably many, and argued that a good tree would not bear such fruit. As time went on, Edwards also found himself fighting against "Enthusiasts" (in eighteenth-

---

[5]For background to the Awakening, George Marsden's recent biography, *Jonathan Edwards: A Life* (New Haven, Conn.: Yale University Press, 2003) is outstanding. Also valuable is *The Great Awakening: Documents Illustrating the Crisis and its Consequences*, ed. Heimart and Miller, (Indianapolis: Bobbs-Merill, 1967).

[6]The original letter can also be found in the Yale *Works*, 4:99-109.

[7]Whitefield's *Journal* for October 19, 1740.

[8]Edwards's most-published sermon. Among many other places, it can be found in the Dwight/Hickman, *Works*, 2:7-12.

century English, the word carried the sense of "fanatics"). These supporters of the revival began to see the whole of God's work in it, and so to decry as ungodly— even unconverted—anyone, particularly any minister, who was not actively engaged in preaching revival.[9] Edwards was thus battling on two fronts, and his response came in an increasingly careful series of treatises analyzing the nature and effects of true spiritual experience: *The Distinguishing Marks of a True Work of the Spirit of God* (1741), *Some Thoughts Concerning the Revival* (1742) and *The Religious Affections* (1746).

The first of these, the *Distinguishing Marks*,[10] was a sermon on 1 John 4:1, "Beloved, do not believe every spirit, but test the spirits to see whether they are from God." In it, Edwards introduced a concept that was to remain important in his analysis, and indeed provided the theme for the second part of the *Religious Affections*: the "negative sign." The negative sign is not, as the name might suggest today, a disproof, but something that proves nothing, that is simply irrelevant to the question of whether spiritual experience comes from the Holy Spirit or some other spirit. Edwards suggested the overzealous supporters and opponents of the revivals were both focusing on the same issues, and that in fact these things proved nothing either way; instead, different questions needed to be asked.

An obvious example might be the strong emotional reaction of someone suddenly and apparently converted that resulted in cries, tears and laughter, and even in physical reactions (people throwing themselves to the floor, shaking and so on). Charles Chauncy, a leading opponent of the revivals, argued that such reactions proved that what was going on was not of God: conversion should be a matter of intellectual conviction of the truth of the gospel, resulting in changed behavior, true, but quiet and reasoned changed behavior. God is "a God not of disorder but of peace" (1 Cor 14:33), and so it is inconceivable that such happenings could be of God's doing. Instead, it was the emotional excesses of preacher and congregation alike that induced temporary mania in such people and that was all there was to it. By contrast, a radical supporter of revival like James Davenport (who, it should be noted, later repented of his excesses) would have insisted that such spectacular manifestations were proof positive that God was at work savingly in that person's life. No other explanation could possibly account for such effects; the Holy Spirit was powerfully at work and whatever happened was to be rejoiced in, not questioned.[11]

---

[9]Representative works of both detractors ("Old Lights") and Enthusiasts can be found in Heimart and Miller, *Great Awakening*.

[10]Found in the Yale *Works*, 4:226-88 and Dwight/Hickman, 2:257-77.

[11]See Heimart and Miller, *The Great Awakening* for further details on, and writings by, Chauncy and Davenport.

Edwards wanted to insist that both sides provide adequate explanations for the events, but neither is right in supposing their explanation is the only adequate one. It is true that a person who is overwhelmed by the presence and action of God's Spirit might well respond in visibly and audibly emotional ways; there is scriptural warrant for such a response (in *Religious Affections* Edwards offers any number of examples of this point, mostly from the Psalms). It is equally true that such a response might be caused by nothing more than a form of religious mania, or by a momentary enthusiasm for religion that has nothing of true conversion about it. The most telling example is the crowd who lined the streets on Palm Sunday, crying "Hosanna to the Son of David" (Mt 21:8-9). Thus, spectacular though they might be, great emotional and bodily effects are a "negative sign": they prove nothing in either direction. To test the spirits we need to look elsewhere.

Some Thoughts Concerning the Present Revival is another attempt to defend the revival, while acknowledging and warning against the errors and failures that Edwards perceived within it.[12] There is much that is wrong, Edwards acknowledged, but it is a failure of logic and charity to judge the whole by the part, and there is also much that is luminously godly and right. He proceeded to offer advice on what should be done to discourage the bad while recognizing and encouraging the good. These first two writings had been occasional, responding to particular circumstances. Before leaving the subject and turning to those things he regarded as more central to his life's work (such as the defense of Calvinism in *The Freedom of the Will* or *Original Sin*), Edwards was to produce one more work which would offer a full account of the nature of religious experience, and how the work of God's Spirit could be discerned. This was *Religious Affections*.

RELIGIOUS AFFECTIONS

Edwards's classic text is, despite its bulk, written in standard Puritan sermon form.[13] The statement of the text (I Pet 1:8) is followed by some exegetical discussion resulting in the statement of a doctrine—a theological proposition that will provide the substance of the rest of the discourse. This doctrine is then developed in various ways (perhaps involving defense, explanation, comparison with other scriptural passages and so on) before finally it is applied, again often in several ways (perhaps to several different groups within the congregation). The method had

---

[12]The text can be found in vol. 4 of the Yale *Works*, or in Dwight/Hickman, 1:365-430.

[13]An extremely helpful discussion of Puritan sermon form, and Edwards's particular employment of it, can be found in Wilson H. Kimnach's "Introduction" to vol. 10 of the Yale *Works*, *Sermons and Discourses: 1720-1723*.

been urged by William Perkins in his *Art of Prophesying* (1592)[14] and was recommended by many other Puritan writers as aiding the congregation to see the connection between text and doctrine, and in remembering the truth and its application that they heard. The form was capable of almost infinite expansion (I have heard that Timothy Edwards, Jonathan's father, once announced "and sixty-sixthly ..." from the pulpit), and also of conveying great rhetorical power (Jonathan's most telling revival sermons were structured like this).

Edwards's exegesis centers on the recognition that I Peter was written to people undergoing persecution, and he suggests that such trials test and refine true religion and even strengthen it as a result. "Although you have not seen him, you love him; and even though you do not see him now, you believe in him and rejoice with an indescribable and glorious joy" (I Pet 1:8). This text describes the purified essence of true religion and it suggests that there are two parts to that: love to Christ and joy in Christ. Both are emotions—"affections" is the common eighteenth-century term. Thus his doctrine: "True religion, in great part, consists in holy affections."[15] He develops this doctrine in two ways: analyzing what he means by "affections" and defending the proposition that they are the heart of true religion. These developments make up the first part of the text. The second and third parts are application: if this is an adequate definition of true religion, then what does this tell us about how we discern whether it is present or not? Edwards is back to the task of "testing the spirits," but his treatment now is exhaustive and based on a solid theological framework. Certain apparently helpful tests are ruled to prove nothing either way by this analysis, and so part two offers a list of negative signs, similar to those developed in the earlier work. Finally, Edwards's theology suggests some ways of testing the spirits that do promise to be effective, and part three (nearly three-quarters of the total work) examines those.

I have already substituted "emotions" for "affections," but this is only a rough equivalent. Edwards himself defines affections as "the more vigorous and sensible [i.e., "sensed" or "felt"] exercises of the inclination and will of the soul."[16] In common with some in the Puritan tradition, Edwards believed that the human psyche was composed of two parts: the will (also called the "inclination" or the "heart") and the understanding (also called the "mind").[17] The latter sees, grasps and inter-

---

[14] Available in the "Puritan Paperbacks" series (Edinburgh: Banner of Truth Trust, 1996).

[15] Edwards, *Affections*, p. 95.

[16] Edwards, *Affections*, p. 96.

[17] Other Puritans often speak of three faculties: mind, will and affections. Edwards here combines the will and affections in his representation.

prets; the former approves, rejects, desires or dislikes. There had been a long-running debate among the Puritans (English and American) as to whether conversion began in the will or the understanding. Clearly, it must affect both (one must love Christ and believe the gospel), but which came first was in dispute.[18] Edwards cut through this with the help of what he had learned from the new philosophy of John Locke, and insisted that conversion involved the whole human person simultaneously. In the *Affections*, however, he suggests that ongoing religion is largely (the qualification "in great part" is important here) a matter of the will, and seeks to derive tests of true religion from that position.

True religion is particularly a matter of vigorous and felt acts of will. The true Christian does not have a mild preference for God, but loves him "with all [one's] heart and . . . soul and . . . mind" (Mt 22:37). This is, of course, a difference of degree, not of kind, and Edwards acknowledges that. I suspect, however, that he would have been impatient with debates about the precise point at which a desire becomes an affection: biblical religion deals in absolutes and superlatives (e.g., "all your heart"; "joy unspeakable" in the text from I Peter), and so asking how small my affections may be and still qualify as saving is both offensive and irrelevant. Finally, Edwards notes that all exercises of the will, and so all affections, are either positive (love and desire) or negative (hatred and repulsion). Both can be a part of true religion: a hatred of sin is, after all, a necessary part of loving God.

Having defined the affections, Edwards defends his doctrine that they are central to true religion. First, he offers a collation of biblical texts stressing the "fervent exercises of heart" to which God calls his people. Second, he suggests that we are so created that our actions generally follow our affections. Thus if we are to be active in our religion, it must have its basis largely in our affections. Third, he notes that many people understand the doctrinal content of the Christian religion very well but are not committed in any way to the Christian life (this point was much stronger in Puritan New England, of course), and so suggests that true religion must lie largely in the will, not the understanding. Fourth, Edwards examines some particular affections that are spoken of in the Scriptures: fear of God, hope, love, hatred of sin, joy, sorrow, gratitude and so on. Of these, fifth, he particularly singles out love as being the chief part of true Christian practice. Then he looks to the religion of the godly people of Scripture, the example of Jesus Christ and what we know of the religion of heaven, and suggests that in each case affections are at the heart of what is going on. There are more proofs but the ones I have listed should

---

[18]For some discussion of this dispute, and Edwards's reaction to it, see Conrad Cherry, *The Theology of Jonathan Edwards: A Reappraisal* (Garden City, N.Y.: Doubleday, 1966), pp. 12-17.

give the flavor: biblically, experientially and theologically we discover true piety in the affections, not merely in ideas.

The conclusion to this section of the book, however, offers an important qualification: "Not that I think these arguments prove that religion in the hearts of the . . . godly is . . . in exact proportion to the degree of affection, and present emotion of the mind."[19] There are several reasons for this: even the saints have much affection that is not spiritual (Edwards simply accepted Chauncy's point that a fervent preacher may whip up an utterly natural emotional storm); bodily condition has a significant effect on our affections (C. S. Lewis once made the point that the degree to which we are uplifted by our prayers can depend as much on what we had for breakfast as on anything else); and so on. As a result, Edwards suggests, we should look at "the fixedness and strength of the habit,"[20] at whether affections remain through thick and thin—sometimes flaring, perhaps, sometimes dipping, no doubt—but still continuing to burn. This will be important before Edwards has finished his exposition.

Edwards continues his development of the doctrine by drawing out some consequences (his word is "inferences") of it.[21] First, we see the error of those "who are for discarding all religious affections, as having nothing solid . . . about them." Once again Edwards acknowledges the errors and failures of some who have been converted in the Awakening, but still, "he who has no religious affection is in a state of spiritual death." Thus, second, preaching and public worship should be designed to stir up affections, and, third, we should be ashamed and convicted of our relative lack of affections. We should be more deeply affected by the gospel of Christ.

How, though, to test the spirits? How can we tell true and gracious religious affections from mere carnal enthusiasm? Edwards offers us twelve "false friends," negative signs that might seem to be discriminating, but in fact prove nothing either way, and twelve signs which do distinguish truly gracious affections. The arguments for the first set are all of the same form: there are (scriptural) examples of true faith marked by this sign, but there are also examples of false belief equally so marked, so nothing may be concluded either way. There is not space here to list the negative signs, but they cover the source, strength, content and effect of the affections. The coming to mind of texts of Scripture is no proof (the tempter quoted Scripture to his own ends when Christ was tested in the wilderness); public zeal, private confi-

---

[19]Edwards, *Affections*, p. 118.
[20]Ibid.
[21]Ibid., pp. 119-24.

dence, and the respect of the saints are alike no proof.

What, then, counts for proof? The twelve positive signs can be grouped into those that describe the *source* of the affections, those that describe their *nature*, and those that describe their *results*. Three relate to the source: truly gracious affections come from the internal work of the indwelling Holy Spirit, enabling the saint to grasp and respond to the beauty and the truth of the gospel. Five more signs relate to the nature of gracious affections. They are a disinterested response to the gospel, rather than a mere calculation of self-interest. They are accompanied by a conviction of the truth of the gospel and a humble awareness of our own sinfulness. As the result of conversion gracious affections are a part of a change of our nature, and they are marked by "beautiful symmetry and proportion";[22] an unbalanced zeal that focuses only on one area of the Christian life is unlikely to be truly gracious. Finally, their result: they produce meekness, a softening of the heart and a desire for their own increase (love for God brings with it a desire to love him more and more). And they result in a lifetime of devoted Christian practice.

LEARNING FROM EDWARDS

Theologically Edwards's points are well-argued and scripturally based. Practically, we might find them either strange or unsatisfactory: strange, because we perhaps don't share Edwards's concern to identify true religious experience; and unsatisfactory because, even if we did, we might notice how difficult it is to actually prove anything with his "positive signs." Both these issues deserve comment.

On the first, most Western churches today are only too pleased to accept claimed experience of God at face value, at least unless and until there seems a very good reason not to (the crossing of some important doctrinal line, or clear immorality in the life of the person claiming the experience). To be specific, a person might come to one of our churches with testimony of having listened to an evangelistic sermon, during which (to invoke some of Edwards's negative signs) texts of Scripture which they could never remember having read before came to their minds, leading them to experience a deep trust in the atoning work of Jesus, and a strong sense of peace, and to respond with a zealous desire to serve God, manifested already by changes of lifestyle and financial commitment to Christian causes. Would not almost all of our churches respond with acceptance and joy that a sinner had repented? Edwards's careful attempts to sift such experiences, and to point out that they might yet mean nothing concerning the person's spiritual state, are foreign to us.

---

[22]Ibid., p. 365.

There are, I suspect, two reasons for this. The first is the changing times: Edwards knew what is again becoming obvious, that human beings are incurably religious. We might not seek or find faith in Christ and new birth, but we long for religious fulfillment and we look to find it wherever we can. ("Thou hast made us for thyself," prayed Augustine, "and our hearts are restless till they find their rest in thee.") Today, a person who knows nothing of the saving work of the Spirit, but desires selfish religious gratification, will no doubt find it in some new spiritual practice that is locally available. Within the broad umbrella that we call the "New Age Movement," after all, are any number of practices promising spirituality without morality. This is in contrast to Christian churches, which are commonly believed to offer precisely the opposite. In Edwards's day it was different; in Puritan New England, the church was the only game in town, and so someone seeking merely selfish and carnal spiritual fulfillment could well have appeared zealous in Christian practice. Thus, Edwards and his fellow pastors perhaps had far more need to "test the spirits" in this way than we have today.

The second reason concerns Edwards's more immediate context: in time of revival, when spiritual fervor is "in the air" because God is powerfully at work, we should expect there to be both natural and spiritual counterfeits. The first because there will always be some people, caught up in the excitement of what is going on, who manufacture their own "spiritual" experience in order to win recognition or approval. The second because, however we chose to understand it, the Scriptures surely tell us that we must expect that there will be spiritual opposition seeking to discredit the work of God's Spirit whenever that work is particularly visible. When God is at work powerfully, we should anticipate that the experiences of people caught up in what he is doing will be more mixed than they are in the general run of things. Edwards recognized this and offers us careful and biblical counsel to help us find our way to the necessary discernment.

The second issue concerns the difficulty of applying Edwards's tests. He does not offer us a form of litmus paper that turns from red to blue if God's Spirit is at work. Rather, we have a series of judgments to make which appear to be uncertain. Sometimes it may be obvious, for instance, that a person's religious response is unbalanced; but if that is not the case, how can we tell with any certainty that it is in fact balanced? The final and crowning test that a truly gracious work of the Spirit results in a lifetime of Christian practice can only really be applied at death—before that moment it is always potentially falsifiable.

It is tempting to find a biographical reason for this qualification: by the time he came to write the *Religious Affections* many of those whom Edwards had seen apparently savingly convicted by the Spirit during the revivals were calling for his dismissal from the pulpit, in part (as he saw it) because he was insisting on standards of Christian practice that they were not prepared to live up to, or see imposed on their children. No doubt this history shook his confidence, but it cannot be the only reason for the difficulty he leaves us with.

At heart, for Edwards, true Christianity is about an internal change: a new birth or new creation, to use the biblical language. This is what the Holy Spirit does. The several effects of this change can be listed, but none of them, according to Edwards, is simple and decisive proof that it has occurred. Instead, it results in a form of life that must be traced carefully over months and years before we can be certain of its authenticity, not because the change isn't immense, but because the admittedly immense change can nonetheless be counterfeited in various ways. Edwards thus paints a picture of true Christianity: not self-interested, but devoted to God, intoxicated with the beauty and rightness of the gospel; built on a firm foundation of reasonable belief and understanding of Christian truth; constantly sorrowing for sin, but also rejoicing in a firm assurance of God's forgiveness of sins through the sacrifice of Christ; of a humble, gentle, meek and loving temper, as Christ himself had while on earth; never satisfied, but always pressing forward to greater depths of love for God, greater heights of holy practice; and finally resulting in a holy and devoted Christian life of service. This is what God gives to his children by the transforming power of his Spirit, and anything less than this is so far from what God wants of us that Edwards would question whether it is built on a true work of the Spirit at all.

These may sound like hard words, but they are gospel words. Edwards's desire for holiness is not based only on a sense that God calls his children to this position, although that is certainly the case. It is also based on the knowledge that this is what God gives to us through his Spirit, and if we do not have all this, then we must ask if we have received the gift Jesus promised. If Edwards believes the gospel asks much of us, it is only because he believes we have been given all that God has to give, and, "from everyone to whom much as been given, much will be required" (Lk 12:48). "Give what you ask," prayed Augustine, "and ask what you will"—an echo of this same high vision of the Christian life.

Edwards's people in Northampton found his uncompromising belief in true holiness uncomfortable too. Eventually, they voted to dismiss him from his pulpit. He took his family to the frontier of the colonies, to Stockbridge, Massachusetts, where, in grinding poverty, he pastored a small church and dedicated himself to the local Native American population, protecting them against greedy merchants and offering them the gospel. From that unlikely outpost flowed a series of works that establish him still as the greatest theological mind to have been born on the American continent: *The Freedom of the Will*, *Original Sin*, *True Virtue*, *Concerning the End for which God Created the World* and several others. Finally his genius was recognized; the college in Princeton invited him to be its president. He traveled there at a time when the smallpox was rife, and so was vaccinated against the disease. Something went wrong, however, and he contracted the disease from the vaccination. At the age of fifty-four, with his projected great summary work on Christian theology unbegun, he lay on his deathbed. He spoke of his love for his wife, and urged his children to find faith in God. He asked that his funeral not be elaborate, but instead that money be given to the poor in his memory. Then it seemed he lapsed into unconsciousness. Those around began to speak of the loss that the college and the colonial churches would have to bear, but he heard them, and spoke one last time: "Trust in God, and you need not fear." Thus ended a lifetime of Christian holiness.

A CHALLENGE FOR TODAY

So what is the significance of the *Religious Affections* for today? Why should we read this Puritan classic? Edwards teaches us how to test the spirits, and there will be times in our own Christian experience when such discernment will become vital, times like the Toronto Blessing. More than that, however, Edwards traces the true work of the Spirit of God in the converted heart, a work that is not, fundamentally, to do with emotional reaction and extraordinary response, although these things might well be present, but is about a humble, cheerful love for God and growth in holiness that lasts a lifetime. Edwards confronts us once again with the high vision of the Christian calling that was perhaps the chief glory of Puritanism, a vision that challenges the carnal and emaciated "Christian" living that is so common in our churches today. We think we have rediscovered the work of the Spirit if we experience warm fuzzy feelings while singing, or see spectacular answers to our prayers. Jonathan Edwards, tracing the teaching of Scripture with care and clarity, would tell us that God has given us immeasurably more than that, more than we have asked, more than we have yet imagined, and would challenge us to show in our lives and our churches all that we have been given. I can imagine no more timely word for God's people and churches in the West today.

SELECT BIBLIOGRAPHY

Primary Works

Edwards, Jonathan. *The Works of Jonathan Edwards*. At the time of writing, Yale University

Press has made eighteen volumes of their edition available; under the general editorship of Harry S. Stout this will be the definitive edition for many years when complete. The old two-volume Dwight/Hickman edition (also called *The Works of Jonathan Edwards*) is still in print from various sources, and contains most of the significant works. There are also many individual editions of particular works of Edwards readily available.

————. *A Jonathan Edwards Reader*. Edited by Stout et al. New Haven, Conn.: Yale University Press, 1995. A one-volume "taster" from the editors of the Yale edition.

Secondary Works

Cherry, Conrad. *The Theology of Jonathan Edwards: A Reappraisal*. Bloomington: Indiana University Press, 1993. Second edition. This is the most useful and accessible of several general accounts of Edwards's theology.

Holmes, Stephen R. *God of Grace and God of Glory: An Account of the Theology of Jonathan Edwards*. Edinburgh: T & T Clark, 2000. My own take on Edwards.

Jenson, Robert W. *America's Theologian: A Recommendation of Jonathan Edwards*. Oxford: Oxford University Press, 1988. This and Pauw's volume are very good books, but not for the faint-hearted.

Marsden, George M. *Jonathan Edwards: A Life*. New Haven, Conn.: Yale University Press, 2003. The best biography on Edwards by some distance.

Pauw, Amy Plantinga. *The Supreme Harmony of All: The Trinitarian Theology of Jonathan Edwards*. Grand Rapids: Eerdmans, 2002.

20

AFTERWORD

THE PURITANS
AND SPIRITUAL RENEWAL

Richard F. Lovelace

FOR MANY YEARS MY TEACHING ROLE HAS BEEN AS A HISTORIAN OF renewal movements in the church—as a "spiritual theologian," a historical theologian of Christian experience. This path led me to some areas not often covered by evangelicals. My favorite region has been the great renewal movement that extends from the Reformation of the sixteenth century through the Evangelical Awakening movements of the eighteenth and nineteenth centuries. In this movement English and American Puritanism had an integral role to play in the development of spiritual awakenings.

I think of this process in the great renewal movement in terms of a rocket that has three stages. The foundational stage is the Protestant Reformation, with its assertion of salvation by grace through faith. The Reformation provides the energy to launch the second stage, expressed in the two sibling renewal movements of the 1600s, Calvinist Puritanism and Lutheran Pietism. These movements balanced the Reformers' emphasis on justification by faith with a strong articulation of the need for sanctification among God's people.

Calvin had begun this understanding of sanctification in a section of the *Institutes*, which replaces the patterns of Catholic asceticism with a biblical model of sanctification drawn from Paul's letters.[1] English Puritans extended and developed this model, aiming at a church composed of "visible saints," Protestants who were

---

[1] John Calvin, *Institutes of the Christian Religion*, ed. John T. McNeill, trans. Ford Lewis Battles (Philadelphia: Westminster, 1960), 3.3.10-15.

not only orthodox, but holy. Puritan pastors aimed at crafting individuals who were filled with what I have called "live orthodoxy."[2]

The third stage of the rocket, the Awakening movements of the next several centuries, simply broadcast this balance more widely among Christians, as the Holy Spirit energized large numbers of Protestants, including those who were formal participants in congregations but who showed little vitality. The renewal of the churches then led to expansive evangelization. But in a way, these awakenings were mainly the lengthened shadow of seventeenth-century Puritanism.

In the first section of this chapter I want to sketch the English Puritan model of Christian experience, the spiritual matrix of the Puritan vision of the Christian life. Sticking with my metaphor, this segment focuses on the second stage of the rocket. Then in the latter section of this essay, I want to look briefly at two exemplars of this model, two pastor-theologians: Cotton Mather and Jonathan Edwards. Mather was really a pre-revivalist, who set the stage for the Great Awakening; and Edwards was of course the main theologian of that revival. So with this material we are actually moving out of the seventeenth century and into the third stage of the metaphorical rocket.

THE PURITAN MODEL OF SPIRITUAL RENEWAL

Between 1600 and 1640, there was a tremendous efflorescence of Puritan literature, most of it focused on the development of a distinctively Protestant spirituality. These works were firmly based on the doctrinal teaching of the Protestant Reformation. However, they insisted that this doctrine be applied by the Holy Spirit in a way that would change lives. Thomas Shepard puts it well in one of his tracts:

> What infinite Cause hath this Age to acknowledge the unspeakable Mercy of God, in affording us such Plenty of spiritual Tractates, full of divine, necessary and Conscience-searching Truths; yea, precious Soul-comforting, & Soul-improving Truths?[3]

In the last third of the twentieth century we have seen a similar flowering of evangelical writings. But there is a difference in these Puritan works. Shepard goes on to say:

> yea, precious Soul-comforting, & Soul-improving Truths? such whereby Head, Heart, and Soul cheating Errors are discovered and prevented, such as soundly Difference true Grace from all seemings and paintings: No Time, no Nation exceeds us herein.[4]

---

[2]Richard F. Lovelace, *Dynamics of Spiritual Life* (Downers Grove, Ill.: InterVarsity Press, 1979), pp. 271-87.
[3]Thomas Shepard, *The Sincere Convert* (London: n.p., 1640), p. ii.
[4]Ibid.

Notice the operative phrases here: the conscience is being searched, and errors are being dissipated. We may ask if this is happening through our current literature. In the same vein, Daniel Featly writes:

> It is Saint Jerome's observation upon the legall sacrifices, that God never appointed hony to bee offered unto him. And the morall truth vailed under that shadow, was that in our spiritual oblations nothing pleaseth God that is onely sweete, and hath not some smacke in it of biting truth.[5]

This is a description of the distinctive character of Puritan devotional material. It is heart-searching. It brings you up against the realities of Scripture like a collision with a brick wall. It measures your life. If we look at the tremendous body of work produced during this period, we are simultaneously challenged, edified and comforted.

The Puritans were Christian humanists—intellectuals with strong mental fiber. But there was also an aura of the presence of the Holy Spirit in their writings. They had Spirit-filled minds. And they were literally the church fathers of English and American theology.

What produced the flowering of Puritan spirituality in the seventeenth century? It appears to be simply an internalized development of the impulse behind the Protestant Reformation. Puritans referred to the "half-reformation" of the sixteenth century—not that the Reformation itself was at fault, but it needed the church to follow through on its teaching. "We have reformed our doctrines, but not our lives," Puritans said.

And so they sought a comprehensive movement of renewal in different areas of the church's life. The name that was applied to them by enemies was not misleading, for their concerns always centered on purity. In the 1570s Puritans were concerned about Roman Catholic remnants in the liturgy and the Anglican *Prayer Book.* Later they complained about the role of bishops. The Synod of Dort (1618-1619) developed a consistent statement of Calvinist theology, and this became another area of purity at which Puritans aimed in the early 1600s. But above all, Puritanism was a movement that sought for purity in the hearts and lives of parishioners, defined as "walking with God" or "walking in the Spirit."

This is not strange, for the first generation of Puritan leaders were pastors like Richard Rogers, William Greenham and John Dod. The second generation brought forth two major theologians, William Perkins and his protégé, William Ames. But their theology was far more pastoral and practical than much of later theology—

---

[5]Daniel Featly, *Ancilla Pietatis,* (London: n.p., 1626), "To the Reader."

including that in our own time.

So Perkins argued that theology is the science of living blessedly forever *(Theologia est scientia beate vivendi in aeternam)*. Knowledge of God is thus inescapably fused with godly living. Similarly Ames claimed that theology is the science of living unto God *(Theologia est scientia de deo vivendi)* and faith is a resting of the heart in God *(Acquiescentia cordis in deo)*.

These theologians were concise in setting forth the essence of their beliefs, but they were also complete in connecting these with Christian experience. So Perkins's tract, *A Golden Chaine*, begins with two chapters on the core of Reformed theology, but follows this with a number of chapters applying this truth to the Christian life.[6]

What was the structure of Puritan spirituality? It was not focused on gifts or passing experiences, but rather on *sanctification*, growth in holiness. We must ask why these words are rare in today's writing. Today we look for add-on experiences that will bolster our faith. But Puritanism was a Reformed *holiness movement*.

The first beachhead of sanctification in the soul is *regeneration*, being born again. This is the initial entry of the Holy Spirit in persons, which engrafts them in Christ and lays the foundation for conscious conversion. Reformed teaching does not say that conversion is what produces regeneration, but rather that regeneration is God's secret, gracious operation in the depths of the soul, which enlivens us and gives us the freedom and the urge to be converted.

Puritans may be said to have founded the first "born again" movement in Christianity, and so they are precursors of modern evangelicalism. But Puritans may have been aiming at a deeper experience than this phrase conveys today. They were aiming at a searching, probing and powerful reconstitution of the souls of persons, which would turn them into "visible saints."

Gordon Wakefield comments that among Puritans, all the developed character and experience of a lifetime of Christian growth is often condensed into the initial encounter with God. I have called this the "loading" of conversion.[7] Born-again Puritan converts could almost be said to be pre-sanctified, compared to converts in our day—like a watch that has been pre-tuned so finely at the factory that it runs long and well after it has been purchased.

In order to promote this depth of transformation at the point of initial conversion, Puritan preachers aimed at what they called a "Law-Work." This was obtained by virtually marinating their hearers in biblical commands and models of

[6]William Perkins, *The Works of William Perkins*, ed. Ian Breward (Abingdon: Sutton Courtenay, 1970), pp. 175-259.
[7]Richard F. Lovelace, *The American Pietism of Cotton Mather: Origins of American Evangelicalism* (Grand Rapids: Christian University Press, 1979), pp. 73-74.

righteousness, stirring the hearts of the audience, creating in them a parching thirst for salvation—for the gospel, the good news coming from a far country.

An aspect of Puritan conversion theory especially interesting to church life today was the handling of assurance of salvation. Some more rigorous Puritans, like Thomas Shepard, argued that the inspection of works was the basis of assurance: "Examine yourselves, whether you are in the faith"; or test yourself by the categories in I John, which indicate passage from death into life. More "evangelical" Puritans, like John Cotton and Richard Sibbes, urged reliance on the internal testimony of the Holy Spirit, who assures us as we pray "Abba, Father."

Both of these methods of assurance have a basis in Scripture. One can imagine Martin Luther wanting to add a third way. Luther seemed to understand that on a bad day believers often cannot find enough good works in their lives to bring assurance of salvation. During such times they might not even hear the voice of the Holy Spirit through the devil's rain of accusations. To such as these, Luther would want to bring encouragement, reminding discouraged believers that they need only exercise bare faith in Jesus Christ; need only look at the serpent raised up in the wilderness. Whatever believers find lacking in themselves, their Savior, reminds Luther, has dealt with it in his atonement.

How did the Puritan model of spirituality interface with the world? Max Weber calls this pattern *Innerweltliche Askese*, "innerworldly asceticism." Puritanism broke down the monastery walls, and took the monastic search for spiritual renewal into the daily life of parishioners. By applying the highest standards of spiritual life to ordinary married laypersons, it universalized the model which Catholic asceticism had confined to "those who would be perfect"—unmarried monks and nuns.

The structured life commonly recommended to modern evangelicals was invented by Puritans: a daily Quiet Time of Scripture reading, meditation and reflection, and prayer rising out of the Scripture texts. Later during the day, Puritans were urged to reflect on symbolic messages in the structure of daily life, a carryover from the mysticism of the Victorine theologians in the Middle Ages. Creation was treated as a great cathedral full of latent symbols that could be discerned and interpreted by Scripture.

Another notable facet of the Puritan model of spirituality was its strong portrayal of indwelling sin. This is another measuring-rod for current evangelical spirituality. How much practical attention is given to this negative factor in Christian experience?

John Owen has a masterful treatise on *The Nature, Power, Deceit and Prevalence of In-*

dwelling Sin in Believers.[8] John Downame has a large volume on *The Christian's Warfarre against the World; the Flesh and the Devil.* Downame observes:

> By the way wee may note a difference betweene the state of Gods children and the wicked. Both fall into sin very often, both also commit hainous and grievous sins; yea sometimes the child of God falleth into more fearefull and horrible sins, than a meere worldling.

But there is a difference: "Herein the chiefe difference betweene them consisteth, that the child of God after his fall is vexed and grieved, and laboureth to rise againe."[9]

Puritans were also realistic about the satanic forces ranged against Christians. If reborn believers fall so often into sin, part of the reason lies with the demonic assault against them. It is hard to understand this without recognizing the invisible forces on the battlefield, whose constant striving is to drag down and disfigure the people of God. So Puritan leaders in the seventeenth century produced a number of "battle manuals" for the Christian warfare, like William Gurnall's *The Christian in Complete Armor,* which was a bestseller well into the nineteenth century, and was reprinted in the twentieth century.

Also in Puritan pastoral theology there was a remarkably balanced and prescient grappling with psychological problems. Puritans traced four causative factors in depression: (1) somatic or biological causes, such as lack of sleep and bad diet; (2) psychological causes, such as "a melancholy disposition"; (3) sin, especially unbelief; and (4) demonic assault, especially accusations of the kind that Luther and Whitefield encountered.

Puritans are often chided for their "precisionism"—a theology of culture which followed the early church fathers in ruling out cosmetics, the dance, and the theatre (this last in the shadow of the great Elizabethan age of Shakespeare and Marlowe!) But these matters were at the periphery, and not at the heart of Puritanism. Robert Bolton puts it well:

> The marrow . . . of Christianitie doth not consist, as too many suppose, in outward shewes, profession, talking: in holding strict points, defending precise opinions, contesting against the corruptions of the times: In the worke wrought, externall forms of religious exercizes, set taskes of hearing, reading, conference, and the like: in some solemne outward extraordinarie abstinences and forbearances, censuring

---

[8] John Owen, *The Works of John Owen,* ed. William H. Goold (Edinburgh: Banner of Truth Trust, 1967), 6:157-322.

[9] John Downame, *The Christian's Warfarre against the World, the Flesh and the Devil* (London: n.p., 1609), pp. 57-59.

others, etc. But, in righteousnesse, peace, joy in the holy Ghost: in meekenesse, ten-
derheartednesse, love: in patience, humilitie, contentedness: in mortification of
sinne, moderation of passion, holy guidance of the tongue: in workes of mercy, justice, and truth; in fidelitie, painefulnesse in our Callings, conscionable conversation
with men: in reverence unto superiors, love of our enemies, and open-hearted reall
fruitfull affectionatenesse, and bounty to Gods people: in heavenly-mindednesse,
selfe-deniall, the life of faith: in disesteeme of earthly things, contempt of the world,
resolute hatred of sinne: in approving our hearts in Gods presence, a sweete communion with him, comfortable longing for the comming of the Lord Jesus, etc.[10]

The real center of the Puritan spiritual model is communion with God. This is
often expressed in terms which are almost charismatic:

> The Holy Ghost at some time falls upon [the Christian], & sets him all on a fire . . .
> both of sudden and violent indignation at sinne . . . as also the fire of holy affections.
> . . . He doth feele his heart oftentimes on a sudden surprized with strange impres-
> sions, sometimes of sorrow, sometimes of feare and awefull dread of God; some
> times of fervent desires after God; some times of strong resolutions of holy duties
> to be done by him. . . . He feeles at some times in the use of Gods ordinances a mar-
> vellous work of the Holy Ghost, in respect of much assurance and strange establish-
> ment of his heart, both in the certaine perswasion of Gods love, and the infallible
> beliefe of the truth. . . . He feeles at some times the unspeakable and glorious joyes
> of the Holy Ghost.[11]

TWO PURITAN LEADERS MOVING INTO AWAKENING SPIRITUALITY

Puritan pastors worked as craftsmen fashioning individual "visible saints." The
awakening tradition of the eighteenth and nineteenth centuries would expand the
reach of this model dramatically—in effect, Puritanizing much larger numbers of
Christians, as the Holy Spirit renewed whole churches and townships in England,
America, Germany and on mission fields abroad. We turn now to look at two
American examples of this third stage of Protestant renewal.

Two of the greatest American Christian leaders were Puritans: Cotton Mather
and Jonathan Edwards. Few theologians have had their reputations so marred by
rationalist and secular attacks as these two. But when we dig through this mass of
accusations, we find two wonderful Christian leaders, who brought forth some of
the finest developments in Puritanism and defined the larger arena of Awakening
spirituality.

---

[10]Robert Bolton, *Directions for a Comfortable Walking with God* (London: n.p., 1609), pp. 57-58.
[11]Nicholas Byfield, *The Marrow of the Oracles of God* (London: n.p., 1630), pp. 172-74.

Cotton Mather. The real heart of Cotton Mather can be found in his *Diary,* which is full of theological and spiritual marrow.[12] His manual for divinity students, *Manuductio ad Ministerium,* is still so relevant for seminarians that it has recently been reprinted.[13]

I recommend also *Bonifacius: Essays Upon the Good.*[14] This was not mere do-good-ism. It was Mather's attempt, at the beginning of the eighteenth century, to develop a new way to transform New England culture, given that the colonial theocracy had been replaced by tolerance and religious freedom.

Mather recognized that Christianity could no longer be imposed from the top down, and he believed that a new strategy had to be developed to seed the culture with Christian values. Mather's new approach was to organize prayer meetings for an outpouring of the Holy Spirit, and then to work to produce lay leaders in all vocations who would live out the gospel in every walk of life. It is fair to say that the "Benevolent Empire" of the nineteenth century works off this model, which seeks to leaven society through spiritual awakenings. As in the book of Acts, the reliance is placed not on theocracy, but on leavening the Christian community.

In some ways Mather was a model pastor. He divided his parish up into seg-ments and put small groups in charge of praying and physically caring for their sec-tions of town. Additionally, he promoted missions to Jews and also to Native Americans. Remarkably, he learned an Indian language in two weeks, in order to write a tract to reach the Indians. Mather was known to have sent bags of gold to the German Lutheran Pietist August Herrmann Francke, for his work with or-phans, Jewish children and foreign missions.

Mather was a classical premillennialist. By 1696, he had concluded that Christ was soon to return. But unlike modern evangelical pessimists, he was praying for signal actions of God in renewing the church as the end drew near. He felt that at the end of history there were going to be both formidable spiritual declensions, and also profound exhibitions of divine power in the outpouring of the Holy Spirit. Mather's *Diary* records that over the decades he spent 390 days and nights in prayer, pleading for the renewal of all churches.

Mather also commented that the church fathers told us not to pray long, but to pray very, very often. Mather recommended short prayers—brief, arrow-like peti-tions sent up to God. He says:

---

[12]Cotton Mather, *The Diary of Cotton Mather,* 2 vols. (New York: F. Ungar, 1957).

[13]Cotton Mather, *Manuductio ad Ministerium* (New York: AMS, 1976).

[14]Cotton Mather, *Bonifacius: An Essay Upon the Good,* ed. David Levin (Cambridge, Mass.: Harvard University Press, 1966).

It has been a frequent Thing with mee, to redeem . . . my Time, in shaping Thousands
of ejaculatory Prayers for my Neighbours. . . . In passing along the Street, I have sett
myself to bless thousands of persons, who never knew that I did it; with secret
Wishes, after this manner sent unto Heaven for them.[15]

There is much in Mather that anticipates the experience of Jonathan Edwards.
Like Edwards, he knew what it was like to be in a congregation that was not responding; but Mather's response was not to scold, but to pray.

Praying for Souls is a main stroke in the winning of Souls. If once the Spirit of Grace
be poured out upon a Soul, that Soul is won immediately. Yea, who can tell, how far
the Prayers of the Saints, & of a few Saints, may prevail with Heaven to obtain that
Grace, that shall win whole Peoples and Kingdoms to serve the Lord? . . . It may be,
the Nations of the world, would quickly be won from the idolatries of Paganism, and
the Impostures of Mahomet, if a Spirit of Prayer, were at work among the People of
God.[16]

In 1716, Mather spent a night in prayer, one of his "vigils." Then he wrote in
his *Diary* what is virtually a prophecy of the Great Awakening that was to come in
a few decades:

We can do very little. Our encumbrances are insuperable, our difficulties are infinite.
If He would please, to fulfill the ancient Prophecy, of pouring out the Spirit on all
Flesh, and revive the extraordinary and supernatural Operations with which He
planted His Religion in the primitive Times of Christianity, and cause them to speak
with the Tongues of Men under the Energy of Angels . . . wonderful Things would
be done immediately; His Kingdome would make those Advances in a Day, which
under our present and fruitless Labours, are scarce made in an Age. I pleaded, that
His Word had given us Reason to hope for a Return of these Powers. . . . I pleaded
. . . for a Descent of His mighty Angels, to give wonderful Shakes unto the World,
and so seize upon the Ministers of His Kingdome, as to do Things which will give
an irresistible Efficacy unto their Ministry; I concluded with a strong Impression on
my Mind; They are coming! They are coming! They are coming! They will quickly
be upon us; and the World shall be shaken wonderfully![17]

Mather died in 1728, with his hopes for a dramatic outpouring of the Holy
Spirit somewhat weakened. But in the year before his death, in Count Zinzendorf's
community of Herrnhut there occurred a powerful renewing work of the Holy

---

[15]Mather, *Diary*, 1:81, 83.
[16]Cotton Mather, *The Nets of Salvation* (Boston: n.p., 1704), pp. 40-42.
[17]Mather, *Diary*, 2:365-66.

Spirit that led to an explosion of Protestant world missions—the overture to the Great Awakening of the next decades in Germany, England and America.

Jonathan Edwards. The great theologian of the Awakening was Jonathan Edwards. Edwards was in many ways the Johann Sebastian Bach of Puritanism. Bach was the late culmination of the baroque era. So Edwards was the apex of the Puritan movement. Just as Bach is recognized as the greatest baroque composer, Edwards may have been the greatest Puritan theologian.

Edwards carries on the Puritan Calvinist tradition. He describes the core of his theology and spirituality as summed up in his "Personal Narrative": "Absolute sovereignty is what I love to ascribe to God."[18] He says that there was a time when this was not so. But then he had an encounter with God, as the Holy Spirit illuminated Scripture:

> The first instance, that I remember, of that sort of inward, sweet delight in God and divine things, that I have lived much in since, was on reading the words, I Tim I:17, Now unto the King eternal, immortal, invisible, the only wise God, be honour and glory for ever and ever, Amen. As I read these words, there came into my soul, and was as it were diffused through it, a sense of the glory of the divine being. A new sense, quite different from anything I ever experienced before.[19]

In his sermon on "The Reality of a Divine and Supernatural Light," Edwards describes this experience as "a sense of the heart" of divine realities.[20] As the Holy Spirit illuminates truth, he transforms and renews the heart. Among all theologians, Edwards is unexcelled in his ability to describe spiritual illumination. He is one of the most powerful writers dealing with Christian experience. His experience centers on Christ as well as the other persons of the Trinity:

> From about this time I began to have a new kind of apprehensions and ideas of Christ . . . and my mind was greatly engaged to spend my time in reading and meditating on Christ, on the beauty and excellency of his person, and the lovely way of salvation by free grace in him.[21]

Edwards was a natural contemplative:

> I walked abroad alone, in a solitary place in my father's pasture, for contemplation. And as I was walking there, and looking upon the sky and clouds, there came into

---

[18]Jonathan Edwards, *The Works of Jonathan Edwards*, with Memoir by Sereno E. Dwight, ed. Edward Hickman, 2 vols. (Edinburgh: Banner of Truth Trust, 1997), I:lv.
[19]Ibid.
[20]Ibid., 2:14-17.
[21]Ibid., I:lv.

my mind so sweet a sense of the glorious majesty and grace of God, as I know not how to express.—I seemed to see them both in a sweet conjunction; majesty and meekness joined together: it was a sweet, and gentle, and holy majesty; and also a majestic meekness; an awful sweetness; a high, and great, and holy gentleness.[22]

But Edwards's Puritan mysticism was not merely solitary; it was accompanied by a fervent concern for the advancement of the reign of Christ:

I had great longings for the advancement of Christ's kingdom in the world; and my secret prayers used to be, in great part, taken up in praying for it. If I heard the least hint of any thing that happened in any part of the world, that appeared, in some respect or other, to have a favourable aspect on the interests of Christ's kingdom, my soul eagerly catched at it, and it would much animate and refresh me. I used to be eager to read public news-letters, mainly for that end; to see if I could not find some news favourable to the interest of religion in the world.[23]

In all of this, Edwards appears to be a remarkably modern Christian, one who travels readily between the Bible and the daily paper. This is not monastic withdrawal; it is a thoroughly world-oriented spirituality. It reaches toward the future— for in the time of John Newton and the Second Evangelical Awakening, the progress of evangelism and cultural reform were dependent on two factors: news, and prayer responding to this.

Edwards, like all Puritans, was relentlessly God-centered. Consider his famous description of his wife Sarah, when he first encountered her in her teens:

They say there is a young lady in [New Haven] who is beloved of that Great Being who made and rules the world, and that there are certain seasons in which this Great Being, in some way or other invisible, comes to her and fills her mind with exceeding sweet delight, and that she hardly cares for any thing, except to meditate on him.[24]

Notice that within the first clause, Edwards has shifted from his beloved almost immediately to the sovereign God. In the rest of this passage he oscillates constantly between Sarah and the Lord. Yet for him there was a clear connection between love for his wife and ascribing absolute sovereignty to God; many writers have said that divine beauty is at the core of Edwards's ethics and theology.

But this did not diminish his love for Sarah. On his deathbed, his last words concerned her: "Give my kindest love to my dear wife, and tell her that the uncom-

---

[22]Ibid.

[23]Ibid., I:lvi.

[24]Ola E. Winslow, ed., *Jonathan Edwards: Basic Writings* (New York: New American Library, 1966), pp. 66-67.

mon union which has so long subsisted between us has been of such a nature as I trust is spiritual and therefore will continue forever."[25]

How did Edwards's development of Puritan spirituality relate to the actual substance of the Great Awakening? We get a glimpse of this in the account of the first Northampton revival. As Perry Miller has shown, New England had been in a long period of spiritual decline from 1652 through the 1730s. The core of the decline was absorption in the pursuit of riches—perhaps the central sin in American culture, when wealth is divorced from concern for Christ's kingdom.

But in 1734, Northampton townspeople suddenly found that they could not get their minds off God, and could barely concentrate on their business. Previously they had what Puritans called a "notional" belief in God, but their ultimate concerns were worldly. Now, suddenly, the whole town was experiencing conviction of sin and conversion, a kind of collective "dark night of the soul."[26]

Was this something abnormal? It certainly did proceed with unusual speed and extent, as did the whole Awakening in Germany, England and the rest of America a few years later. But this experience of spiritual illumination, making truth real in Christian lives, is thoroughly biblical, as Paul says:

> I pray that the God of our Lord Jesus Christ, the Father of glory, may give you a spirit of wisdom and revelation, as you come to know him, so that, with the eyes of your heart enlightened, you may know what is the hope to which he has called you, what are the riches of his glorious inheritance among the saints, and what is the immeasurable greatness of his power for us who believe according to the working of his great power. (Eph 1:17-19)

This is the heart of the Great Awakening, and also the heart of Puritan heavenly-mindedness. And it is undoubtedly something that we should be requesting in prayer, as we move into this new century.

---

[25]Elisabeth D. Dodds, *Marriage to a Difficult Man: The "Uncommon Union" of Jonathan and Sarah Edwards* (Philadelphia: Westminster Press, 1971), p. 201.
[26]Edwards, *Works*, I, 348.

CONTRIBUTORS

William S. Barker is emeritus professor of church history at Westminster Theological Seminary, Philadelphia. He is the author of *Puritan Profiles: 54 Influential Puritans at the Time when the Westminster Confession of Faith Was Written* (Fearn, Ross-shire, Scotland: Christian Focus, 1996) and has published a variety of articles in *Presbyterion, Dictionary of Christianity in America* (Downers Grove, Ill.: InterVarsity Press, 1990), and *The Blackwell Dictionary of Evangelical Biography: 1730-1860* (Oxford: Blackwell, 1995).

Joel R. Beeke is president and professor of systematic theology and homiletics at Puritan Reformed Theological Seminary and pastor of the Heritage Netherlands Reformed Congregation in Grand Rapids, Michigan. His numerous publications include *Assurance of Faith: Calvin, English Puritanism, and the Dutch Second Reformation* (New York: Peter Lang, 1991), and *Reformed Confessions Harmonized* (Grand Rapids: Baker, 1999), which he coedited.

John Coffey is a reader in early modern history in the School of Historical Studies at the University of Leicester, United Kingdom. His recent books include *Persecution and Toleration in Protestant England* (Harlow: Longman, 2000) and *Politics, Religion and the British Revolutions: The Mind of Samuel Rutherford* (Cambridge: Cambridge University Press, 1997). He has also contributed articles to a broad range of journals, including *Historical Journal* and *Evangelical Quarterly*.

J. Ligon Duncan III is the senior minister of First Presbyterian Church, Jackson, Mississippi, and adjunct professor of theology at Reformed Theological Seminary (Jackson). He is founder and editorial director of Reformed Academic Press. He edited, revised and introduced Matthew Henry's *Method for Prayer* (Fearn, Ross-shire, Scotland: Christian Focus, 1994), and edited, annotated and introduced Donald Macleod's *The Humiliated and Exalted Lord: A Study of Philippians 2 and Christology* (Greenville, S.C.: Reformed Academic Press, 1994). He has written for both academic journals and popular magazines.

Sinclair B. Ferguson is professor of systematic theology at Westminster Theological Seminary, Dallas. He is the author of many books, including *John Owen on the Christian Life* (Edinburgh: Banner of Truth Trust, 1987); *The Holy Spirit* (Downers Grove, Ill.: InterVarsity Press, 1996); and *The Grace of Repentance* (Wheaton, Ill.: Crossway, 2000). He also served as coeditor with Donald Alexander for the book *Christian Spirituality: Five Views of Sanctification* (Downers Grove, Ill.: InterVarsity Press, 1998).

Ronald N. Frost is associate professor of historical theology and ethics at Multnomah Biblical Seminary in Portland, Oregon. In addition to his scholarly work on Richard Sibbes and the history of affective theology among Puritans, Frost authored *Discover the Power of the Bible* (Eugene, Ore.: Harvest, 2000).

Randall C. Gleason is professor of systematic theology at the International School of Theology—Asia in Manila, Philippines. He is author of *John Calvin and John Owen on Mortification: A Comparative Study in Reformed Spirituality* (New York: Peter Lang, 1995) and has contributed articles to a broad range of journals, including *Bibliotheca Sacra*, *New Testament Studies* and *Tyndale Bulletin*.

Stephen R. Holmes is a lecturer of systematic theology at King's College, London. He also lectures at Spurgeon's College, London. Most recently he has written *God of Grace and God of Glory: An Account of the Theology of Jonathan Edwards* (Grand Rapids: Eerdmans, 2001) and *Listening to the Past: The Place of Tradition in Theology* (Grand Rapids: Baker, 2002).

Michael S. Horton is the president and chairman of the Council of the Alliance of Confessing Evangelicals, and is professor of apologetics and theology at Westminster Theological Seminary in California. His doctoral work at Wycliffe Hall, Oxford, focused on the theology of Thomas Goodwin. He has written or edited books not only for scholars but also for laypeople, including *Putting Amazing Back into Grace* (Nashville: Thomas Nelson, 1991), *A Confessing Theology for Postmodern Times* (Wheaton, Ill.: Crossway, 2000), and most recently, *Covenant and Eschatology: The Divine Drama* (Nashville: Westminster John Knox, 2002).

Kelly M. Kapic is assistant professor of theological studies at Covenant College in Lookout Mountain, Georgia. He has written "Communion with God: Relations between the Divine and the Human in the Theology of John Owen" (Ph.D., King's College London, 2001). Recently he has also published "The Son's Assumption of a Human Nature: A Call for Clarity" in the *International Journal of Systematic Theology* (July 2001) and "The Humanity of Christ: Looking at Jesus, Ourselves, and Pastoral Ministry" in *Foundations* 45 (2000).

Paul Chang-Ha Lim is assistant professor of historical and systematic theology at Gordon-Conwell Theological Seminary in Wenham, Massachusetts. He is the author of *In Pursuit of Purity, Unity, and Liberty: Richard Baxter's Puritan Ecclesiology in Context* (Leiden: Brill, 2004), and has written articles for *The New Dictionary of National Biography* (Oxford: Oxford University Press, 2004); *The Dictionary of Historical Theology* (Grand Rapids: Eerdmans, 2000); *Persecution and Pluralism: Calvinist Minorities in Early Modern Western Europe* (New York: Peter Lang, 2001); and *Biographical Dictionary of Evangelicals* (Downers Grove, Ill.: InterVarsity Press, 2002).

Richard F. Lovelace is emeritus professor of church history at Gordon-Conwell Theological Seminary in Wenham, Massachusetts. Some of his works include *Dynamics of Spiritual Life: An Evangelical Theology of Renewal* (Downers Grove, Ill.: InterVarsity Press, 1979); *The American Pietism of Cotton Mather: Origins of American Evangelicalism* (Grand Rapids: Christian University Press, 1979); and *Renewal as a Way of Life: A Guidebook for Spiritual Growth* (Downers Grove, Ill.: InterVarsity Press, 1985).

Mark A. Noll is the McManis Professor of Christian Thought at Wheaton College and cofounder of the Institute for the Study of American Evangelicals. His recent works include *America's God: From Jonathan Edwards to Abraham Lincoln* (Oxford: Oxford University Press, 2002); *Protestants in America* (Oxford: Oxford University Press, 2000); *Turning Points: Decisive Moments in the History of Christianity* (Grand Rapids: Baker, 1997); and *The Scandal of the Evangelical Mind* (Grand Rapids: Eerdmans, 1994).

J. I. Packer is the Board of Governors' Professor of Theology at Regent College, Vancouver, British Columbia, Canada, and an executive editor for *Christianity Today*. Among his many publications, two of his most noteworthy contributions include *Quest for Godliness: The Puritan Vision of the Christian Life* (Wheaton, Ill.: Crossway, 1990) and *Knowing God* (Downers Grove, Ill.: InterVarsity Press, 1973).

Leland Ryken is the Clyde S. Kilby Professor of English at Wheaton College, Illinois. His interdisciplinary contributions covering literature, biblical studies and history include *Windows to the World: Literature in Christian Perspective* (Eugene, Ore.: Wipf and Stock, 2000); *Worldly Saints: The Puritans as They Really Were* (Grand Rapids: Zondervan, 1990); *Words of Delight: A Literary Introduction to the Bible* (Grand Rapids: Baker, 1993); and *Redeeming the Time: A Christian Approach to Work and Leisure* (Grand Rapids: Baker, 1995).

Philip G. Ryken is senior minister of the Tenth Presbyterian Church in Philadelphia, Pennsylvania. His academic works include *Thomas Boston as Preacher of the Fourfold State* (Edinburgh: Rutherford House, 1999), and articles in *The New Dictionary of National Biography* (Oxford: Oxford University Press, 2004) and the *Biographical Dictionary of Evangelicals* (Downers Grove, Ill.: InterVarsity Press, 2002). His other works include *The Message of Salvation* (Downers Grove, Ill.: InterVarsity Press, 2002); *The Communion of Saints: Living in Fellowship with the People of God* (Phillipsburg, Penn.: P & R, 2001); and *Jeremiah and Lamentations: From Sorrow to Hope* (Wheaton, Ill.: Crossway, 2001).

Paul R. Schaefer is the chair of the Department of Religion and Philosophy and professor of religion at Grove City College, Pennsylvania. He is author of "The Spiritual Brotherhood on the Habits of the Heart: Cambridge Protestants and the Doctrine of Sanctification from William Perkins to Thomas Shepard" (D.Phil. Oxford University, 1994), which will soon be published by Rutherford House in Edinburgh. He has also contributed to *Protestant Scholasticism: Essays in Reassessment* (Carlisle, U.K.: Paternoster, 1999).

Charles E. Hambrick-Stowe is dean and professor of Christian history at Northern Seminary, Lombard, Illinois, and has served as a local church pastor for twenty-two years. His publications include *The Practice of Piety: Puritan Devotional Disciplines in Seventeenth-Century New England* (Chapel Hill: University of North Carolina Press, 1982) and *Charles G. Finney and the Spirit of American Evangelicalism* (Grand Rapids: Eerdmans, 1996) in addition to numerous academic articles.

Martin Sutherland is professor of systematic theology and the director of the R. J. Thompson Centre for Theological Studies at Carey Baptist College, Auckland, New Zealand, and serves as editor for *The New Zealand Journal of Baptist Research*. His scholarly articles include "Downgrade Down Under: Conflict and Cohesion Among New Zealand Baptists," *Baptist Quarterly* 37 (1998) and "Protestant Divergence in the Restoration Crisis," *Journal of Religious History* 21 (1997). Much of his early work focused on the theology of the puritan John Howe.

Jan van Vliet is assistant professor of theology at Prairie Bible College in Three Hills, Alberta, Canada. His doctoral dissertation is titled "William Ames: Marrow of the Theology and Piety of the Reformed Tradition" (Ph.D. diss., Westminster Theological Seminary, 2002).

Names Index

Subject Index